Law and Social Justice

Law and Social Justice

edited by Joseph Keim Campbell, Michael O'Rourke, and David Shier

A Bradford Book
The MIT Press
Cambridge, Massachusetts
London, England

MIT Press books may be purchased at special quantity discounts for business or sales promotional use. For information, please email special_sales@mitpress.mit.edu or write to Special Sales Department, The MIT Press, 55 Hayward Street, Cambridge, MA 02142.

This book was set in Stone Serif and Stone Sans by SNP Best-set Typesetter Ltd., Hong Kong, and was printed and bound in the United States of America.

Library of Congress Cataloging-in-Publication Data

Inland Northwest Philosophy Conference (5th : 2002 : Moscow, Idaho and Pullman, Wash.)
Law and social justice / edited by Joseph Keim Campbell, Michael O'Rourke, and David Shier.
    p.   cm.—(Topics in contemporary philosophy. A Bradford Book)
"Descendants of presentations given at the 5th annual Inland Northwest Philosophy Conference (INPC) in Moscow, Idaho and Pullman, Washington in April of 2002"—p. viii.
Includes bibliographical references and index.
ISBN 0-262-03340-2 (hc : alk. paper)—ISBN 0-262-53274-3 (pb. : alk. paper)
1. Sociological jurisprudence—Congresses. 2. Social justice—Congresses.
3. Social sciences—Philosophy—Congresses. I. Campbell, Joseph Keim, 1958– .
II. O'Rourke, Michael, 1963– . III. Shier, David, 1958– . IV. Title. V. Series.

K370.I55   2002
340′.115—dc22

2005042147

10 9 8 7 6 5 4 3 2 1

To our parents:
William C. Campbell and Lillian Mumber Campbell;
Lowell Shier and Faith Hubbart Shier;
Robert M. O'Rourke and Keo Helmke O'Rourke

Contents

Part II

Part III

Acknowledgments

These essays are the descendants of presentations given at the Fifth Annual Inland Northwest Philosophy Conference (INPC) in Moscow, Idaho and Pullman, Washington in April of 2002. Hosted by the philosophy departments of Washington State University and the University of Idaho, the INPC brings about a hundred outstanding philosophers and other scholars to the hills of the Palouse region each spring. Presenters are encouraged to submit their work for publication in the associated volume and, after a process of peer evaluation, a few are selected. There were many fine submissions that could not be included owing simply to space limitations, and we regret that we could not publish more of these pieces.

There are many people whose assistance and efforts we would like to acknowledge. We owe special thanks to Harry Silverstein for writing the opening chapter in addition to contributing a piece. Elizabeth Brake, Robert Epperson, Philip J. Ivanhoe, Douglas Kries, Ann Levey, Richard Lippke, Phillip Montague, Clayton Morgareidge, Joseph Pergola, Peter Steinberger, and Brian Steverson refereed submissions. We would also like to thank the members of the editorial board of this series, *Topics in Contemporary Philosophy*, who are listed separately. We are indebted to Kenneth Himma and to Douglas Lind for organizing, respectively, the author-and-critics session on Jules Coleman and the special session on Wittgenstein, and for introducing the corresponding sections of this volume.

Administrators and chairs from both universities, including Robert Bates, Barbara Couture, Kathryn Paxton George, Robert Hoover, Michael Neville, Kurt Olsen, James Peterson, Brian Pitcher, and Lane Rawlins provided support to the conference and thus indirectly to this volume. The conference also received generous financial support through a grant from the Idaho Humanities Council to fund the Public Forum, a community event associated with the INPC in which panelists and audience members discuss an issue of significant public interest related to the conference theme. Both the conference and this book series have benefited enormously from the efforts of departmental administrative managers Laura Stusek and Dee Dee Torgeson.

Finally, we would like to express our gratitude to Delphine Keim Campbell, Rebecca O'Rourke, and Phyllis Shier, without whose support, efforts, and understanding this volume could not exist.

Part I

1 Law and Social Justice: A Framework

Harry S. Silverstein

The Inland Northwest Philosophy Conference (INPC) is a conference hosted annually in Pullman, Washington, and Moscow, Idaho, by the philosophy departments at Washington State University and the University of Idaho. The contributions to this volume are, or are descendants of, some of the presentations made at the Fifth Annual INPC in the spring of 2002. The topic of that year's conference was "Law and Social Justice," a topic whose considerable breadth is illustrated by the breadth of these contributions. In addition to two special parts at the end of the volume on "Wittgenstein and Legal Theory" and "Author Meets Critics: A Panel on Jules Coleman's *The Practice of Principle*" (parts that have their own separate introductions, by Douglas Lind and Ken Himma respectively, and about which I shall therefore say nothing further here), the focus of these contributions ranges from broad, foundational, issues in moral, social, and political theory—instrumentalist versus Kantian conceptions of rights (Wenar), a defense of an egalitarian principle of distributive justice (Christiano), and the implications of a certain conception of "deliberative democracy" (Cohen)—to very specific problems regarding the admissibility of evidence of causation in toxic tort cases (Cranor); from questions concerning the extent to which the initial acquisition of goods yields property rights (Levey) to the treatment of intellectual property in China (Ivanhoe); from the place of "moral luck" in the criminal law (Eisikovits) to the place of strict products liability in business law (Silverstein).

The opening essay is Joshua Cohen's "Privacy, Pluralism, and Democracy," which is derived from his keynote address at the conference. Cohen focuses on the implications of his conception of "deliberative democracy" for privacy, both "privacy rights"—the rights it would be appropriate to honor as part of a society's formal political and legal structure—and

"privacy conventions"—informal social norms specifying conventions as
to what topics are and are not suitable for public discussion. Deliberative
democracy, as Cohen conceives it, contains three key ideas: (1) a conception of citizens as free and equal; (2) the contention that reasonable
citizens do in fact adopt different, conflicting, "philosophies of life" ("the
fact of reasonable pluralism"); and (3) the claim that a society's coercive
collective decisions should be founded on the "public reasoning" of its
citizens. And the crucial implication is that such public reasoning can legitimately be concerned only with considerations that are not restricted to a
particular philosophy of life. For, in Cohen's, words, "People are *reasonable, politically speaking*, only if they are concerned to live with others on
terms that those others, understood as free and equal, can also reasonably
accept"; and given that others may not accept one's particular "philosophy of life," the defense of those terms cannot depend on that
philosophy.

The question, then, is whether, and to what extent, privacy rights and/or
privacy conventions can be defended on the basis of deliberative democracy and its conception of public reason. Though Cohen expresses skepticism regarding the extent to which this framework can be used to defend
informal privacy conventions, he claims that it does provide support for
privacy rights. And one of the more theoretically significant implications
of this claim is that defense of such rights does not depend on political
liberalism; for, as Cohen emphasizes, liberalism is simply one philosophy
of life among others, and, as such, cannot be appealed to in the public reasoning that underlies those rights.

In "An Argument for Egalitarian Justice and Against the Leveling-Down
Objection," Thomas Christiano defends equality as a principle of distributive justice, a principle asserting "that individual persons are *due* equal
shares in some fundamental substantial good" (where a "fundamental
good" is a good "whose value is not derivative from any other good," and
a "substantial" good is one that "any rational being must pursue"). He distinguishes this view from views according to which equality is merely a
"good making property," and also from both (1) a "formal" conception
according to which "one must treat relevantly like cases alike and unlike
cases unlike," and (2) a "moral" conception according to which "all human
beings have the same *fundamental moral status*." The latter two conceptions, however, are included among the premises used in his defense of his

distributive principle, a defense that also appeals to (3) a "principle of propriety," (4) a particular conception of the special significance or status of persons, and (5) a closely related conception of "well-being" as the substantial fundamental good that should be distributed equally. The principle of propriety is simply the principle that justice consists in a person's getting his or her due. Combining this with the "formal" principle, we get the result that "the relevant similarities and distinctions among persons that justify similar or different treatment" must be "ones that are meritorious or features that display a distinctive worth or status in the persons." And our "distinctive worth or status" as persons, Christiano argues, lies in our "humanity" and consists in our "capacity to recognize, appreciate, engage with, harmonize with, and produce intrinsic goods"; the "equal moral status" of human beings then derives from the fact that this capacity is one we all share. Conceiving "well-being" as "that quality of a person's life that involves an appreciative and active engagement with intrinsic goods"—a conception according to which "well-being" is clearly closely connected to that which provides persons their special status— Christiano contends that "well-being" is the good that, according to his principle, should be distributed equally: "only equality of well-being is compatible with the fundamental value of well-being, the formal principle of justice and the absence of relevant differences between persons." The paper concludes with a defense against the "leveling-down objection," the objection that egalitarians are counterintuitively committed to holding, for instance, that if S1 is an egalitarian state, whereas S2 is nonegalitarian but strongly Pareto superior to S1 (everyone has more wellbeing than they do in S1), then S1 is preferable to S2. The heart of Christiano's response is that egalitarians are not committed to holding that every egalitarian state must be superior, in at least one respect, to any nonegalitarian state, but only "that for every nonegalitarian state there is some (not Pareto-superior) egalitarian state that is superior to the nonegalitarian state."

Carl F. Cranor's "Justice, Inference to the Best Explanation, and the Judicial Evaluation of Scientific Evidence" is concerned with the implications of three controversial decisions by the U.S. Supreme Court—*Daubert v. Merrell-Dow Pharmaceuticals Inc.* (1993), *General Electric v. Joiner* (1997), and *Kumho Tire v. Carmichael* (1999)—for the admissibility or inadmissibility of evidence of causation in toxic tort cases. These decisions give judges not only a "heightened duty" to determine whether (alleged) scientific evidence of causality is admissible, but wide latitude both in making, and in deciding how to make, this determination. And, in Cranor's view, the admissibility decisions courts have made on the basis of this heightened duty have often been mistaken, primarily because they have failed to appreciate both the importance of "inference to the best explanation" as a form of scientific reasoning and the various kinds of evidence that can provide a basis for such inferences. The specific mistakes courts have made, according to Cranor, include the following, among others:

1. Demanding that experts base their testimony at least in part on epidemiological studies. As Cranor argues, although good epidemiological studies provide excellent evidence of causation, they are not the only source of such evidence; case studies (to which Cranor devotes considerable attention), animal studies, and diagnostic tests may also provide such evidence, evidence that in many circumstances is sufficient.

2. Regarding negative epidemiological studies as demonstrating lack of causation. This in effect conflates "no evidence of effect" with "evidence of no effect."

3. Excluding specific kinds of evidence, such as case studies and animal evidence—and relatedly, failing to appreciate the "never throw evidence away" principle and "weight of the evidence" arguments. For example, in *General Electric v. Joiner*, the district court excluded each item of evidence piecemeal without considering the weight of the evidence as a whole—a policy that the Supreme Court later strongly endorsed.

And in virtue of such mistakes it may well be that plaintiffs have unjustifiably been denied relief in cases where they were in fact injured by defendants' toxicants.

The problem of "moral luck"—a problem introduced, at least in recent philosophical literature, by Bernard Williams and Thomas Nagel—is the topic of Nir Eisikovits's "Moral Luck and the Criminal Law." As Eisikovits notes, we constantly make moral—and legal—judgments that depend on factors beyond the agent's control, and, thus, on moral luck. For example, if the driver of a school bus dozes off at the wheel and swerves into the opposite lane, our condemnation of him—and the legal punishment he would face—would typically be much more severe if his lapse injures or kills someone than if it "luckily" does not. Yet this obviously conflicts with standard assumptions about the legitimate bases for, and limits of, the ascription of moral responsibility. Following Nagel, who distinguishes four categories of moral luck—"constitutive luck" (which concerns the agent's inclinations, capacities, etc.), "circumstantial luck" (which involves the problems and situations deriving from an agent's specific history), "causal luck" (which has to do with the circumstances antecedent to action), and "outcome luck" (which concerns the way our projects and actions turn out)—Eisikovits begins by discussing the fourth category, outcome luck, which has been the primary focus of the debate regarding moral luck among commentators on the criminal law. He summarizes, and provides some criticisms of, the arguments on behalf of the opposing views in this debate—the "subjectivist view," which holds that, since "only intentions, and the criminal acts they produce, are subject to an agent's control . . . they alone constitute the appropriate basis for responsibility and punishing," and the "objectivist view," which holds that, although intentions do indeed have a role in the ascription of blame and punishment, the amount of harm that an agent's act causes is also a relevant factor. Yet Eisikovits refuses to take sides in this debate, contending that "the problem of moral luck represents a paradox in the heart of our moral practices; it needs to be described rather than 'solved,' since paradoxes cannot be argued away." But what can be done, he claims, is to "elucidate and explain" how the paradox operates. And he concludes his essay by attempting two such elucidations: (1) a demonstration of the significance for the paradox of the distinction between anger and blame, and (2) a discussion of the ways in which, despite the emphasis in the literature on outcome luck, both constitutive luck and circumstance luck are relevant to the criminal law.

In "Intellectual Property and Traditional Chinese Culture," Philip J. Ivanhoe looks at the historical and intellectual background of traditional China in an attempt to explain why China has not developed a strong conception of intellectual property rights. He rejects the explanation propounded by William P. Alford in *To Steal a Book Is an Elegant Offense: Intellectual Property Law in Chinese Civilization*—an explanation whose central contention, according to Ivanhoe, is that "classical, canonical sources" were so revered in traditional China "that no one dared to claim that they had created something new and of sufficient value to bother identifying it as their own." Ivanhoe rejects this explanation on the grounds that, first, it does not distinguish China from the West—indeed, Ivanhoe claims that there were perhaps more competing traditions, and more variety within each tradition, in China than in the West; and, second, that, even if there had been a unified view concerning the significance of certain classical sources in traditional China, "there is no clear conceptual link" between this and opposition to the idea of intellectual property. Ivanhoe's alternative explanation contains two "complementary parts." The first concerns the fact that intellectuals were construed as working for, or at least in support of, the empire, to which, therefore, anything they produced belonged. Hence, "there was little room for personal claims of ownership." And the second concerns the philosophical conception of knowledge, or at least its most important part—knowledge of the *Dao* or "Way." The crucial point here is that, given the *Dao*'s objectivity, activity that conforms to it is regarded as arising "out of spontaneous, natural processes as opposed to calculated, personal schemes," and is thus "thought to be *ziran* 'so of itself' rather than the result of individual effort." Hence, "any idea or cultural creation that is true, good, and beautiful can never belong to an individual, rather, both by nature and function, it belongs to everyone." At the end of his paper Ivanhoe suggests some possibly fruitful modifications to the policies and attitudes we adopt in dealing with China, and with other countries, on the issue of intellectual property.

Property rights are also the focus of Ann Levey's "Initial Acquisition and the Right to Private Property"—though her concerns, and the context of her discussion, are very different from Ivanhoe's. Levey criticizes theories that claim that the initial acquisition of goods yields full ownership rights. "First possession justifications," in her view, depend on the "asymmetry thesis," the thesis that, since later comers are competing with those who are already using the goods or territory in question whereas first comers are competing with no one, there is a significant asymmetry between first possessors and those who arrive later. And the asymmetry thesis in turn rests on two assumptions, the "no antecedent claims" assumption and the "moral meaningfulness of first claims" assumption—assumptions that, she argues, "are at least contentious." One reason one might reject the "no antecedent claims" assumption, Levey suggests, is that one might hold that "everyone has equal competing claims to the world." Such a view she ascribes to Locke; for Locke held that God gave the earth to mankind in common, which means we all have rights to it—and, thus, that it's false to say that, prior to acquisition by a first comer, there are "no antecedent claims." Further, although she admits that asymmetry is part of Locke's account, she contends that his asymmetry "is uninteresting from a justificatory point of view" since it "plays a role in allocation only. The justificatory role is played by one's equal claim to have access to the means of self-preservation." Moreover—and crucially—she argues that accounts such as Locke's fail to justify "full-blown ownership rights." Turning to the moral meaningfulness of first claims assumption, Levey contends that proponents of the asymmetry thesis assume that, given the no antecedent claims assumption, initial acquisition is "morally unproblematic." But although "mere takings" may be morally unproblematic in this context, the acquisition of genuine property rights, she argues, is not. For genuine property rights impose duties on later comers, duties that those later comers need a moral reason to accept; and later comers "appear to have no such moral reason, at least in the absence of already sharing a conception of acquisition with would-be appropriators." In short, the moral meaningfulness of first claims assumption is essentially question-begging.

In "Justice and Strict Liability" I discuss the strict liability policy that most states have applied to product liability since the 1960s. According to this policy, a company is properly held liable for harms caused by a defect in one of its products even if that defect did not result from negligence, or any other fault, on the part of the company. This policy thus conflicts with what seems to be a very plausible principle regarding the conditions under which a person (including a legal person, such as a company) can justly be held responsible for a harm—the principle that, roughly, a person cannot justly be held responsible for a harm unless either (1) that person voluntarily agreed to take responsibility for harms such as the one in question, or (2) the harm resulted from that person's doing something wrong. I argue that neither the two main legal defenses of strict liability—the "make the company shape up" defense and the "distribute the burden" defense—nor two recent philosophical defenses by George G. Brenkert and John J. McCall succeed in defending strict liability against the charge that it is unjust because it violates this principle. I conclude, however, by giving my own defense of strict liability, a defense that attempts to undermine this charge by showing that not only are there a number of noncontroversial cases outside the product liability sphere in which our judgments of responsibility conflict with this principle—cases in which we hold

parents responsible for harms caused by their children, pet owners responsible for harms caused by their pets, and so on—but that such cases share
important features with product liability cases. In short, I attempt to show
that, if this principle is not simply false, it at least has an important class
of exceptions, a class that can properly be taken to include product liability cases. At the end of the paper I make a very tentative suggestion regarding the principle, or type of principle, that may underlie these exceptions.

One of the foundational issues in moral theory—the justification of
rights—is the topic of Leif Wenar's "The Value of Rights." His focus is the
debate between "status-based" and "instrumental" theories of rights, the
former claiming that rights are justified as due the rights-holder in virtue
of his or her status, the latter that they are justified as "instruments for
achieving further state of affairs"—more specifically, as "instruments for
bringing about distributions of advantage." Though this distinction may
sound like the distinction between Kantianism and utilitarianism, Wenar
insists that "the stylized contrast between Kantian theories and utilitarian
theories is misleading." For in the first place this contrast is not exhaustive; the class of instrumental theories, Wenar claims, is a great deal larger
than the class of utilitarian theories and includes, inter alia, egalitarianism, perfectionism, Scanlon's contractualism, both Dworkin's and Posner's
theories of law, and even Rawls's theory of justice. And in the second place,
status-based and instrumental theories, as he construes them, are not
mutually exclusive. Indeed, at the end of the paper he argues not only that
a few rights—for example, the "right in utilitarianism to have one's interests taken equally into account," or the "right in Dworkin's theory to equal
concern and respect"—require a status-based justification, but that such
rights are foundational for instrumental theories. His central concern,
however, is to show that most rights, including "classical individual rights"
such as rights to free speech and bodily integrity, can best be defended
by instrumental theories. Focusing primarily on free speech, Wenar argues,
for example, that instrumental theories, unlike status-based theories, can
appeal not only to the advantages of free speech for those who exercise it
but to its advantages for audiences. And on a more specific issue, he argues
that instrumental theories can do a much better job of explaining "an
interesting and important part of our settled understanding of the right to
free speech," namely, "that there should be a legal right to lie in political
speech, but no legal right to lie in commercial speech."

Despite the great variety of issues and concerns illustrated by these essays, perceptive readers will no doubt be able to find a number of connections among them. I will conclude this introduction by considering one such connection, a focus on the strategy of attempting to derive comparatively specific, and often controversial, judgments from more abstract and putatively less controversial principles. At least four of the eight essays I describe can legitimately be viewed as having at least some concern with this strategy. Levey in effect criticizes an attempted use of it by contending that the relevant grounding principles are more controversial than their proponents assume; I make a similar criticism, but conclude with a brief, tentative, suggestion of my own that in effect adopts this strategy; and the central arguments of both Cohen and Christiano clearly employ it. And it seems to this writer that, though this strategy is of course used often throughout philosophy, it is perhaps used more widely in moral and social philosophy than anywhere else. But of course this strategy faces well-known difficulties; any attempted use of it is subject to the challenge that the supporting principles are no less controversial than the more concrete judgments they allegedly support, and/or that they do not really support those judgments. Despite the admiration many people (including this writer) have for Kant's moral theory, for example, there are very few philosophers who would accept the claim that the categorical imperative is both a logically necessary principle of practical reason and a principle from which specific, concrete, duties can be deductively derived. These problems, moreover, exist even where one does not employ the extreme form of the strategy found in traditional rationalism—that is, even where one does not claim both that the relevant grounding principles are logically or metaphysically necessary and that the derivation of specific judgments from those principles is demonstrative.

In concluding, then, I want to illustrate the force of these problems by showing how one might criticize one of Cohen's attempted applications of, or derivations from, his conception of deliberative democracy. Cohen argues that, on the basis of this conception (and, thus, without appealing to political liberalism), we can defend an essentially permissive, pro-choice policy regarding legal restrictions on abortion. Having contended that, once we accept this conception, "we need to let political ideas of burdensomeness track the weight of reasons within the reasonable views of those we are regulating," Cohen argues that restrictive regulations against abortion are "especially burdensome"—and thus conflict with legitimate privacy rights—because they undermine both the equality of women and the right, in the words of the U.S. Supreme Court's *Casey* decision, "to define one's own concept of existence, of meaning, of the universe, and of the mystery of human life." Opponents of abortion may respond, of course, by arguing that abortion is "the taking of innocent human life." But this argument, he contends, "cannot be made, except by appealing to a particular outlook that is rejected by many who are reasonable, politically speaking"—which means that this argument is illegitimate within the framework of deliberative democracy. The problem with this contention, however, is that, just as the view that abortion is "the taking of innocent human life" appeals "to a particular outlook that is rejected by many who are reasonable, politically speaking," so does any opposing view—from the view that a fetus is just a hunk of organic material with no moral significance to Thomson's view that, even if a fetus has full personhood status, a woman has no obligation to grant it the use of her body. Hence, if arguments in defense of the former view are illegitimate in Cohen's framework, so, it would seem, are arguments in defense of any of the latter. Nor does the appeal to "burdensomeness" help Cohen's position. For from the point of view of opponents of abortion, permitting abortions imposes the ultimate burden—death—on beings who should be given full consideration when burdens are being calculated, namely, fetuses. (Consider, for example, how implausible it would be to use Cohen's argument to defend a policy permitting the killing of infants. And lest this example be dismissed on the ground that such a policy could not be supported by anyone who is "politically reasonable," remember that, in the context of the abortion debate, some philosophers have put forward serious defenses of infanticide.) In sum, it would appear that Cohen's framework cannot, in the end, determine the appropriate legal policy regarding abortion. And since Cohen's framework is essentially procedural, this is just what one would antecedently expect.

My purpose here has not been to attack Cohen's framework, for I think not only that his other attempted applications of it are more plausible but that the framework overall is very interesting and worthy of serious discussion. And I am certainly not challenging the strategy at issue in general—indeed, any such challenge on my part would be inconsistent, since, as I have indicated, I suggest an application of this strategy myself, albeit in a very cautious and limited way, at the end of my own contribution. My purpose, rather, has been to emphasize the difficulties which those of us who attempt to employ the strategy must be prepared to confront, difficulties that serve to remind us (as if any of us needs such a reminder!) how difficult it is to do philosophy—and in particular, how difficult it is to produce arguments sufficient to convince not only ourselves but our philosophical colleagues that the claims and theories we are attempting to defend are both significant and true.

2   Privacy, Pluralism, and Democracy

Joshua Cohen

So the spheres of the political and the public, of the nonpublic and the private, fall out from the content and application of the conception of justice and its principles. If the so-called private sphere is alleged to be a space exempt from justice, then there is no such thing. . . .

Sometimes those who appear to reject the idea of public reason actually mean to assert the need for full and open discussion in the background culture. With this political liberalism full agrees. . . .

—John Rawls, "The Idea of Public Reason Revisited"[1]

Privacy is a controversial idea of law and political morality. The controversy it provokes can be divided into two areas. The first is about the *right to privacy*, which requires protections of certain kinds of information and conduct from public disclosure and regulation. Debate about the privacy right considers how we should characterize its content; whether that content (if there is such a right) transcends concrete rights that protect reputation, property, and bodily integrity; what connection, if any, there is between the protection of interests in personal independence characteristic of constitutional privacy and the protections of interests in nonintrusion and nondisclosure of personal information associated with tort privacy; and what special challenges to such protections may arise from new communications technologies. Stylizing greatly, we might distinguish two parties to the dispute: *privacy skeptics* think we should reject, as uncontrollably capacious, a right to privacy that transcends protections of reputation, property, and bodily integrity; *antiskeptics* think that an expansive privacy right protects a distinct set of interests in personal independence and need not be objectionably open-ended, even if the relevant set of interests is not crisply circumscribed.

A second concern, more cultural than constitutional, is about conventions of privacy—about the informal social norms that distinguish *public* topics, which are fit for discussion, revelation, or disclosure, from topics that are unsuitable for public consideration. Once more, we have two stylized positions. The skeptic worries that solicitude for privacy masks protection for privilege. Fueled by reflection on the history of appeals to the family and firm as spheres of private ordering, skeptics fear that a crisp public–private distinction in cultural debate will put the roots of too much injustice and unreason beyond the reach of public criticism. The antiskeptic argues that inattention to the boundaries between private and public damages both private and public life: it damages private life, because it threatens to "normalize" private diversity and complexity by subjecting it to public scrutiny; it damages public life by swamping deliberation about common concerns with therapeutic *self*-disclosure and the intrusive revelation of personal information. Thus Hannah Arendt expressed concern about our "eagerness to see recorded, displayed and discussed in public what were once strictly private affairs and nobody's business."[2] And Thomas Nagel has urged that "something has gone wrong, in the United States, with the conventions of privacy"—that more or less any topic is now seen as fair game for public discussion.[3]

In this essay, I explore both topics—privacy rights and privacy conventions—within the framework of a deliberative conception of democracy. I will proceed in three steps. First, I sketch the rudiments of the deliberative conception, and indicate how its three essential elements—reasonable pluralism, reasoning, and equality—provide a basis for rights to personal liberties, and thus assign an essential place in democracy to the liberties of the moderns.

Second, I extend this framework to the specific case of privacy rights, and focus on the issues of life, death, and sex that have been the subject of constitutional privacy debates in the United States since the mid-1960s. Rejecting skepticism, I argue that privacy rights—which I understand as protecting *independence of judgment*—have an essential place in a democracy understood as a society of equals. Once we acknowledge the pluralism of philosophies of life characteristic of such a society, I argue, we should understand privacy rights as expressing democracy's central values, not as constraints on such expression.

Finally, third, I discuss conventions of privacy. Here I am more skeptical. Drawing on the distinction between an informal sphere of public

discussion and cultural argument and the formal political sphere of authoritative collective decision making, I argue that the case for strong norms
of reticence is more compelling in the latter than in the former. I accept
what Rawls has called the *duty of civility* in the political public sphere of a
democracy, and agree that that duty imposes restrictions on appropriate
forms of public justification. But I do not think there is a comparable case
for the application of that duty to the informal public sphere: to what I
will call the system of *cultural democracy*. The idea of democracy as a society
of equals has different implications in the political sphere and the informal public sphere. In particular, the fundamental pluralism that makes
privacy rights essential to a deliberative-democratic system of authoritative
collective decision making should achieve more open expression in the
informal, democratic public sphere.

Deliberative Democracy[4]

1. The deliberative-democratic idea is that authoritative collective decisions should issue from public reasoning among equals. Three ideas play
a central role in this conception:
• The fact of reasonable pluralism, according to which citizens endorse a
plurality of politically reasonable philosophies of life;
• The requirement of deliberation, which states that the justification of
authoritative collective decisions should be founded on public reasoning;
• A conception of the members of a democratic society as free and equal.

These three conditions, I suggest, impose restrictions on the principles and
values that provide the proper terms of public-political justification in a
democracy: that is, they circumscribe the content of democracy's public
reason. After sketching these three ideas, then, I will indicate how they
support a conception of the content of public reason that includes a constitutive role of personal, nonpolitical liberties.

First, then, the fact of reasonable pluralism is the fact that there are
distinct and incompatible philosophies of life to which people, who are
reasonable politically speaking, are drawn under favorable conditions for
the exercise of practical reason. By a *philosophy of life*—what Rawls calls a
"comprehensive doctrine"—I mean an all-embracing view, religious or
secular in foundation, liberalist or traditionalist in substance, that includes
an account of all ethical values and, crucially, provides a general guide to

conduct, individual as well as collective. People are *reasonable, politically speaking*—in short, politically reasonable—only if they are concerned to live with others on terms that those others, understood as free and equal, can also reasonably be expected to accept.

I say "politically reasonable" because the relevant notion of reasonableness is suited to the context of political questions. Generically speaking, a reasonable person is someone who gives due attention to the considerations that bear on an issue, and whose judgments and conduct reflect that attention. So a person is politically reasonable if he or she gives due attention to *the facts about the political relation of citizens in a democracy*—in particular, the fact that political power is the collective power of equals: that it belongs to us all, and that government of the people is to be by and for the people. The fact of reasonable pluralism, then, is the fact that when politically reasonable people engage in conscientious, good-faith efforts at the exercise of practical reason—aimed at deciding how to live—those efforts do not converge on a particular philosophy of life, but lead to different views, many of which are compatible with democracy itself.

The fact of reasonable pluralism does not express a skeptical, or nihilist, or relativist view about conceptions of the right way to live and the place of human beings in the world: it does not say that the truth in these matters is unknowable, or that there is no truth, or that the truth varies across persons, or cultures, or places; nor does it deny any of these views. Certainly people who hold different outlooks think of their views as true: they believe them, and believing is believing true. The fact of reasonable pluralism does not conflict with what they believe, but says that the truth in such matters, if there be such, *transcends the exercise of practical reason that we can appropriately expect of others, as equals in the political society*. So it affirms a kind of toleration of reasonable differences in ultimate outlook. As the italicized formulation indicates, when we assert the fact of reasonable pluralism, we are already operating within the domain of political argument. We are not relying on a philosophical theory about the scope and competence of reason that provides common ground for different outlooks: the nature and competence of reason, both theoretical and practical, is one matter on which such outlooks disagree. Instead, we are making a point about what we can appropriately expect of others, as free and equal.

A crucial point for the issue of privacy is that liberalism itself is both a political outlook and a philosophy of life.[5] As a philosophy of life, liberalism emphasizes the importance of autonomous choice—of reflective self-direction—as a guide to conduct. As a political outlook, liberalism is committed, inter alia, to securing basic personal and political liberties through a system of rights, whose precise content is a matter of controversy. One such controversy is about the scope and content of privacy rights, and about whether such rights depend on a liberal philosophy of life. I believe that they do not, for reasons I will discuss later.

Second, the deliberative conception of democracy puts public reasoning at the center of political justification, which I understand as the justification of coercively enforced regulations. To clarify, let's distinguish two conceptions of democracy, *aggregative* and *deliberative*. The basic distinction lies in their interpretations of the fundamental idea of a democratic society as a society of equals, and thus of a collective decision made or authorized by citizens as equals. Both views apply in the first instance to *institutions* of binding collective decision making, and each interprets the basic democratic ideal that such institutions are to treat people bound by collective decisions—subject to them and expected to comply with them—as equals. According to aggregative conceptions of democracy, decisions are collective just in case they arise from procedures of binding collective choice that assign equal weight to—or, more generically, are positively responsive to—the interests of each person bound by the decisions.[6] According to a deliberative conception, a decision is collective just in case it emerges from arrangements of binding collective choice that foster *free public reasoning among equals who are governed by the decisions.*

The two views—aggregative and deliberative—share a conception of political power as the collective power of equals. And they share the idea that that power is exercised over members who typically do not have effective exit options from the political society.[7] The deliberative view then adds that the exercise of this power is rendered suitably collective—appropriately by and for the people—only if the considerations that figure in public argument used to justify its exercise (at least on fundamentals) belong to the common reason of members.

According to the deliberative interpretation, then, democracy is a system of social and political arrangements that ties the exercise of collective power to free reasoning among equals. Which considerations count as reasons? The answer will not take the form of a generic account of what a reason is, but a statement of which considerations count in favor of proposals within a deliberative setting suited to the case of free political association among equals, understood to include an acknowledgment of reasonable pluralism. This background is reflected in the kinds of reasons that will be acceptable: meaning, as always, acceptable to individuals as free and equal.

Third, then, in democratic deliberation, participants are and regard one another as *free*: recognizing the fact of reasonable pluralism, they acknowledge that no comprehensive moral or religious view provides a defining condition of participation or a test of the acceptability of arguments in support of the exercise of political power. Moreover, a democracy is a society of equals. Everyone with the deliberative capacities—which is to say, more or less all human beings—has and is recognized as having equal standing at each of the stages of the deliberative process. Each, that is, can propose issues for the agenda, propose solutions to the issues on the agenda, and offer reasons in support of or in criticism of proposed solutions. And each has an equal voice in the decision.

2. I have sketched the deliberative conception of democracy, with its three main ideas—reasonable pluralism, reasoning, and equality. Subject to these assumptions, political justification cannot proceed simply by advancing considerations that one takes to be true or compelling. For those considerations—whether about the importance of personal autonomy in the conduct of life or the value or rightness of willing submission to divine command—may well be rejected by politically reasonable equals, with conflicting philosophies of life, founded on opposing religious and moral outlooks. One needs instead to find considerations that can reasonably be expected to be acceptable to others, as equals: with political power as the power of all as equals—imposed on all and in the name of all—political justification is to proceed on common ground. Interpreted by reference to pluralism, equality, and deliberation, democracy emerges as an arena not only of public rights but of autonomous public argument—a space of public reasoning and justification open to all on equal terms.

These considerations have implications for the content of democracy's public reason: they constrain suitable political reasons in a democracy. What is of immediate interest is that they provide a way to show the essential place of nonpolitical liberties in a democracy, and underscore that that place does not require an appeal to a moral-liberal philosophy of life. In particular, pressure for liberty comes from at least two sources within the political ideal of democracy.

First, because of the pluralism of philosophies of life among political reasonable citizens, some bases for regulating conduct are politically weightless. To take the clearest case, people hold some commitments on faith, and take those commitments to impose overriding obligations. Such nonnegotiable commitments are not as such unreasonable, nor is there anything unreasonable about embracing them as true. But because they are expressly held as truths known through faith they are matters on which reasonable people disagree, and adherents cannot reasonably expect others to accept those considerations as having any weight, and therefore cannot use them in justifying regulations. And the fact that they cannot will impose pressure for personal liberties—say, religious and moral liberty—which are often restricted for such unacceptable reasons.

Second, acceptable considerations—which are not weightless—will have different weights in political justification. Even if they are not weightless, they may be insufficient to override the reasons that can be acknowledged, consistent with reasonable pluralism, as commending or commanding the conduct whose regulation is under contemplation. And the weight will depend on the nature of the regulated conduct, and in particular on the weight of the reasons that support the conduct.

Take, for example, the value of public order. It provides an acceptable rationale for regulating conduct. Different outlooks have different ways of explaining the value of public order—as a precondition of the full exercise of personal autonomy, as an expression of submission to God's law—and people are bound to disagree about what public order requires. But it will not be acceptable to suppose that, as a general matter, the value of public order transcends all other political values. Except perhaps in the most extreme circumstances, for example, a state may not impose a blanket prohibition on alcohol consumption—including consumption during religious services—in the name of public order. After all, the considerations that support such consumption include considerations of obligation, which will provide a suitable basis for rejecting a justification cast in terms of the value of public order, except in the most extreme conditions. To be sure, not all citizens acknowledge the obligations in question. But even

those who do not can see the weightiness of those reasons, within the outlooks of other politically reasonable citizens.

I will come back later, in the discussion of privacy, to this idea about
the weightiness of reasons that support a course of conduct. Suffice to say
here that if we take these two considerations together, we have the basis
for a strong case for rights to religious, moral, and expressive liberties
as elements of democracy's public reason. Thus, conduct in these areas
is supported by strong (perhaps compelling) reasons, as when religious
exercise is a matter of obligation according to a person's reasonable religious outlook. At the same time, standard reasons for restriction—religious
and sectarian moral reasons—will often be weightless. More generally,
we can see, at least in general terms, how a case for personal liberties
emerges without resting on ideas—of personal autonomy, individuality, or
self-ownership—drawn from liberalism, understood as a general philosophy of life. The ideas of pluralism and deliberative justification addressed
to equals together establish a stricture against religious and moralistic
justification (along with the stricture against secular-liberal moral justification); moreover, they require attention to the burdensomeness of regulations, as defined by the nature of the reasons that support the regulated
conduct.

Given this rationale for personal liberties, we can see why they are elements of democracy. For imposing regulations in the name of reasons that
are either weightless or of insufficient force to override reasonable demands
violates the fundamental democratic idea: the idea that a democracy is a
society of equals and that authorization to exercise state power must arise
from the *collective decisions* of the equal members of a society who are governed by that power, that such authorization must be supported by reasons
that can be shared by the addressees of the regulations.

Privacy Rights

1. Thus far I have sketched a general framework of ideas about democracy,
and indicated how at least some personal liberties might be understood to
have a constitutive place in democracy's public reason. Under conditions
of moral pluralism, the collective authorization that lies at the heart of
democracy has limited scope.

What, then, about the right of privacy—in particular, a right to personal independence in areas of life, death, and sex? Can it be defended without appealing to a liberal philosophy of life? Skepticism in American constitutional argument about a capacious right to privacy derives in part from the concern that such a right *does* depend on a liberal philosophy of life. In particular, constitutional theorists who interpret the constitution as fundamentally a design of democracy, whether aggregative or deliberative, have typically been skeptical about a constitutional privacy right, in part for this reason.[8] Because the constitution is a shared, fundamental, public-political framework, they are troubled—as they should be—by the constitutionalization of a liberal philosophy of life.

Although their concerns are reasonable, their conclusions are incorrect. A fundamental right of privacy does not depend on a liberal philosophy of life. Or so I hope to show.

2. To focus the discussion, I will begin with a widely cited remark in the 1977 Supreme Court case of *Roe v. Whalen*. The details of the case do not matter here. Suffice to say that Justice Stevens there distinguishes two kinds of interests that privacy rights are commonly thought to protect: "the individual interest in avoiding disclosure of personal matters . . . and the interest in independence in making certain kinds of important decisions."[9] The former is the constitutional analogue of one of the interests protected by the privacy tort, and I will not discuss it here—apart from noting that it overlaps the latter, inasmuch as disclosure may itself undermine independence in decision making.[10]

So my focus will be on Stevens's remark about the interest in "independence in making certain kinds of important decisions"—what might be described as *independence of judgment*. The phrase "certain kinds of important decisions" invites the question: which kinds of decisions? One familiar kind of answer strikes me as not very helpful. In particular, I cannot see how we could possibly identify the private arena with the family, or the economy, or with any arena of social life, identified— either spatially or institutionally—prior to normative political argument. My doubts are founded on a familiar line of thought. Once we acknowledge that the organization of any sphere is in part a result of collective decisions, and may have decisive bearing on the lives of equal citizens, then we cannot adopt a hands-off policy to a sphere identified in advance. In the United States, the New Deal taught this lesson about the economy; and feminism, both as a movement and a theory, taught this lesson about the family.[11] Thus the thesis that a decision is private, and ought not therefore to be regulated except for especially compelling reasons, is not best understood as a premise in political argument—*because the decision* is private, we should not regulate it—but as a conclusion of such argument.

3. How, then, are we to characterize the kinds of decisions that ought to be protected as private? I propose that we do so by reference to the weight of the reasons that support them, in the judgments of those who makes the decisions. I do not have a precise characterization of this idea (I am not sure that a precise characterization is appropriate), and I do not wish to suggest that there will be general agreement about the relative weight of different sorts of reasons. Still, the idea strikes me as essential.

Consider some examples that may help explain it. When I say that a course of conduct is a matter of obligation, I claim that it has support from an especially weighty reason. If, in contrast, I say that I prefer one course of conduct to another, even that I prefer it intensely, I am downgrading the kind of reason that supports the conduct. If I say that something is essential to a decent human life, then the reason has considerable weight. If I say that it is a good thing to do, then the weight is greater than if it is a matter of preference (even intense preference), but not as substantial as when it is a matter of obligation or essential to a decent life.

Of course different philosophies of life will interpret these categories differently, and assign different content to them: such philosophies will differ, for example, on the nature and content of our obligations to preserve human life, or on the scope and weight of duties of charity. The essential point is that, once we accept the three essential elements of the deliberative conception of democracy—reasonable pluralism, equality, and deliberative justification—then we need to let political ideas of burdensomeness track the weight of reasons within the reasonable views of those we are regulating. Thus it will not be acceptable to say that we will make special efforts not to burden people by preventing them from fulfilling their fundamental obligations, but then deny that their own politically reasonable views about what those obligations are have any weight—to say that we respect people's obligation to keep the Sabbath, but then to insist that, after all, the only Sabbath they have any obligation to keep falls on Sunday.

4. Consider now how these observations apply to some of the issues about life, death, and sex—issues that are arguably to be covered by a constitutional privacy right, and that have been at the center of the debate about that right in the United States. I will be very brief on these extraordinarily complex issues, because I mean to be illustrating the framework rather than saying anything very distinctive about the issues themselves.

Thus, in the case of abortion, three considerations suggest the conclusion that restrictive regulations are especially burdensome. First, there is the burden on women's equality if women are required to carry unwanted pregnancies to term. This point is acknowledged in the Supreme Court's 1992 *Casey* decision, with reference to the consequences of a twenty-year adjustment to the *Roe* regime—"The ability of women to participate equally in the economic and social life of the nation has been facilitated by their ability to control their reproductive lives"[12]—but the same point could have been made without the reference to issues of adjustment to *Roe v. Wade*.

Second, restrictive regulations burden women's liberty, by restricting choices of a deeply personal kind, thus impinging on a woman's exercise of personal responsibility about the course of her life. They represent a substantial denial of judgment about the conduct of elementary aspects of life. There is of course an equality aspect to the issue here, inasmuch as no comparable denial is contemplated for men. But the relevant burden would not be alleviated by generalizing it.

A third burden—the burden on judgment—results from the kinds of reasons that commonly support decisions about continuing life, and is especially pertinent here. In its *Casey* decision, the U.S. Supreme Court says that "at the heart of liberty is the right to define one's own concept of existence, of meaning, of the universe, and of the mystery of human life,"[13] and it supposes that women take guidance from such judgments in making decisions about childbirth. And in *Life's Dominion*, Ronald Dworkin has characterized the relevant judgments as "spiritual" disagreements about the relative importance of natural and human contributions to the value of a human life.[14]

The burdens on equality and liberty are not especially controversial: someone may think that they are overridden, but surely they are substantial. Moreover, as to the burden on judgment, we can argue over how precisely to characterize the relevant judgments, but however they are characterized, the point is that they have considerable weight. Moreover, we can debate how to explain the disagreements about these judgments, and offer views about why they have the weight that they do. But for the purposes of political argument, this debate is unnecessary. Suffice to say that the judgments are about when we have compelling reason to ensure the continuation of life: that content indicates their weight, and shows why they are covered by a privacy right, and can be overridden only by reasons of considerable weight.

To be sure, that right could be overridden by an argument that abortion is, as the papal encyclical *Evangelium Vitae* asserts, the taking of innocent human life: such an argument would provide grounds for regulation, despite the three burdens.[15] But that argument cannot be made, except by appealing to a particular outlook about the nature and value of life that is rejected by many who are reasonable, politically speaking. This criticism is driven not by the idea that judgments about the continuation of life are in some way intrinsically private: instead the claim that they are private matters expresses the thesis that there is a strong case for leaving women to their own judgment on these matters, in part because of the weight of the reasons that support their conduct. Requirements of reason giving under conditions of a pluralism of philosophies of life drives the argument.

But there may appear to be a sleight of hand at work here. After all, the pro-life and pro-choice positions seem completely symmetrical. That is, either abortions are restrictively regulated or they are not. If they are restrictively regulated, the side that favors restrictive regulation wins. If they are not, then the side that has a liberal view wins. So yes, some people do reject the justification for regulation: and let's say that they are politically reasonable. But why should their objections carry the day? After all, some people reject the current settlement, which permits abortion. Why do their objections to a permissive regulatory regime not carry as much weight as the objections to a restrictive regime?

This alleged symmetry is illusory. The restrictive regime imposes undeniably substantial burdens on women's liberty, equality, and independence of judgment; in a society of equals those burdens need to be justified, and the terms of that justification must carry some weight with those whose liberty and equality are impaired. Otherwise, we fail to respect them as equals. The restrictive regime cannot stand, then, because no such acceptable justification is available.

The case for a right to die, understood as comprising a right to assisted suicide, is importantly different. To be sure, there is a compelling case for the conclusion that regulations of assisted suicide are burdensome: like restrictive abortion regulations, they regulate conduct governed by judgments about when we have compelling reason to ensure the continuation of life. The considerations that support regulations in this area are, however, of a different kind. In particular, the defense of such regulation need not appeal to a conception of when life ends or what makes a whole life (or parts of it) worth living, but only to concerns about when we have a conclusive showing of a person's willing decision to end her own life, and worries about pressures to make that decision as a way to reduce burdens on family and friends. A compelling case for the conclusion that these decisions about death should be treated as private matters would need to address these concerns. Absent such address, it is not unreasonable for a democratic process to regulate, and thus to hold that the interest in independent judgment, although present and substantial, is overridden (though it would also be reasonable to have a more permissive regime).

In the case of sexual intimacy, there is a strong case for concluding that democracy's public reason must treat it as a private matter—an arena to be regulated by the independent and diverse judgments of individuals. On the one hand the reasons for regulation—a religiously founded moral outlook—are arguably weightless because they are objectionably sectarian.[16] Moreover, the regulations are burdensome, for a reason that Justice Harry Blackmun rightly identified in his powerful dissent in *Bowers v. Hardwick*, and which the Supreme Court more recently embraced in *Lawrence v. Texas*: that intimate relations are an important setting in which we do something of fundamental importance in a decently lived life, namely, work out a sense of our identity. But this importance of sexual intimacy—often one aspect of a personal relationship—is contingent in part on its being guided by the judgments, feelings, and sensibilities of the parties to it.[17] Because of the importance of such intimacy, the reasons that support it are substantial.[18] So democracy's public reason provides a compelling case for treating this as a private matter. But, once more, the claim that it is private does not serve as a premise in the case against regulation. Instead it is a conclusion drawn from reflection on the kinds of reasons that support the regulated conduct and the considerations that might be used to defend a case for its regulation.[19]

Conventions

1. I turn now to the second privacy issue: the social conventions that mark the boundaries between the public and the private. This is a sprawling territory, and to narrow it I will focus here on a discussion of these issues by Thomas Nagel. According to Nagel, we ought to embrace strong norms of reticence to preserve "smooth functioning" in the public domain when we don't need collective decisions and cannot expect agreement. Nagel's discussion of these issues was animated by what he perceived as overreaching in the American public debate surrounding Bill Clinton's impeachment—overreaching by the public, media, and political officials who presumed that Clinton's sexual appetites and habits were fit subjects for public discussion. Prompted by the Clinton controversy, Nagel's argument proceeds well beyond Clinton and sex, to a defense of "cultural liberalism." Though fugitive in its precise content, cultural liberalism is (roughly) the view that we ought to respond to fundamental disagreements in our informal public culture with a restraint—a reticence about criticism—parallel to that which we arguably ought to respect in our formal system of law and politics. Let me explain.

In the formal political system—what Habermas calls the "political public sphere"—where the stakes are authoritative, coercively enforced legal regulations, we should not enforce a particular moral or philosophical outlook, and ought to justify laws and policies by reference to values that can reasonably be embraced by reasonable people who endorse different outlooks: that is the idea of democracy's public reason. Similarly, in the public culture more broadly—what Habermas calls the "informal public sphere", and Rawls "the background culture"—where the stakes include discursive presuppositions, as well as social conventions and norms backed by decentralized sanctions, cultural liberalism requires that, as a general matter, we steer clear of controversial topics about which we cannot expect to reach agreement and that do not demand a collective decision. In the particular case of sex, Nagel says: "We should stop trying to achieve a common understanding in this area and leave people to their mutual incomprehension, under the cover of conventions of reticence."[20] Nagel extends these points to religion, and concludes, quite generally, that it would be "a good idea to leave the public space of a society comfortably habitable, without too much conflict, by the main incompatible elements that are not about to disappear."[21] To be sure, in a culturally liberal world, old-fashioned, "healthy mutual contempt"[22]—for example between and among the communicants of different religions—would flourish, but it would be obscured by tight-lipped, ironic smiles.

So cultural liberalism means two things. First, it rejects communitarian aspirations to control the public culture and establish cultural uniformity, and requires instead what might be called a "cultural democracy," in which all members are entitled to participate as equals in shaping the public cultural environment. Second, cultural liberalism takes a particular view about what such participation and cultural democracy involve: it commands reticence about the public expression of fundamental disagreements. These two elements are independent; reticence does not follow from opposition to communitarianism. To be sure, the attractions of permanent Kulturkampf are themselves a matter of persistent conflict. But those who are drawn to it—a group that arguably extends from Machiavelli and Mill to the postmodernist friends of an agonistic public realm—are all anticommunitarian. So we need additional argument in favor of cultural liberalism with its norms of reticence as an alternative to cultural democracy with more open public contestation yet no expectation of agreement. And the case for it does not seem very compelling. The connection observed earlier between democracy and liberalism (including rights of privacy) in the political sphere does not extend to a comparable connection between democracy and reticent liberalism in the cultural sphere.

To explain why not, I will make three points: about the costs of reticence, about why the case for political reticence (a duty of civility) does not extend to a more general case for public reticence, and about the benefits of more open public argument even when no agreement is in view.
2. As to the costs of reticence: let's say that a strong convention of reticence or restraint with respect to some area of disagreement requires that we not get into that area at all (anyway, not outside the sphere of close

friends and intimates). Thus there might be a strong convention against any open, public discussion of sex, or religion, or attitudes toward groups different from one's own. The case for such strong conventions of restraint is that they are mutually beneficial. Still—and as ever—legitimate questions can be raised about the distribution of those benefits.

For example, we are all better off with a norm condemning all discussion of who is sleeping with whom, than with a completely permissive view of sexual gossip. But although such a blanket condemnation is facially neutral, men—especially in positions of power—may be especially large beneficiaries of this particular convention: they get multiple sexual partnerships with reduced danger of discovery (because of the convention). For this reason, strong reticence may be perceived—in Nagel's words—"as a form of male mutual self-protection."[23]

To appreciate the force of this observation about the distribution of such benefits, note that a range of different conventions might be adopted toward regulating discussion in this area—all weaker in the restraints they impose on discussion, but also better for all than an unregulated free-for-all. Consider the norm: "don't talk about who is sleeping with whom, unless the target is a powerful man who should know better." That norm—whatever its ultimate merits—would be better for all than the regime of open gossip, but also less likely to be rejected as a form of male mutual self-protection, and arguably helpful in undermining cultural sensibilities that support the abuse of power.

The general problem is familiar from the discussion of problems of social coordination with mixed motives: we have a plurality of conventions; each such convention is mutually beneficial compared with the absence of normative regulation; different conventions are associated with different distributions of benefits; and there is nothing obviously right about the status quo distribution. Under these circumstances, to opt for strong norms of reticence—to insist on strong cultural norms of privacy that would effectively put existing conventions beyond challenge—seems simply to be a matter of endorsing the current distribution, and seems to deny the importance of cultural democracy. Thus, it is right to worry that the "elevation of reticence" is "too protective of the status quo and that it gives a kind of cultural veto to conservative forces who will resent any disruption," at least if we interpret reticence as requiring a *generalized restraint* on any contentious, open public discussion about a topic.[24]

Nagel acknowledges this concern: "Those who favor confrontation and invasion of privacy will think it necessary to overthrow pernicious conventions like the double standard of sexual conduct and the unmentionability of homosexuality. To attack harmful prejudices, it is necessary to give offense by overturning the conventions of reticence that help to support them."[25] But he appears to believe that these costs must be paid—perhaps worrying, with Lord Devlin, that a rejection of regnant cultural norms may put us on the slippery slope that ends in the rejection of civilization itself, on the road to hell in a handbasket. I conclude instead that there is something to classic worries about conventions of privacy: that under the color of neutral norms of decorum, civility, decency, and sheer discretion, they effectively mute criticism of social practices.

3. Strong conventions of reticence, then, impose costs. But perhaps we ought to bear the costs to avoid even greater damage: after all, less reticence may impose greater pressures to conformity, not more disruption of a stifling status quo. This is a large issue, and I can only address a piece of it here. In particular, I want to consider whether the case for restraint in political argument, aimed at the collective exercise of power, carries over to the informal politics of a democratic public culture—to public conversation and interaction quite generally.

Let's start with the idea—associated with democracy's public reason—that there is a duty of civility that requires that we cast our justifications for fundamental laws and policies on the common ground of political values.[26] Although it is permissible to offer justifications that draw on our own philosophy of life, arguments that lie on the common ground of democracy's public reason must—here I follow Rawls—be available and offered "in due course."[27] Thus moral liberals must, for example, present a case for a right to die that does not rely on the thesis that autonomy is the supreme value, or that individuals own themselves. They can also present arguments that do depend on such premises. But the duty of civility requires that they, roughly speaking, also present ("in due course") *some* argument that lies on common ground. And it requires, too, that when they present an argument on a fundamental political question, and do appeal to their own comprehensive outlook, they are not to expose the underlying philosophical, religious, or moral outlooks of their opponents, and subject those outlooks to challenge: they are beyond reproach. So the duty of civility requires a kind of restraint or reticence in the political arena with respect to matters of fundamental disagreement.

I accept the duty of civility, understood as applying to public political argument. But its plausibility, thus applied, reflects two special features of the political domain. First, political debate issues in collective decisions that are made in the name of all: the majority is the tribune of the people. But the fact that laws are made in the name of all, in the name of citizens as equals, naturally suggests that they ought to be justifiable—and be shown to be justifiable—by reference to values that all can reasonably accept, and that should provide for everyone a secure place in the debate: this, as I indicated earlier, is the deliberative interpretation of the idea that democratic decisions should be suitably collective. When the supreme political authority speaks in a democracy, it ought to be manifest that it speaks in the name of equal citizens. In the informal public culture, we find no such corresponding authoritative statement of a conclusion: "cultural democracy" names a social practice of argument among equals, not a form of authority. With no agent authorized to speak for all, there is no corresponding case for restraint in the terms of debate.

Second, collective decisions apply to all, and are backed by the collective power of the state. If we wish to reconcile this coercive imposition of regulation with the recognition of citizens as politically autonomous self-legislators, then the best we can hope for is that the justification of basic laws and policies rests on political values that can be shared. But, once more, there is no comparable coercive imposition in the case of the public culture, and so no comparable requirement of restraint.

I have said that cultural democracy is not a form of authority, and that it does not involve a coercive imposition of constraints comparable to the formal political system. I do not, however, wish to deny that cultural democracy is a form of power, or to deny that cultural norms constrain conduct. To the contrary. Equal standing in the system of cultural democracy is important in part because of the importance of the common environment of cultural norms and standards of taste and value: we do not want to leave these matters in the hands of others, even if we can count on an exercise of collective political authority that is governed by democracy's public reason. For we may still find the public culture and the constraints it fosters deeply uncongenial. Thus Scanlon says: "I have no desire to dictate what others, individually, in couples or in groups, do in their bedrooms, but I would prefer to live in a society in which sexuality and sexual attractiveness, of whatever kind, was given less importance than it is in our society today." Or again, "What I fear is not merely the legal enforcement of religion but its social predominance."[28] In both cases, it is difficult to see how we can challenge the regnant cultural norms, while remaining within the bounds fixed by a duty of civility extended to the informal public sphere. Nevertheless, the two differences—about authority and constraints—remain, and because of these differences, the case for a duty of civility—for reticence about fundamental criticism—seems less forceful in the informal public sphere. A democratic society is a society of equals; but the implications of this idea for the public political sphere differ from its implications for the informal public sphere.[29]

4. So strong reticence carries costs, and there is no case for it comparable to the case for the duty of civility in the political arena. Still, suppose we accept the fact of reasonable pluralism and reject the communitarian aspiration of achieving agreement on fundamentals through open-ended public discussion. Once we accept that we cannot, in any case, expect agreement on these matters, why bother getting into them? What is the point of a more open, democratic public culture, freed from strong conventions of reticence on matters on which agreement is not in view? Why put up with the conflicts ingredient in the informal public sphere; that's a cost, too. Why not reticence?

Consider three kinds of public speech, each of which might break with strong norms of reticence, none of which is presented with any expectation of achieving deeper agreement, but all of which can contribute something important to informal public argument: bearing witness, the expressive presentation of information, and fundamental criticism.

In bearing witness, I present my stand on an issue, act from a sense of personal responsibility in presenting my view, and may feel it necessary to condemn opponents' views at their roots. I do not aim to change minds or to present someone else with information that they lack, but only to state my convictions.

In the expressive presentation of information, people present their hostility to some aspect of the public culture that they find stifling, oppressive, humiliating, or demeaning, in view of who they are—in view of some particular aspect of their identity. The form of this discourse is, "As an *X*, I feel. . . ." I describe this as an expressive presentation of information because I want to emphasize that others may learn something from the complaint, even if not presented with the aim of enlightenment, but simply as a way of expressing a hostile attitude toward a social practice, perhaps with the suggestion that the speaker's finding the practice objectionable suffices to condemn it. The speaker need not expect a collective response, nor be acting in the hope of prompting agreement, but instead may be seen as providing information about how a feature of the culture is not universally appreciated.

By fundamental criticism, I mean an explicit attack on the moral, religious, or philosophical foundations of someone's political outlook—precisely the kind of thing that violates the duty of civility when it happens in political discourse. But there are three reasons for pursuing fundamental criticism rather than adopting a general policy of reticence as a response to fundamental disagreements.

The first reason is, once more, simply informational: I may want to let my opponents know that others who share the public culture with them find their public displays of religiosity creepy, or find their views false, or childish.

Second, I may entertain the more ambitious thought that an awareness of deeper and persisting disagreements will result in some modification of opposing views, particularly if fundamental criticism is coupled with the political respect reflected in the duty of civility. This point has particular force when there are political disagreements that we think are probably rooted in deeper religious or moral disagreements: certainly true in issues about sexuality, life, and death that provided the focus of my discussion of privacy rights. If a duty of civility restrains us from pursuing these disagreements in the political arena, it will be important that there be a setting in which they can be openly aired. Here I offer a speculation about the cultural basis of political democracy: namely, that we are more inclined to keep political deliberation within the confines of democracy's public reason and to respect the duty of civility if we think that opponents have been subjected to more open-ended pressure elsewhere. A vibrant cultural democracy may be supportive of a liberal political democracy, and not only philosophically consistent with it.

Third and finally, I may think that the public culture itself is now one-sided: that it is far easier to express conventional religious sentiment or deploy conventional religious symbols than to express skeptical or hostile views about religion, or to embrace unconventional religious views. Think again of Scanlon's examples. Believing that the public culture is important—that cultural norms do constrain conduct—and rejecting the idea of regulating the culture politically, I think it important that it be open to expressions of fundamental disagreement that do not have a proper place in politics. The point of such expressions is not to produce agreement, or create a comfortably communitarian public culture. Instead, the point is to create a public culture more fully expressive of the pluralism that democracy promises.

To be sure, there are dangers here. As Nagel says, "revolution breeds counterrevolution." Nagel is surely right about the United States: the cultural revolution of the 1960s eventually bred a cultural counterrevolution, filled with nonsense about how the civilization was in much better shape in the 1950s when it was dominated by white Protestant men. More fundamentally, though, my argument here suggests an answer to worries about counterrevolution in response to cultural democracy: with strong protections of privacy rights acting as limits on the exercise of political authority by a society of equals, the informal public sphere of that same society of equals can more easily afford to reject cautious reticence —really, deference to the status quo—as a response to persistent disagreement.

Acknowledgments

I presented earlier versions of this essay at a meeting of the Eastern Division of the American Philosophical Association, at the Universidad Torcuato di Tella, the University of Georgia, as a Donald Kalish Memorial Lecture at UCLA, at the Graduate Center, City University, and at the Inland Northwest Philosophy Conference. I am indebted to Martha Nussbaum, Judith Thomson, Frances Kamm, David Estlund, Andrew Sabl, Seana Shiffrin, Eduardo Rivera-López, and Erik Olin Wright for their helpful comments on earlier versions. I would like to think that my friend Don Kalish would have endorsed the combination of privacy rights and cultural democracy that I endorse here.

Notes

1. Rawls 1997, pp. 791, 769.

2. Cited in Benhabib 1999, p. 45.

3. Nagel 2002, p. 3.

4. The discussion that follows draws on Cohen 1998.

5. A central point of Rawls's political liberalism is to show that liberalism as a political conception does not depend on liberalism as a broader philosophy of life, with a distinctive moral, metaphysical, and epistemological outlook. See Rawls 2001, pp. 153–157. For the alternative view, see Unger 1974 and Sandel 1982.

6. See, for example, the discussion of intrinsic equality and equal consideration in Dahl 1989, pp. 85, 87; and Christiano 1996. Also, conditions imposed on social choice functions—in particular, anonymity and independence—are sometimes motivated in ways that suggest an identification of the requirement that people be treated as equals with the requirement that interests be given equal consideration. See Riker 1982.

7. Rawls (1997, p. 769) suggests that we model the political relation by thinking of it as a relation in a "structure we enter only by birth and exit only by death." To be sure, this modeling assumption is not literally true, but it captures the idea that political decisions are binding on citizens, and that they cannot be made compatible with the freedom of citizens simply by establishing a right to emigrate.

8. See Ely 1980, and Sunstein 1999, esp. pp. 250–252.

9. *Roe v. Whalen.*

10. If having an abortion, for example, meant that your name appeared in the newspaper, then the decision about whether to have one would to that extent be less independent.

11. See the quote from Rawls about the public–private distinction at the start of the essay.

12. *Planned Parenthood v. Casey.*

13. Ibid., p. 851. In *Lawrence v. Texas*, Justice Scalia disparages this remark as the "famed sweet-mystery-of-life passage." He finds two problems with it: laws, he says, never restrict the right to define concepts (he has "never heard of a law" that restricts the "right to define" concepts); and laws standardly restrict conduct based on a self-defined "concept of existence." Thus the famed passage is either vacuous or massively destructive ("the passage that ate the rule of law"). But some laws do restrict beliefs—for example, they attach sanctions to holding them—and laws restricting

beliefs do not contain escape clauses that permit defendants to plead that their belief is a matter of definition ("it is impermissible to deny the Trinity, except when the essential unity of God is asserted to be a matter of definition"). As for "eating the rule of law": the famed passage asserts that conduct that is closely associated with certain kinds of important beliefs (say, in the way that wine consumption is closely associated with belief in the doctrine of transubstantion) should only be regulated for especially compelling reasons. To be sure, it is important to say which beliefs and in what way the conduct is closely associated. But it is not clear why the effort to draw such distinctions is bound to undermine the rule of law, except of course if the rule of law means a law of rigid rules. See Scalia 1989.

14. Dworkin 1993, p. 91.

15. See Pope John Paul II 1995.

16. The majority opinion in *Lawrence v. Texas* notes that the moral reasons that support regulation have, among other things, a religious background (they are "shaped by religious beliefs, conceptions of right and acceptable behavior, and respect for the traditional family"), and asserts their weightlessness, though the weightlessness does not turn on their provenance in religious morality.

17. *Bowers v. Hardwick.*

18. The majority in *Lawrence* cites *Casey's* "sweet-mystery-of-life" passage in explaining the importance of the conduct regulated by restrictions on sexual intimacy. Autonomy in intimate conduct is important because such conduct is tied to independent self-definition.

19. The issue of gay and lesbian marriage raises questions that extend beyond my concerns here, though the considerations I have presented bear on the issue in three ways, which I will simply mention. First, the regulated conduct is supported by important reasons. Second, some of the considerations appealed to in arguments against legal status are weightless: for example, the argument in the Vatican's "Considerations Regarding Proposals to Give Legal Recognition to Unions Between Homosexual Persons" that "marriage is holy, while homosexual acts go against the natural moral law." Third, although arguments about the "best interests of the child" (also in the Vatican statement) are certainly not weightless, they need to be made in a sufficiently compelling way, given the importance of the regulated conduct. The statement is available at http://www.vatican.va/roman_curia/congregations/cfaith/documents/rc_con_cfaith_doc_20030731_homosexual-unions_en.html.

20. Nagel 2002, p. 23.

21. Ibid., p. 24.

22. Ibid.

23. Ibid., p. 23.

24. Ibid., p. 25.

25. Ibid.

26. On the duty of civility, see Rawls 1995, p. 216, and Rawls 1997, pp. 768–769.

27. Rawls 1997, p. 793.

28. Scanlon 1996, p. 30.

29. On this point, see my discussion of the distinction between equal opportunity for electoral, political, and public influence in Cohen 2001.

References

Benhabib, S. 1999. "The Personal is Not the Political." *Boston Review* 24: 45–48.

Bowers v. Hardwick, 478 U.S. 186 (1986).

Christiano, T. 1996. *The Rule of the Many*. Boulder, Colo.: Westview.

Cohen, J. 1998. "Democracy and Liberty." In J. Elster, ed., *Deliberative Democracy*. Cambridge: Cambridge University Press.

———. 2001. "Money, Politics, Political Equality." In A. Byrne, R. Stalnaker, and R. Wedgwood, eds., *Facts and Values*. Cambridge, Mass.: MIT Press.

Dahl, R. 1989. *Democracy and Its Critics*. New Haven, Conn.: Yale University Press.

Dworkin, R. 1993. *Life's Dominion*. New York: Knopf.

Ely, J. 1980. *Democracy and Distrust*. Cambridge, Mass.: Harvard University Press.

Lawrence v. Texas, 123 Sup. Ct. 2472 (2003).

Nagel, T. 2002. "Concealment and Exposure." In *Concealment and Exposure and Other Essays*. Oxford: Oxford University Press.

Planned Parenthood v. Casey, 505 U.S. 833 (1992).

Pope John Paul II. 1995. *The Gospel of Life [Evangelium Vitae]*. New York: Random House.

Rawls, J. 1995. *Political Liberalism*. New York: Columbia University Press.

———. 1997. "The Idea of Public Reason Revisited." *University of Chicago Law Review* 64: 765–807.

———. 2001. *Justice as Fairness: A Restatement*. Erin Kelly, ed. Cambridge, Mass.: Harvard University Press.

Riker, W. 1982. *Liberalism against Populism: A Confrontation Between the Theory of Democracy and the Theory of Social Choice*. San Francisco: W. H. Freeman.

Roe v. Whalen, 429 U.S. 589, 599–600 (1977).

Sandel, M. 1982. *Liberalism and the Limits of Justice*. Cambridge: Cambridge University Press.

Scalia, A. 1989. "The Rule of Law as a Law of Rules." *University of Chicago Law Review* 56: 1175–1188.

Scanlon, T. 1996. "The Difficulty of Tolerance." In D. Heyd, ed., *Toleration*. Princeton, N.J.: Princeton University Press.

Sunstein, C. 1999. *One Case at a Time*. Cambridge, Mass.: Harvard University Press.

Unger, R. 1974. *Knowledge and Politics*. New York: Free Press.

3 An Argument for Egalitarian Justice and against the Leveling-Down Objection

Thomas Christiano

I propose in this essay to give an argument for the principle of egalitarian justice. The argument attempts to establish the intrinsic justice of equality for at least a limited but important range of cases. I refute the often-made leveling-down objection to egalitarianism and show how the principle of equality that I argue for supports Pareto improvements over equality.

What I will do is give an account of egalitarian justice as I understand it. I will then say why an argument for equality is desirable, and I will lay out and defend the principles of formal justice and propriety from which I proceed, as well as a number of subsidiary principles. I will then give the basic argument for egalitarian justice, criticizing sufficiency theories along the way. Subsequently I will show how the traditional leveling-down objection to egalitarian justice fails to impugn the justice of equality, and I will outline some ways in which equality can justly be abridged.

What Is Egalitarian Justice?

We need to distinguish distinct conceptions of equality here. To begin, we might think of equality merely as a good-making property of states of affairs in the sense that Larry Temkin conceives of it. Temkin seems to think of equality as a kind of intrinsic good along with other intrinsic goods such as well-being and that we should try to bring about as much of it as possible. On this view, equality of well-being among persons is a good to be promoted.[1] We can also think of equality in a purely formal sense as understood by Aristotle when he says that justice is equality. This principle states that one must treat relevantly like cases alike and unlike cases unalike. This is distinct from the principle of equality that

I will defend but it is a premise that I will use in the defense of egalitarian justice. In addition, we can understand equality as fundamental equality in the sense that all human beings have the same fundamental moral status. This too is a premise that is required for defending egalitarian justice.

None of the above principles are the same as egalitarian justice. As I understand egalitarian justice, it is a principle of distributive justice. It states that individual persons are *due* equal shares in some fundamental substantial good. This principle is a comparative principle of justice: it makes the share that each person is due a comparative function of what others are due. Distributive justice, as I understand it, is a *condition* among persons wherein each person's good is advanced in a way that is due to him or her. Saying that distributive justice is a condition among persons implies that it is not merely a property of actions. Actions are just to the extent that they ensure that each person receives what is due to him or her. Distributive justice is, at its root, an impersonal notion. That is why, at the limit, we can think that it is just that a person receives his just reward, even if no actions are at the basis of this distribution. It is why, traditionally, it has been thought just that the virtuous are happy and the vicious unhappy. It is also why it is thought unjust when a person is convicted for a crime he did not commit even though the conviction was obtained through the completely conscientious use of an excellent criminal trial procedure and no one is at fault for having made this mistake.

Distributive justice is a condition under which the advantages and disadvantages among persons are distributed in a way that is responsive to the relevant inherent qualities of those persons. The distribution of advantages and disadvantages ought not to be arbitrary or based on considerations that do not reflect the relevant qualities of each person. As a principle of justice, the principle of equality states more than that equality is a good thing to bring about, it states a condition on what human beings are due.

A fundamental substantial good is one whose value is not derived from any other good. The good is substantial in that it is a good any rational being must pursue. Examples of such a fundamental substantial good are well-being and capability in the sense characterized by Amartya Sen.[2] What is crucial about fundamental substantial goods is that they are indeterminate goods in the sense that although more of these goods are better than less for any particular person, what each person ought to have is not settled merely by reference to the nature of the good. Another principle must come in to determine how much of the good a person ought to have or ought to pursue.

In this essay I will argue that the principles of equality in the formal and moral senses in conjunction with some principle of a good life imply a principle of equality of condition. This principle is not a principle for assessing the goodness of states of affairs simpliciter. It is meant to be a principle of justice.

Why Do We Need an Argument for Equality?

Some might say that we already have an adequate reason for thinking that equality of condition is a principle of justice. They may say, for example, that the principle of equality is self-evident. Or they may say that some presumption in favor of equality is self-evident. But this seems to be false or in any case unjustified. It seems false because so many people have thought about the question and have rejected the idea that equality of condition in any form is a principle of justice. And contemporary opponents of equality have been exposed to the idea in its most desirable forms as presented by its most thoughtful and devoted exponents. At the very least, this suggests that the idea that equality of condition is self-evidently a principle of justice is as yet undefended.

A common way of defending equality in recent years has been to say that justice forbids that some people's lives should go worse than others through no fault of their own. These thinkers argue that departures from equality of condition can be justified only by pointing to facts that show that the worse-off people are somehow responsible for their situations. Equality is a way of eliminating the effects of brute luck on the distribution of advantages.[3] But this idea, although quite illuminating, does not give us an argument for equality. It presupposes the idea that we ought to start with equality and only allows departures from it when people are responsible for it. But the question we need to ask is, why ought we think of equality as a starting point from which departures need to be justified? Surely most nonegalitarian thinkers would reject this starting point. Indeed, for most nonegalitarians, this starting point is precisely the principle that they reject.[4] And it is this principle that I wish to defend in this essay.

In addition, an argument for equality as a principle of justice can illuminate the nature of the value of equality. In the argument I give below I show how, and in what circumstances, equality can be intrinsically just. But the argument also shows that equality is a conditional good. It is not the right distribution under all circumstances. Indeed, one advantage that my argument and conception of equality has is that it allows for departures from equality when they work to everyone's advantage. Hence, the conception of equality defended here is not subject to the leveling-down objection. In other words, when we see what reason there is for thinking that equality is just, we will have a clearer idea of the limits on and qualifications of egalitarian justice.

Two Basic Ideas of Justice

There are two fundamental ideas about justice that will play a role in my argument. The first is that justice consists in each person receiving his or her due. We might call this the *principle of propriety*. The second is the commonly accepted principle that one ought to treat relevantly like cases alike and relevantly unlike cases unalike. This principle, called the *formal principle of justice*, is sometimes taken as directly supporting a principle of egalitarian justice. Many authors infer a principle of egalitarian justice once they have shown that there are no relevant differences between persons. I want to show that this inference, in the form that it usually takes, is mistaken but that there is a sound form of the inference.

The formal principle of justice is a principle of *reason*, in part. It assumes that reasons are general and so the same reasons can apply to many like situations. It merely requires that one act in accordance with the relevant reasons relating to a particular situation and it requires that one's treatments of different situations be consistent with the same set of reasons. In this respect it is a principle of rationality; it requires that one's treatment of situations be in accord with the reasons that apply and not with irrelevant considerations. And since the reasons are general, when two situations are relevantly alike the reasons that apply are the same.

But as I shall understand it, it is a principle of *justice*. As a principle of justice the cases it deals with are persons. So it tells us to treat persons who are relevantly similar alike. And, it deals with those persons in a particular way. This is where the principle of propriety comes in. It requires that the relevant similarities and distinctions among persons that justify similar or different treatment be ones that are either meritorious or contain features that display a distinctive worth or status in those persons. The properties of persons in virtue of which they are to be treated similarly or differently from others may not be incidental or relational properties of those persons. And this is my gloss on the idea of the notion of what is due a person. What is due a person is what ought to be done or ought to be had by a person by virtue of meritorious features or features that display the worth or status of that person such as are relevant to the ownership. What the person ought to have is a fitting response to the worth of the person in question.

For example, consider the already mentioned notion that it is fitting that a virtuous person be happy or that a vicious person not be happy. Here the idea is that happiness is the virtuous person's due and unhappiness is the vicious person's due. Virtue and vice are relevant qualities of persons, many have thought, by virtue of which a person ought to be happy or unhappy. Happiness seems a fitting response to virtue and unhappiness seems a fitting response to viciousness, on these accounts.

Let me illustrate the way in which relevant meritorious qualities function in reasoning about justice by way of a contrast with utilitarian reasoning. Utilitarianism at least logically permits that one do something harmful to one person merely in order to advance the interests of others. One might suppose that there are circumstances where a harm to one person will benefit others whereas the very same harm to another, who is similar in other respects, will not benefit others. E. F. Carritt's example of a utilitarian judge who convicts an innocent person of a crime in order to stop a crowd from rioting comes to mind here.[5] Here the mere principle of reason that says treat like cases alike, with no restriction on the nature of the likeness, would not rule out that one harm the one and not the other.

But this action would not be just, whatever else one might think of its justification.[6] And the reason it would not be just is that it predicates the difference in treatment between the two people on the basis of something that is not a difference of merit or status between the two. It predicates the treatment of the one on the basis of something that somehow does not have to do with his or her distinctive worth. Justice, in contrast, requires that what we do to people should depend on morally relevant facts about them. And the formal principle, to the extent that it includes the principle of propriety, requires that the differences and similarities among people that ground different or similar treatments ought to be based in facts about the worth or status of those people.

I will say more in this essay about the features that determine the worth or status of a person as opposed to the incidental features of persons. Suffice it to say for the moment that only those features of persons that make their lives better or worse whether morally or prudentially can be relevant features of persons to which justice must be responsive. A partial list of these things would be the moral goodness of a person, the moral quality of a person's actions, the capacity of a person for living a flourishing life, and the interests that a person has in life, liberty, and property. Here the crucial idea is that there is something about that person in virtue of which one *owes it to that person* to treat them a certain way.

The formal principle is a *second-order principle*. That is, it is a principle that regulates the operation of other principles. And in some cases the principle merely requires a second-order equality. It functions in a merely second-order way when *determinate* normative considerations already apply to the cases at hand. Determinate normative considerations are ones that yield determinate requirements on action in a way that is independent of context. An example of a determinate normative consideration is the consideration that one ought to comply with one's contractual obligations. Here, what one is required to do is specified exactly by the contract. And this requirement is dependent only on the conditions for a valid promise and not otherwise on the context in which it is found. Of course, determinate normative considerations are only *pro tanto* considerations so they may be overridden by other considerations.

The formal principle does have some bite even in the case of determinate normative considerations. For if one realizes that some of one's conception of what one ought to do is inconsistent with what one is planning on doing in the future, then one must either change one's conception or one must change one's plans. Furthermore, in the case of considerations of justice, the principle imposes a constraint of *generalization* over what is due to persons on the agent's reasoning. For example, if one believes that each person is owed the complete product of the things that they help produce, then one will not be able to satisfy everyone's claim and the principle is self-defeating. Or a principle of justice that required that each person have unlimited liberty would also be self-defeating. So the formal principle of justice imposes a constraint of generalization on determinate normative considerations.

Why Does Justice Matter?

In this essay, my concern is mainly to show that the principle of egalitarian justice can be defended as a principle of distributive justice. In principle this is compatible with justice being merely an instrumental good that may promote overall utility. It is even compatible with the idea that justice is of no importance in moral considerations. These would, I think, be implausible claims, but the main thrust of this essay does not undermine them. Rather I will sketch an argument for why these claims are implausible and for why we ought to see justice as a fundamental moral value.

The importance of justice, that is, the importance of giving each person his or her due, is grounded in the special significance of persons. It is grounded on a value that cannot be fully grasped if we attend only to the values of pleasure or other forms of utility as consequentialists do. In addition to the values of pleasure, happiness, beauty, and others that can be promoted, I believe we must acknowledge another kind of value that is not ordinarily promoted, and that is the value of *humanity*. The fact of humanity confers a special status on human beings that ought to be honored.[7]

The humanity of a person is that person's capacity to recognize, appreciate, engage with, harmonize with, and produce intrinsic goods.[8] It is in virtue of this feature of human beings that they bring something unique and distinctive to the world. They are capable of seeing the value in the world. They see the values of life, beauty, and pleasure, among other things. They are also capable of appreciating these values. They enjoy them; they celebrate and affirm these values. And, the appreciation, enjoyment, and love of valuable things are in themselves of great value. Human beings are also capable of engaging with these values and harmonizing with them. They can build their lives in harmony with the values of life and beauty, and they do this because they appreciate and love these values and want to be part of a world that includes them. They are also capable of producing valuable things. They produce justice, beauty, culture, and happiness for others. Once again, they do this because they appreciate and love these values.

Humans do not merely cause these things to come about as, say, a river causes the conditions of life to come about; they bring about these things self-consciously and through their own activity because they appreciate them. And it is the fact that they bring them about self-consciously and as a result of their appreciation that gives these values their special quality. Consider the difference between looking at a particular formation of stone as merely a natural object and looking at that same formation as the product of a self-conscious attempt by a human being to realize beauty and express something about the values of life. We can appreciate the beauty of the natural rock formation, but when we look at it as the product of self-conscious human activity, it takes on a whole new dimension of value.

This new dimension of value derives from the fact that we perceive human beings as a kind of authority in the realm of value. Humans are authorities in the realm of value to the extent that they are uniquely capable of recognizing and appreciating value as well as self-consciously producing it, and to the extent that the exercise of this authority is itself intrinsically valuable. By analogy, we value the love that someone has for us because it comes from an independent being who does it self-consciously and in a way authoritatively. Similarly, the value that human beings bring to the world, in their appreciation of the world, is partly constituted by the fact that it comes from independent beings that are authorities in the realm of value.

It is the fact that human beings have this highly significant authority in the realm of value that gives them their special status. To fail to acknowledge this is to cut oneself off from all values that are realized in this way. Think again of the stone sculpture. If we were to think of it as merely the product of natural forces, we would recognize and appreciate beauty, but we would fail to see something fundamental about the sculpture's value. It is only once we see it as the product of a human being and we think of this human as not being merely a set of causal forces but in addition being a kind of authority in the realm of value that we come to see the full value of it. Moreover, to treat human beings as mere means for bringing about more of the goods they produce (such as the appreciation of intrinsic good, the creation of intrinsic good) is to fail to acknowledge their special status. It is a status that may not be sacrificed merely for the sake of these goods because it is more important than the goods themselves; it is the very ground of their value. It is only because the appreciation of the values in the world comes from a being with the kind of authority that human beings have that the appreciation is so important. Indeed, the appreciation of, production of, and harmonization with value by human beings derives its distinctive character from the fact that it is an activity engaged in by a being with this unique kind of authority.

The only way to acknowledge the special status of human beings as authorities in the realm of value is to guarantee that what happens to them and what we do with them is responsive to their special worth as human beings. In other words, it is the status in virtue of which we must make sure that we give each person his or her due. And what is due to this kind of being is that he or she be enabled to exercise his or her enormously valuable authority.[9] In my view, the happy exercise of this authority is the distinctive form of human well-being.

The Principle of Egalitarian Justice

The principle of egalitarian justice is itself a first-order principle. It states that how much one person ought to receive of some important good can be ascertained only relative to what others can receive. Egalitarian justice is not the only such comparative principle; some principles of desert are comparative as well. I will argue in what follows that egalitarian justice follows from the formal principle in conjunction with what I call the principle of well-being.

The principle of well-being states that to the extent that it is feasible, and with other things being equal, it is better that individuals have more well-being rather than less. The principle of well-being is an *indeterminate* requirement. What does it mean to say that the principle is indeterminate? It means that, at least under certain circumstances, the principle states that more well-being is better than less, but it does not specify a definite amount of well-being that the person *ought* to have. What the person ought to receive is to be determined partly by reference to the context the person is in and partly by some other principle.

In contrast, the principle of need states that each person ought to have a definite amount of good. And some think that the principle of retribution requires that the committing of a crime be followed by a definite amount of hard treatment. Similarly, some say that the activity of production implies that the producer ought to receive a definite amount of the good produced. For example, a contract implies that each person ought to receive a definite amount of some good, an amount specified by the contract. In these cases, the principle specifies a particular quantity of good or evil to be assigned to the individual by virtue of some action or character trait of that person and that such a quantity ought to be specified independently of the contingent circumstances.

The indeterminacy of the principles of opportunity, political power, and well-being implies that such principles must be supplemented by another principle in order to determine what a person ought to have. And for different kinds of questions, this indeterminacy might be resolved in different ways. For instance, a person might think that he ought to pursue as much well-being as possible. But we might also think that individuals ought to be equally well off. Some other theorists might think that well-being ought to be maximized as in utilitarianism.

The argument I want to lay out is that when applied to indeterminate principles, the formal principle of justice does in fact generate a first-order requirement not already present in the indeterminate principles. Indeed the idea is that the formal principle itself determines what justice requires regarding the realization of indeterminate principles.

The Basic Argument

The basic argument involves three main premises. First, the argument states the truth of the formal principle of justice as elaborated above. Second, the argument states that there are no relevant differences between human beings that can determine that one person ought to receive more well-being than others. Third, it states that well-being has a fundamental value that gives reason for moral agents to promote it in other beings. Here the idea is that more well-being is better than less and that the worth of well-being is not derived from any other value. And this value of well-being gives each person a reason, albeit indeterminate, to enhance other people's well-being.

One additional feature of the argument is that it occurs in different stages. In the first stage it is concerned only with a fixed stock of divisible goods. In the second stage of the argument we will give up this restriction.

No Relevant Differences

To start with, human beings have *equal moral status*. Since the status of humanity derives from the fact that humanity is a kind of authority in the realm of values, equal status is based on the fact that human beings all have essentially the same basic capacities to be authorities in the realm of value. This does not mean that they appreciate the same values. The realm of value is an extremely pluralistic world. No one can experience and appreciate more than a small proportion of that realm. Indeed, to be able to appreciate some values requires a discipline and focus that necessarily excludes other values. The development of these capacities are suppressed in some people as a result of poor education and other adverse circumstances, but, I will argue, this is a product of injustice and not a suitable basis for grounding a principle of distribution.

What kinds of differences are relevant reasons for treating people differently with respect to their well-being? The usual relevant differences are connected to considerations of desert, reciprocity, productivity, and need. These include whether one person deserves more than another, whether one person is more productive than another, and whether one person is needier than another. These are the traditional bases of differential treatment.

In order to establish no relevant differences, I propose here to narrow the scope of the argument. The argument is now to be applied to people before the age of adulthood. At this stage in life, it is generally thought that individuals are not deserving of greater fundamental goods than others; nor are people's relative productivities thought to be such that they entitle them to greater shares of fundamental goods.[10]

Well-Being

People are nevertheless capable of well-being to some extent, and this is the quality that is relevantly similar among them when other considerations do not differentiate them. That well-being is a fundamental good can be seen from the fact that societies are devoted to realizing the common good and that the common good is to be understood in terms of well-being.

Well-being can also be seen to be a fundamental good. I understand well-being as that quality of a person's life that involves an appreciative and active engagement with intrinsic goods. For example, a person's well-being is enhanced when that person is enjoying a work of art. Or, a person's well-being is enhanced when that person happily acts morally. The account of well-being presupposed here is neither subjective nor objective, strictly speaking. It includes both an objective factor and the subjective appreciation of the objective good as it is realized in that person.[11]

In terms of the conception of the status of humanity I sketched earlier, the well-being of a person is, broadly speaking, the happy exercise of the distinctive authority of human beings. We can see why well-being ought to be promoted: it is an intrinsic good that contributes to the good of the world. And we can see why a person is due well-being: to the extent that well-being consists in the happy exercise of the distinctive authority of human beings and each person is due the ability to exercise that distinctive authority, well-being is due each person.

The more a person has well-being, in general, the better. Each person is capable of having an overall good set at an unattainable maximum, at least for practical purposes. But how much well-being ought we to try to ensure that a person has? This is not immediately determined by the fact that more well-being is better than less for each person; that is why well-being is an indeterminate principle. The nature of well-being does imply that a person ought to have his or her well-being advanced. But the principle of well-being does not specify exactly how much for most circumstances.

Maximization

We might say that if a person's well-being is the one and only moral basis for treating a person and that person is the only person under consideration, then we ought to maximize that person's well-being. Furthermore, if more well-being is better than less, and well-being is the only consideration that ought to inform our moral duty to a particular person, then we ought, other things being equal, to make that person as well off as possible. This is where the formal principle of justice comes in. Once we take into account the fact that there are many individuals, we can see that if one person ought to be made as well off as possible, then every other like-situated person ought to be made as well off as possible. If we apply the principle of maximum well-being to one person then we must apply it to everyone.

But here the application of the formal principle to the maximization of well-being leads to a problem. The idea that one ought to maximize each person's well-being cannot be satisfied even in principle since it requires the maximization of more than one independent variable. Hence, when we apply the formal principle to the principle of the maximization of well-being we run into a kind of generalization problem: when generalized, the maximization of one person's well-being implies that we ought to maximize each and every person's well-being separately. But this is impossible.

Notice that *maximization of the well-being* of all persons is not a way of maximizing the well-being of each and every person independently. Total maximization cannot maximize the well-being of each and every person because this is impossible. Furthermore, the formal principle of justice is one that requires us to consider each person separately and maximize his well-being separately, which cannot be done by total maximization.

Another possibility is a *sequential maximization* of each person's well-being. What we do here is maximize the well-being of one person and then, given what is left over, maximize the well-being of another, applying this procedure until we have reached everyone. The consequence of this in many cases is that the persons at the end of the procedure will get very little or nothing. But is this a conceivable application of the formal principle with no relevant differences to the principle of maximization of well-being?

This proposal suffers from violating the formal principle itself. It does not treat each relevantly like person alike. First of all, one must choose a sequence of persons as recipients of the maximization procedure. The first are likely to do well and the later are likely to do poorly. Are there reasons, grounded in the persons themselves, why some should come first and others should come later? By hypothesis, there are no such reasons. The sequential maximization procedure seems to be an arbitrary procedure.

This conclusion is interesting since it displays how the formal principle can have some bite. The requirement to maximize a person's well-being cannot be conjoined with the formal principle of justice if one thinks that each person's well-being is important. To treat everyone alike in the way specified by the principle of maximization is impossible. But this implies that there is injustice when one maximizes the well-being of any arbitrary person.

The conclusion shows us that we ought to pursue for each person some level below what is the best for him or her in order to satisfy the principle of formal justice while advancing the well-being of all persons. This leads to an interesting result in the subsequent stretch of argument. It enjoins us to find a level that is consistent with the formal principle.

Sufficiency

One level of well-being that would be consistent with the formal principle is *sufficiency*. We might think that there is a level of well-being that we can bring about for all people that is enough for each person. This is, in other words, an adequate level of well-being. And to the extent that this is not a maximum of well-being, this principle can be made consistent with the formal principle at least under certain circumstances. There may be circumstances in which everyone has enough well-being so that the formal principle conjoined with the principle of sufficiency can yield a determinate and plausible answer.

Sufficiency is a complex notion and it is important to be clear about it. It is generally thought to be above the level of mere subsistence but beneath the level that would make a person as well off as possible. The idea is that there is some adequate level of well-being that can be improved upon but that does not really matter morally.[12]

There are problems with the standard of sufficiency itself. If we accept the importance of sufficiency as part of a conception of justice, does justice have nothing to say when there are conflicts of interest above the level of sufficiency? Surely this cannot be right. An example of this might be the division of office space in an academic building. Let us suppose that each person thinks that a single office is quite enough for doing work, receiving students, relaxing by listening to music or reading a novel, and so forth. Surely no one will quarrel with this. Now suppose that there are four similar rooms to be divided between two people. The chairman gives one to one of them and gives three to another. He does not ground this difference on differential need or on greater merit. He reasons that one is sufficient for the one and three is more than sufficient for the other, and that there is no reason to be concerned about the inequality. The person with three offices will now have separate offices in which to receive students, work, and relax. Let us suppose that both can get along with only one office but that they also both like the idea of having separate rooms for separate activities. Is there no injustice here? Surely there is, and one of these people will complain loudly about the unequal treatment over and above the adequate. Indeed, short of arguments connected with the common good or perhaps with those of greater need or merit, the idea is that a less than equal division is unjust.

Finally, since the level of sufficiency is greater than the level of satisfying biological needs, it is important to know what one must do when there are conflicts of interest between those who do not reach the level of sufficiency. The solutions to such conflicts require that one invoke a principle in addition to that of sufficiency. And that is a very large set of cases. Human beings tend to have capacities for well-being that far outstretch what they have available to them. It is hard to see how, for most people, the level of sufficiency could be met.

In general, then, the idea that there is a level of sufficiency above which moral concern does not extend is implausible. And the idea that distributive concerns ought to be limited to a principle of sufficiency is also quite implausible. For the moment, let us put aside this answer.

Equality

Once we put aside the sufficiency principle of justice, we are not left with any suitable alternative principle that can be used to assign well-being to each individual on his or her own. But this need not mean that there is no principle. The only principle that can help us is the formal principle of justice.

The key idea is that if there is a reason for any person to be brought to a certain level of well-being, then the same reason holds for every person to be brought to that level of well-being. The formal principle itself can serve as a constraint on what reasons we act on, as we saw earlier, because it establishes a criterion of generalization that must be met by the reasons. This is what ruled out maximization of everyone's well-being. The question is, does the formal principle determine the level we ought to bring

about when we are dealing with the principle of well-being or any analogous principle?

What we need to do is select levels of well-being until we come to the
point that is consistent with the formal principle of justice, and the only
such point is equality of well-being. Hence, there is a reason for a person
to be made as well off as possible consistent with everyone else being that
well off. Any other distribution of well-being would violate either the
formal principle of justice or the fundamental value of well-being.

Therefore, only equality of well-being is compatible with the fundamental value of well-being, the formal principle of justice, and the absence
of relevant differences between persons.

Here is a way of making this argument intuitive. If there are two people
and we believe that one person ought to be better off than the other, it
follows that we think that there is a reason for the better-off person to be
better off than the other. But, by hypothesis, there is no relevant difference, so it follows that the same reason holds for the other person to be
that well off. If the other person is not so well off, then that person is being
treated in violation of the formal principle of justice. Hence, either the
better-off person does not have reason to be treated that way or there is a
relevant difference or the formal principle is false. By hypothesis there is
no relevant difference, and the formal principle of justice is true. Therefore, the better-off person does not have reason to be treated as well as he
is. There is only one level of well-being that can satisfy the formal principle of justice, the fundamental value of well-being, and the fact of no
relevant difference, and that is the level at which there is equality of well-
being.

Here we have derived the principle of equality of condition from the
formal principle of justice and the fundamental value of well-being.

The Leveling-Down Objection

It has been said by some that the principle of egalitarian justice is subject
to a fatal intuitive flaw. The objection is that the principle of equality
defended above has an extremely implausible implication. Suppose there
are two alternative states S1 and S2 such that in S1 everyone is equally well
off and in S2 everyone is better off than in S1 but some in S2 are better
off than others in S2. The principle of equality appears to say that S2 is

worse than S1: S1 is egalitarian whereas S2 is not. So S2 represents a departure from equality while S1 does not. Thus the principle of equality implies that, at least as far as equality is concerned, if given such a choice we ought to make everyone worse off. Of course, other principles may contend with equality and override its recommendation in any particular case. But the worry is that, to the extent that the principle of egalitarian justice makes the recommendation that everyone be made worse off, that is a strike against the principle.[13]

Not everyone agrees that this objection is a strike against the principle of egalitarian justice. Temkin argues that there are other principles that may have strongly Pareto-inefficient implications. He cites the case of principles of desert as ones that imply that everyone ought to be worse off than they might be if they are to receive what they deserve. Further, he argues that many accept such a view despite its welfare-diminishing character.[14]

Temkin is right to point out that not every principle is likely to be tarnished by the implication that some states can be better than others in certain respects even though everyone is worse off in them. But it is not clear to me that most egalitarians can agree with this. For most egalitarians seem to hold both to the idea that equality is important and to the idea that well-being is important (or at least the opportunity for well-being). And these two judgments seem to come together in their egalitarianism. Their principles invoke equal opportunity for or equal access to welfare, and the reasons given for this idea is that welfare is intrinsically important. This suggests to me that these egalitarians cannot be indifferent between two equal states S1 and S2 that are such that everyone is better off (or has more opportunities or access to being better off) in S2 than in S1. Since the importance of well-being or opportunity for well-being seems to be built in to the principle of equality—it is the reason for the principle taking the shape that it does—they cannot be indifferent between these two states.

Moreover, unlike a desert principle, the principle of equality has no component that justifies lowering the welfare of a person (or the opportunity for welfare). It makes sense for a desert principle to favor a Pareto-inefficient outcome in those circumstances where everyone deserves to be worse off. But this is part of the value theory of desert. In some sense, it is better for a person who deserves it to be worse off. We may reject this value theory, but it is at least internally coherent. But there is no analogous feature in egalitarian principles.

One possible analogy is that if a person is responsible for having less well-being than someone else, then that person's being worse off may not be unjust. But now consider a situation in which every person is responsible for having less well-being than they might have had. Each decided not to make the extra effort that would have brought him or her more well-being overall. Then, unexpectedly, a new set of resources becomes available such that each can bring himself or herself to the higher level of well-being without any extra effort. Most egalitarians would say that this increase in good for everyone was an improvement.

But the same would not hold for desert. If every person in a society turned out to be vicious, then each might deserve to be badly off. Then the introduction of a new set of resources that could make everyone better off would not be an improvement. Indeed, on the desert theory if as a consequence everyone were made better off than they deserved to be, that would be worse. So the desert theorist would be within her rights to respond to the objection that her theory endorses Pareto-inferior states that that is not an objection to her theory but a statement of it.

The egalitarian theorists are not in such a position. For them, the leveling-down objection is a genuine objection, if it works. But I do not think that it works. And the fact that it does not work can be seen in a number of ways.

A Gap in the Leveling-Down Objection

The leveling-down objection derives its apparent strength from the claim that an egalitarian must think that something is lost when there is some inequality. From this it is inferred that any egalitarian state must be better than any nonegalitarian state, at least in one respect. And from this it is further inferred that there is one important respect in which an egalitarian state is better than a strongly Pareto-superior state (one in which everyone is better off).

But the first inference is not valid. From the fact that there is loss from inequality it does not follow that any egalitarian state is better with respect to equality than any nonegalitarian state. All that an egalitarian need say is that for every nonegalitarian state there is some (not Pareto-superior) egalitarian state that is superior to the nonegalitarian state.

Consider three states: S1, S2, and S3. S1 and S3 are egalitarian and S2 is nonegalitarian. S3 and S2 are both strongly Pareto superior to S1. But S3 is egalitarian and S2 is not. The difference is that in S2 at least one person is better off or worse off than in S3. All the egalitarian is committed to asserting is that there is something lost in S2 because all the people in S2 are not equally well off. This may merely imply that S3 is better or more just than S2. It is compatible with this to say that S2 is better or more just than S1, as is S3. This set of claims is also sufficient to ground the claim that for every inequality, there is something lost with respect to equality.

Of course, S3 may not be feasible, but this is not a reason to think that a failure to be equivalent to S3 is not the defect of S2. All that is needed for the egalitarian is to say that relative to some nearby equality that is set at the level of well-being of, or between, the persons in the unequal state, the unequal state is missing something or is unjust because it is not equal.

What my argument so far has shown is that there is a significant gap in the leveling-down objection against equality. It has shown that a crucial inference is unsupported by the objector and that alternatives to that inference are logically possible. What I want to show in the next section is that the logically possible alternative missed by the proponents of the leveling-down objection is in fact the one supported by my argument for equality.

An Argument for the Least Unequal Pareto-Optimal Inequalities

The first important extension of the argument for equality of condition generates an account of justice in the cases of Pareto improvements over equality of condition. I have in mind *strong* cases of Pareto improvement, that is, where everyone would be better off if there were some inequality. A *weak* Pareto improvement is one in which some but not all are better off under inequality than under equality, and no one is worse off. Let us consider cases of strong Pareto improvements where everyone is better off under inequality than under equality. There are a number of cases of this sort. In one type of case, some goods are "lumpy", so we cannot achieve a completely egalitarian distribution. Another case involves production. In this kind of case, the complexities and uncertainties of production require that incentives be offered to those who are most suited to the tasks to be performed. Here, inequalities arise as a kind of by-product of the production process.[15] My thesis is that if every person can be made better off than under efficient equality, then each person ought to be made better off than under efficient equality.

In the following case, I shall consider whether it is just to bring about a strong Pareto improvement over equality given the argument I have made above. I will discuss a case of lumpy goods where, if one insisted on equality, one would have to throw away some of those goods in order to achieve equality. And I shall consider this for just two persons: A and B—a narrow idealization, but firm enough to grasp it properly. The argument proceeds by comparing two states: S1, in which A and B are equally well off, and S2, in which both are better off than in S1 but A is better off than B.

Let us suppose that A and B are both made better off under an unequal distribution of well-being than under an egalitarian distribution. Hence it looks like the Pareto improvement in S2 pushes us beyond the equality of S1. It pushes us in a direction that does not allow us fully to satisfy the constraint on reasons stated by formal equality. Someone is not being treated fully in accordance with the reasons that apply to him. Either someone is being treated better than the reasons applying to him allow, or someone is being treated worse than the reasons applying to him allow, or both of these are true. So there is some kind of failure of justice in cases of unequal distribution. In our example, either A is being treated better than the reasons allow in his case or B is being treated worse than the reasons allow in his case.

If we compare S1 (equality) and S2 (Pareto improvement), the formal principle of justice says that there is something wrong with S2 because it is not equal. But I will argue that there is something even worse with S1 with regard to justice. And so, from the point of view of justice, we have reason to prefer S2 to S1.

The argument starts from the observation that in S2, either A is better off than he ought to be or B is worse off than he ought to be. But if we look at S1, we notice that *both* B and A are worse off in S1 than they are in S2. Both B and A are worse off in S1 than B is in S2; so at the very least, both the principle of well-being and the formal principle of justice pick out the level of well-being of B in S2 as the minimum that everyone ought to have. So ideal justice seems to require that everyone be at the level B is at in S2. The egalitarian level in S1 is worse for both A and B. So, to the extent that A and B ought to be at the level of B in S2, there are two failures from the point of view of justice in S1: two people are worse off than justice says they ought to be. It seems to me, then, that from the point of view of justice, S1 is worse than S2 even though S1 is egalitarian and S2 is not.

This seems to me to give exactly the right result. The idea is that there *is* injustice in an unequal condition when there are no relevant differences between the persons between whom the inequality holds. But, there is *less* injustice in such an unequal condition than in an equal condition that is strongly Pareto inferior to the unequal condition. So though there is something wrong with the Pareto-improving inequality, it is less problematic than the Pareto-unimproved equality.

But this also shows that although there is something problematic in efficient inequality, it does not follow that egalitarians are committed to the proposition attributed to them in the leveling down objection. For that objection to work against an egalitarian principle of justice, it is not enough that the egalitarian is committed to the injustice of inequality. The leveling-down objection applies to equality only if the egalitarian is also committed to the claim that inequality is worse from the point of view of justice than a Pareto-inferior equality. But it is this last claim that the egalitarian need not be committed to, as I have argued.

Equality, Productivity, and Desert

Does the principle of equality extend beyond birth and childhood? It would appear that it at least extends as far as the point where considerations of desert and productivity arise. But does it extend to these considerations as well? Here is a way in which it might. Each person's well-being matters equally, and so conditions for well-being ought to be equal. Productivity and desert, if they are legitimate principles of justice, require the modification of the well-being of each person. Therefore, each ought to have equal conditions for being productive and deserving *if* productivity and desert are legitimate principles by which the society ought to be organized.

Is this an arbitrary claim about productivity and desert? I don't think so. Both of these principles require that prior conditions be in place in order for them to be legitimate. In order for a person to be productive, a person must have the necessary tools for productivity. The right to these tools cannot be given by the principle of productivity itself, but by a prior principle. To the extent that we have argued for the great and universal importance of equality of well-being, the right of each person to the conditions of productivity is implied by the principle of equal conditions for well-being. Shouldn't the right to the conditions of well-being also determine the shape of the principle of productivity as well? It is hard to see why not in the light of the previous considerations.

The same kind of consideration applies to comparative positive desert claims but for different reasons. Comparative positive desert claims can be justified only when there is a prior baseline where each person has similar opportunities to engage in the deserving action. One person cannot deserve more than another for an action he performed and the other did not, in the comparative sense, if the other person did not have the opportunity to engage in the action. That itself is not sufficient to show that equality is the necessary baseline. But desert does require a baseline, and the principle of egalitarian justice determines justice in the absence of considerations of desert. It appears that complete justice would require that at least at the start each have an opportunity to engage in deserving actions, where that opportunity is consistent with equal conditions for well-being.

Conclusion

I have argued that egalitarianism is the principle of justice that ought to regulate the distribution of goods during the preadult phase of life and that equality of condition is the basis for a kind of equality of opportunity for well-being at the onset of adulthood. This equality of condition can be suspended only if there are defensible principles of desert or productivity that justify inequalities. I have also argued that equality can be abridged (in a way that is consistent with its underlying rationale) when everyone can be made better off as a consequence. Thus we avoid the leveling-down objection.

I think that there are other contexts in which equality of condition ought to hold sway. In particular, I think that there are grounds for saying that egalitarian justice ought to hold for the political sphere, since this is a sphere of activity wherein principles of justice are debated and called into question.[16] But I cannot go into that here.

One last remark: this paper defends only a very abstract principle of justice. I do not claim that this principle is the only principle of justice or even that it is the only component of justice. Indeed, I think that justice is something that must be observed in addition to being done. So justice requires publicity as well as fair distribution. A full account of just institutions would require therefore a much fuller treatment than the one I have given here.

Acknowledgments

I would like to thank John Christman, Craig Duncan, Houston Smit, and Andrew Williams for their helpful comments on previous drafts of this paper.

Notes

1. See Temkin 1993.

2. See Sen 1992.

3. See Arneson 1989 and Cohen 1989 for excellent accounts of this approach to equality. It is not clear that these authors endorse the argument I briefly described above but it is often attributed to them and merits some response.

4. Two other efforts to defend equality should be mentioned here. Rawls (1971) provides a defense of a principle of equality with his original position argument. This is a powerful and illuminating argument but it has been subject to a great deal of persuasive criticism starting with Barry (1973). Also Thomas Nagel has defended equality in "Equality," in his 1979. The principle he ends up defending is closer to the principle of priority than a principle of equality.

5. See Carritt 1947.

6. This is not a criticism of utilitarianism. I take it that most utilitarians would accept the point and then go on to say that utilitarianism is the underlying principle behind the principle of justice and that it gives considerations that ought to override justice under some circumstances. See for instance, John Stuart Mill, *Utilitarianism*, chapter 5. I do think that justice is a deeper value than utilitarianism can allow, but I will sketch an argument for this below.

7. See Pettit 1994 for the helpful distinction between promoting and honoring.

8. The notion of humanity I sketch here owes much to Immanuel Kant's conception of humanity in his *Groundwork of the Metaphysics of Morals*. It is also quite different in that the value of humanity, in my view, connects human beings with the realm of value in the world and is not the ground of all value, as many Kantians would have it.

9. The notion of the status of humanity that I have sketched here bears some resemblance to the idea of the status of inviolability that has been discussed by Kamm (1992, p. 385). It is also similar to that discussed by Thomas Nagel in "Personal Rights and Public Space," included in Nagel 2002, p. 91. It is also quite different as they ground this conception in the Kantian conception of the person and the idea grounds negative rights primarily. I do not see why the notion of humanity that I have sketched should give preference to negative rights over positive rights as long as the authority is given the ability to exercise its distinctive authority.

10. One relevant difference that merits discussion but that I do not have the time to discuss here is inheritance. For those who regard private property as a basic component of justice and who assert that that right includes a full right of bequest, one child might have a right to greater resources than another because someone has given those greater resources to him. See Nozick 1974 for a view of this sort. See Christman 1994 and Cohen 1995 for some quite persuasive criticism of this whole approach.

11. For an account of well-being that is very similar to the one here see Darwall 2002, chapter 5.

12. See Frankfurt 1997 for this kind of view.

13. See Parfit 1991, p. 23, for an account of the objection. See also Narveson 1983 and Frankfurt 1997, p. 266, for other sympathetic accounts of this objection.

14. See Temkin 2000, esp. p. 138.

15. See Christiano 2000.

16. I argue for this in part in Christiano 2001.

References

Arneson, R. 1989. "Equality and Equal Opportunity for Welfare." *Philosophical Studies* 56: 77–93.

Barry, B. 1973. *The Liberal Theory of Justice*. Oxford: Oxford University Press.

Carritt, E. F. 1947. *Ethical and Political Thinking*. Oxford: Oxford University Press.

Christiano, T. 2000. "Cohen on Incentives and Inequality." In G. Gaus and J. Lamont, eds., *Ethics and Economics*. Buffalo, N.Y.: Humanities Press.

———. 2001. "Knowledge and Power in the Justification of Democracy." *Australasian Journal of Philosophy* 31: 23–38.

Christman, J. 1994. *The Myth of Property*. Oxford: Oxford University Press.

Cohen, G. A. 1989. "The Currency of Egalitarian Justice." *Ethics* 99: 906–944.

———. 1995. *Self-Ownership, Freedom and Equality*. Cambridge: Cambridge University Press.

Darwall, S. 2002. *Welfare and Rational Care*. Princeton, N.J.: Princeton University Press.

Frankfurt, H. 1997. "Equality as a Moral Ideal." In L. Pojman, ed., *Equality*. Oxford: Oxford University Press.

Kamm, F. 1992. "Non-Consequentialism, the Person As an End-in-Itself, and the Significance of Status." *Philosophy and Public Affairs* 21: 354–399.

Kant, I. 1990. *Groundwork of the Metaphysics of Morals*. M. Gregor, trans. Cambridge: Cambridge University Press.

Mill, J. S. 1979 (1861). *Utilitarianism*. G. Sher., ed. Indianapolis, Ind.: Hackett.

Nagel, T. 1979. *Mortal Questions*. Cambridge: Cambridge University Press.

———. 2002. *Concealment and Exposure and Other Essays*. Oxford: Oxford University Press.

Narveson, J. 1983. "On Dworkinian Equality." *Social Philosophy and Policy* 1: 1–22.

Nozick, R. 1974. *Anarchy, State, and Utopia*. New York: Basic Books.

Parfit, D. 1991. "Equality or Priority?" *The Lindley Lecture*. Lawrence, Kans.: Department of Philosophy, University of Kansas.

Pettit, P. "Consequentialism." 1994. In P. Singer, ed., *A Companion to Ethics*. Oxford: Blackwell.

Rawls, J. 1971. *A Theory of Justice*. Cambridge, Mass.: Harvard University Press.

Sen, A. 1992. *Inequality Reexamined*. Cambridge, Mass.: Harvard University Press.

Temkin, L. 1993. *Inequality*. Oxford: Oxford University Press.

———. 2000. "Equality, Priority and the Leveling Down Objection." In M. Clayton and A. Williams, eds., *The Ideal of Equality*. New York: St. Martin's Press.

4 Justice, Inference to the Best Explanation, and the Judicial Evaluation of Scientific Evidence

Carl F. Cranor

Science and the law are two major institutions that have substantial impact on our lives. As our society has become much more technological, the interaction between these institutions has greatly increased. For example, scientific developments lead to new technologies that result in beneficial products. Yet some of these technologies may result in risks or injuries by means of their products, by-products, or pollutants, which in turn may subject them to regulation by federal or state administrative agencies or to "legal regulation" through personal injury (tort) law.

The law is one institution that sets the terms of social interactions—inter alia, it adjudicates the distribution of risks and harms among people and aims to provide justice between parties when legal conflict arises. Both administrative and tort law need science, its principles, and tools to help set regulations, to diagnose the adverse effects of a technology, and to resolve disputes in activities where scientific research is of key importance. Science also provides a model of some of the best procedures for discovering objective support for factual propositions, some of which are needed in law.

In a trilogy of cases, two of which were toxic tort cases, beginning with *Daubert v. Merrell-Dow Pharmaceuticals Inc.* (1993), (hereinafter referred to as *Daubert*) the U.S. Supreme Court gave federal judges a heightened duty to review scientific evidence and expert testimony that are proposed for admission into civil and criminal litigation (see also *General Electric v. Joiner* [1997] and *Kumho Tire v. Carmichael* [1999] [hereinafter referred to as *Joiner* and *Kumho Tire* respectively]). An admissibility review of the evidence is not aimed at adjudicating between the scientific claims submitted by the parties; that is an issue that is left (or should be left) to juries. Rather, according to *Daubert*, courts should ensure that the *scientific* evidence and expert testimony to be introduced and considered during a trial are based on a reliable scientific foundation. The legal interpretation of this point is that the evidence and testimony must be "ground[ed] in the methods and procedures of science," and they must fit the facts of the case (*Daubert* 1993, p. 588). The subsequent *Joiner* and *Kumho Tire* decisions held that judges have considerable latitude in determining how decisions to admit or exclude evidence are to be made and in making them. Once district courts have decided an admissibility issue, they can be overturned only if the decision is "manifestly erroneous" (*Joiner* 1997, p. 147). A typical legal gloss on this is that if the court's view of the evidence is plausible, given the record before it, its decision cannot be overturned (*Cooter and Gell v. Hartmarx Corp.* 1989).[1] This is not an impossible review hurdle to overcome, just a very difficult one. Thus, a district court judge's decision stands unless a clear error is shown in the admissibility decision.

This heightened duty has posed problems for the courts. Except for some high-profile mass torts, toxic tort cases are not frequently encountered by the courts and, perhaps partly because of this, they have struggled to make law and science function well together. Moreover, scientific evidence is not easy to interpret for those not trained in assessing it. Although in the abstract the aims of science and the law do not appear to conflict, problems can arise in adjudicating legal relations between people when substantial scientific evidence is needed. There can be a variety of tensions between law and science, including tensions between the epistemic virtues of research science and the public health protection and justice virtues of legal institutions (Cranor 1993). As a result, the admissibility of scientific evidence has become a subject of substantial focus in court cases and in the recent legal scholarly literature.

What evidence is admitted into a trial can have a substantial impact on the justice of the decision between parties. If judges do not review scientific evidence and expert testimony well, they put at risk the accuracy of legal decisions, justice between the opposing parties, and plaintiff access to the law. If courts mistakenly admit plaintiffs' experts to testify who are charlatans or who base their testimony on grossly mistaken science, this may result in adverse legal decisions that result in the withdrawal of beneficial products from the market. If courts exclude reputable plaintiffs' experts whose testimony is scientifically reliable, they may preclude a plaintiff from trial at all and send the wrong message about a potentially dangerous product.

The focus of this essay is to consider an aspect of the admissibility of scientific evidence and expert opinion testimony into toxic tort suits, with one aim of addressing some of the tensions between science and the law, and another of helping to ensure more accurate and just legal decisions in cases that significantly rely on scientific evidence. I explore, but do not seek to prove, a conjecture, namely that judges in reviewing scientific evidence in toxic tort suits have underappreciated a form of inference that is central to scientific inquiry and reasoning—inference to the best explanation. If courts do not understand this form of inference, they risk mistakes in evaluating scientific evidence and thus risk adversely affecting justice between parties.

I begin the exploration by briefly summarizing examples of one kind of scientific evidence—case studies (taken from a companion article being developed simultaneously to this one). A case study or case report "is a detailed report by a physician, [or] other healthcare provider . . . of the profile of single individuals. . . . Case reports . . . tend to document unusual occurrences and may provide early clues about the development of a disease or the occurrence of rare [events]" (Strom 2000, p. 77). Case studies or reports are utilized extensively in trying to identify adverse reactions to vaccines, drugs, poisons, and some anesthetics. A few have been used to identify carcinogens and, perhaps, some other toxicants.

Scientifically, case studies are not regarded as the best evidence for causation, especially when compared with double-blind clinical studies involving large numbers of people. In addition, in many legal cases, case studies are rejected by courts as primary evidence of causation. Case studies lack features typical of other kinds of evidence that courts routinely admit, such as epidemiological studies, that have control groups for comparison and background rates of disease against which to assess a disease rate and assist in determining causation.

Nonetheless, these somewhat controversial kinds of evidence can provide good evidence of causal relationships—scientists and physicians regard *good* case studies as good evidence for causal relations between exposure to a substance and a disease. If case studies can be good evidence of causal relations, they can shed light on the reasoning that supports causal inferences when features typical of statistical inference of causation are absent. A widely endorsed methodology that scientists utilize to infer causation from case studies is simply *inference to the best explanation*, provided it is well founded.

After briefly summarizing some persuasive case studies and the methodology underlying them that scientists utilize to infer causation, I will sketch in more detail this concept of inference to the best explanation, the foundation of most nondeductive reasoning. Once that form of reasoning is articulated and compared with some of the mistaken judicial reasoning in admissibility cases, we can see various ways, some subtle, some not, that judicial evaluation of scientific evidence has been mistaken.

Courts, seemingly insensitive to aspects of scientific reasoning and inference, appear to have adopted various mistaken "causal templates" for interpreting scientific evidence that most scientists would argue are not necessary forms of inference. In this, courts appear not to have recognized the more fundamental form of inference in causal explanation—inference to the best (causal) explanation.

It is plausible to suppose that had courts better understood inference to the best explanation, they would have evaluated evidence differently, and most likely, more accurately. Understanding the importance of inference to the best explanation helps to put other kinds of causal evidence into a better perspective and suggests ways that courts can improve their review of the admissibility of scientific evidence in toxic tort suits. The ultimate result would be better and more just outcomes in toxic tort suits that depend centrally on scientific evidence.

Institutional Background

Tort law is one of the legal institutions that functions to "regulate" exposures to toxic substances. It is not a regulatory institution as that term is typically understood, however. That is, it does not issue rules about how much exposure to potentially toxic substances humans should have. Rather, tort law dictates public standards of conduct concerning the extent of care with which individuals or firms must behave toward members of the community, or in the cases of products (a typical concern in product liability law aimed at potentially toxic substances), public standards concerning the degree of safety that products must exhibit. Tort law is privately enforced by the injured parties or their surrogates. Those who are exposed to substances that they believe harmed them may file suits seeking compensation for injuries suffered in order to restore them to the *status quo ante* and to annul wrongful gains and losses. This retrospective aspect of tort law, when successful, sends some (probably weak) deterrence signal that future plaintiffs may receive compensation for conduct similar to that of the defendant. There is also a general deterrent effect presented by the mere possibility of tort law sanctions.

In order to successfully bring a suit in cases involving scientific claims, plaintiffs must present sufficient scientific evidence to persuade courts that they have been harmed by exposure to the substances in question and that as a consequence they deserve compensation for the injuries from which they suffer. However, the two institutions—science and the law—must function well together in order to provide guidance foward the appropriate outcome of such a suit.

Good Case Studies Are Good Evidence for Causation

Case studies are one kind of scientific evidence used in support of expert testimony with which courts have struggled. Tort judges tend to reject them as a reasonable foundation of expert testimony on causation in toxic tort cases. As I (and a coauthor) argue elsewhere, *good* case studies, those that satisfy certain criteria, *are* good evidence of causation in the appropriate toxic tort cases. This is not a tautology: case studies in which the author has followed certain procedures in reviewing the evidence revealed in a particular event tend to be good evidence for causation. A scientist or physician may have made a mistake or missed something, but if he followed well-recognized procedures, such studies must be considered presumptive evidence for causation. The data for my claims are what scientists and methodologists in the field judge to be good evidence of causation.

Also, good case studies, even though based on a singular event or a small number of events, can reveal causal relations. They provide important insights into the nature of causal judgments and the reasoning supporting them, as examples from science show. In fact case studies rest on a principle of reasoning quite familiar to philosophers and utilized in many fields—inference to the best explanation. This form of reasoning supports the soundness of good case studies (that reveal causal relations) and is the foundation for many other evidentiary inferences in science and in law.

(Moreover, inferences to the best explanation are those that judges them-selves use, or would use if they considered the basis of much, perhaps nearly all, legal reasoning.)

Finally, once inferences to the best explanation are understood, it becomes clear why several causal templates that have been utilized by judges are inadequate. Courts have posed problems for themselves or mis-conceived a number of problems because they failed to recognize the significance of inference to the best explanation.

Even in scientific inquiries, singular or small numbers of events can be good evidence for a causal relationship between exposure and an adverse effect on humans. Ordinarily, the best experimental evidence for deter-mining causation is the result of a randomly assigned experimental group of subjects subjected to a particular exposure (or therapeutic regime) com-pared with a randomly assigned control group not exposed. Scientists, using sufficiently large numbers of research subjects, are thus able to rule out other explanations, such as the adventitious contraction of disease as correlated with exposure, common causes, and so on. Singular or a small number of events often are not as reliable as statistical studies as evidence for causation. Nonetheless, although they may not be as good as statisti-cally based clinical or epidemiological studies, they can be good evidence for causation.

Case studies or reports are utilized extensively in trying to identify adverse reactions resulting from exposure to vaccines, drugs, poisons, some anesthetics, and even an occasional carcinogen or other toxicants. Case reports for vaccines and drugs often tend to be part of what health pro-fessionals call "passive reporting schemes that rely on the vigilance of health care providers to detect events that are felt to be due to the admin-istration of a drug product . . ." (Collet et al. 2000). They are also utilized to provide early warning of adverse reactions to occupational exposures. Such systems rely on the collection of case reports for some centralized agency, such as the Centers for Disease Control in the United States or the Vaccine-Associated Adverse Events Surveillance Program of the Division of Immunization, Bureau of Infectious Diseases in Canada. These are then uti-lized to provide early warnings of adverse health effects. Case series provide "a description of a number of patients who exhibit the same exposure, disease or [unusual drug events]. . . . A single case report may indicate an individual reaction and/or an extremely rare phenomenon. A case series provides evidence that a finding, even though still rare, is repeated" (Hartzema, Porta, and Tilson 1998).

Case Studies in the Law

Case reports and case series have tended to fare very badly in the law; they are usually dismissed out of hand as evidence of causation. Judges and legal commentators have roundly criticized the use of case studies in the law, but often for poor or misleading reasons. Their criticisms can be summarized as follows.

• "Such case reports are not reliable scientific evidence of causation, because they simply described reported phenomena without comparison to the rate at which the phenomena occur in the general population or in a defined control group; do not isolate and exclude potentially alternative causes; and do not investigate or explain the mechanism of causation. Even if some credibility were given to the study, it does not have the degree of clarity required for a validation of its results or its methodology which is sufficient for objective and independent peer review" (*Casey v. Ohio Medical Products* 1995, p. 1385).

• Case reports often merely reveal a temporal relationship, which alone cannot establish causation. To infer causation from the temporal relationship is to exhibit the logical fallacy "*post hoc ergo propter hoc,*" or "after that, because of that."

• They focus on one or a few people, thus lacking controls to provide a background rate for the disease in question.

• Case reports don't explore the mechanisms of causation. "Unlike epidemiological studies, they (case reports) do not contain a testable and systematic inquiry into the mechanism of causation. As such, they reflect reported data, not scientific methodology" (*Brumbaugh v. Sandoz Pharmaceuticals* 1999, p. 1156).

• Courts often complain that case reports offer a basis for a hypothesis about general causation, but not a conclusion. "[T]he generally accepted view is that [the expert's] methodology (animal studies and case reports) can be used to generate hypotheses about causation, but not causation conclusions" (*Haggerty v. Upjohn Co.* 1996, p. 1165).

There is some truth in each of these objections, especially for poorly done or merely *descriptive* case reports—reports that do not rule out alternative causes of disease, do not assess features of a patient that might have led to an adverse reaction, do not address the biological plausibility of the adverse reaction, or are not at all subtle about the temporal relations involved. Often case reports fail to provide evidence of causation because they are simply instances of physicians or nurses noticing adverse effects in a patient following exposure to a drug, vaccine, environmental contaminant, or poison, and reporting these facts to a governmental agency or a journal. (These would indeed be instances of *post hoc ergo propter hoc*.) Health care workers are strongly encouraged to issue such reports in order to facilitate monitoring—to provide a basis for early warnings if significant patterns of adverse effects emerge. Adverse drug reaction reports can be particularly useful to an administrative agency monitoring the safety of drugs that it has approved in order to see whether wider exposure results in adverse health effects.[2]

However, each of the above criticisms about case studies is misleading if they are meant to be universally correct claims. There are good and bad case reports. What constitutes a good case report, and can good case reports provide reasonable evidence of causation in toxic tort cases?

The argument proceeds by several steps: I briefly summarize five case studies (described in more detail elsewhere) in which the studies provide good evidence of causation. I then review science methodologists' procedures for accepting case studies as evidence for causation. Finally, I show how the inferences from case studies are founded in inference to the best explanation, a much more fundamental form of reasoning.

The Scientific Data

In one case, physicians diagnosed the cause of an adverse reaction to the anesthesia halothane based on a single case study. The individual, an anesthesiologist exposed to halothane in his work, experienced hepatitis shortly after his first exposure and on about five other occasions. Each time he had even modest exposure to halothane over a six-year period he contracted hepatitis. When exposure to halothane was removed, he recovered within a reasonable period of time. Finally, realizing that this might shorten his career as an anesthesiologist, he underwent deliberate exposure to halothane under controlled conditions and suffered an acute attack of hepatitis within twenty-four hours (Klatskin and Kimberg 1969).

Physicians found expected liver abnormalities and were able to draw on background knowledge to rule out alternative explanations for the hepatitis and to find biologically plausible temporal relationships between his exposure and the disease. They also found plausible temporal relationships between the removal of exposure and disappearance of the disease. The only times he experienced halothane exposure but did not contract hepatitis was when he was taking prednisone, a drug that appeared to block the effect. The authors of the study concluded that "it is highly probable that halothane was responsible for the recurrent attacks of hepatitis in this case" (ibid.).[3]

In a different case, a forty-two-year-old man developed Guillain-Barré syndrome (GBS), a disease affecting the peripheral nervous system following receipt of a tetanus vaccine. Three times over a thirteen-year period he received tetanus shots and on each occasion he contracted GBS within biologically plausible time periods. Following each episode he made a fully functional recovery. Scientists reviewing his case and ruling out other explanations for his condition based on general biological theory and background knowledge concluded that the "relation between tetanus toxoid and GBS is convincing at least for that one individual, even though this man [subsequent to his last episode of GBS caused by tetanus toxoid] experienced multiple recurrences of demyelinating polyneuropathy, most following acute viral illness. . . . [Two other cases] are recorded in enough detail to be accepted as GBS" (Stratton, Howe, and Johnston 1994, p. 89). Finally, independent evaluators in the U.S. Institute of Medicine report on adverse vaccine reactions noted that "because [this] case . . . demonstrates that tetanus toxoid *did* cause GBS, in the committee's judgment tetanus toxioid *can* cause GBS" (ibid., p. 86).

In a further example, a few case studies, some animal evidence, pathological evidence, and finally a blind study on several tissue samples were sufficient to identify the liver carcinogen dimethylnitrosamine as a cause of death that led to the conviction of a suspect in a murder case. The scientific and forensic investigators ruled out various causes partly based on symptoms, partly on the context of the poisoning, partly on laboratory tests, and partly on tissue damage similar to that in animals exposed to dimethylnitrosamine. This example has become a classic case study in toxicology. Moreover, the authorities were *certain* about causation without having the kinds of evidence that courts have insisted on in many tort cases—no human epidemiological studies and no knowledge about background rates of liver damage. The causal judgment *in this murder case* was sufficiently certain to establish causation beyond a reasonable doubt as required in criminal law.

Finally, in 1974 Creech and Johnson, two occupational physicians, diagnosed that exposure to vinyl chloride monomer (VC) in a polyvinyl chloride plant was the cause of a rare form of liver cancer on the basis of three cases of the disease (Creech et al. 1975, p. 231). They concluded: "The reason an *etiologic association between VC work and tumor* could be inferred so readily on the basis initially of only 3 cases is that ASL [angiosarcoma of the liver] is extraordinarily rare" (ibid., p. 234). They estimated an approximate relative risk of about 400:1 on the basis of ASL in the general population compared with the rate of ASL in the polyvinyl chloride plant in Kentucky.[4] This persuasive case study is widely acknowledged in toxicology.

Scientific Methodological and Theoretical Considerations behind Good Case Studies

The above constitute clear case studies accepted by experts in the field in which a singular or small number of events led to conclusions that the exposures in question *caused* or *probably caused* the adverse effect. In the argot of philosophy, these examples are comparatively fixed points for theorizing about causal judgments and quite important evidence to use in assessing judicial decisions concerning the admissibility of expert testimony based on case studies.

The persuasiveness of the examples is strengthened by the considerations utilized by the U.S. Institute of Medicine (IOM) in assessing whether vaccines cause or probably cause an adverse reaction in a person. As they pose it, this is the "did it?" question—*did* the substance in question cause the adverse reaction? The IOM specifically considers evidence from case reports that bear on the likelihood of a causal relation between exposure to a vaccine and an adverse reaction. They utilize the following considerations that we might regard as *defeasible criteria* that must be taken into account in assessing the quality and plausibility of case reports for inferring causes.[5]

1. Previous general experience with the vaccine   How long has it been on the market? How often have vaccine recipients experienced similar events? How often does the event occur in the absence of vaccine exposure? Does

a similar event occur more frequently in animals exposed to the vaccine than in appropriate controls?

2. Alternative etiologic candidates   Can a preexisting or new illness explain the sudden appearance of the adverse event? Does the adverse event tend to occur spontaneously? Were drugs, other therapies, or diagnostic tests and procedures that can cause the adverse event administered?

3. Susceptibility of vaccine recipient   Has he or she received the vaccine in the past? If so, how has he or she reacted? Does his or her genetic background or previous medical history affect the risk of developing the adverse event as a consequence of vaccination?

4. Timing of events   Is the timing of the onset of the adverse event as expected if the vaccine is the cause? How does that timing differ from the timing that would occur given the alternative etiologic candidate(s)? How does the timing, given vaccine causation, depend on the suspected mechanism (e.g., immunoglobulin-E versus T-cell-mediated)?

5. Characteristics of the adverse event   Are there any available laboratory tests that either support or undermine the hypothesis of vaccine causation?

6. Dechallenge   Did the adverse event diminish as would be expected if the vaccine caused the event? (Stratton et al. 1994, pp. 23–24). (They note that this feature rarely contributes useful information [ibid., p. 26].)

7. Rechallenge   Was the vaccine readministered? If so, did the adverse event recur? (They note that this will often have "a major impact on the causality assessment" [ibid.].)

Moreover, the committee endorsed the view that

[I]n the absence of epidemiologic studies favoring acceptance of a causal relation, individual case reports and case series were relied upon, provided that the nature and timing of the adverse event following vaccine administration and the absence of likely alternative etiologic candidates were such that a *reasonable certainty of causality* could be inferred . . . from one or more case reports. (Ibid., p. 31)

In making overall assessments the committee adopted the following criteria. The evidence *"favors acceptance of a causal relation,"* when

the balance of evidence from one or more case reports or epidemiologic studies provides evidence for a causal relation that *outweighs* the evidence against such a relation. Demonstrated biological plausibility was considered supportive of a decision to accept a causal relation but was insufficient on its own to shift the balance of evidence from other sources. . . . [And the evidence] *establishes a causal relationship* when epidemiological studies and/or case reports provide *unequivocal evidence* for a causal relation, and biological plausibility has been demonstrated. (Ibid., pp. 32–33)

Such unequivocal evidence favored a causal assessment in the case of tetanus toxoid causing GBS.

Different considerations were relied on in the examples mentioned above to assist in revealing causality—sometimes one was more important, for example, the particular timing in one case, sometimes another, for example, the repeated GBS reactions following tetanus shots, and the repeated contraction of hepatitis resulting from exposure to halothane, specifically augmented by the rechallenge under controlled conditions.

Moreover, the considerations advanced by the IOM are not unusual; they have been endorsed by other national or international bodies and leading scientific methodologists. For example, the World Health Organization (WHO), after explaining the number of considerations it uses to guide causal assessment, gives the following summary guidelines: a causal relation is defined as "very likely/certain," when a "[c]linical event with a plausible time relationship to vaccine administration . . . cannot be explained by concurrent disease or other drugs or chemicals." A causal relation is "probable" when there is a "clinical event with a reasonable time relationship to vaccine administration, and is unlikely to be attributed to concurrent disease or other drugs or chemicals." Similar considerations are endorsed by thoughtful methodologists in the biomedical sciences (Hutchinson and Lane 1989, pp. 10–11; Kramer and Lane 1992).

The Reasoning Underlying Causal Inference

The examples of case studies that scientists have accepted as evidence of causation, together with the IOM's, WHO's, and other methodologists' considerations, should be sufficiently persuasive for accepting causal judgments based on singular or a small number of events, since such reasoning is widely accepted in the scientific and medical community.[6] Moreover, courts should recognize the evidentiary value of causal relations revealed by good case studies. They are based on reasoning and methodologies that are noncontroversial and widely accepted in the scientific community.

However, we can strengthen the argument above by anchoring it to a deeper form of reasoning that is operative in these cases—inference to the best explanation, or what some call "diagnostic arguments," which are also related to what physicians call "differential diagnosis." That is, the inferences that scientific methodologists utilize to draw conclusions concerning causation in such cases are simply inferences to the best explanation. This form of inference underlies the inferences in the case studies just reviewed, as well as the general methodological considerations endorsed by consensus bodies of the scientific community, including the IOM and the WHO. It is (at least implicitly) widely shared across many fields and accounts for the particular characteristics of causal inferences to which methodologists and others call attention in good case studies.

As philosophers are well aware, inferences to conclusions are of two kinds: deductive and nondeductive. The defining feature of valid deductive inferences, typical of mathematics and formal logic, is that the conclusion is guaranteed logically or semantically by the premises: if the premises are true, the conclusion must be true (Wright 1989, pp. 38–46).[7]

By contrast, nondeductive inferences are simply those whose conclusions are supported but not guaranteed by their premises. Even if the premises are true, the nondeductive link between premises and conclusions will have varying degrees of strength, unlike a deductive argument (which is either valid or invalid). Thus, a nondeductive argument will be strong, modest (in between), or weak, but not valid or invalid. If the premises are true, they may offer much, modest, or little (to no) support for the conclusion in question (Wright 1989, pp. 48–54). Nondeductive inferences are sometimes called "inductive," but the better term for many of them is, as Gilbert Harman argues, "inference to the best explanation" (Harman 1965). Moreover, the given premises will provide support for different possible conclusions (or as the literature puts it, support different explanations). The task of evaluating such inferences is to determine which conclusion is the most plausible or which explanation best accounts for the evidence.

How does one infer the best explanation of an event? Harman sketched the generic inferential process, but some elaboration is needed.

In making this inference one infers, from the fact that a certain hypothesis would explain the evidence to the truth of that hypothesis. In general, there will be several hypotheses which might explain the evidence, so one must be able to reject all such alternative hypotheses before one is warranted in making the inference. Thus, one infers, from the premise that a given hypothesis would provide a "better" explanation for the evidence than would any other hypothesis, to the conclusion that the given hypothesis is true. (1965, p. 89)

This form of inference has been elaborated into an extensive account of reasoning by Larry Wright in several books (1989; 2001). Since his account provides more detail, I follow it in sketching the inferential process.

Inference to the best explanation involves a *process of reasoning*. The process begins with the consideration of some phenomenon to be explained. Next, one must ensure that *all* plausible rival explanations for the phenomena to be explained are considered (e.g., why an automobile does not run or a person has a disease). That is, one begins with any plausible and perhaps even implausible legitimately rival explanations that might account for the evidence and other support available. These rival explanations are then ranked by the expert (or reasoner) according to their plausibility based on the evidence available at the time of this initial ranking (including both evidence collected at the time of the investigation and background knowledge about the subject being studied).

"Plausibility rankings" refers to "the list of rival explanations [to explain on the basis of the evidence what is going on] in the order of their plausibility" (Wright 1989, p. 101). Thus, "[w]hen we judge the [explanatory] rivals [of nondeductive arguments] to be more or less plausible, we are estimating how well or badly they explain what happened, or what is going on, given what we know about it" (ibid., p. 107). Such plausibility and associated judgments have many degrees of strength (ibid., p. 47). (Individuals can develop their skills in ranking the different conclusions from the premises based on their plausibility. Such skills are quite important for scientists and the explanations they consider within their fields. Courts need to recognize the importance of these skills in implicit scientific inferences to the best explanation.)

Next, one would use the initial plausibility rankings to try to discern what other evidence might be available that would distinguish between the explanations—to separate more plausible from less plausible explanations—and seek it out. For example, in the dimethylnitrosamine case described above the toxicologists looked for any tests, animal data, background information, and other considerations that might point to a comparatively tasteless, water-soluble substance that would cause liver damage of the kind seen in the case. Background information narrowed the search to a small class of alkylating agents. Then, investigators sought information that would permit them to distinguish between different alkylating agents.

Based on additional evidence and its strengths, plus evidence initially available (and its strength), and what both show about the plausibility of different explanations, one then may be able to modify the initial explanations as to their plausibility. One might find that the initial rankings were correct, but that the top-ranked explanation was either better or worse than one thought initially, or one might find that the ranking of explanations needs to be modified. In the dimethylnitrosamine case investigators modified the initial diagnosis from Reyes's syndrome to the ingestion of a toxic substance. Based on additional information they then narrowed the explanation further to identify a particular substance.

The goal in reasoning to the best explanation is to find the most plausible or best explanation of the rivals available to account for the evidence, and, one hopes, to find a quite good explanation out of those considered. In pursuit of that goal, one would seek evidence that would increase the plausibility gap between the highest-ranked explanation and the next highest-ranked one. That is, during one's investigation the particular top-ranked explanation may gain in strength and plausibility; or it may lose strength, and, hence, the gap between it and other possible explanations would narrow, showing that its strength and plausibility compared with rival explanations is weakening (or that the others have risen in plausibility). On Wright's view, one does not so much *reject* all other explanations as one finds evidence or relies on background knowledge that permits one to judge that one explanation is more or less plausible than others. If additional evidence or background knowledge is persuasive, then one might even reject all other hypotheses in favor of one supported by the bulk of the evidence and background knowledge.[8] Of course, if two hypotheses are approximately equally plausible, there might be no best explanation, but two equally plausible rivals. In other cases, the plausibility of hypothesis might be so great compared with the others that it clearly stands out as highly probable.

In the dimethylnitrosamine poisoning case, the explanation that dimethylnitrosamine was the cause of liver damage and death not only rose to the top of the plausibility rankings, but in the end was so far above all the others that it was presumably established beyond a reasonable doubt as the proximate cause of death, providing much of the factual foundation for a criminal prosecution for murder. In the second example, the patient's GBS following the injection of tetanus shots was so consistent and so related to the receipt of each of the three tetanus shots, that the explanation of tetanus-toxoid-caused GBS was much more probable than any alternative explanation.

Implications of Inference to the Best Explanation for the Law

A reasonable conjecture is that judges and perhaps legal scholars have underappreciated inference to the best explanation as a form of inference in science, and that this failure has resulted in a number of problems currently plaguing the legal screening of scientific evidence. Once it is understood that inference to the best explanation is a fundamental principle of reasoning, especially for scientific inferences, we can see various ways, some subtle, some not, in which the judicial evaluation of scientific evidence has been problematic.

One problem begins with the language of the *Daubert* decision. The court insisted that expert testimony must rest on "valid science." In one sense this may not be misleading, if it is referring merely to the scientific research results underlying an expert opinion. Experiments might be judged to be valid or invalid, although they are probably better described as well or poorly designed and well or poorly executed. Instead the court appears to be referring to the opinion offered by the scientific expert at the bar, which risks being more misleading.

If inference to the best explanation is the proper form of reasoning providing support for nearly all scientific inferences, then an expert's *inferences* to the best explanations might be said to be *strong, weak,* or *in between.* They are not "valid or invalid." Validity is typically the language of deduction, not of inference to the best explanation.[9]

There is a second problem related to the first. The Supreme Court has given trial court judges an enhanced legal duty to evaluate an expert's testimony before admitting the expert into court and even before proceeding with a trial of the issues. A judge must address a *dichotomous* issue: is the testimony *admissible* or *inadmissible*? However, the judge, if she understands the idea of inference to the best explanation, will see that the phenomena to be evaluated—the strength and quality of an expert's inferences based on scientific evidence—is a *continuous* phenomena. That is, courts are being asked to assess continuous phenomena with dichotomous categories.

Assessing such phenomena is not an easy task. Where on a continuum of well-supported to poorly supported scientific explanations for disease does one draw the line for a dichotomous cutoff? Neither is it a unique situation, for in other rulings courts may have to apply "yes–no" criteria to assessing continuous phenomena. However, in this case it may be more problematic because judges may not understand that scientific inferences are inferences to the best explanation; that an explanation can strongly, weakly, or only modestly account for the evidence. Judges' understanding of the nature of scientific reasoning and evidence evaluation, as revealed by their written opinions, often appears to be problematic.[10] Some courts, thus, have used categorical language—evidence is "invalid"—rather than language suggesting continuous phenomena that may be strong to weak to nonexistent. The Fifth Circuit Court of Appeals, for example, in *Allen v. Pennsylvania Engineering* ruled that Allen's expert testimony that ethylene oxide (ETO) caused brain cancer "was not scientifically valid . . . and [additionally that it] was not based on facts reasonably relied on by experts in the field" (*Allen v. Pennsylvania Engineering* 1996, p. 194).

The above are only preliminary linguistic issues, however, and hardly decisive (although as philosophers know linguistic and conceptual confusion can be quite problematic). A vastly more serious set of issues concerns some courts' apparent failure to recognize inferences to the best explanation in their various guises and instead impose what we earlier called "templates for causal inference" (or "causal templates" for short) to guide the admissibility of scientific testimony. Many of these templates, I submit, are misleading or mistaken in important ways. Moreover, it appears that courts may not recognize the nature of inference to best explanation and what must be taken into account in assessing evidence according to this principle.

Misleading Causal Templates

Some court decisions have required certain kinds of evidence that scientists themselves would not necessarily demand for causal inference. Others have excluded kinds of evidence that scientists themselves would utilize in causal inference and that, on the inference to the best explanation model, should not be ruled out of bounds a priori. Both kinds of decisions on the part of courts impose a misleading template for causal judgments on expert scientific testimony; they impose requirements on expert testimony and causal inferences that are contrary to how scientists themselves think about causal inferences.

Demands for particular kinds of evidence   First, a few early decisions post-*Daubert* insisted that an expert's opinion must rest *collectively on all the kinds of evidence* that are typically discussed in toxicological textbooks—multiple epidemiological and animal studies, as well as various short-term tests—in order to be admitted. Even though such evidence might be ideal, not all of it is necessary for an admissibility decision (*Wade-Greaux v. Whitehall Lab., Inc.* 1994). This also approaches a demand that toxicologists be highly certain that a substance is a teratogen before that conclusion could even be *admitted* for tort law purposes. The ideal, thus, became the enemy of the good.

Second, other courts, although not making the first mistake, appear to have demanded that experts base their testimony on epidemiological studies; without such studies experts in some cases have been excluded. This is a mistaken demand that has been well documented by legal scholars, some courts, and scientists. *Well-designed, well-conducted, and large* epidemiological studies (there is much conceptual baggage built into the idea of a well-done study), especially when there are many such studies done in a variety of circumstances using different study populations, can be one of the best kinds of evidence to reveal causal relations in *populations*. Unfortunately, large, well-done epidemiological studies of potentially toxic substances appear to be the exception rather than the rule (Cranor and Eastmond 2001, pp. 35–39).

Epidemiological studies are, however, just one kind of evidence. In order to make an inference to the best explanation, alternative explanations of the disease in question must be either ruled out or placed low enough on a plausibility ranking that the most likely explanation of an injury in question is a particular exposure. Epidemiological studies can provide particularly good means of doing this, but just as important, they are not the only way to do so. Other kinds of evidence, including case studies, animal studies, diagnostic tests, and so on, can help support a causal inference. The case studies sketched above reveal good inferences showing that there is a probability or certainty of a causal relation between exposure and disease, even though in none of those cases were there good epidemiological studies to support the inference. Similarly, there is good epidemiological evidence for only about half or less of the known or likely carcinogens assessed by national or international scientific bodies (Cranor and Eastmond 2001). How widespread a problem this is for other toxicants is difficult to know.

Third, on a related issue, judges seem to regard negative epidemiological studies as showing that substances do not cause disease. By contrast, scientists are quite reluctant to take one or a small number of negative studies as showing that a substance does not have an adverse effect because "no evidence of effect" (the only result of a typical negative study) is quite different from "evidence of no effect" (IARC 1999). (This mistaken inference is one of the first that students of epidemiology learn.) Using inference to the best explanation, *no evidence of an effect* from an exposure might have other explanations than that *an exposure had no effect.*

Fourth, if courts insist, as a few have, on mechanistic biological evidence for a disease, this too is an unreasonable demand. By understanding the biological mechanism by which an exposure produces a disease, for example, think of bacteria or viruses, an inference about causation would be greatly strengthened. However, this is rarely available, and certainly not a necessary condition of causal inference. It is asymmetrical evidence: when present it can be quite compelling, but when absent, it does not necessarily undermine the causal inference. This is another instance in which a few courts have conflated *particularly good evidence* with *necessary evidence* for causal inference.

The mistaken exclusion of evidence   The pertinence of animal evidence: Some courts have excluded animal evidence as pertinent to making causal judgments about the effects of toxicants on humans. Yet this is a particularly important kind of information on which toxicologists and other scientists routinely rely for making causal assessments (recall the dimethylnitrosamine example). The U.S. National Academy of Sciences, the International Agency for Research on Cancer (a prestigious international environmental health organization that issues consensus judgments about substances that are carcinogens), and the U.S. Environmental Protection Agency (as well as many other scientific organizations and virtually all toxicologists) endorse animal studies as important evidence to consider when assessing the carcinogenicity of substances in humans (National Research Council 1994, p. 120; U.S. Environmental Protection Agency 1996, pp. 40–45; IARC 1999).

Animal studies do not provide mathematically certain means by which to infer the causal effects of a toxicant on humans, but they are good and pertinent evidence, and, in most circumstances, quite good evidence for identifying substances as human toxicants. In making an inference to the best explanation about whether an exposure to a substance contributes to a disease, animal evidence is clearly presumptively pertinent evidence (Cranor and Eastmond 2001, pp. 39–45 and notes therein).

Nonetheless, animal studies have frequently not fared well in the courts. For example, in *Allen v. Pennsylvania Engineering* both a district court and the Fifth Circuit Court of Appeals rejected the plaintiff's evidence and held that the fact that ethylene oxide caused brain tumors in rats could not be evidence for the claim that EtO could cause brain tumors in humans, because EtO did not correspondingly cause brain tumors in phylogenically similar mice. Considered by itself this is bad reasoning; it shows a generic mistake. Even though mice and rats are phylogenically closer to each other than to humans—sometimes one provides a better model for human toxicity responses than the other—there is no necessity that rats and mice should be more similar to each other than either is to humans for modeling disease processes in a particular case. Toxicologists develop expertise at identifying the appropriate animal models for humans (Cranor and Eastmond 2001, pp. 39–45). However, the reasoning on scientific grounds appears to be even worse in this particular case. The reason the rat studies were so important is that they show that the small molecule of EtO can cross the blood-brain barrier, something that is quite difficult to do (because this provides a protection of brain tissue from invasions). If EtO can cross the blood–brain barrier in rats, this provides a good reason to believe that it can do so in humans, which is what the plaintiffs had argued (Kelsey and LaMontagne 1992). Toxicologists would explain EtO's inability to cross the *mouse* blood-brain barrier as based on special features of mice (e.g., their high metabolism rates, which result in the excretion of EtO before it can cross the barrier). The courts, by contrast, *assumed* that there was something special about rats not applicable to mice and humans, when it was very likely that mice exhibited the special features that distinguished them from rats and humans (Eastmond, pers. comm.). In short, the court misunderstood the significance of the evidence in question, excluded both the evidence (as well as other evidence it had difficulty with) and the expert testimony based on it, and denied the plaintiff her day in court (*Allen v. Pennsylvania Engineering* 1996, p. 197).

Chemical structure–biological activity evidence   Many courts have routinely excluded the use of chemical structure–biological activity relationships as pertinent to assessments of causal effects of toxicants on humans, arguing that at best they form the basis of a hypothesis, not evidence, of causation. Indeed, structure–activity relationships have a number of well-known difficulties. However, properly understood they can provide substantial evidence of causation in certain contexts and would be part of any scientifically reasonable composite pattern of evidence of causation. In general, it is not a *scientifically* strong inference to argue from similarity in chemical structure to similarity in biological activity, since even some specific similarities in chemical structure with minor dissimilarities elsewhere can result in fairly significant differences in biological effects.

However, for some chemical families with certain properties, there are scientifically strong inferences that can be made. For example, molecules with chemical groups that are known to interact with mammalian DNA or proteins provide strong, but not infallible, reasons for thinking that substances with chemical similarities have similar biological activity (Ashby and Tennant 1988; Eastmond, pers. comm.). On balance, if courts were to adopt a *general* policy to utilize structure–activity relationships, this would likely lead to scientific mistakes and not provide particularly accurate identifications of toxic substances. However, adopting a more fine-grained structure–activity approach aimed at identifying classes of substances that acted on proteins or on DNA would be much more defensible and in keeping with current scientific methodology.

Case studies as evidence   As already noted, courts have tended to reject the use of case studies at least when they constitute major evidence of causation in toxic tort cases (they tend to permit them if they are supportive of more robust evidence, but then they have minimal decisive relevance). Like structure–activity relationships, case studies are *in general* not *mathematically certain* guides to causal relationships, because, although some case studies are good guides for this purpose, many others are not. Thus, not every positive case study provides evidence of causation. However, not every positive epidemiological study or every positive animal study provides evidence of causation as well. Courts must learn to evaluate and sift the evidence at the bar in order to admit the biological evidence that does provide evidence of causation, including case studies.

Good case studies are less rare than the recitation of a few examples might suggest. The World Health Organization has found that about 17 percent of the case studies they have considered are the basis of certain or probable casual relationships between vaccine exposure and adverse reactions. Seventeen percent is a comparatively small percentage, but it is not negligible. Moreover, since courts are required to review carefully all the evidence litigants present that might assist the jury in coming to its decision, they need to consider whether the case studies at the bar are among those providing good evidence of causal relationships or not.

Never throw evidence away   In order to evaluate possible explanations of a phenomenon a scientist must consider *all the evidence* available that might assist one in making an inference to the best explanation. Several scientific methodologists and consensus committees make the point in quite strong terms. For example, a large group of scientists and physicians involved in assessing adverse events from immunizations propose a method for assessing vaccine-caused adverse effects that is "based on the best available information, [such that] [m]aximum use is made of all available information and nothing is arbitrarily discarded" (Fenichel et al. 1989, p. 290). Hutchinson and Lane make the same point in even stronger terms: "A causality assessment method must respect Fisher's fundamental rule of uncertain inference—*never throw information away*. That is, any fact, theory or opinion that can affect an evaluator's belief that [a particular exposure] caused an adverse event E must be incorporable by the method into the 'state of information' on which the assessment is based" (1989B, p. 10 [emphasis added]). Thus, any piece of evidence that "can affect" a scientist's belief with regard to the toxicity of a substance according to this principle should be admitted into evidence.

The application of the aphorism, "never throw information away," to the law suggests that if a particular kind of evidence can affect scientists' causality judgments, it should be equally applicable to judges reviewing the plausibility of scientists' causal inferences. This suggests that presumptively courts should admit any individual fact, theory, or opinion that can affect a scientist's belief that a particular exposure caused an adverse event. Such evidence might ultimately be inadmissible if *taken in conjunction with all the other scientifically relevant evidence* it were "scientifically unreliable" or did not fit the facts of a case. Yet courts have excluded individual kinds of evidence that are pertinent to a scientist's judgment concerning causation. The important point, developed next, is that evidence is plausible or not when considered in the context of all the evidence taken as a whole.

Weight-of-the-evidence arguments   Up to this point I have focused on particular kinds of evidence that courts have demanded or excluded. However, the Supreme Court's evaluation of evidentiary reasoning in one of its leading cases was so misleading, and so at odds with inference to the best explanation and scientific inferences in general, that it merits discussion.

Particularly disturbing was the district court's exclusion of each piece of evidence in *Joiner* (1997) without considering whether the evidence taken as a whole was admissible. In effect the court rejected the plaintiff's weight-of-the-evidence argument in *Joiner*. On appeal, the Supreme Court, when it could have remanded the issue to lower courts, went out of its way to endorse the district court's reasoning:

The District Court agreed with petitioners that the animal studies on which respondent's experts relied did not support his contention that exposure to PCB's had contributed to his cancer. The studies involved infant mice that had developed cancer after being exposed to PCB's. The infant mice in the studies had had massive doses of PCB's injected directly into their peritoneums . . . or stomachs. Joiner was an adult human being whose alleged exposure to PCB's was far less than the exposure in the animal studies. The PCB's were injected into the mice in a highly concentrated form. The fluid with which Joiner had come into contact generally had a much smaller PCB concentration of between 0-to-500 parts per million. The cancer that these mice developed was alveologenic adenomas; Joiner had developed small-cell carcinomas. No study demonstrated that adult mice developed cancer after being exposed to PCB's. One of the experts admitted that no study had demonstrated that PCB's lead to cancer in any other species. (*Joiner* 1997, pp. 144–145)

The Court then found, with the district court, that none of the human epidemiological studies on which the plaintiff's case rested was *singly* or in combination sufficient to overcome the admissibility barrier plaintiffs faced (ibid., pp. 145–147). Although the Court referred to epidemiological studies "in combination," it only considered the adequacy of each piece of evidence taken by itself.

A better approach, as Justice Stevens articulated in dissent, would have been whether the evidence taken as a whole—the infant mice studies at that exposure level together with information about the lung cancers involved and the epidemiological studies—constituted a sufficiently respectable form of scientific reasoning or pattern of evidence to be admitted into evidence about which litigants could then argue before a jury (*Joiner* 1997, pp. 151–155).[11] Or was the evidence taken as a whole and the reasoning utilized so far beyond the pale of what constitutes respectable scientific reasoning that it should be ruled inadmissible? Neither the district court nor the Supreme Court majority asked this question, although the Eleventh Circuit did. Their failure to recognize the importance of inference to the best explanation in assessing evidence may have deprived Mr. Joiner of his day in court and the possibility of justice.

The disturbing feature of this opinion is that it endorses the rejection of evidence piece-by-piece without requiring the district court to consider whether the evidence taken in combination met admissibility standards. Yet it is precisely the evaluation of all the evidence taken together that inference to the best causal explanation requires of scientists. By rejecting this alternative, the Supreme Court placed its imprimatur on rejecting precisely the kind of reasoning and methodology on which scientists routinely rely in their laboratories for evaluating the toxicity of substances.

Courts' apparent failure to understand inferences to the best explanation has led to another confusion about weight-of-the-evidence arguments (*Allen v. Pennsylvania Engineering* 1996).[12] The term "weight of the evidence" is often utilized by regulatory agencies when they assess the plausibility of a causal relation between exposure to a potentially toxic substance and the contraction of a certain disease or groups of diseases. Some courts, noting that regulatory agencies utilize this term and that agencies are interested mainly in assessing *risks* not causal relations as required by torts, dismiss weight-of-the-evidence arguments in torts either (1) because they are merely about risks, not retrospective causation, or (2) because the standard of proof may be lower. There are at least two confusions here.

First, the term "weight-of-the-evidence argument" is merely a label for an inferential process of weighing and evaluating evidence for a causal relation that explains a harm. Weighing and evaluating the extent to which evidence supports one explanation or another is pertinent to assessing both risks *and* retrospective causation; it is not necessarily restricted to assessing risks.[13]

Second, the level (standard) of proof is not a function of inference to the best explanation (or weight of the evidence). Instead, it is a function of how plausible the causal explanation between exposure and disease must be for some legal (or social) purpose compared with other explanations of the same phenomena. Is it certain, highly probable, or only marginally probable compared with alternative explanations? The standard of proof for the argument lies not in the form of the argument, but in how strongly supported one explanation must be compared with alternative explanations for the institutional purposes in question.

Confusion of Certainty of Causation with Frequency of Adverse Effects

Some courts have insisted, following certain results from statistical studies, that before a plaintiff can make a case that the defendant's substance more likely than not caused the plaintiff's disease, the plaintiff must show that exposure to the defendant's substance *doubled* the risk of the background rate of disease. *Daubert v. Merrell-Dow Pharmaceuticals Inc.* (1995) represents one of the most prominent examples, but by no means the only one in which courts have required such evidence. This doubling of the background rate of disease is thought to be needed for proof of causation. It is argued that only if there is a doubling of the background rate of disease as a result of exposure to a substance can the court be assured that it is more likely than not that the plaintiff's disease resulted from the defendant's substance. The reason for this is that if exposure doubles the disease rate above background, then a court would have *a general statistical reason* to believe that at least half of the diseases in an exposed population would be attributed to the exposure, and, thus, that it was at least 50 percent likely that any instance of the disease was attributable to the exposure. The requirement that disease rates be doubled above background has, thus, served as a surrogate for probability of causation in individual cases.

This demand, almost a mantra in some courts, suggests a confusion between *the degree of certainty of causation* and *the frequency with which a disease occurs* in an exposed population. The fundamental legal issues are what is the likelihood that a particular exposure can cause a disease (general causation), and what is the likelihood that a particular exposure in fact caused a particular plaintiff's disease (specific causation). In both cases the issue is what is the likelihood of disease causation. However, statistical evidence is not necessarily needed to show probability of causation. Above I sketched four examples of disease causation based on singular (or a small number of) events. For each of them exposure to the substance in question certainly or probably caused the adverse reaction, but there were no statistical studies that revealed a doubling of disease rate above background on which to base the probability or certainty of causation. In example (1), physicians were virtually certain that the anesthesiologist contracted GBS as a result of exposure to halothane, even though such exposure did not double the GBS rate and even though few others had such reactions. In example (2), the experts asserted that exposure to tetanus toxoid more likely than not did cause GBS even though there had been only a few other case studies reported. In example (3), there were no statistical studies whatever showing any relationship between ingestion of dimethylnitrosamine and acute poisoning, but there was quite sufficient proof of causation in that particular case. For the vinyl chloride exposures in example (4), there had been no epidemiological studies on VC exposure at the time scientists concluded that VC likely caused ASL.

The conclusion: to the extent that courts demand statistical evidence of a doubling of background rates of disease as evidence for probability of causation, they have it *backward*. What must be shown is that it is more likely than not that exposure to the defendant's substance can cause injuries like the plaintiff's and more likely than not did cause the plaintiff's injury. Statistical evidence is merely one way, sometimes the only way, and even a particularly strong way to establish this claim, but there may be many others depending on the evidence that is available in a particular case. The above examples of good case studies show this quite clearly.

We can enhance this point by considering the general-versus-specific-causation issue further. In toxic torts courts tend to insist that a plaintiff must first show that it is more likely than not that a substance *can cause*

the disease in question (general causation), and then show that the substance *did cause* the particular plaintiff's injury (specific causation). Courts
and some recent articles in the literature have, moreover, insisted on the
order of showing—first, general causation and then specific causation. This
makes sense in many cases, but there is no necessity to the order. Consider
the second case study example. In that case, scientists explicitly concluded
that "because [this] case . . . demonstrates that tetanus toxoid *did* cause
GBS, in the committee's judgment tetanus toxioid *can* cause GBS" (Stratton, Home, and Johnston 1994, p. 89). That is, because a specific case of
causation had been shown, by conceptual reasoning they concluded that
the possibility of general causation followed as a logical consequence. Now,
it is likely that such cases will be rare, but not unheard of. Consequently,
courts and commentators must exercise care in laying down hard and fast
rules about the order of demonstration between general and specific
causation.

Consider this point with respect to what is called "differential diagnosis," yet another term, I believe, for inference to the best explanation. Joe
Sanders and Julie Machal-Faulks have argued that the majority of decided
legal cases suggests that in differential diagnosis, a physician or scientist
must "rule in" the possibility of a general causal relationship between an
exposure and a disease before ruling out all other possible explanations
(Sanders and Machal-Faulks 2001, p. 107). It is not enough, most courts
have held, in differential diagnosis or inference to the best explanation
that an expert can rule out all other explanations and then find that the
remaining one—that the defendant's substance caused the plaintiff's
disease—can be ruled in and the only explanation left standing.

There is much to this suggestion, but no necessity. A particular explanation must be a plausible one—it must be biologically plausible, typically
must be consistent with what is known (although even these two considerations can be overemphasized), and satisfy other explanatory desiderata.
However, as the tetanus toxoid and vinyl chloride cases show, given background information, particular exposures, and the ruling out of other
explanations, a previously unsuspected causal relationship can be revealed
on the basis of a singular event or small number of events. Moreover,
because a particular exposure *did cause* an adverse reaction, it follows
that the exposure *can cause* that reaction. In such cases specific causation implies general causation. In the tetanus vaccine-GBS example a

particular explanation was ruled in by compelling singular circumstances and background information without general causation having been established. A similar inference occurred in the vinyl chloride case. Although such cases may not be common, in the spirit of *Daubert* courts must allow for this in their evidence evaluation.

We can understand courts' and public health officials' concern with statistical studies, since the rate of disease above background is important for both purposes. For public health, if exposure to a vaccine or an anesthetic greatly increases disease rates, this is important information concerning whether or not to pursue a vaccination program or allow exposures to an anesthesia. If exposure only slightly increases disease rates above background, there may be little or no public health concern; if there is a great increase, there is a correspondingly greater concern (the background rate of disease is also important).

For legal purposes, if courts have such statistical information, this can provide some evidence about the likelihood of causation, but it is not necessary. On a separate legal issue, if a defendant is subject to a negligence standard of liability, a plaintiff must show that the defendant failed to exercise the kind of care a reasonable person in those circumstances would. Thus, in order to establish the defendant's liability, the plaintiff would need to show that the harm was foreseeable. The foreseeability requirement would need some substantiation that an *ex ante* risk was being imposed on those exposed to a product or substance. Thus, having a disease rate elevated above background would be one kind of evidence to show foreseeability, but this is a separate issue from showing causation.

The last two points raise a significant underlying point that suggest a conjecture for which I will not argue, but one that seems plausible. Certainly courts, and perhaps much of the scientific world more generally, has become captivated by the idea that various kinds of statistical support are needed for scientific conclusions. This is not surprising, not even remarkable, given the methodological and other progress that has been made with statistical reasoning in the twentieth century and the myriad inferential mistakes that can be made in causal reasoning. Moreover, certain kinds of statistical evidence—in particular double-blind clinical trials with large numbers in both the control and the exposed groups—can be paradigmatic of excellent empirical studies in identifying the causes of disease. The mistake, and it is a mistake, is to confuse a common and frequent example of good scientific reasoning for what is required of *all* scientific and factual reasoning.

Causal inference is needed in science. Inference to the best explanation is the form of reasoning by which scientists infer that a causal relation holds between exposure and disease. There are a variety of kinds and patterns of evidence that could be used in inferences to the best explanation to conclude that a causal relationship more likely than not existed. Statistical studies of one kind or another are merely *one* means (one pattern of evidence, if you will) of supporting causal inferences, not the only one and not a necessary form of evidence that must be present for every causal inference.

The conjecture is that courts have mistaken one species of causal inference for the genus or necessary condition of *all* causal inferences. Instead they should recognize that the fundamental issue is the causal relationship between exposure and injury and that there are a variety of kinds and patterns of evidence that would license an inference to such conclusions. A variety of patterns of evidence—utilizing all the kinds of evidence available in a particular case—can support causal inferences.

Expert Judgment in Inference to the Best Explanation

In *Joiner* the Supreme Court noted "nothing in either *Daubert* or the Federal Rules of Evidence requires a district court to admit opinion evidence that is connected to existing data only by the *ipse dixit* of the expert" (a bare assertion resting on the authority of an individual [Black's Law Dictionary 1968, p. 961]). "A court may conclude that there is simply too great an analytical gap between the data and the opinion proffered" (*Joiner* 1997, p. 146). This statement is in general correct, since, simply because an expert *says* that existing data support his or her conclusion, this does not make it so.

However, the Court's assertion is misleading if it suggests that there should be little or no *individual judgment* in expert inference. Experts' inferences about causation typically rest on individual assessments by the person involved at several points in the inferential process, as I have argued elsewhere (Cranor forthcoming).

Conclusion

Contemporary toxic tort law with its causation requirement and a significant need for scientific evidence to substantiate causal claims results in significant tensions between science and the law. Some courts have exacerbated these tensions by how they have screened evidence (Cranor and Eastmond 2001). If the two institutions are to function well together, judges must screen scientific evidence more sensitively than some have to date. Failure to do this will frustrate the Supreme Court's aim of resting legal decisions on a reasonable scientific basis (when scientific evidence is central) and typically result in little compensation for technological accidents involving toxicants. By contrast, if judges recognize the wide range of evidence that bears on the human toxicity of substances, legal cases will be more nearly scientifically accurate. This in turn enhances the possibility of justice for plaintiffs who have in fact been harmed by defendants' toxicants.

Central to the scientific evaluation of evidence are inferences to the best explanation of the evidence available. Judges and perhaps legal scholars appear to have underappreciated this form of inference that is fundamental to science and other nondeductive reasoning. That failure has resulted in a number of problems that currently plague the legal screening of scientific evidence. Once it is understood how fundamental inference to the best explanation is used in scientific reasoning, we can see various ways, some subtle, some not, that judicial evaluation of scientific evidence has been problematic. Understanding the importance of inference to the best explanation helps to put other kinds of causal evidence into better perspective, thus helping to correct some of the misleading and mistaken causal templates adopted by courts to date. A better understanding of these issues should lead to more accurate judicial decisions concerning the admissibility of evidence and increase the possibility of justice for those affected by admissibility rulings.

Acknowledgments

Research for this essay was supported by NSF grant 99-10952, a grant from the University of California's Toxic Substances Research and Teaching Program, and a University of California, Riverside, intramural research grant. David Strauss, a Ph.D. candidate in philosophy, provided valuable research assistance and discussions on portions of the essay. I have also received quite useful comments from members of the Southern California Law and Philosophy Discussion Group.

Notes

1. *Cooter and Gell* 1989, 400, quoting *Anderson* v. *Bessemer City*, 470 U.S. 564, 573–574 ("[If] the district court's account of the evidence is plausible in light of the record viewed in its entirety, the court of appeals may not reverse it even though convinced that had it been sitting as the trier of fact, it would have weighed the evidence differently. Where there are two permissible views of the evidence, the choice between them cannot be clearly erroneous.")

2. The FDA, for example, removed Parlodel (bromocriptine), a postpartum lactation suppression drug from the market simply on the basis of a series of case reports indicating a relationship between the use of Parlodel and patients suffering strokes or heart attacks, although it was working under a somewhat different authority.

3. Inferences such as this in which the exposure was present, followed by the adverse reaction, contrasted with circumstances in which the exposure was absent with no adverse reaction, each repeated several times followed by a deliberate challenge under controlled conditions (which was preceded by no exposure and no adverse conditions) is very close to John Stuart Mill's method of difference. The method of difference is to "have every circumstance in common save one, that one occurring only in the [circumstance in which the phenomenon under investigation occurs]; the circumstance in which alone the two instances differ is the effect, or the cause, or an indispensable part of the cause, of the phenomenon" (Mill 1941, p. 256).

4. It is unusual for carcinogens to be identified mainly on the basis of case studies. Cancers tend to be fairly common diseases, making it more difficult to identify common cancers on the basis of a small number of cases. However, when the disease is quite rare, as is ASL, it becomes comparatively easier. In addition, cancers are multifactorial diseases with typically long latency periods. Consequently, since over a long period of time a person will be subjected to a number of bodily insults that might contribute to the contraction of cancer, it can be difficult to identify one factor as a significant causal contributor to the disease. Moreover, when cancers caused by workplace or environmental exposures are elevated only slightly above background rates of disease, this, too, complicates the identification of the cause of the disease, since even the best scientific tools are comparatively insensitive. However, when the disease is rare, highly elevated above background with few other exposures likely to cause the particular disease in question, the evidentiary value of case studies rises and may be quite compelling for identifying the cause of disease as they were in the case of VC-caused ASL.

5. By "defeasible criteria" I suggest that these are features of a reasoning process that a scientist might follow, and if the features are present, he/she will likely arrive at a correct causal conclusion. However, these criteria are *defeasible*, that is, they do not guarantee, or are not sufficient for, a correct outcome. A scientist might make a mistake, ignore some important background information, etc., even though he/she was formally following all the steps that one should in coming to a conclusion about causation. I owe this point to my colleague Peter Graham.

6. Moreover, in another venue the National Transportation Safety Board usually has only case studies, single accidents, by which to evaluate the cause of airplane accidents.

7. Another way to put this point is to say that if one finds the conclusion to be false in a valid argument, at least one of the premises must be mistaken as well. Or, if one accepts the truth of the premises, but rejects the truth of the conclusion in a valid argument one contradicts oneself.

8. Harman (1965) appears to be thinking of clear cases in which one explanation is so superior to all others that one can properly be said to *reject* them.

9. I was once asked to advise a defense attorney on the evaluation of a plaintiff's expert's reasoning in a worker's compensation case. After reading the documents and discussing the issue with the attorney, it became clear that the defense attorney was trying to evaluate the reasoning as *deductive* reasoning, not as it more properly should have been assessed, as an inference to the best explanation. Once the difference between the two different kinds of inferences was clarified, it became obvious that the attorney's first argumentative strategy would not work and that he would have to attack the plaintiff's expert in a different way. He could not show that the plaintiff's expert was committing a particular deductive fallacy, but he had to engage the expert on the issue of what was the best explanation to account for the evidence in question.

10. It is difficult to obtain very good evidence on this issue, since courts express opinions on the admissibility of evidence only when they are ruling that it is not admissible. If it is admissible and they admit it, they typically write no opinion on the issue at trial court (at the appellate court level this is a different matter, since an appellate court might rule that evidence excluded by a district court was in fact admissible). However, in reading a number of appellate and some district court cases, a large number appear to have misunderstood the nature of evidence evaluation in science as revealed by their discussion of the issues.

11. "Unlike the District Court, the Court of Appeals expressly decided that a 'weight of the evidence' methodology was scientifically acceptable. . . . To this extent, the Court of Appeals' opinion is persuasive. It is not intrinsically 'unscientific' for experienced professionals to arrive at a conclusion by weighing all available scientific evidence—this is not the sort of 'junk science' with which *Daubert* was concerned.

After all, as Joiner points out, the Environmental Protection Agency (EPA) uses the same methodology to assess risks, albeit using a somewhat different threshold than that required in a trial. . . . And using this methodology, it would seem that an expert could reasonably have concluded that the study of workers at an Italian capacitor plant, coupled with data from Monsanto's study and other studies, raises an inference that PCB's promote lung cancer. . . . [W]hen qualified experts have reached relevant conclusions on the basis of an acceptable methodology, why are their opinions inadmissible?" (*Joiner* 1997, pp. 153–154)

12. "We are also unpersuaded that the 'weight of the evidence' methodology these experts use is scientifically acceptable for demonstrating a medical link between Allen's EtO exposure and brain cancer. Regulatory and advisory bodies such as IARC, the Occupational Safety and Health Administration and EPA utilize a 'weight of the evidence' method to assess the carcinogenicity of various substances in human beings and suggest or make prophylactic rules governing human exposure. This methodology results from the preventive perspective that the agencies adopt in order to reduce public exposure to harmful substances. The agencies' threshold of proof is reasonably lower than that appropriate in tort law, which 'traditionally make[s] more particularized inquiries into cause and effect' and requires a plaintiff to prove 'that it is more likely than not that another individual has caused him or her harm' " (quoting *Wright v. Willamette Industries, Inc.* 1996, p. 1107).

13. Moreover, weighing and evaluating evidence of the relation between exposures and risks is not substantially different from weighing and evaluating evidence for evidence of a retrospective causal relation between exposure and harm. In fact, scientists regard both activities as like those of scientific detectives, since the evidence for *risks* from exposures is likely to be some kind of harm that the exposures have caused to people, animals, mammalian cells, organs, or DNA, or some combination of these; the same kind of evidence scientists would use for assessing the *causes* of harm (Eastmond, pers. comm.).

References

Allen v. Pennsylvania Engineering Corp., 102 F. 3d 194, 197 (5th Cir. 1996).

Anderson v. Bessemer City, 470 U.S. 564 (1985).

Ashby, J., and R. W. Tennant. 1988. "Chemical Structure, Salmonella Mutagenicity and Extent of Carcinogenicity as Indicators of Genotoxic Carcinogensesis among 222 Chemicals Tested in Rodents by the U.S. NCI/NTP." *Mutation Research* 204: 17–115.

Black's Law Dictionary. 1968. Fourth ed. St. Paul, Minn.: West.

Berger, M. A. 1997. "Eliminating General Causation: Notes Towards a New Theory of Justice and Toxic Torts." *Columbia Law Review* 97: 2117–2152.

———. 2000. "The Supreme Court's Trilogy on the Admissibility of Expert Testimony." In Federal Judicial Center, ed., *Reference Manual on Scientific Evidence*. Washington, D.C.: Federal Judicial Center.

———. 2001. "Upsetting the Balance between Adverse Interests: The Impact of the Supreme Court's Trilogy on Expert Testimony in Toxic Tort Litigation." *Law and Contemporary Problems* 64: 289–326.

Black v. Food Lion, Inc., 171 F. 3d 308 (5th Cir. 1999).

Breyer, S. 2000. "Introduction." In Federal Judicial Center, ed., *Reference Manual on Scientific Evidence*. Washington, D.C.: Federal Judicial Center.

Brumbaugh v. Sandoz Pharmaceuticals, F. Supp. Ct. 2d 1153, 1156 (D. Montana 1999).

Casey v. Ohio Medical Products, 877 F. Supp. Ct. 1380 (1995).

Cavallo v. Star Enter., 892 F. Supp. Ct. 756 (E. D. Va. 1995).

Clayson, D. B. 2001. *Toxicological Carcinogenesis*. New York: Lewis.

Collet, J. P., N. Macdonald, N. Cashman, R. Pless, and the Advisory Committee on Causality Assessment. 2000. "Monitoring Signals for Vaccine Safety: The Assessment of Individual Adverse Event Reports by an Expert Advisory Committee." *Bulletin of the World Health Organization* 78: 178–185.

Cooter and Gell v. Hartmarx Corp., 496 U.S. 384 (1989).

Craighead, John. 1995. *Pathology of Environmental and Occupational Disease*. St. Louis, Miss.: Mosby.

Cranor, C. F. 1993. *Regulating Toxic Substances: A Philosophy of Science and the Law*. New York: Oxford University Press.

———. Forthcoming. "Scientific Inferences in the Laboratory and the Law." *American Journal of Public Health*.

Cranor, C. F., and D. A. Eastmond. 2001. "Scientific Ignorance and Reliable Patterns of Evidence in Toxic Tort Causation: Is There a Need for Liability Reform?" *Law and Contemporary Problems* 64: 5–48.

Creech, J. L., and M. N. Johnson. 1974. "Angiosarcoma of Liver in the Manufacture of Polyvinyl Chloride." *Journal of Occupational Medicine* 16: 150–151.

Daubert v. Merrell Dow Pharmaceuticals Inc., 509 U.S. 579 (1993).

Daubert v. Merrell Dow Pharmaceuticals Inc., 43 F. 3d 1311 (9th Cir. 1995).

Donaldson v. Central Illinois Public Service 199 Ill. 2d 63 (2002).

Faigman, D. L. 1999. *Legal Alchemy: The Use and Misuse of Science in the Law*. New York: Freeman.

Falk, H., J. L., Creech Jr., C. W. Heath, Jr., M. N. Johnson, and M. M. Key. 1974. "Hepatic Disease among Workers at a Vinyl Chloride Polymerization Plant." *Journal of the American Medical Association* 230: 59–68.

Fenichel, G. E., D. A. Lane, J. R. Livengood, S. J. Horwitz, J. H. Menkes, and J. F. Schwartz. 1989. "Adverse Events Following Immunization: Assessing Probability of Causation." *Pediatric Neurology* 5: 289–290.

Finley, L. M. 1999. "Guarding the Gate to the Courthouse: How Trial Judges Are Using Their Evidentiary Screening Role to Remake Tort Causation Rules." *DePaul Law Review* 49: 335–375.

Fisk, M. C. 1999. "Chicago Hope: A $28M Verdict." *National Law Journal* November 10: A10.

Federal Rules of Evidence.

Frye v. U.S., 293 F. 1013 (D.C. Cir. 1923).

General Electric Co. v. Joiner, 522 U.S. 136 (1997).

Gillette, C. P., and J. E. Krier. 1990. "Risk, Courts and Agencies." *University of Pennsylvania Law Review* 138: 1027–1109.

Globetti v. Sandoz Pharmaceuticals Corp., 111 F. Supp. Ct. 2d 1174 (N. D. Ala. 2000).

Graham, M. H. 2000. "The Expert Witness Predicament: Determining 'Reliable' Under the Test of Daubert, Kumho and Proposed Amended Rule 702 of the Federal Rules of Evidence." *University of Miami Law Review* 54: 317–357.

Green, M. D. 1999. "The Road Less Well Traveled (and Seen): Contemporary Law Making in Products Liability." *De Paul Law Review* 49: 300–403.

Haggerty v. Upjohn Co., 950 F. Supp. Ct. 1160, 1165 (S. D. Florida 1996).

Harman, G. 1965. "The Inference to the Best Explanation." *Philosophical Review* 74: 89–90.

Hartzema, A. G., M. Porta, and H. H. Tilson, eds. 1998. *Pharmacoepidemiology: An Introduction.* Cincinnati, Ohio: Harvey Whitney Books.

Heath, Jr., C. W., H. Falk, and J. L. Creech, Jr. 1975. "Characteristics of Cases of Angiosarcoma of the Liver among Vinyl Chloride Workers in the United States." *Annals of the New York Academy of Sciences* 246: 231–248.

Huff, J., and D. P. Rall. 1992. "Relevance to Humans of Carcinogenesis Results from Laboratory Animal Toxicology Studies." In J. M. Last and R. B. Wallace, eds., *Maxcy-Rosenau Last Public Health and Preventive Medicine*, thirteenth ed. Norwalk, Conn.: Appleton and Lange.

Hutchinson, T. A., and D. A. Lane. 1989a. "Standardized Methods of Causality Assessment of Suspected Adverse Drug Reactions." *Journal of Chronic Disease* 39: 857–860.

———. 1989b. "Assessing Methods for Causality Assessment of Suspected Adverse Drug Reactions." *Journal of Clinical Epidemiology* 42: 5–16.

IARC (International Agency for Research on Cancer) Monograph Series. "Preamble." Located at http://193.51.164.11/ monoeval/StudiesHumans.html. Last updated 17 December 1999; visited 3/4/2002.

James, R. C. 1985 "General Principles of Toxicology." In P. L. Williams and J. L. Burson, eds., *Industrial Toxicology*. Belmont, Calif.: Lifetime Learning Publications.

Kelsey, K. T., and A. D. LaMontagne. 1992. Plaintiff's Expert Opinion Affidavit in *Allen v. Pennsylvania Engineering Corp*. 5th Cir. Court of Appeals court files. October 13.

Klatskin, G., and D. V. Kimberg. 1969. "Recurrent Hepatitis Attributable to Halothane Sensitization in an Anesthetist." *New England Journal of Medicine* 280: 515–522.

Kramer, M. S. and D. A. Lane. 1992. "Causal Propositions in Clinical Research and Practice." *Journal of Clinical Epidemiology* 45: 639–649.

Kuhn, T. 1977. "Objectivity, Value Judgement and Theory Choice." In T. Kuhn, *The Essential Tension*. Chicago, Ill.: The University of Chicago Press.

Kumho Tire Co. v. Carmichael, 526 U.S. 137 (1999).

Mill, J. S. 1941. *A System of Logic: Ratiocinative and Inductive*. London: Longmany, Green.

Moore v. Ashland Chemical Inc., 151 F. 3d 269 (5th Cir. 1998).

National Research Council. 1994. *Science and Judgment in Risk Assessment*. Washington, D.C.: National Academy Press.

Ozonoff, D. 2000. "A Fish Out of Water: The Scientist in Court." Presented at the National Academy of Sciences Scientific Evidence Workshop, September 6.

Roueché, B. 1982. "The Lemonade Mystery." *Saturday Evening Post*. May/June: 59, 120.

Sanders, J., and J. Machal-Faulks. 2001. "The Admissibility of Differential Diagnosis Testimony to Prove Causation in Toxic Tort Cases: The Interplay of Adjective and Substantive Law." *Law and Contemporary Problems* 64: 107–138.

Stratton, E. R., C. J. Howe, and R. B. Johnston, eds. 1994. *Adverse Events Associated with Childhood Vaccines: Evidence Bearing on Causality*. Washington, D.C.: National Academy Press (Institute of Medicine).

Strom, B. L., ed. 2000. *Pharmacoepideimology*, third ed. New York: John Wiley and Sons.

United States v. Posado, 57 F. 3d 428 (5th Cir. 1995).

U.S. Environmental Protection Agency. 1996. "Proposed Guidelines for Carcinogen Risk Assessment." *Federal Register* 61 (79): 1796–18011.

Wade-Greaux v. Whitehall Lab., Inc., 874 F. Sup. Ct. 1441 (D.V.I.), affirmed, 46 F. 3d 1120 (3d Cir. 1994).

Wright, L. 1989. *Practical Reasoning*. New York: Harcourt Brace Jovanovich.

———. 2001. *Critical Thinking: An Introduction to Analytical Reasoning and Reading.* New York: Oxford University Press.

Wright v. Willamette Industries, Inc., 91 F. 3d 1105, 1107 (8th Cir. 1996).

5   Moral Luck and the Criminal Law

Nir Eisikovits

The problem of moral luck springs from a discrepancy between our notion of responsibility and the actual manner in which we make moral judgments. We tend to think people are only responsible for what they can control, but we are also inclined to judge them on the basis of what they cannot. The problem was introduced by two seminal articles written by Bernard Williams and Thomas Nagel[1] and has generated a good deal of interest since. Scholars concerned with the criminal law have found it especially rich. Most lawyers have focused on Nagel's account of moral luck, perhaps because it is more concerned with external judgments of an agent's action (which are the kind of judgments the law makes), whereas Williams focuses on self-evaluation.[2] As a matter of fact legal scholars have focused especially on one aspect of Nagel's account, namely luck in the outcomes of our actions, or *outcome luck*.

This paper begins with a short example aimed at bringing out some of the questions involved in the notion of "moral luck." It then proceeds to give a critical account of the debate concerning the role of fortuity in the moral assessment of criminal actions and in their punishment. I preface the final part of the essay with a cautionary note about taking sides in this debate. The problem of moral luck represents a paradox in the heart of our moral practices; it needs to be described rather than "solved," since paradoxes cannot be argued away. I then go on to describe aspects of the relationship between law and luck that have been largely neglected by the literature.

What is moral luck?

Max, a bus driver, is taking a group of thirty schoolchildren home after a day trip to the local zoo. He is quite tired, and occasionally doses off at the wheel. After several minutes of monotonous driving he awakens, startled, to find himself in the opposite lane. He sharply jerks the steering wheel to the right, and manages to steer the bus back to safety. He sighs in relief, marking that he should never agree to work more than one driving shift a day, even if he is threatened by his employers with termination. The children reach their homes safely, and excitedly recount their zoo experiences, quite oblivious to how close they were to catastrophe. Max mentions the incident to his supervisor and insists on a reduction in his daily workload. The supervisor agrees, although he makes it clear that Max's salary will be diminished accordingly. Two weeks later Max, unable to make ends meet, is back working two shifts a day.

None of us has ever heard of Max or of the company he works for. His story as recounted above is quite uninteresting. It is not the stuff news is made of. But if there had been an oil spill in the exact spot where Max regained his consciousness, or if there had been a car in the opposite lane at that exact time, or if Max had been naturally endowed with weaker instincts, or if a loud song had not come on the radio shaking Max from his slumber, the situation would have been very different. His name and image would be mentioned in every household in the community. He would be subject to criminal and then civil proceedings. Some of the enraged parents would refer to him as a murderer. For Max the difference between obscurity and notoriety boils down to the location of an oil spill, the velocity of muscular reflexes, the editorial choice of music. None of these are subject to his control. Whether we ever hear of Max or not, whether we condemn him or continue to be oblivious to him is a question of moral luck.

According to Thomas Nagel, the term "moral luck" describes a state of affairs "where a significant aspect of what someone does depends on factors beyond his control, yet we continue to treat him in that respect as an object of moral judgment. . . ."[3] If people can only be held responsible for what they control, judging them on the basis of what they cannot is problematic. Yet we make such judgments all the time. Whether we treat Max as a negligent killer or not depends, considerably, on factors he could not influence. What he ends up having done is, to an important extent, not up to him. It seems, then, that the phenomenon of moral luck denotes a paradox embedded in our notion of responsibility. As Nagel so succinctly puts it: "A person can be morally responsible only for what he does; but what he does results from a great deal he does not do; therefore he is not morally responsible for what he is and is not responsible for."[4]

Nagel provides us with four categories for classifying cases of moral luck.[5] The first is *constitutive luck*. This concerns the kind of person the agent is, and it includes one's inclinations, capacities, and temperament. The speed of Max's reactions and his physical propensity to dose off under certain conditions would be subsumed under this category. The second category, *circumstantial luck*, relates to the kinds of situations and problems one's specific history presents one with, or in Nagel's words, "the things we are called upon to do, the moral tests we face. . . ."[6] To use Nagel's own example, most Germans complied with the diabolical Nazi regime they lived under, and we condemn them for this. But whether or not one lives in a society where he has to face such moral challenges is a question of luck. Correspondingly, whether or not one ends up in a line of work like Max's, where the chances of being involved in a road accident are relatively high is also, to some degree, a matter of circumstantial luck. The last two forms of luck "have to do with the causes and effects of action."[7] Following Daniel Statman, I will call the third category *causal luck*.[8] This kind of luck concerns the circumstances antecedent to action, which may often determine whether or nor the action is performed. A loud song comes on the radio and shakes Max from his sleep an instant before it is too late. Yigal Amir decides to assassinate Yitzhak Rabin, but the latter unexpectedly catches a bad cold and stays home on the designated day, thus aborting the plan. Finally, *outcome luck* concerns the way our "actions and projects turn out."[9] Max does not wake up at the last moment, but miraculously none of the children are hurt in the accident. Yigal Amir shoots at Rabin but misses and manages to get away in the commotion that is created. Subsequently, Max is never treated as a negligent killer; Amir is never regarded as a murderer.

The Moral Luck Debate

The problem raised by the notion of moral luck has generated a lively debate among commentators on the criminal law. As I have already indicated, the discussion has, for the most part, focused on Nagel's fourth category, namely outcome luck. Writers have dealt with four kinds of scenarios under this category: creation of risk versus causation of risk, attempts versus completed offenses, impossible attempts, and proximate causation. Corresponding examples of questions arising under these scenarios are: should our evaluation of Max's behavior differ according to whether the accident actually took place? Should our treatment of Yigal Amir differ according to whether he hit or missed his target? Should our treatment of someone who buys talcum powder, thinking it is a drug, differ from that of someone who buys actual cocaine? Should our treatment of a fact pattern in which a woman shoots at her husband and misses, only to find that he dies in a car crash while fleeing the scene,[10] differ from that of a woman who shoots and hits her husband directly? The first two scenarios have received most of the attention, and I shall focus on them here.

The question underlying the debate concerns the appropriate basis for moral evaluation of action, and, more specifically, the appropriate basis for punishment. Should we restrict ourselves to examining an agent's intentions and actions, or should we allow the consequences those actions brought about (or the more subtle questions of whether they could have brought about any consequences, in the case of impossible attempts and the causal route between actions and consequences in the case of proximate causation) to weigh in? I shall now move on to discuss the main arguments supporting these two alternatives. For the sake of brevity, I will refer to the first view as the subjectivist view and to the second as the objectivist view.[11]

The Subjectivist View

The general argument for the subjectivist view is simple enough: only intentions, and the criminal acts they produce, are subject to an agent's control. Therefore they alone constitute the appropriate basis for responsibility and punishing. The practical upshot of this is that attempts, or risk creation, become the basis for criminal responsibility.[12] Thus, if Yigal Amir aimed and shot at Rabin with the intention of killing him, he has done everything that is within his power to bring about that result. Whether Rabin is hit, or whether he dies is immaterial. Similarly, if Max drove in spite of the fact that he was too tired to competently control the bus, he has created a risk. Whether or not an actual accident resulted is, again, irrelevant.[13]

The first argument in support of this view proceeds from the *purposes of punishment*.[14] Punishment is, among other things, a means for deterrence. The occurrence of harm is said to be irrelevant both for specific deterrence and for general deterrence. The aim of specific deterrence is to reduce future danger from the offender at issue. This goal is not served by taking harm into consideration because the amount of harm caused is not a competent indicator of dangerousness. An offender who did not bring about harm might be just as dangerous as one who did, and therefore if punishing may be said to deter from future criminal activity at all, there is no justification for punishing lightly when no or little harm is caused. Insofar as general deterrence is concerned, basing punishment on the acts rather than results is said to decrease the possibility that offenders will engage in the creation of risks. This argument is more relevant to negligent creators of risk than it is to those engaged in premeditated criminal activities. As Yoram Shachar puts it: "[The reckless risk creator] may be indifferent to the harm, or wish it would not occur, but finds it expedient to take the risk. . . . From the point of view of deterrence . . . the reckless perpetrator gambles on non-occurrence of the harm and can therefore be effectively persuaded to desist only if a high price is set on the act of gambling itself."[15] The attempted murderer, on the other hand, assumes that he will bring about the harmful result. It is therefore unlikely that basing responsibility on attempts would have any influence on him.

The second argument attempts to establish that we naturally gravitate toward intention-based judgments. Larry Alexander argues, quite compellingly, that there are cases in which we intuitively disregard the identity of the agent causally responsible for the harm, and focus instead on the intentions of all of those involved:[16] our attitudes toward a member of a firing squad would not change if we knew he had fired a blank shell. When our two children break a vase during a play sword-fight (an activity we strictly prohibited them from engaging in), we do not mind which of the two struck it. What we care about in both these instances is that the agents exhibited the willingness to participate.

This seems a bit too weak to make the point. The argument only proves that at times we do not care about the specific identity of the agent causally linked to the occurrence of harm. It does not establish that we are intuitively indifferent to the question of whether harm was caused or not. It is this indifference that needs to be addressed if Nagel's challenge is to be met. The fact that we don't mind which of our children actually hit the vase still leaves room for us to be much less concerned or altogether oblivious of the swordfight, had it ended without consequences.

A third argument maintains that basing our moral evaluation on harm rather than intent introduces a problem in the long-term judgment of actions. Today's harms can turn into tomorrow's benefits. Thus, for example, if we judge Hitler by the amount of harm he has brought about, how will we maintain our unequivocal condemnation of him if it turns out that in the long run his actions created such a universal feeling of shock that they averted further killings of similar magnitude?[17]

This does not seem like a fair argument to make against the objectivists. Objectivists do not necessarily base responsibility on consequences. Their claim seems to be, rather, that the severity of consequences may serve as an aggravating factor in our evaluations. In other words, the incredible number of people murdered is not the exclusive basis for condemning Nazism; it is, rather, a reason to condemn it more vehemently.

Proximate causation provides the basis for the next argument. If one ties culpability and punishment with the causation of harm, we encounter problems with cases in which the causal chain between the agent and the consequences is unusual. Consider the scenario, mentioned earlier, of a husband who is shot at by his wife, is not injured, but dies in a car crash while driving away hurriedly from the scene of the assassination attempt. How do we determine whether the wife actually brought about this result? If responsibility is correlated with outcomes, it matters a great deal whether we can tie the agent to the results, yet it is hard to find reliable tests for establishing this causal link (if the example presented seems unproblematic, one could conjure up others. X shoots Y in an open field but misses. Y faints from terror. X leaves him for dead. While Y is lying unconscious in the field he is struck by lightning or attacked by wild animals, and dies). The point of the argument is that only by disregarding consequences can we avoid proximate causation puzzlers.[18]

Finally, it is interesting to note an attempt to provide empirical grounding for the moral superiority of intention-based judgments. On the basis of research conducted by developmental psychologists from Piaget onwards, Yoram Shachar attempts to establish that harm-based moral judgment represents a lower level of moral development than judgments founded on intentions. The former are taken to rely on instincts, whereas the latter are assumed to be grounded in rational consideration. The studies he quotes allegedly confirm that both types of judgment exist concurrently, but that harm-based judgments are characteristic either of children in the early stages of their development or of adults acting without full rational consideration.[19]

A detailed exposition and evaluation of this intriguing attempt is beyond the scope of this paper. For our present purposes it is enough to note that the effort to ground moral hierarchies on empirical data is not without problems. Even if the studies do establish that judgments based on harm are instinctual and those based on intention are rational, that cannot establish the general superiority of reason over instinct. People have been known to act laudably on the basis of instincts and despicably on rational grounds.

The Objectivist View

As I have already indicated, objectivists do not deny that intentions have a role in the allocation of moral blame and punishment. Some writers even go so far as to state explicitly that although the existence of a criminal intention is both independently necessary and independently sufficient for punishment, the existence of harm in itself is neither.[20] Nevertheless, the gist of the objectivist argument is that the amount of harm caused by an agent's act can and should serve as a factor in our judgments of that act.

The argument begins by challenging the subjectivist contention that results are an improper factor in determining responsibility since they are beyond our control. Any reasonably foreseeable outcomes, so the argument goes, are ones that we have full control over. Following Hart and Honore, Moore gives the following four scenarios to demonstrate this point: (1) D culpably throws a lighted cigarette into a group of bushes. The bushes catch fire, but would burn themselves out if not for a standard breeze that begins blowing and causes the fire to spread to a nearby forest. (2) Same as (1) except the intervening force is not a normal breeze, but a freakish and rare storm. (3) Same as (1) but this time the intervening factor is a would-be extinguisher of the fire who catches fire himself and runs to the forest, causing the forest to burn down. (4) Same as (1) except that P, on seeing that the bushes are about to burn themselves out, creates a trail of gasoline from the locus of the fire to the forest. None of the factors (1)–(4) were in D's control. Nevertheless, because he could have reasonably foreseen the occurrence of (1) and (3), he can be held responsible for the resulting destruction of the forest in those cases.[21] In short, there is no real problem of moral luck with outcomes that are reasonably predictable. Objectivists, then, take the separation between actions and consequences made by the subjectivists as artificial. As Moore claims, when we contemplate possible courses of action we contemplate their possible outcomes at the same time. Results (or at least the predictable ones) are taken to be integral parts of our activity.[22]

To this Moore adds a reductio argument according to which if people can't be held responsible for the consequences of their actions, they can't be held responsible for any earlier stages of activity either. If factors like wind velocity, for example, negate control over whether our shot actually hits its target, factors influencing our opportunity to shoot (such as visibility, and whether or not the victim can be easily located, etc.) may be said to extinguish our control over performing an activity. Similarly factors prior to forming the decision to assassinate may eliminate our control regarding the decision itself, and so on until any form of responsibility is completely obliterated.[23]

The metaphor of a "penal lottery" is used to ground the next argument,[24] which proceeds something like this: upon attempting to commit a crime all perpetrators have an equal chance of succeeding and, consequently, of being punished. Therefore, there is no unfairness involved in the heavier punishment of those who actually brought about the harm. Lighter punishment represents good luck, not less guilt. The obvious objection, as Kadish effectively presents it, is that "the two offenders end up being punished differently even though they are identical in every non-arbitrary sense."[25]

A fourth attempt to justify the objectivist view is based on the need for frugality in punishment. Punishment, so the argument goes, is a necessary evil inflicted on people, and therefore, if there is a manner in which it can be used economically while still achieving its purposes, that way must be pursued. Thus for instance, if we examine crimes of intent, we discern that they represent instances in which the offenders expect to achieve their purpose. Now, if such perpetrators have not been deterred by the punishment for success why would they be deterred by equal punishment for failure? If this is the case, lighter punishment of those who fail can economize on the usage of punishment without loss in terms of deterrence.[26]

Another, stranger, version of the frugality argument runs as follows: since there is a larger chance that the public would become aware of those crimes that succeeded, punishing them more severely than attempts would be profitable in terms of both deterrence and frugality.[27] In other words, by punishing attempts lightly, one economizes on punishment without losing in deterrence, since attempts are bound to attract less attention. The argument, in both versions, raises some burdensome empirical questions: First, is it in fact the case that all perpetrators of crimes of intent are so focused on achieving the harmful results that they would not consider the possibility of failure and its relative cost? Kadish mentions cases "where potential offenders know there is a greater chance of being caught and punished if they fail than if they succeed" as a counterexample.[28] Treason and sting operations are given as examples. Second, is it indeed the case that the public is always more aware of completed offenses than it is of attempts? What then would we make of the attempted murder of celebrities? The first version of the argument raises a further, nonempirical question: what is the rationale for singling out the attempter (rather than perpetrator of the completed offense) for lighter punishment? If both have their minds set on bringing about the harmful consequences, how does frugality determine that it is the attempter who should be punished lightly?[29]

The fifth argument simply states that our own sentiments are a competent index for determining the amount of punishments perpetrators deserve. We feel more resentment at successful wrongdoing than we do at mere attempts and the creation of risks. This enhanced sense of outrage serves as an indication that completed offenses merit a higher level of moral condemnation than attempts.[30] The objection is obvious: can people's feelings of outrage serve as a reliable guide for the moral evaluation of an action? People have been known to feel delight at atrocities and outrage at morally commendable developments. Quite often, their amount of indignation is inappropriate given the circumstances. Thus people may feel more resentment at the burning of a flag than at the murder of a homeless person. Does this indicate that the former is morally graver than the latter? Furthermore, what is there to guarantee that this emotional index, once applied to the evaluation of punishment would not be turned toward other aspects of public policy? Would we want to live in a place where it was? All of this is of course separate from the proposition that legal systems must adhere, to some degree, to public sentiment in order to maintain their legitimacy and efficacy. This may be true, but it is a strictly descriptive point, not a claim regarding the probative value of such sentiments.

A related argument concerns the moral weight of private (as opposed to public) sentiments. We feel, so the argument goes, more guilt for successful wrongdoing on our part than for attempts. A variation of the argument is the claim that we feel guilt when we cause damage, but only shame when we fail to bring it about. Yet another variation is that the person who did not bring about the harm may feel a sense of relief that the person who did cannot.[31] Again, sentiments (this time our own attitudes toward our actions) are taken as competent indicators of the gravity of the act. Apart from the previous objection, this argument seems much more applicable to cases of risk creation versus realization than to cases of attempts versus completed offenses. If Max actually kills any of his passengers, he will, indeed (assuming that he is generally of a normal mental constitution), feel far more guilty than if the accident ends without any casualties. But can the same be said of an attempted murderer? Isn't it plausible that he would feel regret for not fulfilling his original intention rather than relief? Furthermore the capacity to feel shame and guilt assumes internalization of and consent with social norms. It is not obvious that violators of the law, who often originate from social groups that feel they have not benefited from existing social structures, would easily adopt such attitudes.[32]

Finally, let us consider the argument from the communicative or declarative functions of criminal law. The argument claims that by inflicting lighter punishment on attempters we communicate a sense of relief that a worse state of affairs has been averted.[33] A reformulation would be that dispensing equal punishment for attempts and completed offenses sends a message according to which the causation of harm does not matter.[34] This, the argument asserts, is the wrong message to send out. Kadish's criticism of the first formulation of this argument seems in order. It is quite unlikely that most of us need the criminal law to tell us that a criminal act ending in death creates a worse state of affairs than one ending in light injury.[35] As for the second formulation, it seems a bit too strong. Equating the punishments for attempts and completed offenses conveys that harm does not matter for allocating guilt and punishment, not that it does not matter, period.

Arguing Away a Paradox?

There is something strange about taking sides in the debate sketched above. Nagel's insight about "moral luck" is descriptive rather than prescriptive. He claims that the way we make moral judgments is paradoxical: we hold people responsible only for what they can control, but tend to judge and punish them on the basis of what they cannot. To be an objectivist or a subjectivist is to argue away one side of this paradox.

The resulting simplicity might be tempting, but, to use vaguely Aristotelian language, it does not do justice to the phenomenon. In order to make well-informed legal decisions we need to understand rather than obscure the complexities inherent to our intuitions about punishment. If these intuitions are paradoxical, we must do everything we can to comprehend rather than discard the paradox.

In light of this, I opt out of the debate and concentrate on further description of the problem. I am not claiming that it is impossible to take sides on this issue. I am even willing to admit that there are circumstances under which one should. We might want to tighten or loosen our punishment practices for public policy reasons. An administration interested in increasing its tax revenues might push for legislation imposing more severe penalties for inaccurate tax returns, regardless of criminal intent. Such an approach disregards our subjectivist intuitions, but may still be effective in obtaining policy goals. Philosophically, however, the best that can be done for a paradox is to further elucidate and explain the manner in which it operates. This is what I propose to do here. In the first section below, I make explicit an important distinction underlying the moral luck paradox. In the second section, I illustrate how other varieties of moral luck (beyond outcome luck) shape the criminal law.

Anger and Blame

It seems that the problem of moral luck comes about largely because our intuitions regarding blame and the manner in which we become angry often pull us in opposing directions. It is worthwhile, then, to say a bit more about this tension.

Our feelings of anger and blame can overlap, but they don't have to. It is possible to blame someone without being angry at her, just like it is possible to be angry with no one to blame. Perhaps the following taxonomy can help clarify this:

(1)   Blame without anger

I decide to risk parking my car in a forbidden spot in Cambridge, Massachusetts and end up getting a ticket. Abstracting from the fact that this would probably be defined as a strict liability offense, I have committed a culpable act. I can be blamed for it. But my act generates very little, perhaps even no anger on the part of those who learn about it.

(2)   Overlap between blame and anger

Yigal Amir cold bloodedly murders Yitzhak Rabin. We blame him for Rabin's death. We are also outraged with him for killing Rabin. Our feelings of anger at Amir more or less overlap with the degree of blame we attribute to him. Everything that happened to Rabin is Amir's fault. We are angry at Amir because of everything that happened to Rabin.

(3)   Surplus anger

Sam pushes Kate lightly in order to intimidate her, but Kate, due to a rare neural anomaly affecting her sense of balance, falls, hits her head on the curb, and dies. We are outraged with Sam because of Kate's death, although he can only be blamed for wanting to intimidate her.[36] We are angry at Sam for more than he can be blamed for. Let's call the increment of anger beyond the amount that would be felt for an act of intimidation "surplus anger."

(4)   Blameless anger

Mark's entire family is wiped out in a natural disaster, or he gets a rare and untreatable form of cancer at the age of thirty, or his parked car is hit and damaged by another driver who was trying to avoid a cat, or his young son trips (through no fault of his own) and breaks an expensive vase. Mark will be angry in all these cases (to varying degrees), in spite of the fact that there is no one to blame for the events. I call this kind of anger "blameless anger."

Although the problem of moral luck does not arise in categories (1) and (2), categories (3) and (4) must be examined more carefully. The extra increment of anger over blame that is evident in categories (3) and (4) is quite natural, perhaps even necessary. It makes perfect sense to be mad at Sam for more than just wanting to scare Kate, just like it makes perfect sense for Mark to be very irritated by the sight of his disfigured car. The ability to enjoy our possessions, our bodies, and our friends depends on their physical integrity. In other words, the persistence of anger at the sight of damage, even when there is no one to blame for it, is very natural. It springs from the knowledge that harm hinders the preconditions for usage and pleasure. We cannot drive our smashed cars nor delight in the company of our dead friends. These states of affairs are distressing regardless of the fact that there is no one to blame for them. Perhaps the fact that there is no one to blame for them makes them even more distressing.

The four categories sketched above allow us to crystallize the question underlying the problem of moral luck: when we experience surplus anger or blameless anger, are we angry at an agent or at a state of affairs? If the latter is the case, can anger that is directed primarily or exclusively at a state of affairs serve as the basis for punishing an agent? If it can't, why do our practices suggest otherwise?

Other Categories of Moral Luck
Perhaps the most peculiar feature of the debate outlined in this essay is the fact that it focuses, for the most part, on Nagel's fourth category of moral luck, namely outcome luck. The question of whether constitutive, circumstance, or causal luck have any important bearings on the criminal law is almost completely overlooked. I am not sure why this is the case. Perhaps it is due to the fact that both sides share a compatibilist assumption concerning the relationship between free will and determinism. According to such a view, the first three categories do not raise serious moral problems, as they all concern fortuity prior to choice. We may be constituted in certain ways, we may be lucky to live under these or other circumstances, we may encounter different causal factors that influence our choices, but none of these negates our ability to choose, which is the basis for responsibility. It is possible that we would not have killed if we were more tolerant by nature, or if we had grown up in a different neighborhood, or if there had not been perfect visibility on the day of the event; nevertheless, none of these factors *made* us kill, we could have still avoided killing if we had so chosen, and therefore we are still accountable.[37] Bad luck prior to choice is just bad luck on this view. It cannot affect our responsibility.

But it seems that the law does pay a good deal of attention to fortuity before choice (and thus to Nagel's first three categories). In what follows I try to make good on my promise to further describe the workings of Nagel's paradox by pointing out the significance of constitutive luck and circumstance luck in the criminal law.

Constitutive luck   Defenses against criminal responsibility often involve proving an element of reasonability. If I kill my neighbor after an incident in which he severely provoked me, I might be able to avoid a murder conviction if I successfully establish a claim of "provocation." To do so I would have to demonstrate that any reasonable person would have been similarly provoked. If I wish not to be charged with murder for shooting my daughter's boyfriend, as he climbed through her window, I would need to show that someone else would have mistaken him for a burglar too. To be successful in such a claim I need to establish that the fact pattern I assumed to exist was reasonable.

The test for reasonability might be more or less subjective. It might pertain to a reasonable person under circumstances similar to my own (perhaps I am naturally more prone to provocation because of a brain tumor, or perhaps I am more prone to making mistakes because of a certain neurotic tendency I possess), or it may pertain to a reasonable person, regardless of those circumstances. The main point is this: the more subjective the test for reasonability, the more it takes into consideration questions of constitutive luck. A subjective test would take the tumor or the neurosis into account when assessing the reasonability of my actions. It would allow my physical or mental constitution, which is largely beyond my control, to determine my level of guilt. An objective test, on the other hand, would mean that such factors would be ignored. The tumor or the neurosis would be considered irrelevant. That, of course, amounts to allowing bad constitutive luck to determine my fate.

Circumstance luck   The "normal science" of provocation claims requires that the defendant's action be an immediate response to a provocation carried out by the victim. Buffered reactions do not usually satisfy this requirement. We can, however, imagine scenarios in which the demand for temporal contiguity could be eased. Suppose the defendant is a battered woman who has taken the life of her husband. In such a case a judge might see the husband's history of violence as constituting sufficient provocation (even if he was not violent just before he was killed). The wife would be charged with manslaughter rather than murder. This would signal that sometimes people's actions are a result not so much of their choice, as of the circumstances under which they live. A refusal to ease the requirement of temporal contiguity would imply that such circumstances are irrelevant for determining guilt. In that case the battered wife's conviction and punishment is, to a significant degree, the result of bad circumstance luck.

Take another example that has to do with the authority to grant clemency: Dudley, Stephens, and Parker were shipwrecked for days. At a certain stage, Dudley and Stephens reverted to murdering and cannibalizing the ailing Parker in order to survive. Upon their return to England they were convicted of murder and sentenced to death, only to have their sentence commuted to a mere six months by the queen.[38] The two spent six months in jail because they had bad circumstance luck. On the other hand, they were not executed because someone had acknowledged their bad circumstance luck. They were spared, in other words, because the queen realized, like we all do, that misfortune can present people with moral tests they simply cannot pass.

Conclusion

Daniel Katz was the owner of a successful firm providing private security services. Due to the nature of this line of work, he was licensed to carry a gun. On December 13, 1998, Daniel planned to take his family to a wedding party. He returned from work early that evening, and handed his pistol to Mona, his wife, expecting she would put it away in the safe while he took a shower. This had been the long standing routine between the couple. But Mrs. Katz was in a rush: she could not find her earrings, the kids were half dressed, and there wasn't really enough time to go up to the third floor and start fidgeting with the safe's combination. So she put the gun in her purse and proceeded to scold her daughter for endlessly vacillating between her different outfits.

Three hours later the family was back home. Daniel, who needed to use the restroom urgently, was the first one through the door. As he was washing his hands a sharp, loud noise rang through the elegant duplex.

Mr. Katz darted out of the bathroom and up the stairs. What he saw froze the blood in his veins. His wife of fifteen years was lying motionless on the floor of the master bedroom, a gunshot exit wound visible beneath her left shoulder. His six-year-old son, Tom, was standing next to her, screaming. On the floor next to his feet rested a smallish black nine-millimeter CZ pistol.

The police investigation yielded a partial picture of what had happened. According to testimony gathered from the boy and his nine-year-old sister, who witnessed the events, Mona stepped into the bedroom, removed her evening dress, and sat in front of the bedside mirror to wipe off her make-up. She left her purse on the bed. Little Tom followed Mona into the bedroom, looked through the bag and found the handgun. He played with the weapon until it misfired, hitting and killing his mother.

What do we do with Mr. Katz?[39] How is the law to process his case? We could indict him for negligent manslaughter. After all, he is largely to blame for his wife's death. The gun was his and he should have taken better care in handling it. But something seems awry with putting him on trial. We shudder at the thought. It breaks our heart. Nevertheless, simply letting him off the hook does not sit too well with us either. Perhaps, we think, all that really matters is Daniel Katz's reckless conduct, his casual attitude toward human life. After all, if his son had played with the gun during the wedding rather than after it, if he had killed one of the guests rather than his mother, we would be inclined to indict Mr. Katz.

Somebody is going to have to decide. It might be a prosecutor with the authority to close the case, or a judge with the power to determine the punishment. Either way, a well-balanced decision would have to be rooted in an understanding of the case's complexity rather than in a strict adherence to rules: it would have to consider Daniel's recklessness, as well as the horrific misfortune that befell him; both subjectivist and objectivist considerations will have to be taken up. Eventually something will tip the scales. The law will deal with Daniel. But a mature legal answer should be the result of recognizing rather than overcoming the problem of moral luck. It must signify the realization that there are situations in which one important moral intuition can be served only by discarding another. In these cases there is no triumph of one sort of principle over another. There is only imperfect, incomplete, unsatisfying human justice.

Acknowledgments

I wish to thank David Lyons, Ken Simons, Maria Granik, Ajume Wingo and the participants of the INPC conference on Law and Social Justice for their helpful comments on various drafts of this essay.

Notes

1. Nagel 1993, p. 57, and Williams 1993, p. 35.

2. See Williams 1993, p. 36: "the agent's reflective assessment of his own actions . . . it is this area I want to consider." See Statman 1993, supra note 1, 5.

3. Nagel 1993, p. 59.

4. Ibid., p. 66.

5. Ibid., p. 60.

6. Ibid., p. 65.

7. Ibid., p. 60.

8. Statman 1993, p. 11.

9. Nagel 1993, p. 60.

10. See Alexander 1994, p. 14, for further examples.

11. Other names in the literature for the subjectivist view are: the Kantian position, the standard educated view, and the equivalence theory. Other names for the objectivist view are the anti-Kantian position, the Harm doctrine, and the nonequivalence theory.

12. Fletcher 1998, p. 173.

13. For different versions of this argument see generally Kadish 1994, Ashworth 1993, p. 107, and Alexander 1994, supra note 10.

14. Kadish 1994, pp. 684–688.

15. Shachar 1987, p. 14.

16. Alexander 1994, pp. 8–12.

17. Ibid., p. 12.

18. See generally Sverdlik 1998, p. 79, and Alexander 1994, pp. 14–17.

19. See generally Shachar 1987.

20. Moore 1994, pp. 238, 280–281.

21. Ibid., pp. 254–258.

22. Moore, p. 270; R. A. Duff as quoted by Ashworth (1993, p. 109).

23. Moore 1994, pp. 271–274.

24. Kadish, p. 691.

25. Ibid.

26. Kadish 1994, p. 686.

27. J. Stephen as quoted in Shachar 1987, pp. 14–15.

28. Kadish 1994, p. 686.

29. Shachar 1987, p. 15.

30. Moore 1994, pp. 267–268.

31. For the different variations of this argument see Moore 1994, pp. 268–269, Fletcher 1978, p. 483, and R. A. Duff as quoted in Ashworth 1993, pp. 112–113.

32. Criminological research shows that a preponderance of criminal offenders see themselves as victims of systematic injustice on the part of the legal system. This being the case, why should we assume that they feel guilt for their actions rather than rage, or even satisfaction for injuring a social structure they conceive as unfair? As a reference for criminological findings see Matza 1964.

33. R. A. Duff as quoted in Kadish 1994, pp. 694–695.

34. R. A. Duff as quoted in Ashworth 1993, pp. 112–113.

35. Kadish 1994, p. 695.

36. I tried to pick an example in which Sam could not foresee the consequence of Kate's death, in order to meet Moore's objection according to which we can be held responsible for those results we could have predicted.

37. Evidence of the general acceptance of compatibilism on both sides of this argument can be found in Kadish 1994, pp. 689–691, and in Moore's reductio argument (1994, pp. 271–278).

38. *The Queen v. Dudley and Stephens.*

39. The events described here took place in Tel Aviv in 1998. They are taken from an actual case I was involved in evaluating (and eventually closing) while working as a junior prosecutor at the district attorney's office. Names have been changed to protect the privacy of those involved.

References

Alexander, L. 1994. "Crime and Culpability." *Contemporary Legal Issues* 5: 130.

Ashworth, A. 1993. "The Problem of Luck." In S. Shute, J. Gardner, and J. Horder, eds., *Action and Value in Criminal Law*. New York: Oxford University Press.

Fletcher, G. 1978. *Rethinking the Criminal Law*. New York: Oxford University Press.

———. 1998. *Basic Concepts of Criminal Law*. New York: Oxford University Press.

Kadish, S. 1994. "Forward: The Criminal Law and the Luck of the Draw." *Journal of Criminal Law and Criminology* 84: 679–702.

Matza, D. 1964. *Delinquency and Drift*. New York: John Wiley and Sons.

Moore, M. 1994. "The Independent Moral Significance of Wrongdoing." *Journal of Contemporary Legal Issues* 5: 237–281.

Nagel, T. 1993. "Moral Luck." In D. Statman, ed., *Moral Luck*. Albany: State University of New York Press.

Shachar, Y. 1987. "The Fortuitous Gap in Law and Morality." *Criminal Justice Ethics* Fall: 12–36.

Statman, D. 1993. "Introduction." In D. Statman, ed., *Moral Luck*. Albany: State University of New York Press.

Sverdlik, S. 1998. "Crime and Moral Luck." *American Philosophical Quarterly* 25: 79–86.

The Queen v. Dudley and Stephens, 14 Q.B.D. 273 (1884).

Williams, B. 1993. "Moral Luck." In D. Statman, ed., *Moral Luck*. Albany: State University of New York Press.

6 Intellectual Property and Traditional Chinese Culture

Philip J. Ivanhoe

Although officially denounced, the violation of intellectual property rights is still widespread in both the People's Republic of China (PRC) and the Republic of China (ROC).[1] This continues to generate considerable friction between the governments of these countries and Western countries, which object to the pirating of what they regard as legally protected property. This state of affairs has generated a growing literature on the history of intellectual property law in China.[2] Although many of the scholars who produce such work seek to avoid casting the issue as "why China failed to develop intellectual property rights," there is a tendency to take the development of intellectual property rights in the West as a norm or standard, and to read other cultures like China as deficient or deviant for not following the path taken in the modern West. This makes the discussion of intellectual property rights in China similar in structure to the question of the development of modern science. The latter problem often is cast as "why did China fail to develop modern science?"[3] However, in either case, this is not the right way to proceed. We don't tend to ask, why didn't Western countries invent paper, gun powder, the compass, or printing? For often the only clear answer to such a question is, because they didn't.

Taking "the West" or any particular country as the norm, almost inevitably leads to the uninteresting and unproductive conclusion that each country has its own history. Even if we could get clear on how something like a conception of intellectual property took shape in say England, this would not give us the necessary or sufficient conditions for its development elsewhere. For there could be alternate routes to the same end, and in a different context, what worked in the case of England might fail to produce a similar result. It would be much more sensible and productive to ask questions like, "why did intellectual property rights develop *when they did* in the West?" or "why did modern science develop *when it did* in the West?" It might be equally interesting to ask why intellectual property rights or modern science developed at all. They surely are not necessary for human existence or a complex society, for human beings did without them for much of their history.

However, these are large questions. My present aim is much more modest. I want to explore some aspects of the intellectual and historical background of traditional China in order to show that certain features of this landscape were not particularly fertile soil for cultivating a conception of intellectual property rights. In other words, I am not attempting to show why intellectual property rights *could not* have developed but that certain aspects of Chinese thought and society made such a development less likely. In doing so I will take issue with the most widely accepted account of why something akin to intellectual property rights did not develop in premodern China, that found in William P. Alford's monograph, *To Steal a Book is an Elegant Offense: Intellectual Property Law in Chinese Civilization.*[4]

Alford's Account

After a brief review of certain economic and technological features of premodern Chinese society, which he admits may have played some role in the development of a conception of intellectual property, Alford claims that, "it is to political culture that we must turn for the principal explanation as to why there were no indigenous counterparts to contemporary ideas of intellectual property law throughout Imperial Chinese history."[5] In this Alford may well be correct. He surely is right in noting that, "one must avoid construing the path that intellectual property law in the United States or other jurisdictions has followed as providing a 'normal' or inevitable course against which Chinese developments are to be evaluated."[6] The reasons for this, or at least my reasons, have been noted above, where I argued that the question of the development of modern science offers a similar case and an illuminating comparison. Alford still believes, and I agree with him here too, that we can produce a convincing explanation of why a robust conception of intellectual property did not develop in traditional China. However, it is not easy to discern precisely what aspects of traditional Chinese political culture Alford sees as constituting the "principal explanation" for this course of events. The title of his second chapter, "Don't Stop Thinking about . . . Yesterday: Why There Was No Indigenous Counterpart to Intellectual Property Law in Imperial China," clearly implies that beliefs and attitudes about the normative force of the past played a central role. This is the claim with which I shall take issue.

Alford identifies two "functions" of the past that he claims, "militated against thinking of the fruits of intellectual endeavor as private property."[7] First, he tells us that the past was "the instrument through which individual moral development was to be attained and the yardstick against which the content of the relationships constituting society was to be measured. . . ."[8] In the remainder of the chapter, Alford seeks to illustrate these ideas with examples from various aspects of traditional Chinese culture. His main point seems to be that classical, canonical sources played such a strong and pervasive role in the ethical, political, and social aspects of traditional Chinese society that no one dared to claim that they had created something *new* and of sufficient value to bother identifying it as their own. This idea is summed up in the epigram to the chapter, which comes from Confucius' *Analects* and which Alford repeats in the course of his remarks. Confucius is said to have insisted, "I transmit rather than create; I believe in and love the Ancients." The idea is that even the greatest sage of all did not claim to be the author much less the owner of any intellectual property. His teachings were not his own. His life's work was merely the preservation and passing on of earlier truths and these were the only things worth knowing.

This account suffers from a variety of weaknesses. First, claiming that there was a strong commitment to a traditional canon of classical texts that was "the instrument through which individual moral development was to be attained and the yardstick against which the content of the relationships constituting society was to be measured" in no way distinguishes the Chinese tradition from the various societies that constitute the West. For precisely the same thing can be said about the basic scriptures of Western religion. In a single sentence Alford asserts that the Chinese classics were authoritative, "to a further-reaching and more enduring degree than even the Bible in the Judeo-Christian world or the Koran in Islam."[9] However, simply invoking such a claim does nothing to establish its truth and even a moment's reflection will reveal that it is a highly dubious claim. For one thing, in China, unlike most Western countries, there were several competing canons, for example, Confucian, Buddhist, and Daoist, none of which commanded complete control either of people's conception of "moral development" or the "content of the relationships constituting society." Moreover, within each of these traditions there was a vast and diverse range of different interpretations as to what their respective canons were saying. Alford cites the neo-Confucian thinker Wang Yangming as representative of a seamless Confucian orthodoxy that purportedly presented a united front on the veracity and indispensability of the classical canon. However, this is remarkably inaccurate. Wang likened Confucius' editing of the classics to the First Emperor's burning of the books and clearly implied that had Confucius had his way, he would have *gotten rid of* all the classics. For Wang, the classics not only are not necessary for moral enlightenment, they often prove to be a major impediment to spiritual and social well-being. Wang Yangming and his school were widely considered unorthodox and often denounced as heretical. Later Confucian critics went so far as to blame Wang and his school for the collapse of the Ming dynasty.[10]

Second, and perhaps more telling, even if it had been the case that there was a single uncontested view concerning the importance of some set of classics in premodern China, there is no clear conceptual link between this and an environment inhospitable to the development of a robust conception of intellectual property. One can believe that something one creates, discovers, or invents reflects some deeper truths embodied in some ancient sacred text or canon while at the same time still regarding one's creation, discovery, or invention as one's own. The link between what one creates, discovers, or invents and the canon may be exceedingly indirect and tenuous. We have no evidence that those Chinese inventors who first produced paper, gunpowder, the compass, or printing, or those who were among the first to develop deep drilling technology, somehow understood their work in terms of the *Book of Poetry* or any other classic. Indeed we have no reason to believe that these innovative individuals adhered to *any* particular tradition or even were members of the literati class. And so even if they were under the constraint of an alleged authority of the past, what difference would it have made in regard to whether or not they thought of their inventions as private property? It seems equally plausible to imagine that they would seek to identify themselves with their inventions and discoveries as a way to escape the purported authority of the past. And so, even if we were to grant Alford's improbable scenario of an oppressively authoritative past, this alone does not explain traditional Chinese attitudes regarding intellectual property. The story appears to be more complex and subtle. At the very least, it must be more compelling than what Alford has given us. This is not to say that Alford's general strategy of looking to cultural factors is in error, nor does it mean that some of the evidence he musters does not in fact help us to understand the cultural conditions that militated against the emergence of a robust conception of intellectual property. In fact, several sources that he cites, when interpreted differently, do point in the right direction. And so let us now follow these and turn to explore an alternative account.

A Universal State and the Nature of Knowledge

The alternative story that I have to offer consists of two complementary parts. The first concerns the political and cultural context of imperial China and the reflections and echoes of this context in the modern PRC and ROC. The second concerns widespread beliefs and attitudes about the nature of truth and, most significantly, the proper relationship one should have to the truths that one discovers. I will argue that it is the confluence of these two factors that created an environment that was not conducive to the development of a robust conception of intellectual property. In my conclusion I will go on to suggest that appreciating these two factors not only will help us to understand better how modern conceptions of intellectual property relate to enduring aspects of Chinese culture but also will lead us to appreciate more important aspects of the development of such ideas in the West.

Alford's account of the features of traditional Chinese society that may have contributed to an environment not conducive to the development of a robust conception of intellectual property is laudable for avoiding a common type of argument, one that moves quickly from some crude claim about the "totalitarian" nature of Chinese monarchy to its desired conclusion. At the same time, he sees the important role that the state played in regard to intellectual property. He shows clearly that "[v]irtually all known examples of efforts by the state to provide protection for what we now term intellectual property in China prior to the twentieth century seem to have been directed overwhelmingly toward sustaining imperial power."[11] As Alford notes, this is quite similar to what we see in the case of Western nations as well. The early development of patent law in the West was intimately tied up with the desire on the part of various states to strengthen themselves and maintain their power. Early legislation regarding copyrights and patents was not motivated by or designed to maintain the rights of authors or inventors but rather at increasing the power of states. This is seen for example in the case of England where, "the throne awarded patents to foreigners who introduced new products or processes to the British isles, even if those persons were not themselves responsible for the innovation in question."[12] Another example is the United States, which for most of its history was notorious for its flagrant violation of copyright and "did not grant even formal protection for foreign copyrighted materials until 1891—by which time we had passed through what arguably might be termed our period as a developing country."[13]

One important difference between the cases of China and the West in this regard is that the Chinese monarchy sought to control the internal production of valuable goods and materials while Western states were seeking to monopolize lucrative ideas and inventions in external competition with neighboring states. Until the confrontation with the West, China was never in anything like this kind of competitive context and hence was not inclined to develop ways of protecting the works of its subjects or gaining and maintaining control of the original discoveries of foreigners.[14] It may well be that the development of intellectual property rights for individuals in the West was in some sense an echo of practices and ideas that first developed within the context of competing states. In any event, I would like to focus on another aspect of what we might call the "Imperial" context.

It is often remarked that in imperial China everything "under Heaven" belonged to the emperor. In some sense this was true and of course the same was true for every European monarchy as well. We also should not forget that in times of national crisis or cases of great public need our own right of ownership often gives way to the state's claims of eminent domain or national security. What often gets less attention in the case of imperial China is the degree to which most intellectuals—as well as many people who were not—were, in one way or another, in the employ of the state. For most of the last two thousand years China has been ruled by various forms of state bureaucracy, staffed by individuals selected for government service through a variety of means, including a system of civil service examinations. Even many who were not officially members of this system still earned their living by preparing people for it, supporting people in it, or through the patronage of the more successful and powerful members of it. The most influential members of society, for the most part those directly in the employ of the state, were in a position not wholly unlike a contemporary civil servant, a researcher in a government lab, or, more close to home, a member of an academic institution. As we know, people in any of these contemporary occupations have only weak if any legal right to much of their intellectual property. Since they are employees of larger institutions, the things they create, at least those that they do on or in relation to their jobs, belong to their institutions and not to themselves.[15] In the case of China, such a state of affairs not only was not in any way conducive but in fact quite hostile to the development of a robust sense of intellectual property. Since everyone was working for the empire, everything they did and produced belonged to the state. There was little room for personal claims of ownership and it is not too much to say that such claims were regarded with suspicion. For any good subject would put the well-being of the empire before personal profit, power, or fame. As many have noted, within such an environment, there is a sense in which strong claims to privacy of many kinds carried a connotation of selfishness. And so the first part of my explanation is that the institutional structures of imperial China militated against the development of any strong sense of intellectual property. The vast majority of intellectuals were in one way or another working for or at the very least could not be seen as working against the state. Since the Chinese state lacked the kinds of interstate competition that gave rise to early Western legislation on patents and copyrights designed to protect and strengthen the state, there was little incentive to develop any distinctive sense of intellectual property.

The second part of my argument concerns a constellation of beliefs and attitudes about the nature of the most important kind of knowledge—knowledge about the *Dao* or "Way"—and the proper relationship one should have to such knowledge.[16] Although the claims that I will make here are not universally true of all Chinese thinkers, they hold for the most part for a wide range of thinkers and find clear representatives throughout the history of Chinese philosophy. They also cut across the three grand traditions of Confucianism, Daoism, and Buddhism.

The Dao is the underlying patterns and processes of the universe that offer a normative standard for all events, actions, and activities and every state of affair. Those who understand and act in accord with the Dao work to realize and maintain an inherent harmony in the universe, one that tends toward the good of not only human beings but also the world in general. Since such actions arise from and follow deep-grained natural patterns, they are marked by spontaneity, ease, and efficacy and possess a deep and inherent appeal. Through them we sense our harmonious connection with the rest of the world. Thus the Dao not only describes how things are in the world, it also is the source of both an ethical and aesthetic order.[17]

This general cluster of ideas is seen in such early thinkers as Liu Xin (ca. 46 B.C.E. to 23 C.E.), a court librarian during the Han dynasty. In the preface to his catalog of imperial holdings, Liu argued that all of the different philosophical schools in Chinese history had arisen out of different governmental departments of the past golden age of the Zhou dynasty. This idea in turn was based on his belief that during the time of the Zhou, all teaching and writing was done by specialists who were at the same time court officials. Teaching and writing were produced in the course of people performing their various official duties in the different departments of the state. Only with the collapse of the Zhou and the disintegration of their ideal form of government did various individuals begin to write in a private capacity and claim various branches of knowledge as their own. In an ideal society, all writing and teaching were functional and anonymous. People wrote what needed to be written in order to carry out their official duties, and they handed these skills and records down to posterity, but they did not produce private works of their own. All of their intellectual products were expressions of the Dao. This is why later people looked backed to the classics not only as repositories of truth but also as paradigms for what is good and beautiful. As strange as these ideas may seem, at least in part they are probably an accurate description of early human history. As David Nivison has pointed out, "the insight that human knowledge must at first have been functional within society, and anonymous, and only later became the teachings of nameable individuals, is probably right.[18]

These ideas reappear in various guises throughout Chinese history and one of their most developed and interesting expressions is found in the writings of the later Confucian philosopher of history, Zhang Xuecheng (1738–1801). In an essay entitled "Yangong" ("Words for Everyone"), Zhang argues that any idea or cultural creation that is true, good, and beautiful can never belong to an individual. Both by nature and function, such things belong to everyone.[19] It is simply part of the nature of whatever is true, good, and beautiful that it belongs to all, for such things are reflections of the Dao, which runs throughout and unites everything. Every part of the Dao works for the greater good and so whatever one might discern or discover about it has a role to play in the common well-being of all. Not to see this involves a *moral* failing, a failing that in one way or another will preclude one from ever fully realizing the true, good, and beautiful.

Those who pursue the Dao motivated by a desire for personal fame, fortune, or power will often fail. Since they are attempting to force their way to what is spontaneous, natural, and efficacious, their efforts always will fall short of the ideal. Those in the grip of such motivations, who still manage to grasp some aspect of the Dao, will be led by their desire for recognition and their mistaken belief that they in some way own the true, good, or beautiful to misuse the knowledge that they have attained. They either will hide it away, fearful that others will steal their glory, keep it from wide circulation, in order to nurture their delusions of ownership, or they will misuse what they know in order to win fame, fortune, or power. In any event, they will keep what they know from fulfilling its proper role, that of serving to help human beings and the rest of the world realize and maintain the harmony of the Dao.

This constellation of beliefs and attitudes constitutes the second part of my argument concerning the true nature of the social and cultural conditions that created an environment inhospitable to the development of a robust conception of intellectual property. For according to such a view, to hold back knowledge in any form and claim it as one's own is not only to misconstrue the nature of the best that human beings can achieve, it constitutes a profound moral failing. It would be like insisting on a patent for the principles of geometry, defending a copyright on the beauty of nature, or insisting that one's virtue is such a valuable commodity that others must pay you to exercise it.

Conclusion

William P. Alford argues that a constrictive dedication to the past was the chief force working against the emergence of a robust conception of intellectual property. I have argued against this view. On the one hand, such an explanation fails to distinguish the Chinese case from what one finds in the West. If anything, the multiple traditions of Chinese culture, including Confucianism, Daoism, and Buddhism, offered a much less intellectually restrictive environment than the monotheistic religions of the West. On the other hand, even if there had been a fierce and narrow dedication to a past canon, there is no conceptual link between this state of affairs and the development of a robust sense of intellectual property. In light of the remarkable history of scientific and artistic innovation in premodern China, Chinese veneration of the past, in whatever form it took, did not appear to inhibit people's creativity or expression.

In place of Alford's account, I offered an alternative explanation according to which the institutional structure of traditional China, together with certain beliefs and attitudes about the nature of knowledge, worked to inhibit the growth of a strong sense of intellectual property. The former factor meant that everyone, or at least the vast majority of intellectuals, were in one way or another working for the state. This meant that most of the products of their endeavors would fall under our definition of "work made for hire" and as such would not be regarded as their personal property even by contemporary Western standards. I also suggested that in the premodern period China did not find itself faced with strong competition from surrounding states and so there was little impetus to develop the kinds of state-centered protections that one sees in the history of the development of intellectual property law in the West. The second part of my argument is more philosophical and concerns widely held beliefs and attitudes about the nature of knowledge and the proper relationship one should have toward it. Briefly, the idea is that the most important kind of knowledge is knowledge about the Way. Anyone who discovers some truth about the Way is uncovering some facet of a much greater pattern, something that by its very nature cannot be owned by any one person, for it belongs to everyone. Moreover, because the Way nurtures and benefits all under Heaven, knowledge about it exists for this greater good. On such a view, to regard any discovery or invention as one's own property mani-

fests a profound ignorance of the nature of such truth and tends to interfere with the role that such knowledge is to play in the greater scheme of
things. To put this in terms that were in use for much of the Chinese philosophical tradition, this would violate both the *ti*, "substance," and *yong*,
"function," of one's discovery.[20]

The two parts of my account apply with almost equal force to the situation in both the PRC and ROC over the course of their respective histo-
ries and down to the present day. It is only most recently that significant
numbers of intellectuals in either of these states are working with anything
resembling complete independence from government sponsorship, and
many of the beliefs and attitudes that I have described still inform or at
least influence many contemporary people's views.

In conclusion I would like to say a bit in defense of the philosophical
motivations that I have described as part of my explanation, and close with
some suggestions on how to shape policy in light of the two factors that
I have argued have militated against the development of a robust sense of
intellectual property.

The idea that all of the most important truths are in some irreducible
sense public is not wholly without merit. We tend to agree that things like
the principles of geometry or proofs of various kinds are not owned by
anyone. Our intellectual property laws do not apply to algorithms. The
very nature of such discoveries seems to make them everyone's, and the
good that such knowledge can bring is an important part of human flourishing in general. Indeed many people believe that possessing such knowledge is good in itself. Furthermore, we tend to believe that all truth is
objective and in this sense at least, shared by all people who are able to
see it. Admittedly, this is still a long way from the idea that all the most
important truths are also good and beautiful. However, there is something
in these notions as well. For many people believe that anything that is
worth knowing must be good to know. It surely is the case that certain
kinds of knowledge are so good to have that there is something morally
wrong with withholding them from others. This seems to be the primary
justification for a general policy requiring the state to ensure universal
public education.[21] It also appears to be the basis for our view about
specific cases where eminent domain or national security override claims
to personal property. Claims to intellectual property are not going to slow
the production and distribution of a lifesaving vaccine in the midst or even

at the threat of an epidemic. A more radical expression of this kind of view appears to be the primary justification for the free software movement.[22] The driving idea here is that anything worth having that can be shared, should be shared. Similarly, any work or idea that is worth having must on some level produce some sense of appreciation in those contemplating it. Given this, there seems to be something wrong with withholding from view or even destroying a great work of art. Many Americans agree with this sentiment, though we don't embody it in law: if you own a great work of art you can do with it what you will, even destroy it. We do, however, protect certain architectural treasures and parts of nature based on something like this idea. Except for a small minority of people who clearly were motivated by narrow and dogmatic views, most people were outraged when the Taliban destroyed the monumental Buddhist statues located in Afghanistan. Apart from their religious value, these figures were widely regarded as a common human treasure.[23]

So it seems that something like the spirit of the beliefs and attitudes that I described earlier as characteristic of traditional Chinese culture animates some of our own views and practices. We don't, however, share the deeper assumptions about the Way that play an important part of this constellation of beliefs. And of course, many of us believe that even if one's overall goal is to benefit others, there are good reasons for protecting intellectual property. For such protection is what enables people to develop the kinds of things that really prove to be of the greatest benefit to us all.

The most widely cited and plausible justification for protecting intellectual property is broadly consequentialist. We protect people's ideas because such a policy tends to benefit both individuals and the societies in which they live.[24] We should draw on this justification in working to move other countries and people to something closer to what we regard as a reasonable view. One of the first things that we should do in this regard is to take a lesson from our own history and work to persuade foreign governments that it is in the state's best interests to foster and enforce respect for intellectual property. Such protections will enable the state to defend its own intellectual property, both that which comes forth from its own citizens and that which it can attract through foreign application, from infringement by other individuals and states. At the same time, we should make the case that a general policy of protecting individual intellectual property is good for both states and the individuals within them. Such protection is needed in order to ensure that people can reliably invest time, effort, and capital into the research and development that is required for so many useful ideas, inventions, and discoveries. The same point applies in the case of foreign companies who locate production or research facilities in or establish joint ventures with a given state. Arguments such as these can easily be cast in ways that appeal to many of the beliefs and attitudes described earlier as characteristic of traditional Chinese thought. For the gist of such consequentialist justifications is that people in general—all under Heaven—are better off when such policies are advocated and enforced.

However, in order to make these ideas more appealing and compelling we will have to work harder to enforce them on ourselves in a consistent manner. This should lead us to reconsider and reform some of our own policies. For example, the kind of justification that I have been advocating as the best foundation for the protection of intellectual property should at the very least move individuals and corporations to stop insisting on intellectual property rights as if they had some kind of occult ontological status, or that they are indistinguishable from basic human rights. Recognizing that intellectual property rights are socially constructed mechanisms for maximizing certain kinds of goods should lead companies to reconsider some of their policies, for example, their blanket pricing policy in lesser developed countries. If Western companies want to avoid pirating and make money in these countries, they will have to price their goods lower in markets where income levels prevent most people from purchasing them. Such a policy would have the further advantage of allowing these companies to develop relationships with customers who will buy and use their future products, and will do so as their economic situation and ability to pay improve. By developing appropriate agreements with host countries, companies could ensure that their goods are not resold and make significant headway against the rampant pirating that currently costs them so dearly. In the case of software—a type of product that is at the heart of much present tension—there is a clear precedent for the kind of policy I am advocating very close to home. What I am recommending is essentially a site license for certain markets.

Recognizing that intellectual property rights are socially constructed mechanisms that when properly adjusted work to the advantage of all can open up possibilities for engaging some of the very forces—both institutional structures and standing beliefs and attitudes—that have worked against their acceptance in China. Appreciating some of the deep reasons that inform and animate Chinese beliefs and attitudes toward the notion of intellectual property is an important part of forging better relationships between our two countries on many levels. Although I do not claim to have provided an exhaustive description of the causes and conditions that have tended to inhibit the development of a robust conception of property rights, I believe the account that I have provided identifies several of the most important aspects of this complex story. I have argued that such an understanding can help to alleviate some of the difficulties Western companies have faced in China and help to reduce some of the tensions that this issue has generated between the governments of our two nations. I also have argued that such an understanding will lead us to appreciate new and interesting aspects of our own conception of intellectual property; in certain cases, aspects that we tend to neglect or undervalue. This in turn will lead us to reexamine and in some cases revise not only our own beliefs and attitudes but our practices and policies as well. A great deal more work needs to be done before any of these goals can be achieved. However, such work must begin from a more accurate and clear understanding of the Chinese context and the nature of our own conception of intellectual property. The degree to which this will lead us toward the belief that everything true is also good, beautiful, and the common heritage of all under Heaven is an open question. However, a deeper appreciation of this kind of view might well recommend it, in at least some form, as an inspiring ideal.

Acknowledgments

Thanks to Eric L. Hutton, T. C. Kline III, and participants of the Fifth Annual Inland Northwest Philosophy Conference on Law and Social Justice, held at the University of Idaho, April 5–7, 2002, for helpful comments and suggestions on an earlier draft of this essay.

Notes

1. "Intellectual property rights" includes a broad range of different legal protections including but not limited to copyright, patents, and trademarks. There is considerable variety among modern Western nations in how these are conceived but there

is a general consensus that those responsible for the invention, discovery, or creation of certain types of devices, products, ideas, or processes have certain rights in regard to these that in some way parallels the rights people have in regard to more tangible types of property.

2. The most comprehensive and thorough study to date is Alford 1995.

3. My views regarding the question of the rise of modern science in China and the West owe a great deal to the analysis of Angus C. Graham in his 1973. Unlike Graham though I think there is a fairly clear reason why modern science did not develop in China or anywhere else before it did in seventeenth-century Europe and I argue for this view in an as yet unpublished essay of my own. Graham allows that such an explanation is possible (p. 54) but he tends to be pessimistic that it can be found.

4. See above. This is a thorough and revealing study of intellectual property law in China, the best work to date on this topic. It is filled with useful information and careful analysis and written in a lucid and engaging manner. My disagreements with Alford's view concern only his account of the historical reasons that militated against the development of intellectual property law in China. This is found in chapter 2 of his work.

5. Alford 1995, p. 19.

6. Ibid., p. 4.

7. Ibid., p. 20.

8. Ibid.

9. Ibid., p. 26.

10. Alford was quoting James Cahill on traditions of painting (ibid., p. 28), but the point would be the same regardless of this quote. The Confucian tradition does not speak with anything approaching a single voice even on an issue as basic as the status of the classics. One clear illustration of this lack of consensus, which sharply distinguishes many East Asian traditions from monotheistic faiths, is the considerable variation concerning what *constituted* the classical canon. For an introduction to Wang's thought see my 2002. For a discussion of his understanding of Confucius' editing of the classics, see pp. 122–123. Some of Wang's harshest critics were members of the Donglin Academy. For a thorough account of the academy and Wang's critics within it, see Bush.

11. Alford 1995, pp. 16–17. I will argue that the nature of Chinese state institutions played a critical role in regard to Chinese conceptions of intellectual property, though one that Alford does not consider. The view I defend bears certain similarities to the work done by G. E. R. Lloyd comparing early Greek and Chinese science. For example, see Lloyd 1990. Thanks to T. C. Kline III for pointing out this similarity.

12. Alford 1995, p. 18.

13. Ibid., p. 5. In his footnote to this quote, Alford notes, "In one of the more celebrated examples, Charles Dicken's work was sold in the United States in numerous pirated editions. *A Christmas Carol*, for instance, was offered for as little as six cents in the United States (as opposed to the equivalent of $2.50 in Great Britain) and altered in different parts of the United States to suit local tastes."

14. Even once China had come into contact with other technologically advanced civilizations, its profound confidence in its own superiority tended toward a policy of sharing its inventions, discoveries, and products as a sign of its greatness. This general policy of course began to change as the strength and threatening nature of Western nations became increasingly obvious.

15. The strength of this claim varies across the cases I have noted and there is considerable contention concerning what gets protected. A great deal turns on whether or not the work was produced as part of one's contractual agreement with one's employer. This idea is discussed at length in Title 17 of the United States Code, § 101, which in part says that "a 'work made for hire' is a work prepared by an employee within the scope of his or her employment." At present, this does not include the scholarly works that, for example, a philosopher produces in the course of her career. And yet, since *research* clearly is part of her job description—the core of her work at most research universities—the current interpretation is by no means self-evident.

16. The precise nature of the Way differs considerably across traditions and among thinkers. However, most Chinese philosophers would agree that it is the deep structure and true nature of the world, which at the same times defines the proper place for human beings. It offers an objective standard, which is independent of any text, even though certain texts were highly valued as repositories of knowledge about the Way.

17. A related and familiar view is that one can only come to an understanding of the Dao by being a certain kind of person. One needs to cultivate oneself to fulfill one's proper place in the grand scheme of things and understand and endeavor to carry out one's role. Imposing one's individual will or personal preferences on the Way or trying to force one's way to knowledge would only keep one from attaining it.

18. Nivison 2003.

19. Nivison discusses this essay in his masterful study of Zhang's thought. See Nivison 1966, pp. 127–133. Note that he employs an older romanization scheme in which Zhang's name appears as "Chang" and "Yangong" appears as "Yen Kung," Nivison translates the title of this essay as "If Your Words Are Everyone's."

20. For a discussion of these ideas see my 1998b. With the rise of neo-Confucianism in the Song dynasty, the view that I am describing here became even more pronounced. Most neo-Confucian thinkers believed that all of the underlying

li "principles" or "patterns" that gave sense to the world were in one way or another available within every human mind. Even something as apparently personal and particular as a poem was at least potentially available to anyone through the right kind of intuition. This view—like Plato's theory of recollection—was used to explain how we both recognize and appreciate the truth when we see it. For a discussion of the concept of *li*, see my 1998a. For a discussion of this view of *li* in the thought of the most influential neo-Confucian, Zhu Xi, see my 2000, pp. 48–49, 57. Thanks to Eric L. Hutton for suggestions on how to develop this point.

21. This idea also seems at least consistent with the general approach to social welfare in terms of basic capacities as developed by Amartya Sen and Martha Nussbaum. See, for example, Nussbaum and Sen 1993.

22. For an introduction to the history and philosophy of the free software movement, see DiBona, Ockman, and Stone 1999.

23. This kind of attitude is embodied in the UNESCO designation of certain natural features and cultural artifacts as World Heritage Sites. For a description of the 721 sites that have earned this designation and an introduction to the work and principles of the World Heritage Committee, see: http://www.unesco.org/whc/nwhc/ pages/sites/main.htm. Thanks to Eric L. Hutton for alerting me to the importance of UNESCO's work in this regard.

24. The consequentialist justification of copyright laws, which are the only type of intellectual property guaranteed by the U. S. Constitution, is clear from how they are described, "The Congress shall have power . . . To promote the progress of science and useful arts, by securing for limited times to authors and inventors the exclusive right to their respective writings and discoveries." *United States Constitution*, Article 1, section 8, clause 8. This wording makes it abundantly clear that such rights enjoy no ontological status and are in force for a limited time in order to promote the common good.

References

Alford, W. P. 1995. *To Steal a Book is an Elegant Offense: Intellectual Property Law in Chinese Civilization*. Stanford, Calif.: Stanford University Press.

Bush, H. 1949–1955. "The Tung-lin Academy and Its Political and Philosophical Significance." *Monumenta Serica* 45: 1–163.

DiBona, C., S. Ockman, and M. Stone, eds. 1999. *Open Sources: Voices from the Open Source Revolution*. Electronic version: http://www.oreilly.com/catalog/opensources/ book/intro.html.

Graham, A. C. 1973. "China, Europe, and the Origins of Modern Science: Needham's *The Grand Titration*." In S. Nakayama and N. Sivin, eds., *Chinese Science: Explorations of an Ancient Tradition*. Cambridge, Mass.: MIT Press.

Ivanhoe, P. J. 1998a. *"Li."* In E. Craig, ed., *Routledge Encyclopedia of Philosophy*, vol. 5. New York: Routledge Press.

————. 1998b. *"Ti* and *Yong."* In E. Craig, ed., *Routledge Encyclopedia of Philosophy*, vol. 9. New York: Routledge Press.

————. 2000. *Confucian Moral Self Cultivation*, revised second ed. Indianapolis, Ind.: Hackett Publishing.

————. 2002. *Ethics in the Confucian Tradition: The Thought of Mengzi and Wang Yangming*, revised second ed. Indianapolis, Ind.: Hackett.

Lloyd, G. E. R. 1990. *Demystifying Mentalities*. Cambridge: Cambridge University Press.

Nivison, D. S. 1966. *The Life and Thought of Chang Hsüeh-ch'eng (1738–1801)*. Stanford, Calif.: Stanford University Press.

————. 2003. "Chinese Philosophies of History." In A. S. Cua, ed., *Encyclopedia of Chinese Philosophy*. New York: Routledge Press.

Nussbaum, M., and A. Sen, eds. 1993. *The Quality of Life*. Oxford: Clarendon Press.

UNESCO. "World Heritage Sites." http://www.unesco.org/whc/nwhc/pages/sites/main.htm.

United States Code.

United States Constitution.

7   Initial Acquisition and the Right to Private Property

Ann Levey

Many people share the intuition that something like the familiar child-hood saying of "finders keepers" must be right, at least for those things for which a previous owner cannot be found. Our legal code agrees; first pos-session is the foundation of title to a range of things from salvage to wild animals, and first finders of lost goods have a claim over subsequent finders. The idea that property rights can arise via some act of initial acqui-sition has a long history in philosophical writing on property and the homesteading history of the European colonization of North America gives first possession a secure place in popular North American thought. Some-thing this pervasive seems worth analyzing in greater detail.

My aim in looking at first possession is to elucidate the nature of initial acquisition justifications of property and to ask what kind of moral claims, if any, acts of initial acquisition generate. My motivation is the frequency with which initial acquisition theories are used as part of an argument justifying full ownership rights. I think these arguments don't work. I hope to offer an account of initial acquisition that does not readily lend itself to these uses. In the first part of the essay I examine what I take to be the main assumptions required by first possession justifications of property rights: the presumption of negative community and the moral meaning-fulness of first possession. In the second and third sections, I look in more detail at each of these assumptions. Although I offer no knockdown argu-ments against these assumptions, I hope at least to suggest that they cannot be taken as obviously true. In the final section of the essay I sketch where I think initial acquisition does give rise to moral claims, to claims that limit what other people can then do with respect to what has been possessed or acquired. I think, however, that the scope of these claims is limited. I argue that acts of initial acquisition require uptake on the part of those who are thereby disallowed from interfering with what has already been so acquired. The claims that can be generated by first possession are context dependent. Although they can give rise to genuine property rights in things, these rights will only hold in contexts where other (later) comers share the relevant conception of property. This limitation has consequences. Initial acquisition stories might explain, for instance, why a person's ordinary property rights hold against people who are similarly situated, but they won't give reason to think such rights hold against those who are outside the community whose conception of property underlies the possibility of acquisition. These are genuine property rights. However, they are special rather than general rights. A second consequence is that initial acquisition cannot be used to justify an institution of private property. Instead, it presupposes such an institution.

Before I turn to the body of this essay I need to comment briefly on its terminology. By "property rights" I mean moral rather than legal rights, as I am concerned with the claim that such rights can arise in advance of legal institutions of private property and can be used to justify such institutions. I take property to be a set of rights, liberties, and powers held against other people with respect to resources. These generally include a right to exclude others, a liberty of use, and a power of transference, though a form of property could be said to exist without the full powers of transference. How strong these rights are I leave open. Although claims that are too easily trumped seem not to be rights at all, the notion of property allows some leeway with respect to the strength of the claim. So, for instance, one still has a property right when it can be overridden by other's needs, or is subject to taxation or expropriation by the state, but if people's possessions were routinely expropriated or seized for taxes then we would hesitate to say the person had property rights to those possessions.

I take an initial acquisition theory of property to be any theory that takes individual property claims to come into being from a state of nature as a result of some initial acquisitive act. That is, it makes some appeal to what Judith Thomson calls an "acquisition schema": "if a thing is unowned, then if X does alpha to it, X thereby comes to own it" (1990, p. 324). Acquisition theories hold that first possession, at least under the right circumstances, gives rise to property rights. The activities that might be taken to constitute first possession are multiple; they have in common that all involve a kind of use that precludes the simultaneous use and possession by others.[1]

Asymmetry

A basic idea underlying contemporary initial acquisition arguments is that there is an asymmetry between first possessors and subsequent arrivals. Later comers who make claims are competing with the claims of those who are already using the goods or territory. First comers, however, are competing with no one, because no claims to the land exist when they arrive. As David Schmidtz puts it in *The Limits of Government*, there is no question of consent for first possessors because there is no one of whom consent may be reasonably asked. All subsequent claimants, in contrast, must make their claims in the face of the claims of those who were there first (1991, p. 15). My focus is on arguments that rely on the asymmetry thesis as part of a general justification for ownership rights.[2]

The view that there is an asymmetry is often presented as if it were a simple and obvious (even empirical) observation. In fact, it rests on two substantive assumptions. The first assumption is that no claims to the world exist until specific individuals make claims. That is, the view assumes that the appropriate description of the original state of nature is one in which there are no general antecedent claims to the world. The second assumption is that the claims of the first comers are morally meaningful. That is, it assumes that acts of occupation or possession are themselves claims or can serve to ground claims, since later comers are taken to be positioned differently from first comers.

Even were we to grant to Schmidtz that there are no claims that need to be acknowledged by first comers, it does not follow immediately that someone's being the first to possess generates claims; it does not follow that later comers must get consent from or otherwise acknowledge the claims of those who had first possession. Possession is not identical to property; it implies physical control, but not yet moral rights. Property is a moral relation between people with respect to goods in the world, and possession is neither necessary nor sufficient for property.

Although the asymmetry thesis is presented as part of an argument for the justification of property by initial acquisition, the assumptions underlying it are far from being obviously true. Why then, is the asymmetry thesis so pervasive? One reason for its pervasiveness is an assumption that the relevant question to be asked is whether some item X should be owned by the person who first possessed it, or owned by some later comer. The situation of first and second arrivals then appears to be asymmetric because we ask, "who should have this; Lilith, who was here first, or Adam, who came along later?" Being first has an air of naturalness as a criterion, a naturalness that is had by no other place in a numerical ordering. If the relevant criterion were being the third possession, one's immediate response would be "why not second or fourth or any other place in the order?"— think how arbitrary radio contests seem when they award the prize to the fourth rather than the first caller. When we see the problem in terms of deciding between two people as owners, in the absence of some morally compelling feature about Adam, choosing him does appear to ignore a claim of Lilith. If we must choose someone, since it seems arbitrary that it be Adam, it must be Lilith. Then if we want to point to something about Lilith, it seems that what there is to point to is just the fact that she was there first; she, unlike Adam, did not have to confront the previous claims of another person.

We do not, however, need to think of the issue in terms of whether Lilith or Adam should have the thing; several other questions could be asked and several other stories could be told. Here is one story. Lilith might have a claim to use of the whole only until Adam shows up and then she has a claim only to half. There is an asymmetry here; Lilith, but not Adam, was able to make rightful use of the whole because there was no one else around when she did so. However, the asymmetry here is not connected to a story about Lilith getting property rights that holds against later comers. Lilith and Adam in turn may each have a right to half until Eve shows up, and so on. Eventually, if enough people show up, subdividing might cease to work and a different sharing arrangement will need to be made. Only if we already assume that someone must have a claim to the thing that holds against all others will we be tempted to think of the issue as deciding between Lilith and Adam and so be tempted to see an interesting asymmetry. Indeed, we need not think of property rights as things that are allocated sequentially in the order that people show up. Granted, it would seem like gratuitous interference on the part of Adam were he to insist on having the bit that Lilith is already using, provided that he has other options. However, the naturalness of that intuition tells us little about the institution of property, or about whether some form of first possession can generate property.

Two features make the asymmetry thesis tempting. Initial acquisition stories invite us to think of property as arising through a sequence of individual acts by people who have no connection with each other. And initial acquisition stories invite us to think that what is gained through initial acquisition is a set of modern ownership rights that once gained must be rights in perpetuity and rights that hold against all comers. Without these assumptions, when we ask instead what kinds of property relations should hold between people, the asymmetry seems less intuitively compelling. I turn now to a brief discussion of the substantive assumptions underlying the asymmetry thesis and suggest that they are at least contentious.

The "No Antecedent Claims" Assumption

One might deny the first substantive assumption and instead hold that everyone has equal competing claims to the world. This is the view that James Tully ascribes to John Locke.[3] Here, although no particular claims have yet been made by particular others, anyone's use of the world is always subject to the equal claims of others to have access to the world. If those who arrive first are to acquire property rights in particular bits of the world, they must be able to address the claims of others. This questions whether there is, after all, a morally interesting asymmetry between first comers and later comers. If there are equal antecedent claims to the world, then everyone will have these claims equally. Although there is an asymmetry in Locke's account of how property can get started, that asymmetry plays no significant role in the justification of property rights.

A distinction used in seventeenth-century discussions about the origins of property was the distinction between positive and negative community.[4] Positive community is already a kind of property relation in that it is a claim to the world that goes beyond mere liberty of use. Negative community, in contrast, is the liberty of all to make use of the world. It is false on a positive conception of community that first comers compete with the claims of no one, whereas later comers compete with the claims of those who were here first. On a positive conception of community, any would-be appropriator must deal with the common claims of all.

The seventeenth-century discussions about positive and negative community were connected to a debate about how property could arise given that God gave the earth to all mankind in common. Grotius and Pufendorf held that, beginning from negative community, the consent of all is required for appropriation. Filmer (1991, pp. 19–20) argued that since such consent is not obtainable, we could explain property only on the assumption that God gave the earth to Adam and his heirs. Locke entered this debate to argue that, beginning from the assumption that God gave the earth to all mankind in common in the positive senses, he can show how individual property can be derived without any need to appeal to express consent. Positive community is Locke's solution to the problem of explaining the origins of property without appeal to consent.[5]

Tully ascribes to Locke the view that the earth is held in common in the sense that each individual has rights to it. This is an inclusive right—the right to be included.[6] An inclusive right is not yet the right to a particular thing, but is a claim that there be some particular thing or other available that one can claim. This includes two components. First, it requires that others not exclude you. Second, it requires that you can come to make use of or to hold an item of the sort you have an inclusive claim to. An example is the right given to a person as the holder of an unreserved seat at a bas ball game. The ticket picks out no particular seat. The person has no claim violated if her preferred seat happens to be already occupied; but she has a claim that some seat be available for her. She has a legitimate complaint if all the seats are taken. Having found a particular seat, she has some kind of claim to that seat, though precisely what kind of claim is a matter of convention. We can think of positive community as the case where everyone is a ticker holder.[7]

External resources, of course, are not individuated as neatly as seats at a baseball game. There are questions about what kind of specific property claim would count as the analogy of having a seat; the world does not come predivided. Locke, famously, made use of two constraints on acquisition; that one has a claim only to what one needs for self-preservation and that enough and as good be left for others. Thus, one may take no more than what one has an inclusive right to and others must be able to exercise their equal rights. One's claim is based on the need for self-prese vation and so does not extend beyond that, and others have equal co peting claims on the same basis, so any given individualized claim must be compatible with others, like the exercise of an equal claim. Thus for Locke, the basis of initial acquisition provides a natural limit to what one could rightly remove from the commons.

Locke argues that consent is not required to move from positive community to individual claims to specific parts of the world. His argument turns on two assertions. First, God gave the earth to mankind in order that people be able to preserve themselves. Second, in order to make use of the earth for self-preservation, a person must be able to appropriate it; "there must of necessity be a means *to appropriate* them some way or other before they can be of any use, or at all beneficial to any particular man."[8]

Locke's reasoning in this passage has been criticized. John Simmons describes Locke as making the not very convincing claim that productive use requires private property (1994, p. 71, n. 17). However, Locke's reasoning is convincing given two features: the original community is positive, and Locke takes property to be something less than full ownership rights. Simmons finds Locke unconvincing because it seems to him that the claim to self-preservation can be met by merely making use of the commons as commons, rather than by individual appropriation. However, if Locke's conception of original community is characterized by inclusive rights, any particular piece of the world can be rightfully used by an individual only if it is no longer a part of the commons; that is, it must no longer be a part of what others have a general (inclusive) claim to. Simmons is right that productive use does not require private property in the form of ownership rights. Locke, however, does not distinguish between two ways of making use of the world—free use of the commons as commons and private property removed from the commons. For Locke, to take anything from the commons for one's own use is to make it exclusive to oneself. One has a moral claim to what one has removed from the commons provided that the limitations are respected. In that sense, one has a property in what one has removed.

He that is nourished by the Acorns he pickt up under an Oak, or the Apples he gathered from the Trees in the Wood, has certainly appropriated them to himself. Nobody can deny but the nourishment is his. I ask then, When did they begin to be his? When he digested? Or when he eat? Or when he boiled? Or when he brought them home? Or when he pickt them up? And 'tis plain, if the first gathering made them not his, nothing else could. That *labour* put a distinction between them and common.[9]

In the context of Locke's argument, labor is a natural way of staking out particular claims because self-preservation, which is the basis of the original claim, creates the need for individual title, and one preserves oneself by making use of external goods. The examples of labor that Locke gives are all examples of using external goods for one's self-preservation. The labor of self-preservation makes use of, and so makes useful, external goods. Trivially, an acorn is of no use for self-preservation unless one makes use of it by picking it up and putting it in one's mouth, or storing it and consuming it later. One transforms a general claim to external goods into a particular claim to particular goods by making use of those goods, just as one claims a particular stadium seat by sitting in it. The same could be said of stadium seats as Locke says about resources. Until a particular seat has been appropriated, it is of no use for watching the game.

The case is no different when what is removed from the commons is the land itself, through enclosure and cultivation.[10] People need to have sufficient stable access to resources if they are to make use of the earth to preserve themselves. What kind of access will depend on how the land gets used. Hunting, herding, and grazing permit multiple people to use the same land. Farming requires that no one else be using it, at least for the duration of the season. Since privatization of fixed resources is not necessary for preservation, Simmons is quite right that the argument from preservation shows at most that private property in these resources is permissible. Privatization of the earth itself is on the same footing as any other use. Land, like anything else, may be privatized by its removal from the commons; there is no basis in Locke for treating it differently from consumables. The Lockean proviso that enough and as good be left for others ensures that the equal claims of others to the world are met; it ensures that they will suffer no diminution in the ability to exercise that claim as a result of the appropriation of others, no matter the form of that appropriation.

There is an asymmetry in Locke. One turns an inclusive claim into an exclusive claim by being the first to remove something from the commons. That asymmetry, however, is uninteresting from a justificatory point of view. The asymmetry plays a role in allocation only. The justificatory role is played by one's equal claim to have access to the means of self-preservation.

Locke's account does not justify private property in the earth in perpetuity; the property rights are not yet full-blown ownership rights. It cannot justify unequal resources and it cannot justify removal from the commons when the effect is to leave others without a means to exercise their common claims. At that point, the original appropriations lose their justification. They were permissible only because leaving enough and as good for others ensured that all antecedent claims could be met. Locke recognizes this point when he says that where the invention of money has led to an increase of people and a scarcity of land, consent settles property.[11] The original right to self-preservation remains as a right to charity, the right to have what one needs to survive.[12]

The point about Locke for my purposes is simply that it provides an alternative model to the negative community that is assumed by modern asymmetry theorists and a model that seems no less plausible. Although the claim that God gave the earth to mankind in common won't do, one might hold instead that an equal claim to the earth and its benefits is part of the moral endowment of all human beings. Such a view is at least compatible with the kind of natural rights view that often accompanies initial acquisition theories of justification. However, beginning from positive community limits the kinds of claims that one can make to the world. It fails to provide a justification for full-blown ownership rights.

There is a basic problem with any state-of-nature initial acquisition argument; one needs to build in sufficient moral richness to generate property rights. Unlike the model of negative community, positive community can provide an account of our moral relation to the world that explains why acts of first possession are morally meaningful. The problem that negative community accounts seem to set themselves is the problem of tying property rights to other rights deemed to be less substantive or generating new obligations *ex nihilo*.

The "Moral Meaningfulness of First Claims" Assumption

I turn now to the second assumption of the asymmetry thesis: the view that first possession is morally meaningful. Here I will assume that the state of nature is to be characterized as negative community; although people are equally at liberty to make use of the world, there are no antecedent general claims to the world. Claims are to arise from the actions of individuals. Assuming nothing more than the equal liberty of all to make use of the world, the challenge is to move from it being morally permissible for each individual to make use of resources without the consent of others to the state where particular items are in the exclusive control of particular individuals.

Proponents of the asymmetry thesis assume that initial acquisition is morally unproblematic once we have the first substantive assumption, namely that there are no antecedent competing claims to the world.[13] But this is to confuse initial acquisition of property rights with mere takings. Mere takings are morally unproblematic if no one has claims to the world—but there is no prima facie reason to think that takings get us to property rights. One might deny that the claims of first comers are morally meaningful; that is, one might deny that they can straightforwardly give rise to duties on the part of others. Pufendorf, for instance, thought that beginning from negative community, property is only possible by consent. As he put it, "assuming an equal faculty of men over things, it is impossible to conceive how the mere corporal act of one person can prejudice the faculty of others unless consent is given."[14] Appropriation of property imposes new obligations and duties; hence, those on whom the duties are to be imposed must agree to the enlargement of their obligations. Jeremy Waldron echoes a similar concern when he notes that acts of acquisition involve imposing onerous burdens on others, burdens that may even jeopardize the survival of others. He suggests that an acquisition principle that justifies the unilateral imposition of onerous duties on others is radically unlike other moral principles (1988, pp. 265–271).

John Simmons has argued that the unilateral imposition of duties on others is not the radically unfamiliar idea that Waldron claims it to be. Simmons offers the following examples: using a public tennis court, filing a patent, making a legal will, and buying a rare stamp (1994, pp. 83–84). Most of these examples are not of the right sort to do the job that Simmons uses them for. Using a public tennis court leaves intact the liberty of others to use the tennis court, though it prevents one from exercising the liberty at that point. The liberty to use a tennis court was already only the liberty to use it when free. Buying a rare stamp, similarly, leaves intact the power and liberty of others to purchase it, though it removes an opportunity to do so. These differ in kind from the burdens placed by initial acquisition if we take it to be the acquisition of rights; the acquisition of new rights extinguishes the liberty of others to make free use of what is acquired. The burden imposed on others is thus onerous in a way that the burdens imposed in using a tennis court or buying a rare stamp are not. Filing a legal will is not different from any other transference of owned goods. Others cannot dispose of what I own without my consent; a legal will extends that control beyond my death. Others will have duties owed to new people, as happens whenever property is transferred, but these are not new duties; no new duties arise without consent. The executor is free to decline her duties and those due to inherit property are free to decline their inheritance along with any encumbrances that may accompany it.

Of the examples that Simmons mentions, only that of filing a patent appears to involve the imposition of new and onerous duties. Filing a patent is a kind of initial acquisition, and like any initial acquisition, it involves extinguishing the liberty of others with respect to the thing owned. We can grant Simmons the point that the power to impose uni-lateral duties is not completely unfamiliar. Notice, though, Simmons's only persuasive appeal is to what is already a case initial acquisition. Notice also that patents on products like medicine or genotypes are controversial pre-cisely because of the onerous burdens they impose on others. Finally, observe that how long a patent on a particular good can be held is a matter of complicated legal negotiation, and to that extent, patents scarcely func-tion as a paradigm unilateral imposition of duty.

What Pufendorf and Waldron serve to highlight is that initial acquisi-tion understood as the acquisition of rights involves the unilateral impo-sition of duties on others and that such an imposition requires that others have moral reason to accept that imposition. If we think about it from the point of view of later comers then we can see that what is needed is a reason for them to refrain from interfering with the claims of earlier comers. The burden of proof is on the proponents of initial acquisition. On the face of it, second comers appear to have no such moral reason, at least in the absence of already sharing a conception of acquisition with would-be appropriators.

Suppose that Abraham has arrived first in an unoccupied territory and that he has set about making use of a piece of land, clearing out the trees, putting up fences to contain his sheep, building a well and a residence, and so forth. When Daniel arrives some time later, what moral reason has he to respect Abraham's possessions? There are a variety of options open to Daniel. He might simply take over all or part of Abraham's holding, raise sheep, and farm it, thereby profiting from Abraham's labor. He might take over all or part of Abraham's place and start a trout-fishing operation on the stream that runs through Abraham's property. He might negotiate with Abraham to share the territory, and so on. If Abraham has fenced in the whole of the valley for his sheep, if Abraham has taken the best or most fertile part of the valley, what reason has Daniel to respect his claims? From Daniel's point of view, if he has to choose between Abraham and Daniel, then why not choose Daniel? If Daniel can take over from Abraham without violating Abraham's other rights or liberties, what reason could Daniel have not to take over? From Daniel's point of view, there needs to be some reason for thinking that claim is morally meaningful. The kinds of contexts where we are familiar with the unilateral imposition of duty are contexts where there are already in place conventions and practices against which to justify the imposition of duties, against which they are morally meaningful. The task for an initial acquisition justification of property will be to explain that moral meaningfulness.

There are two basic approaches that can be used to derive property rights starting from negative community. First, someone might argue that the exercise of other rights that are not themselves rights to resources will in certain contexts amount to the exercise of property rights because respecting those rights will require respecting possessions. Alternatively, someone might argue that people, as a brute fact, have the moral power to create the kinds of moral relations with others that constitute property rights. That is, under the right circumstances, engaging in certain acts just does constitute the acquisition of a property right.

There are a variety of standard arguments purporting to derive property rights from the exercise of rights such as the right to one's labor or to bodily integrity or a right to liberty. The standard form of argument is to hold other rights or liberties fixed and then to show that property rights will arise from the exercise of the other rights or liberties. I think these arguments don't work. I briefly sketch why, below.

The argument from a right to labor begins with the claim that laborers have the exclusive right to the use of their labor.[15] Laboring involves, at least typically, laboring on the world. Were the laborer not to own the goods labored on, then others would be able to make use of his labor without his permission, and that violates the right to the exclusive use of one's labor. Hence, the laborer must own the goods that he labors on. The argument from liberty claims that interfering with what a person has acquired is an interference with their liberty. These arguments are familiar. The objections are equally familiar.

The labor argument is subject to the objection that labor gives title at most to the fruits of the labor rather than to what is labored on, since the object labored on exists prior to the labor and hence can be made use of without making use of the labor. This objection is strengthened when we notice that underlying material resources may have more than one use so that someone may make use of preexisting resources without reference to the labor of others. Suppose Abraham has cleared and ploughed a piece of land. Abraham has contributed to the value of that land relative to its use as a farm. Now, let us suppose that uranium is discovered in the area, and that it is highly likely that there is uranium underneath the land that Abraham is farming. The land now has value as a potential mining site, and Abraham's labor has not contributed to that value; clearly, he has no rights of ownership over the uranium—it just happens to be on land that he is farming. We must also observe that those who want to move in and start mining do not owe Abraham anything; his labor does not contribute to the use they want to make of the land. No one is making use of his labor without his consent—no one is forcing him to do anything. Others can make use of the same resources as Abraham labors on without thereby making use of Abraham's labor. If this is so, the argument from Abraham's ownership of his labor to ownership of what he labors on does not go through. We get no stable ownership of underlying resources.

The liberty-based argument appears to be a nonstarter; since initial acquisition just does interfere with the liberty of others, a right to liberty counts against the power to acquire property. Jan Narveson (1988) argues that one's liberty to pursue ongoing projects is what needs to get protected and that its protection will generate property rights. However, this does not help. Abraham might insist that Daniel is interfering with his, Abraham's, liberty to farm if Daniel moves in and starts a trout-fishing operation where Abraham has been farming; but Daniel might equally claim that if Abraham prevents him, Daniel, from starting a trout-fishing operation then Abraham is interfering with Daniel's liberty. Daniel, like Abraham, just claims the right to do his own thing. Either the interference with liberty is mutual or Daniel is not interfering with any natural right that Abraham might have, barring a natural right to acquire property by an act of first possession.

We can generalize about why these arguments go wrong. For any non-property rights we might use, and for any favored conception of property, we will be able to find significant classes of situations where respecting that other right just won't map onto the favored conception of property. Rights like the right to liberty, labor, or bodily integrity can be minimally met without thereby instituting property.

Moral Powers and First Possession

The second basic approach I mentioned above is to postulate a moral power to acquire property rights via acts of initial acquisition. Someone might argue that although the rights in which property consists are acquired, the moral power to acquire property is part of the natural moral endowment of humans. A moral power is simply the ability to alter the moral relations between people, the ability to bring into being new rights and duties. The power to make promises is a familiar kind of moral power. We are also familiar with a variety of legal powers with respect to external goods, like the power to sell or acquire legal property including the legal power to acquire property by first possession. We might, then, think there are also moral powers to acquire property.

Moral powers to acquire property are often taken to be universal powers that operate unilaterally—that is, accounts of such powers often focus only on the possessor and the possessive act that is meant to give rise to the property claims. They rely on some universal claim that doing alpha to X brings about a property claim in X. However, this is implausible. Human communities do not need property to exist as moral communities. However we identify alpha, there will be cases where doing alpha fails to bring about property rights because the relevant context is lacking. An act that is taken to be an act of possession in one context will fail to be so taken in another.[16] Thus the early European explorers in the Americas took themselves to be acquiring in the name of the king, whereas the natives did not recognize these activities as acquisitive acts. If there are moral powers to acquire property, the most plausible account will be one that takes such powers to be morally meaningful only within specific moral communities.

The most familiar example we have of a moral power is promise keeping; hence it might be useful to compare initial acquisition to promising. I suggest that acquisitive acts are performatives, just as promises are performatives. However, plausibly, like promises, they require intention and uptake. For promising to exist at all there needs to be a general recognition of promise keeping, and there needs to be a general notion of uptake. A society might fail to have promise keeping altogether because it failed to have the relevant performatives—that is, things we take to be performatives simply might not be recognized as performatives. Similarly, a community might lack uptake for acquisition; it might not distinguish property from mere possession, or even mere transient possession. For acquisition to take place there needs to be a background recognition of property. Without the recognition, there is no performative and without the performative there is no property. There must be conventions in place that recognize particular acts as acts of acquisition rather than mere use or possession.

In addition, a promise requires something like specific uptake. A promise is not unilateral. As a promiser, you need to involve the promisee—that is at least part of the difference between a promise and a vow to oneself.[17] Acquisition has the same feature. Unless it somehow involves the people against whom the obligation holds, what reason have we to distinguish between possession and property, between physical control and rightful physical control?[18] At a minimum, second comers must recognize first comers as having acquired property, as having performed an acquisitive act. Without such recognition, what could count as a moral reason for respecting possessions?

These considerations suggest that property is best understood within the context of specific communities; what gets recognized as being first possession, as being an acquisitive act, will depend on the background, including background about the kinds of things that resources get used for and how they get used. Whether something is recognized by a specific individual as an acquisitive act will depend more generally on the existence of moral relations between the claimant and the people against whom the claims are made. In short, we can allow a moral power to acquire property, just as we acknowledge a moral power to make promises without supposing that there is anything that counts as an acquisitive act outside a convention or practice recognizing it as such. But then initial acquisition justifications don't get claims that must be recognized outside of those communities that have the conventions. This account of how moral powers work greatly limits the kinds of claims that can be made for the scope of property rights acquired by some acquisitive act. That is, it limits the extent to which acquisition stories can be used as state-of-nature justifications of private property institutions.

It might seem that first possession generates at least minimal moral claims, even outside the context of specific communities with acquisitive practices or conventions. It might be thought there is at least a minimal asymmetry; later arrivals, unlike earlier arrivals, at least get confronted with existing occupation, and so it might be thought that there is at least one circumstance under which there would be something wrong with Daniel's simply taking over what Abraham claimed first. If there is "enough and as good" left for Daniel, then his taking over what Abraham possesses would be a gratuitous interference with Abraham. Someone might agree that when Daniel has to choose between himself and Abraham there seems no good moral reason why he must choose Abraham. But, the argument goes, when there is enough and as good left for Daniel, then Daniel does not have to so choose. His displacing Abraham then seems to be unmotivated interference.

Even here, we need to appeal to the recognition of an acquisitive act. Taking something to be an unmotivated interference with another's possession requires recognizing what they are doing as possessing, and as having an intent to continue possessing. But that seems to already presuppose the recognition of acquisitive acts. Furthermore, the whole notion of "enough and as good" is already predicated on certain ideas of what land is appropriately used for. Think about the failure of European settlers to have recognized the natives in North America as first possessors, or even about the failure of the natives to have had a concept of first possession at all, at least with respect to land.

If we think about it from the point of view of the later comers the question we are led to ask is "why should later comers respect what earlier arrivals have done?" Part of the answer at least is that as long as there is enough and as good left for others then later comers have moral reason to respect the possessions of earlier comers because a minimal moral claim against others is the claim not to be gratuitously interfered with. This kind of answer presupposes that the arrivals in question share enough of a conception of property to recognize the acquisitive acts.

Where there is not shared recognition of what counts as an acquisitive act, an act of first possession, I don't think first comers have any moral claims at all against later comers. John Simmons (1994, p. 76) thinks that original acquisition stories can justify at least minimal claims. If someone has a modest holding, he argues, and there is no evidence of force or fraud, then the person who acquired it has a claim to it. I disagree in this respect; the person has a claim at most against others like her, people who share her community and its concept of acquisition. There is no reason to think that this claim holds generally against the world. We tend to think of property rights as holding in general against all others, unless trumped by something like needs. However, we need not think of them this way. They might be claims that hold against some people, but not against others. If we reflect on how property plays a role in moral lives and when and why initial acquisition stories make sense, we should expect first possession to generate special and not general obligations.

Conclusion

Commonsense history suggests that property arose as a result of people's occupying and using pieces of land. That commonsense history fails to provide a justification of the institution of private property. I have suggested that acts of initial acquisition can have real moral import; they can give rise to genuine property rights in the thing acquired. These property rights are genuine in that they do obligate others to refrain from interfering with what has already been acquired. I suggested, however, that this moral import occurs only where there are conventions recognizing the acts as acquisitive. Furthermore, these property rights hold only against those who share the relevant conception of property. Notoriously, the Europeans largely failed to recognize any act of acquisition on the part of natives in the Americas. Early explorers claimed the land for their sovereigns without regard to any claims of existing possessors. On my view, they were not wrong to do so: they failed to share a convention with the natives that would allow them to recognize the natives as having acquired the land. Nor were the natives bound to respect the claims of the newcomers. The claims made by the Europeans held at most against other Europeans. This account suggests that although intitial acquisition is a morally useful concept for us, it does not function as a presocial moral act that constrains later social relations. If acts of acquisition are performatives in the way that promises are performatives then they will not be useful as a way of justifying contemporary institutions of property. The kinds of

acquisitive acts that are appealed to in initial acquisition accounts seem
to already presuppose something like a contemporary background of
property relations.

Acknowledgments

I would like to thank Elizabeth Brake, David Kahane, Mark Migotti, and
the members of the University of Calgary Ethics Research Group for useful
feedback on earlier drafts of this essay.

Notes

1. A group might collectively make use of a territory as a hunting ground or range-
land in such a way as to preclude simultaneous use by others. In these cases, it is
reasonable to say that the group collectively possesses the territory.

2. Other writers do not state the asymmetry thesis as clearly as does Schmidtz, but
Nozick seems to be assuming something like this when he takes initial acquisition
to be unproblematic beginning from Hofeldian liberties, and Gauthier also when he
argues that a first appropriator worsens no one's position but a second comer
worsens the position of the first if she appropriates what the first comer has already
appropriated.

3. Tully 1993. See also Simmons 1992 for a somewhat different interpretation of
Locke's claim that God gave the earth to all.

4. The distinction is clearly stated by Pufendorf (1964) book IV, chapter IV, section 2. Pufendorf took positive community to be a form of proprietorship in
which several people own a thing in the same way. Because he took ownership to
be something that excludes others, he thought that original community could not
be positive since original community includes all.

5. In the *Second Treatise* section 26, Locke notes that on the assumption that God
gave earth to mankind in common, "it seems to some a very great difficulty, how
anyone should ever come to have a *Property* in anything." Laslett (Locke 1988) notes
that this is a clear reference to Filmer. Locke also argued extensively against Filmer
(1991) in the *First Treatise* that it is inexplicable how property could have become
divided if it were given solely to Adam.

6. Simmons (1992, p. 238) distinguishes three forms of positive community: joint
positive community, inclusive positive community, and divisible positive community. He takes inclusive community to be the view that each has only a protected
right to free use of the commons. He takes divisible positive community to be the
view that each person has a claim to an equal share of the earth, though not yet

possession of any particular share. The view that I attribute to Tully under the label "inclusive rights" comes closer to what Simmons takes to be divisible positive community.

7. The example is an adaptation of the simile of a theater seat that Grotius borrowed from Cicero. Grotius (1901), book II, chapter 2, section 1, uses the example to show how a kind of property can arise from negative community, namely the claim to exclusive use of an item as long as it is in one's possession. I have adapted the example by looking at the kind of claim one has as a ticket holder. See also Tully 1993, pp. 107–108, and Waldron 1988.

8. Locke, *Second Treatise*, section 26.

9. *Second Treatise*, section 28.

10. Locke also offers an argument from labor based on the claim that the bulk of the value of natural resources is contributed by the labor. I take this to be independent of the commons argument that I have been discussing. The labor as value argument does not require a positive conception of community; but nor does Locke's argument from positive community require that labor add value.

11. Second *Treatise*, section 45.

12. *First Treatise*, section 42. Locke is explicit here that those in need are entitled to the surplus of those that have as a matter of God-given right.

13. Nozick, for instance, takes initial acquisition to be morally unproblematic provided that the proviso is met that no one be worsened by the appropriation.

14. Pufendorf (1964), book IV, chapter IV, section 5.

15. Becker (1977, pp. 32–57) offers a lengthy analysis of labor derivations of private property.

16. Harris (1996, p. 215) notes that social or legal conventions may award first occupants title based on grounds other than natural rights given no other claimants and present possession.

17. I owe this point to Mark Migotti.

18. Thomson (1990, p. 322) says that uptake is required for transference of property.

References

Becker, L. 1977. *Property Rights*. London: Routledge and Kegan Paul.

Filmer, Robert. 1991. *Patriarcha and Other Writings*. Johann P. Sommerville, ed. Cambridge: Cambridge University Press.

Gauthier, D. 1986. *Morals by Agreement*. Oxford: Clarendon Press.

Grotius, H. 1901. *The Rights of War and Peace*. A. C. Campbell, trans. Washington and London: M. Walter Dunne.

Harris, J. W. 1996. *Property and Justice*. Oxford: Clarendon Press.

Locke, J. 1988. *Two Treatises of Government*. Peter Laslett, ed. Cambridge: Cambridge University Press.

Lomasky, L. 1987. *Persons, Rights, and the Moral Community*. Oxford: Oxford University Press.

Narveson, J. 1988. *The Libertarian Idea*. Philadelphia: Temple University Press.

Nozick, R. 1977. *Anarchy, State, and Utopia*. New York: Basic Books.

Pufendorf, S. 1964. *De Jure Naturae et Gentium Libri Octo*, vol. 2. C. H. Oldfather and W. A. Oldfather, trans. New York: Oceana Publications and London: Wiley and Sons.

Ryan, A. 1987. *Property*. Minneapolis: University of Minnesota Press.

Schmidtz, D. 1991. *The Limits of Libertarianism*. Boulder, Colo.: Westview Press.

———. 1994. "The Institution of Property." In E. F. Paul, F. D. Miller, Jr., and J. Paul, eds., *Property Rights*. Cambridge: Cambridge University Press.

Simmons, J. 1992 *A Lockean Theory of Rights*. Princeton, N.J.: Princeton University Press.

———. 1994. "Original Acquisition Justifications of Private Property." In E. F. Paul, F. D. Miller, Jr., and J. Paul, eds., *Property Rights*. Cambridge: Cambridge University Press.

Thomson, J. 1990. *The Realm of Rights*. Cambridge, Mass.: Harvard University Press.

Tully, J. 1993. *An Approach to Political Philosophy: Locke in Contexts*. Cambridge: Cambridge University Press.

Waldron, J. 1988. *The Right to Private Property*. Oxford: Clarendon Press.

8 Justice and Strict Liability

Harry S. Silverstein

I

Despite much grumbling by business interests and their supporters, the "strict liability" approach to product liability has been the dominant approach in most states since the 1960s. According to this approach (which I shall dub "SL"), if Ann, for example, is injured using a power saw made by Tools Inc., then to provide legally sufficient proof that Tools Inc. is liable, and thus must compensate her for her injuries, Ann need only show (and let's suppose that she can indeed show) the following:

1. that the power saw in question was defective;
2. that the power saw came from Tools Inc.; and
3. that the power saw's defect was the cause of her injuries.[1]

Significantly absent from this list is any requirement that Ann demonstrate that Tools Inc. was negligent, or was in any other way "at fault." Hence, even if Tools Inc. did nothing wrong—their product's design was flawless, their quality-control procedures for the production phase were the best that could possibly be implemented, and so on—SL still finds them liable. Thus, SL conflicts with the following "conditions of responsibility principle" (CRP):

No person (including a legal person, such as a company), P, can justly be held responsible for a harm, H, unless either
1. P made a prior, voluntary, agreement to take responsibility for harms such as H, or
2. H resulted from some fault on P's part, from P's doing something wrong.

Assuming, as I shall, that the (1) clause of CRP is inapplicable to Ann's case—that is, assuming that Tools Inc. did not offer a warranty covering cases like Ann's—Ann's case does not satisfy CRP; yet according to SL, Tools Inc. is nonetheless liable for Ann's harm. Yet at first blush, CRP seems extremely plausible; hence, it seems natural to conclude that SL is unjust. Suppose, for example, that Jack is a member of the audience at a philosophical presentation by Jill, and that he is shot in the leg by a stray bullet during the course of Jill's talk; and suppose further that Jill did not voluntarily agree to take responsibility for any such harms, and that Jack's being shot was in no way the result of anything Jill did wrong. In such a case any attempt by Jack to hold Jill responsible—and thus obligated to pay his resulting medical bills—would be outrageous. And note in particular that this remains outrageous even if he can demonstrate a causal connection between Jill's doings and his harm (he demonstrates, for example, that he would not have been shot had he not been in this room, and that he would not have been in this room had Jill not prepared a talk that he thought would be interesting). The only way for Jack to justify holding Jill responsible, it seems reasonable to say, would to be show that his harm resulted from Jill's doing something wrong;[2] otherwise, holding Jill responsible is an injustice to Jill. Similarly, critics of strict liability contend, holding companies liable when they have done nothing wrong is an injustice to them.

The argument that strict liability is unjust to companies because it violates CRP I shall call the "conditions of responsibility argument" (CRA). CRA will be the focus of the remainder of my essay. In the next section I shall consider the standard legal defenses of SL, as well as two recent philosophical defenses, and attempt to show that none of these defenses provides a successful response to CRA. In the final section I will give my own argument against CRA, an argument that (of course!) I think succeeds.

II

The two main legal defenses of SL[3]—defenses provided, at least implicitly, in judicial rulings—are what I shall call the "make the company shape up argument" (SUA) and the "distribute the burden argument" (DBA).[4] According to SUA, SL is justified by the fact that it will force companies to make safer products: a company that knows it will be held liable for any harm-causing defect will, it is claimed, take greater care regarding safety both in design and in manufacture than a company that knows it will be held liable only for negligence. But this argument faces obvious objections. For one thing, no amount of pressure from an SL system can prevent defects that cannot reasonably be foreseen or controlled—which presumably applies to most cases where companies are not negligent. Furthermore, if we are focusing on consequences, we have to consider the bad consequences of SL as well as the good—driving some useful companies out of business, either directly through high SL judgments against them, or indirectly through skyrocketing insurance costs; preventing the production of useful goods and services simply because of fears relating to SL; and so on. But the main problem with SUA is that it is indeed merely a consequentialist argument; it does not even address the question of justice, and thus does nothing to undermine CRA.[5]

Turning to DBA, its claim is that SL is justified by the fact that it provides an "equitable" distribution of the financial burden faced by the injured consumer. If Ann is seriously injured by Tools Inc.'s defective power saw, then if Tools Inc. is held liable, the financial burden is not borne by Ann but by Tools Inc., which in turn can "distribute it equitably"—it can cover the cost by, for example, raising the price of the relevant item slightly, so that the cost is borne by a large number of customers, no one of whom has to pay very much. But however the crucial notion of "equity" is construed here, this argument fails as a response to CRA. If equity is construed along the lines suggested by CRA itself—or, indeed, by any plausible view that attempts to link "equitable distribution of the burden" to responsibility—then of course it is *not* equitable to make Tool Inc.'s other customers[6] pay, even if no single customer has to pay very much; for those customers are, of course, not responsible for Ann's injury. But if equity is not conceived this way, then the only content left seems to be the bare idea of "spreading the burden to lots of people so that no one person has to pay very much."[7] But apart from the fact that this is a highly dubious conception of "equity"—if, for example, a professor suddenly announced in one of his large lecture classes that all the students in the room that day would be required to pay for his dinner that evening, I seriously doubt that any of the students would regard that as equitable merely because no one student was being required to pay very much—it does not yield the desired results. For if the sole aim at issue is indeed spreading the burden to lots of people so that no one person has to pay very much, then presumably the wider the distribution, the better. And there are many other possible distribute-the-burden arrangements that would be perfectly workable in practice and would spread the burden even further: for example, (1) an industry-wide fund used to pay for all injuries caused by defective products in the entire industry (a fund that could be financed, for example, by annual assessments against all companies in the industry based on market share)—this would spread the burden not just to customers of a particular company, but to customers of the entire industry; or (2) a general fund maintained by the government and derived from general tax revenues, a fund set up to pay for *all* damages from *all* defective products—this would spread the burden further still, to all taxpayers; and so on.[8] Indeed, if spreading the burden is the sole relevant aim, then it would not seem to matter whether the product causing the harm was even defective. And this, in my view, is a final reductio ad absurdum of DBA. For this means that, insofar as DBA could be used to support SL, it could also be used to support what George G. Brenkert would call an "absolute liability" system,[9] a system in which companies are held liable for harms caused by their products not merely when they are not negligent, but even when their products are not defective. And not even the most passionate supporter of SL would want to defend that.

I turn now to the argument proposed by Brenkert in "Strict Products Liability and Compensatory Justice" (1984). Brenkert agrees that SUA and DBA fail, but contends that SL can be justified as a matter of compensatory justice on the basis of the assumptions or requirements underlying the "free enterprise system." Specifically:

1. the free enterprise system involves competition, not only among businesses, but between each business and its customers;
2. "such competition must be fair" (ibid., p. 349);
3. "Crucial to the notion of fairness of competition is . . . that each person . . . be given an equal opportunity to participate in the system in order to fulfill his own particular ends" (ibid., pp. 349–350);
4. "If . . . a person . . . is injured by a defective product, . . . his equal opportunity to participate in the system in order to fulfill his own ends will be diminished" (ibid., p. 350);
5. Hence (ibid., pp. 350–351):

[I]t is fair that the manufacturer compensate the person for his losses. . . . That is, the user of a manufacturer's product may justifiably demand compensation from the manufacturer when a product of his which can be shown to be defective has injured him and harmed his chances of participation in the system of free enterprise.

Hence, strict liability finds a basis in the notion of equality of opportunity which plays a central role in the notion of a free enterprise system. . . . [T]he basis upon which manufacturers are held strictly liable is compensatory justice.

And Brenkert provides an analogy from rule violations in games (ibid., p. 351):

[The] situation is analogous to a player's unintentional violation of a game rule which is intended to foster equality of competitive opportunity. A soccer player, for example, may unintentionally trip an opposing player. He did not mean to do it; perhaps he himself had stumbled and consequently tripped the other player. Still, he is to be penalized. If the referee looked the other way, the tripped player would rightfully object that he had been treated unfairly. Similarly, the manufacturer of a product may be held strictly liable. . . . Even though he be faultless, it is a causal consequence of his activities that renders the user of his product less capable of equal participation. . . . The manufacturer too should be penalized by way of compensating the victim.

In my opinion, however, all this fares no better as an argument against CRA than do SUA and DBA. For even if we grant—as I am happy to do—that equal opportunity is a basic right, and that one's equal opportunity is undermined when one is seriously injured by a defective product, it does not follow that *the relevant company* is the one obligated to supply—or restore—equal opportunity *when that company is not at fault*. Why not, again, have the government (i.e., all taxpayers), or the entire industry—or, alternatively, the injured consumer's own insurance—do it? Apart from the game analogy, to which I shall return, Brenkert's discussion contains very little that can be regarded as a response to this question—that is, as a defense of the claim that the relevant company can justifiably be forced to be the "equal opportunity restorer"; and this little is clearly insufficient. At one point Brenkert considers the possibility of having the government do it, but rejects this on the ground that, if one accepts a free enterprise system, "this alternative must be rejected because it permits the interference of government into individual affairs" (ibid., p. 353). This argument does not, of course, apply to nongovernmental alternatives; but even if we ignore that point, the argument seems clearly to fail. For any policy here—

including SL, the policy favored by Brenkert—involves "the interference of government" (it is the government, after all, that, through its legal system, enforces SL). Indeed, a system in which government tax revenues compensated those injured by defective products would very probably involve less, or at least less invasive, interference than SL. This would almost certainly be true for companies, who now would have very little to do with such cases;[10] and it would probably be true for the injured customers, who, instead of having to go through a trial, would now merely have to fill out government forms.

The only other defense of requiring the relevant company to be the "equal opportunity restorer" suggested in Brenkert's discussion is the idea that such a requirement is justifiable because the harm was *caused* by that company (note, for example, his emphasis, at the end of the passage setting out the soccer analogy quoted above, on the fact that the harm to the consumer was a "causal consequence" of the company's activities). But this also is plainly inadequate. If Brenkert is thinking of "cause" in the relevant normative sense, a sense according to which to say that a company "caused" a harm *just is* to say that the company is properly held liable for it, then of course his argument is straightforwardly question-begging; whether or not companies are properly held liable in the relevant circumstances is precisely the question at issue. But on any standard descriptive interpretation of "cause" there are many cases where a company's product causes a harm and the company plainly should *not* be held liable—including the "absolute liability" cases that Brenkert himself rejects. Suppose, for instance, that Harry refuses to buy, or use, a ladder, because he regards ladders as intrinsically unsafe, but that Tools Inc. produces a ladder with so many brilliant safety features that Harry is won over. But suppose further that, when Harry is up on his new "super safe" ladder he is startled by a loud noise and—through no fault of the ladder—falls off. Here Harry's injury is a "causal consequence" of Tools Inc.'s actions—if that company had not made, and sold, such an enticingly safe product, then Harry would have been sitting comfortably on his couch rather than falling off the ladder. But since the ladder is not defective—indeed, it is the most profoundly nondefective ladder on the market—it would be absurd to hold Tools Inc. liable for Harry's injury.[11]

Finally, Brenkert's game analogy has two related defects, and thus also fails as a defense of SL. First, in the game case there are only two participants in the competition; hence, the only place compensation *can* come from is the other team. But of course this is not true in a defective product case; compensation can come from the government, or an industry-wide fund, or what have you. Second, and relatedly, the only way to restore equal competitive opportunity in the game case is to impose a penalty on the offending team; but in the defective product case, a penalty against the company is not necessary, or even relevant, to restoring the injured consumer's equal opportunity.

None of the defenses of SL considered so far directly confronts, or even explicitly considers, CRA. This is not true of the argument advanced by John J. McCall in "Fairness, Strict Liability, and Public Policy" (2000). McCall sets out a principle similar to CRP, which he calls the "fault/control" principle. In defending SL, however, McCall does not challenge the truth or correctness of the "fault/control" principle; his contention, rather, is that, in the relevant cases, this principle is "inapplicable." After articulating the argument that SL is unjust to businesses because it violates the "fault/control" principle, McCall defends this contention as follows (ibid., p. 328, emphasis mine):

We should look a bit closer . . . before concluding that strict liability is unfair. By definition, a strict liability standard applies to cases of accidental injury related to product defects. A consumer who is injured by a defective product is not at fault for the injury just as the business is not at fault. In an equally important way, then, the consumer is harmed by something beyond his or her control. . . .

If we accept the argument that strict liability is unfair to business, the paradoxical conclusion is that the alternative for cases of non-negligent defects is also unfair to the injured consumer. So, rather than drawing conclusions on the basis of the . . . fault/control principle about the fairness of strict liability, we instead should recognize that this principle *is simply inapplicable* when no one bears moral responsibility for the harm, that is, when the harm is purely accidental.

And if we apply this argument to CRA, the obvious conclusion is that, since the CRP is "inapplicable" to strict liability cases, CRA fails to show that SL is unjust. But I think this argument is confused. For CRP does not say that any time there is no fault (or voluntary agreement), there is injustice or unfairness; it merely says that, where there is no fault (or voluntary agreement), then it is unjust *to hold the relevant agent(s) responsible,* and is thus unjust to say that they are *morally required* or *obligated* to pay. And this claim can be applied, without any paradox whatever, to both sides. When Ann is injured by the defective power saw in circumstances where neither she nor Tools Inc. is at fault, we can say simply that neither is responsible, and thus neither is morally obligated to pay for the harm. Now in practice this does normally mean that, if Ann wants her injuries fixed, she will have to pay. However—and this is perhaps where McCall goes wrong—to say this is not to say, or imply, that Ann is responsible, and thus morally obligated, to pay; it is merely to say that, since no one is responsible, and thus, presumably, nobody else *will* pay (since, in the absence of responsibility, nobody but Ann has a reason or motive to pay), if she wants the requisite medical treatment, she will have to be the one to pay. But this result is not only completely nonparadoxical, but—so far as any argument yet given is concerned—entirely reasonable. thus, McCall has failed to show that CRP is "inapplicable"; and, thus, he has failed to undermine CRA.

III

The only way to undermine CRA, in my view, is to mount a direct, frontal attack on CRP. This is what I shall now attempt to do. Specifically, I shall argue, first, that there are a number of cases (cases that do not involve product liability and thus are not question-begging in the present context) where the claim that the relevant agent is properly held responsible even without fault or voluntary agreement seems entirely noncontroversial—cases that thus show clearly that, if we do not simply reject CRP, we do at least acknowledge a significant class of exceptions; and, second, that these cases share a number of features with product liability cases and thus give positive support to the view that CRP's class of exceptions properly includes product liability cases—in short, that these cases give positive support to the view that SL is not unjust. I shall assume that in all the following cases there was no voluntary agreement to take responsibility and shall thus focus on the (2) clause of CRP, the issue of fault.

Consider, to begin with, the responsibility that is standardly ascribed to principals for the conduct of their agents. Principals are typically held liable for the misdeeds of their agents even where they (the principals) are not negligent or in any other way at fault—even where, that is, they have taken all reasonable care in the selection, training, and supervision of those agents.

Admittedly, the liability of principals for their agents might be regarded as an arbitrary legal convention, and thus as a less than compelling exception to CRP. But the same cannot be said for my next example, the responsibility standardly ascribed to parents for the conduct of their children. If Ann and Bill's young son Charlie carelessly breaks a neighbor's window with a baseball, then virtually everyone would agree that Ann and Bill are properly held responsible and are thus obligated to pay for the window's replacement; and this is true, again, even if Ann and Bill are in no way at fault—for example, they have done all that could be expected by way of teaching Charlie to respect other people's property and to be careful when playing with potentially harmful objects like baseballs. Also on the subject of children, a quite different sort of case where we have no qualms about assigning responsibility where there is no fault is a case where the child himself is harmed by nature in a way that imposes unusually heavy burdens on his caregivers. Thus, if Charlie were born with serious spinal problems that required a series of operations and special, time-consuming therapy from ages two to ten, there would be no question but that Ann and Bill would be responsible for providing that special care even if the problems in no way resulted from any fault of theirs.

Further, just as faultless parents are responsible for the behavior of their children, so faultless pet owners are responsible for the behavior of their pets. If Ann and Bill have a rambunctious dog who manages to escape from his fenced-in area and then tears up a neighbor's garden, then even if Ann and Bill have taken all reasonable care to ensure that such escapes do not happen, virtually all of us would agree that Ann and Bill are responsible for the harm and obligated to pay for the needed repairs. And what goes for pets goes also for the "behavior" of one's inanimate possessions. For example, if Ann and Bill have a tree that falls over onto their neighbor's house, severely damaging the roof, we would again agree that Ann and Bill are responsible for paying for the damage even if they were in no way at fault (though the tree was presumably defective, we can suppose that the defect was a hidden one that was not discoverable even by conscientious oversight).

In all of these sorts of cases, then, we routinely ascribe responsibility to faultless agents. Hence, according to standard, apparently noncontroversial, moral views and practices, it is *not* invariably unjust to ascribe responsibility to faultless agents. Thus, if CRP is not simply false, it at best has a number of important exceptions. And given these exceptions, showing that an act or policy violates CRP is not sufficient to show that it is unjust; in short, CRA fails. Moreover, the sorts of cases just discussed— the cases where we routinely ascribe responsibility to faultless agents—typically share a number of important features with product liability cases. Specifically, in both these cases and product liability cases it is typically true that (1) the agent in question performed some relevant voluntary acts (the parents voluntarily had a child; the pet owner voluntarily acquired a pet; the company voluntarily manufactured a product; etc.); (2) that for which the agent is held responsible is something that the agent created, or acquired, or that in any event is something that in some reasonably straightforward sense can be regarded as "that agent's own" (the child is his or her child; the pet is his or her pet; the product is his, her, or its product; etc.);[12] and (3) the relevant agent is held responsible where, but only where, the entity causing the harm (the child, or pet, or product, or etc.) was itself, even if only in an entirely nonmoral sense, "at fault" (the child was misbehaving, or at least being careless; the product was defective; etc.).[13] And the fact that product liability cases share these important features with the other cases I have described—cases where ascribing responsibility to faultless agents seems noncontroversial—allows us, I think, to draw a stronger conclusion. We can now say not merely that a particular argument (viz., CRA) fails to show that SL is unjust to companies, but that it is highly unlikely that any persuasive argument in support of that conclusion could be constructed; in short, we can now regard it as reasonable to hold that in fact SL *is not* unjust to companies. For the similarities between product liability cases and these other, noncontroversial cases gives strong support to the view that including product liability cases within CRP's class of exceptions is not merely possible, but morally correct.

Even this stronger conclusion, of course, entails only that SL is compatible with considerations of justice; it does not entail that SL is required by considerations of justice. And this means that even if opponents of SL cannot argue that SL is unjust, they can still argue on other grounds that it is not the best policy. In short, the argument of this section, even if it is correct as far as it goes, is not, and does not claim to be, the final word on SL. But in this connection I would like to note the following: though if I am right arguments of the sort criticized in section II above fail as arguments against CRA, that does not mean they are entirely worthless; it simply means they could not meet CRA's charge that SL is unjust. But if the justice of SL is no longer at issue—as it is not if the argument of the current section is successful—so that the question of whether SL is an appropriate policy must be debated on other grounds, then those sorts of arguments, including the purely consequentialist arguments, are back in the game. And when those sorts of arguments are added to the argument presented in this section, I think they give significant support to the view that SL is not simply morally permissible, but morally desirable.

I would like to conclude with a very brief consideration of one final question: given that the cases where it seems legitimate to ascribe responsibility to faultless agents share a number of important features, is there a single principle underlying these cases, and if so, what is it? My extremely tentative answer is that there is indeed a single principle, a principle that goes something like this:

It is morally justifiable to require any entity given moral agent status (which includes, in the present context, "artificial persons" such as companies) to take responsibility for his, her, or its own person[14] *and all extensions thereof.*

Admittedly this is extremely vague—if nothing else, an adequate exposition would require a detailed explanation and defense of what is and what is not to be counted as an "extension." But this is a topic for another occasion.

Acknowledgment

Thanks to my INPC commentator, Brian Steverson, for helpful criticisms.

Notes

1. This is of course a bit rough and oversimplified. To take just one example, if the power saw was indeed made by Tools Inc. but became defective only because, and only after, it was mishandled by a retailer, then the retailer, not Tools Inc., would be held liable. But the above characterization is sufficient for the purposes of this essay.

2. In my view the requirement is actually somewhat stronger; roughly, Jack would have to show not merely that the harm resulted from something Jill did wrong, but

that the harm had an appropriate connection with the wrongness. E.g., although it would clearly seem legitimate for Jack to hold Jill responsible if Jill had arranged for the shooting (Jill had decided, let's suppose, that everyone was becoming too comfortable and thought a few stray bullets flying around were needed to wake them up)—or even if Jill knew the stray bullets were coming and gave no warning—it would not seem legitimate for Jack to hold Jill responsible if her fault consisted simply in misleading him about the topic of her talk as a way of ensuring his attendance.

3. A third defense is provided by the "difficulty of proof argument," which contends that SL can be justified pragmatically on the ground that, given the difficulty of proving negligence and the fact that companies typically have far greater resources than consumers, a negligence system has the result in practice that companies are seldom held liable even when they are negligent (consumers have great trouble winning; hence, they seldom sue even when justice is on their side). I won't focus on this argument because it does not really question the legitimacy of a negligence system in principle; it contends, rather, that best way in practice to get the desired effect of a negligence system is via a strict liability system. (Moreover, a proponent of a negligence system has obvious rejoinders. E.g., one could argue that to get around the problem of the difficulty of proving negligence, it is not necessary to switch to a strict liability system; we could, rather, simply modify the rules regarding the burden of proof. Specifically, we could adopt a system where, if the consumer succeeds in demonstrating that product was defective and that defect was the cause of his/her harm, then the company has the burden of proving that it was *not* negligent.)

4. Both arguments are at least implicit in the case that is generally regarded as the first case to approve SL, the case of *Henningsen v. Bloomfield Motors Inc.* decided by the Supreme Court of New Jersey in 1960. The decision in this case contends that (United States Interagency Task Force on Product Liability 1985, p. 55; reprinted from *Final Report*, United States Interagency Task Force on Product Liability):

When a seller places a defective product into the stream of commerce, the loss should fall on that seller, who is in a position to control the danger and to distribute the losses equitably, rather than on the innocent plaintiff.

The idea that "the loss should fall on that seller who is in a position to control the danger" is a brief expression of SUA; and the idea that "the loss should fall on that seller who is in a position to distribute the losses equitably" is a brief expression of DBA.

5. As Brenkert notes in his criticism of SUA (1984, p. 345), it is arguable that a policy of punishing a convicted criminal's entire family—spouse, children, etc.—would be more successful as a deterrent to crime than our current policy; but (presumably) we would all nonetheless condemn such a policy on the grounds that it is unjust.

Similarly, proponents of CRA would argue, SUA must be condemned on grounds of injustice even if it has desirable consequences.

6. Or, depending on how the company decides to absorb the cost, their employees, or their senior management, etc.

7. A possible alternative conception, as Brian Steverson pointed out, is one according to which a distribution of burdens is equitable if it is spread among those who receive the benefits of the relevant "practice." But apart from the fact that supporters of CRA would quite properly reject this conception (since it is not relevant to CRP), it does not in any case provide significant support to SL. For in the first place, SL does not dictate how companies are to spread the burdens imposed by strict liability judgments. Thus, in response to the judgment against the company in Ann's case, Tools Inc. could spread the burden by raising the price of the model of power saw Ann was using, or by raising the price of all its power saws, or by raising the price of all its products, or by reducing employee raises in the next contract negotiations, etc. Hence, whatever antecedent conception one has as to who the beneficiaries of the relevant practice are, there is no reason to suppose that the burden will be spread among all and only those beneficiaries. And in the second place, and more fundamentally, there seems to be no independent reason for conceiving the relevant practice in a way that has any hope of matching SL to begin with. In Ann's case, for example, there seems to be no more reason for conceiving the relevant practice as including all and only the users of Tools Inc. power saws, or Tools Inc. products in general, etc., than there is for conceiving it as including, e.g., all users of power tools (which would require some sort of industrywide distribution), or all those involved in the American economic system (which would require a distribution among all those living in this country plus many millions living elsewhere), etc. Compare the discussion of an analogous suggestion by John J. McCall in the next footnote.

8. John J. McCall rejects the sort of criticism I am articulating here on the following grounds (2000, p. 329):

Making society at large bear the cost through some form of socialized product liability insurance violates the principle of "user pays." . . . In ordinary circumstances, then a strict liability standard is preferable to its alternatives.

But McCall not only fails to provide any defense of "the principle of 'user pays' "; he fails to provide any specific interpretation—in particular, he fails to provide any guidelines as to who, in any particular case, counts as a relevant user. And without such specification, his appeal to this principle is entirely vacuous; for any of the possible policies I've suggested—as well as any other alternative one might suggest—can provide a stipulation of the relevant users that would support the policy in question. Suppose, for example, that Joe is injured by a defective red Dodge sedan. Who are the relevant users? McCall would presumably give an answer like "the users of Dodges," since that is the sort of answer that supports his conclusion. But why not instead say "the users of sedans" or "the users of red cars" or "the users of motor vehicles"? The latter answer would, of course, support an "industrywide fund" policy. And an answer that would support, e.g., a government fund financed by general tax revenues would also be easy to provide; we need merely say that the relevant users are, for example, "the users of the services and protection provided by the government."

9. See Brenkert 1984, p. 344.

10. If, e.g., the system envisaged is one in which companies are still held financially liable when they are negligent, then companies might still face government interference in the form of inquiries into such negligence. But even in such a system, negligent companies would be no worse off as regards government interference than they are now, and nonnegligent companies would remain better off.

11. Brian Steverson objected that the ladder example ignores the fact that the causality relevant to SL is causality related to a product *defect*. But this point about SL is irrelevant to the question at issue, which is whether the fact that the relevant company was a cause of the harm can be used as a *justification* for SL—and specifically, for the contention that that company (rather than the government, or the entire industry, etc.) should be the "equal opportunity restorer." And since the ladder example is a case where the company was indeed a cause of the harm and yet clearly has no obligation to be the "equal opportunity restorer," it remains a perfectly legitimate counterexample in this context. Moreover, it is simple enough in any event to construct a counterexample where causality is related to a product defect. Suppose, for instance, that Bill is injured by a defective product made by XYZ Corp, a product that XYZ Corp could not have made without using one of the unique tools produced by Tools Inc., a tool that itself, however, is entirely free of defects. Here Bill is injured by a defective product, an injury that, paraphrasing Brenkert, is "a causal consequence of Tools Inc.'s activities"; yet no one would say that it would be justifiable to hold Tools. Inc. liable for Bill's injury, or, thus, that Tools Inc. has any obligation to be the "equal opportunity restorer."

12. The sense in which the thing in question is the agent's own is of course not constant throughout these examples. Pets and inanimate objects are the agent's own in the sense that they are his-her-its property. But a company's products are its creations, not (after they are purchased) its property; and children are their parents' creations but no one's property. An issue that it would be useful to examine further in this context is the extent to which there are significant commonalities underlying the use of the possessive in all these sorts of cases.

13. Contrast, for example, the baseball case in the text with the following case. Charlie is playing catch with a friend; one of Charlie's throws hits his friend in the head; but this occurs, not because Charlie has done anything wrong (he is taking all reasonable care), but because the friend's mitt is defective—the webbing suddenly breaks, allowing the ball to go right through it. In this case we would all say that

Charlie's parents are not responsible because Charlie's behavior was in no way faulty (this despite the fact that Charlie's behavior is as much a cause of the harm in this case as it is in the text case).

14. Note here that another entity, not mentioned above, for which we all think one is properly held responsible even when one is guilty of no *moral* fault is *oneself*. E.g., if I stumble in a friend's house and inadvertently knock over a valuable vase, then even if am morally faultless (I am cold sober, taking all reasonable care, etc.), virtually all of us would agree that I am obligated to reimburse the friend for the value of the vase.

References

Brenkert, G. G. 1984. "Strict Products Liability and Compensatory Justice." In W. M. Hoffman and J. M. Moore, eds., *Business Ethics: Readings and Cases in Corporate Morality*. New York: McGraw-Hill.

McCall, J. J. 2000. "Fairness, Strict Liability, and Public Policy." In J. R. DesJardins and J. J. McCall, eds., *Contemporary Issues in Business Ethics*, fourth ed. Belmont, Calif.: Wadsworth.

United States Interagency Task Force on Product Liability. 1985. "An Overview of Product Liability Law." In J. R. DesJardins and J. J. McCall, eds., *Contemporary Issues in Business Ethics*. Belmont, Calif.: Wadsworth.

9   The Value of Rights

Leif Wenar

There are, in the broadest terms, two views of the value of the right to free speech. On the first view, speech rights are good in themselves. To respect a person's speech rights is simply to respect the inherent dignity and worth of that person as a rational and autonomous being. On the second view, speech rights are means to ends. We ascribe speech rights because doing so will help us to achieve desirable states of affairs like democratic stability, market efficiency, and greater enlightenment.

Thomas Nagel labels these two perspectives on the value of speech rights the "intrinsic" and the "instrumental" views. Nagel, following Frances Kamm and Warren Quinn, favors the intrinsic. For these authors, speech rights are not means to some further end, but are rather "a nonderivative and fundamental element of morality."[1] Indeed these authors hold this view not only for speech rights, but for *all* fundamental individual rights. All fundamental rights express the intrinsic value of each person as an end in herself, and so all fundamental rights are themselves intrinsically valuable. The rational nature of each person determines her moral status as a sovereign and inviolable being, and the dimensions of her sovereignty and inviolability are marked out by the fundamental rights that entitle her to protection against oppression and abuse.

Nagel contrasts this intrinsic view to the utilitarian thesis that fundamental rights are merely instrumentally valuable. For a (rule) utilitarian, individual rights are simply tools for increasing weal and decreasing woe. If ascribing a right will maximize utility, a utilitarian will ascribe it; if not, not. Interests, not dignity, have justificatory priority for the utilitarian, and the value of rights derives entirely from the goodness of the states of affairs in which the agglomeration of interests is largest.

The general lines of the conflict between these two views of rights are familiar. Opponents say that the instrumental view of rights cannot plausibly account for the strength of individual rights. The instrumental view must struggle to explain, for instance, why one should not violate the speech right of one person in order to prevent the violation of the speech rights of two other persons. On the other hand, as Nagel says, the challenge for the intrinsic view is that "it has proven extremely difficult to account for such a basic, individualized value such that it becomes morally intelligible."[2] The idea of individuals as ends-in-themselves is compelling, yet a cogent explanation for the intrinsic value of rights has remained elusive.

Nagel's work presents an excellent opportunity for evaluating these two views of the value of rights, and of the right to free speech in particular. For Nagel considers rights at a much finer level of detail than is normally done. Nagel is not content to show how the intrinsic view might account for "manifesto" rights like a vaguely defined right to free speech. Rather, he argues that the intrinsic view explains why it would violate individual rights to prosecute pornographers, or to prosecute Holocaust deniers; to prosecute those who make hateful statements about racial minorities, or those who make unwanted sexual proposals to others. Nagel's advocacy of the intrinsic approach at this level of specificity puts clear space between the intrinsic and the instrumental views; this will enable us to test which approach captures better the nature of our reasoning about rights.[3]

Here I will first lay out the general features of the intrinsic and the instrumental views of rights, focusing on the right to free speech. The first important conclusion here is that many more theories than utilitarianism take an instrumental approach to rights. Since several of these other theories do not share utilitarianism's problems with weak rights, the comparison between the intrinsic and instrumental views begins to look more like a real contest. We then isolate specific, uncontroversial examples where the intrinsic and the instrumental views favor different speech rights. The aim is to run controlled experiments on these examples to evaluate which view of the value of the right to free speech is more plausible. These comparisons will lead to the final conclusion that the two views do not—as is often held—characterize different types of theories of rights. Rather, the two views work at different levels of familiar rights-oriented theories.

Rights as Intrinsically Valuable

Nagel joins Quinn and Kamm in defending the view that rights are intrinsically valuable. Quinn explains the connection between a rational being and his rights in this way:[4]

A person is constituted by his body and his mind. They are parts or aspects of him. For that very reason, it is fitting that he have primary say over what may be done to them—not because such an arrangement best promotes overall human welfare, but because any arrangement that denied him that say would be a grave indignity. In giving him this authority, morality recognizes his existence as an individual with ends of his own—an independent *being*. Since that is what he is, he deserves this recognition.

Intrinsically valuable rights are *status based*, whereas utilitarian rights are *interest based*:[5]

Fundamental human rights, at least, are not concerned with protecting a person's interests, but with expressing his nature as a being of a certain sort. . . . They express the *worth of the person* rather than the *worth of what is in the interests of that person*, and it is not unimaginable that it will be harder to protect the other interests of a person just because of the worth of his person.

Because of their focus on status, theorists like Nagel and Kamm and Quinn are relatively unconcerned with the consequences of ascribing rights. Rights are ascribed because they are appropriate to persons, not because their ascription will bring about some further state of affairs. As Quinn puts it, "It is not that we think it fitting to ascribe rights because we think it is a good thing that rights be respected. Rather we think respect for rights a good thing precisely because we think people actually have them—and . . . that they have them because it is fitting that they should."[6]

Consequences are not wholly irrelevant on the intrinsic view of rights. If respecting a right would have consequences that are above some threshold level of badness, then the right no longer holds. As Nagel says, there may be "evils great enough so that one would be justified in murdering or torturing an innocent person to prevent them."[7] Yet on the status-based approach, consequences are only grounds for qualifying rights—they are not the basis for justifying rights. Below the threshold of very bad consequences, individual rights are grounded solely by the status of the individual as a sovereign and inviolable being.

Thus a status-based argument for entrenching an individual right within a legal code will not be an argument based on the good effects of doing so. A status-based argument for entrenching a legal right "is not supposed to be merely an argument for *creating* or *instituting* rights, through laws or conventions. In a sense the argument is supposed to show that the morality that includes rights is *already true*—that this is the morality we ought to follow independently of what the law is, and to which we ought to make the law conform."[8] On this view, we know which rights people have before we look at legal institutions and we make institutions fit the rights that are set by the nature of persons. This does not mean that legal institutions must be the same everywhere—as Nagel says, different institutional setups can instantiate the same entitlements. But whatever the institutional arrangements are, they must realize the same preestablished rights. When a status theorist argues that a legal right should be "ascribed" to citizens, he is arguing that the legal code should be brought into line with the fundamental rights that are known to be appropriate to sovereign and inviolable persons.[9]

An instrumental approach to rights is quite different. When an instrumental theorist recommends that a legal right should be "ascribed" to individuals, he is saying that the entrenchment of that right in the legal code will promote better results overall. Rights are not justified by the antecedent nature of the individual, but by the desirable states of affairs subsequent to their recognition.

The two views thus approach rights from opposite directions. A status-based justification begins with the nature of the rightholder and arrives immediately at the right, with only a brief nod to the negative effects that respecting the right may have on others' interests. The instrumental approach starts with the desired consequences (like maximum utility) and works backward to see which rights-ascriptions will produce those consequences.

Status theorists like Nagel and Kamm aim to rescue the right to free speech from the vagaries of instrumentalist calculation. On their view the justification for free speech must be more immediate, and deeper, than the instrumental view provides. Speech rights must flow directly from the nature of persons:[10]

The right to speak may simply be the only appropriate way to treat people with minds of their own and the capacity to use means to express [them]. . . . It fails to respect people not to give them the option of speaking. Someone may waive (or perhaps even alienate) the right in order to promote his greater interests. But to say that any given person is not entitled to the strong right to free speech is implicitly to say that no one person is so entitled noninstrumentally. That is, it is a way of saying that certain crucial features of human nature are not sufficient to generate the right in anyone. And this seems to be a mistake. [On the status-based account of rights] we might say that some rights are a response to the good (worth, importance, dignity) *of* the person and/or his sovereignty over himself, rather a response to what is good *for* the person (what is in his interests).

The sovereignty of individuals "with minds of their own" is crucial both for those who would speak and for those who would hear:[11]

The sovereignty of each person's reason over his own beliefs and values requires that he be permitted to express them, expose them to the reactions of others, and defend them against objections. It also requires that he not be protected against exposure to views or arguments that might influence him in ways that others deem pernicious, but that he have the responsibility to make up his own mind about whether to accept or reject them.

The essence of the status-based position is that speakers must be allowed to speak, and audiences to listen, out of respect for the sovereignty of each person's reason over his own beliefs and values.

Nagel's status-based position on speech has two striking features. The first is that the justification for speech rights is content neutral. The only valid reason for restricting speech, Nagel says, is when this is "clearly necessary to prevent serious harms *distinct from the expression itself.*"[12] On Nagel's account, speech rights flow immediately from the nature of persons as reasoners and not from the interests that people may have in speaking on particular topics or in listening to others speak on particular topics. Whatever the issue at stake, people must be allowed to exchange their views so that they can form their own opinions. To censor speakers because of the content of their views is, Nagel says, "an offense to us all."[13]

The second striking feature of Nagel's status-based justification for speech rights is that (short of catastrophe) it permits restrictions on speech only for the sake of limiting *direct* harms—harms inflicted by the speech act as such. Speech, for example, can be deafening if it is amplified too greatly, and speech can wake the sleeping if shouted in residential areas at night. In these cases the sovereignty of the speaker encroaches too much on the inviolability of those who would be subject to his speech, and Nagel allows that such directly harmful speech may be restricted. Nagel also grants that graphic images can be kept off the newsstands if the public would find them genuinely revolting, and that "extreme cases" of direct personal insult "can legitimately be considered a form of assault liable to legal action."[14]

What Nagel denies, however, is that speech rights may be qualified out of concern for the *indirect* effects of speech. Speech may not be restricted, that is, because it convinces one person to act in a way that is harmful to another person. Sexist or racist speech, for example, must not be restricted on the ground that it encourages the spread of false beliefs about women or minorities, which beliefs then make audiences more likely to harm women or minorities. Speech that directly harms may be restrained, but speech that convinces audiences that they have reason to harm must remain free. We must not restrict speech for the sake of preventing indirect harms, Nagel says, because we must respect each listener's capacity to decide for himself what courses of action are worth taking.[15]

An instrumental account of speech rights will of course have quite a different character. An instrumental account will likely not be content neutral, as people can have very different interests in speaking and in hearing speech on different topics. Moreover, an instrumental account will be concerned not only with the direct harms that speech can inflict on listeners, but with all the benefits and burdens of speech whether directly or indirectly produced. Indeed an instrumental account will see the entire justification of speech rights as hanging on the benefits and burdens that their ascription generates—however these benefits and burdens are produced and to whomever they accrue. John Stuart Mill, for example, favored speech rights similar in robustness to those favored by Thomas Nagel. But Mill rested his case for strong speech rights on both the direct and indirect effects of their exercise. Mill recognized that strong speech rights will engender indirect harms, but also thought that these harms will be more than compensated by the tendency of such rights to further the discovery of truth and to discourage a deadening social conformity.[16] Instrumental justifications of speech rights thus embrace facts about indirect harms and benefits that intrinsic justifications spurn.

Yet it is the expansive and contingent nature of the utilitarian calculus that has generated the general suspicion about the weakness of utilitarian rights. If Mill were really to carry through a full utilitarian defense of speech rights, it is said, he might well have to concede that the rights that he could derive were not as strong as he had hoped.[17] If the sheriff could stop the riot by framing an innocent man, would utilitarianism not require him to do so? Instrumentally justified rights have seemed to many to be simply too flimsy to be plausible, and the weakness of instrumentally justified rights has attracted many to the status-based alternative.

These complaints about the weakness of utilitarian rights may be correct. However, we should not rush to hand the laurel to the status-based approach. For utilitarianism is in fact just one of many contemporary theories that view individual rights as instrumentally justified. Moreover, as we will see, it is features specific to utilitarianism that generate the familiar worries about weak rights. Other theories that take an instrumental approach to rights do not share these features. Before comparing the intrinsic and instrumental theses in detail, we need a broader view of the conceptual terrain.

Rights as Instrumentally Valuable

Consider a utilitarian engaged in evaluating a particular right to free speech. In order to determine whether this right is a good instrument for reaching the fundamental goal of his theory, the utilitarian will need information about the impact of ascribing the right on the interests of all of the parties concerned. Figure 9.1 shows in schematized form the

	With right ascribed	Without right ascribed
Speakers	i_1	i_4
Audiences	i_2	i_5
Third parties	i_3	i_6

Figure 9.1
A matrix of interests for a right to free speech.

information that a utilitarian will require in deciding whether to ascribe such a right.

The three categories in the rows indicate the types of individuals who would be affected by the ascription of this right.[18] They are speakers; their intended audiences; and third parties (third parties are affected by speech without being its intended audience—for example, third parties are those affected by the litter and congestion caused by protest rallies, and those affected by the policies that emerge from political debates they do not take part in). The letters i_{1-6} in the matrix represent the long-term utility levels of these three types of individuals in a world in which the right is ascribed, and in a world in which the right is not ascribed. A utilitarian will ascribe this right to free speech only if the total utility in the left column is greater than the total utility in the right. .

As the example illustrates, utilitarianism views rights as *instruments for achieving an optimal distribution of interests* among all those who will be affected by the rights' ascription. For the utilitarian, an optimal distribution is simply one that maximizes the sum (or the average) of the interests of all parties. Yet seen in these general terms, utilitarianism is just one theory within a large set of theories that takes an instrumental view of rights. Many contemporary normative theories see rights as instruments for achieving an optimal distribution of interests. They differ from utilitarianism primarily in what they view an optimal distribution as being.

An egalitarian theory, for example, ranks distributions according to their degree of inequality. An egalitarian will require the same type of information as a utilitarian regarding the distributions of interests that the ascription of a particular right will engender. But because he is looking for equal instead of maximal distributions, an egalitarian will evaluate the information contained within a matrix of interests differently. An egalitarian will ascribe a right only if its ascription will lead to a less unequal distribution of interests—that is, only if the distribution in the left column is less unequal than that in the right. To take another example, a prioritarian theory resembles a pure egalitarian theory except that its specification of the optimal distribution gives extra weight to the interests of the worst off.[19]

Each of these theories sees rights as instruments for achieving an optimal distribution of interests. These theories may also of course differ in how they *measure* individual interests. They may differ, that is, as to what the variables in figure 9.1 should be taken to represent (what Sen calls their "informational bases").[20] A utilitarian theory will require a matrix in which i_{1-6} represent levels of utility. Posner's normative theory of law uses a metric of wealth instead of utility.[21] Hurka's perfectionism uses a metric of human excellence instead of utility.[22] The various contributors to the "equality of what" debate have their own interpretations of how to measure interests: capabilities (Sen), resources (Dworkin), opportunities for welfare (Arneson), opportunities for advantage (G. A. Cohen), and so on. All of these theories aim for an optimal distribution of interests, whatever they take interests to be.

Indeed, once we see the instrumental approach as including all those theories which view rights as instruments to engendering an optimal distribution of interests, we discover that the range of instrumental theories is quite wide indeed. It includes, for instance, Rawls's justice as fairness, Scanlon's contractualism, and Dworkin's normative theory of law. Rawls seeks a fair distribution of interests (represented by primary goods), where the fairness of distributions is discovered through the original position thought experiment.[23] For Scanlon's contractualism, the optimal distribution of interests is one that no one could reasonably reject. If a right produces a distribution of interests that is not reasonably rejectable then a contractualist will ascribe it, otherwise not.[24] Dworkin's theory of legal rights, like utilitarianism, seeks a maximal distribution of utility—but only after utility has been sanitized of "external" preferences.[25] Each of these theories evaluates potential rights according to whether these rights engender what is regarded to be an optimal distribution. As with utilitarianism, egalitarianism, prioritarianism, and perfectionism, these theories begin with a fundamental distributive goal and work backward to the find the rights that will produce the distributions they want.

The initial concern about instrumentally justified rights was that they would be implausibly flimsy. Yet with our wider view it now appears that weak rights are a problem for utilitarianism specifically, but not for the instrumental approach more generally. Utilitarian rights may be weak, but this is because utilitarianism's drive toward maximal distributions make it insensitive to other features of distributions—such as whether some individuals are required to make large sacrifices for the sake of others. There is no reason to think that instrumental theories that aim for equal distributions, or fair distributions, or distributions that no one could reasonably reject will also suffer from this defect. Indeed, the Rawlsian case demonstrates that an instrumental approach can require rights that are neither limited, nor marginal, nor flimsy. The parties in the original position agree to a principle of robust individual rights that "have an absolute weight with respect to reasons of public good and perfectionist values."[26] Here rights are instruments, yet they are anything but weak. They are, as in Dworkin's theory, trumps.

What distinguishes the intrinsic and the instrumental views is not the strength of their rights but the style of their justifications. Quinn, in explaining the intrinsic view, says that it is *fitting* for beings with a certain nature to have particular rights, and that the former *deserve* the latter. Kamm prefers to speak of what rights are *appropriate* to beings who are ends in themselves. An instrumental justification of rights, by contrast, will turn on facts about interests and consequences. An instrumental theory will evaluate a right by investigating what interests will be affected by that right's ascription, and how the ascription of that right will affect the distribution of those interests within a specific causal environment.[27]

The contrast in justificatory style is stark in the case of free speech. As we have seen, a status approach will ground speech rights directly in the sovereign reason of speakers and listeners with minds of their own. An instrumental inquiry into speech rights, by contrast, will be more complex. An instrumental theorist will first seek to catalog the many particular interests that will be at stake for the speech in question. For example, a speaker may have interests in influencing the votes, or the purchases, or the cultural attitudes of his fellow citizens. Audiences will have interests in greater access to information and opinions, but also interests in being protected against deceptive and offensive expression. Third parties will have interests in peace and quiet, but also in healthier political and economic systems. Moreover, an instrumental approach will be concerned not only with the content and strengths of these interests, but also in understanding how they may push in different directions in particular contexts. For example, an advertiser's desire to sell cars may conflict with audience interests in truthful expression and with third parties' preferences for fewer garish billboards. Finally, an instrumental approach will take into account what is known about the institutional context in which legal rights will be enacted. For example, an instrumental approach will take into account the facts that government officials are especially prone to use their power to silence the speech of their political opponents, and that vaguer and more punitive laws restricting speech will have a chilling effect on people's willingness to express themselves.

Hustler Magazine v. Falwell is a typical legal case in which the decision turned on instrumental reasoning. In this case the televangelist Jerry Falwell sued *Hustler* magazine for the intentional infliction of emotional distress arising out of a *Hustler* ad parody suggesting that Falwell's first sexual experience was a drunken encounter in an outhouse with his own mother. In their decision the justices of the U.S. Supreme Court acknowledged that *Hustler's* interest in ridiculing Falwell was relatively trivial, and that Falwell's emotional distress was significant. Yet the Court ruled unanimously for *Hustler*, on two main grounds. First they found that although *Hustler's* parody was itself speech of slight worth, there was no plausible criterion that juries could use reliably to separate this crude lampooning from the more general category of political cartoons and caricature. Second, they found that political cartoons and caricature were important contributions to the "robust" and "uninhibited" debate on public issues that is "essential to the common quest for truth and the vitality of society as a whole."[28]

The justices here came to their decision by weighing the conflicting interests of *Hustler*, Falwell, and the general public within the context of a particular causal environment. They kept a close eye on institutional capacities (like the ability of juries to discriminate worthless from worthwhile satire), and on indirect effects (like the indirect effects of caricature on the public good). They found that the broad societal interests in truth and social vitality outweighed the harm to public figures like Falwell. Although the justices did not explicitly commit to a particular distributive goal such as fairness or maximization, the instrumentalities of ascribing the relevant speech right were decisive in their reasoning.

Comparison of the Two Approaches

Having outlined the major differences between the intrinsic and the instrumental approaches to rights, we are now in a position to compare the two approaches in more detail. If rights have intrinsic value, we should expect our understanding of speech rights to turn on:

1. the nature of persons in relation to the speech; and
2. the direct harms that the speech may inflict on audiences.

Alternatively, if rights have instrumental value we should expect our beliefs about speech rights to be sensitive to:

3. facts about the wider causal environment in which the rights are ascribed, including the indirect effects of the rights and how institutions would enforce the rights; and
4. the benefits and burdens of the speech for speakers, audiences, and third parties.

These specific comparisons will reveal that both of the approaches have weak points. However, a repeated theme throughout the comparisons to come will be that the status approach lacks the resources to make the kinds of distinctions that we clearly do make in our reasoning about rights. The status approach, though resonant with our deep intuitions about human dignity, often appears unable to match the subtlety of our reasoning about rights. The instrumental approach, on the other hand, can capture this subtlety.

The *Hustler* case just mentioned gives an initial indication of the kind of difficulty that the status approach faces. The justices in the *Hustler* case ruled that Falwell would have to bear the emotional distress caused by *Hustler*'s speech for the sake of the broader political benefits engendered by caricature of public figures. In the Court's reasoning it was crucial that Falwell was a public figure. Had *Hustler* targeted a random private citizen instead of a famous televangelist there is no question that *Hustler* would have lost its case. Attacking private citizens in print does not after all further "robust political debate." Moreover, this seems correct—it seems appropriate to distinguish the right to caricature public figures from the right to caricature private citizens because caricaturing public figures can promote wider societal interests in a way that caricaturing private citizens cannot.

So the instrumental reasoning of the justices in this case seems apt. Yet it appears difficult for a status-based account of rights to reach the desired result. How could a status-based account distinguish the right to caricature public figures from the right to caricature private citizens? What separates public and private figures as targets of speech will not be found within the nature of persons as rational beings. Nor are public figures any more or less likely to be harmed by wounding speech. It seems that only the instrumental approach has the resources to distinguish public from private individuals as targets of speech. This gives the instrumental approach the edge in this initial comparison.[29] It also foreshadows the kind of result that we will find throughout the specific comparisons to come: the status approach often seems unable to make the kinds of distinctions that we routinely make when we reason about which specific speech rights we should ascribe.

Rights and the Content of Speech

We are looking to run controlled experiments on cases in which the intrinsic and the instrumental views give different results. We need to find cases in which the nature of persons and direct harms remain constant, but in which the causal environment and indirect effects are allowed to vary.

We focus first on the content neutrality of Nagel's status-based account of speech rights. Recall that on Nagel's view speech rights flow immediately from the nature of persons as reasoners, and not from the interests that people may have in speaking on particular topics or in listening to others speak on particular topics. We can test this feature of the status-based approach by examining whether our reasoning about speech is in fact content neutral in specific, uncontroversial cases.

Consider the following three cases, each of which asks us to compare two billboards. In each case, the question is whether we think that there are more reasons for permitting one billboard than the other, or whether we think that the two billboards should be equally permissible.

(1) Billboard 1 displays in large letters the word "F***," while Billboard 2 displays in large letters the motto "F*** George W. Bush."

(2) Billboard 3 displays a picture of a vivisected human corpse, while Billboard 4 displays the same picture with the caption: "Global Capitalism."

(3) Billboard 5 displays a photo of a platter of filth, while Billboard 6 displays the same photo with the logo of a tabloid newspaper in the background.

A status-based approach would deem the two billboards to be equally permissible in each case. This is a result of the content neutrality of the status approach. The speakers who design the billboards and the audiences who see them remain beings with minds of their own regardless of the content of the speech involved. Nor can direct harms distinguish the two bill-boards, since the two billboards are equally disgusting or equally offensive in each case. Although we do not know whether a status-based approach will endorse or deny the rights to put up any of the billboards, we do know that in each of the three examples a status-based approach will say that speakers have just as much right to erect the first billboard as the second.

An instrumental approach will distinguish the billboards in each case, because the two billboards will affect interests differently. Speakers have different interests in shocking audiences for the sake of it, and in shock-ing audiences for the sake of spreading a political message. Audiences can be benefited or harmed by exposure to unwanted political messages, especially if these messages prompt them to reconsider their stands on important issues. And third parties who never see the billboards can be affected—positively or negatively—by the debates that the billboards stimulate. A given instrumental theory may accept one billboard and reject the other in a particular case, or it may accept both or reject both in all three cases. But all instrumental theories will say that the reasons bearing on the permissibility of the two billboards differ significantly within each comparison.

These examples speak strongly, I believe, in favor of the instrumental approach. We do tend to think that there are different reasons bearing on the acceptability of the billboards in each case, because of the different interests involved. And we tend to think this even if we believe that ulti-mately neither (or both) billboards should be permitted. Our reasoning about these cases, and about similar cases we can construct, does appear to track a wide range of speaker, audience, and third-party interests rather than simply the nature of persons and direct harms.[30] The content neu-trality of the status approach appears to be a liability here, because our reasoning about speech rights in specific cases is not neutral in this way.

Rights and Indirect Effects

The second test case focuses on the second striking feature of Nagel's status-based justification of speech rights. This is Nagel's insistence that (below the threshold of catastrophe) speech rights may only be limited for the sake of preventing direct harms inflicted by speakers on audiences.

Speech may not be restrained out of concern for its indirect effects—out of concern that it will convince an audience to act in ways that are harmful to others.

The status-based account of free speech taken by Nagel and Kamm is essentially libertarianism for expression. The idea of inviolability invoked by Nagel and Kamm descends ultimately from Kant; but its immediate ancestry is within the neo-Kantian theory of Robert Nozick. In Nozick's terms, status-based speech rights are "side constraints" grounded in the dignity of the individual, which are limited only by the dignity-based rights of others against attack. Just as Nozick advocated strong property rights limited by a restriction against battery, so Nagel advocates strong speech rights qualified by a restriction against assaultive speech.[31]

The instrumental approach, on the other hand, yields what Nozick called end-state or patterned views.[32] An instrumental approach to rights will aim to bring about a particular distribution (end state, pattern) of interests, and will ascribe whatever rights are necessary to achieve this distribution. For example, Rawls's justice as fairness will ascribe property rights to individuals, but Rawls's property rights will be qualified so as to allow whatever taxation is necessary to give effect to the difference principle.

The two approaches to rights obviously disagree on the reasons for ascribing rights. What sets them apart in practical terms, however, are the reasons that they acknowledge for *restricting* rights. A status-based approach may restrict a right if A's exercise of that right would directly harm B. These are cases where the sovereignty of A—for example, in amplifying his speech—intrudes too far on the inviolability of B—for example, by having his eardrums shattered. An instrumental approach may of course also restrict a right out of concern for direct harms, because direct harms damage audiences' interests. Yet an instrumental approach may in addition restrict a right if its exercise, though innocuous on any particular occasion, leads to a distribution of interests that is objectionable on other grounds. This disagreement over the relevance of patterns defined one dimension of the debate over Nozick's Wilt Chamberlain example. In this example, Nozick argued against restricting property rights by stressing the harmless freedom exercised in each act of property transfer. Nozick's critics objected that although any given transfer of strong property rights may be free, the patterns of holdings generated by the exercise of such rights will eventually generate unfairness, especially for the descendents of current transferors.[33] Insofar as strong property rights engender unfair patterns, an instrumental view may require that strong property rights be qualified.

Speech is more difficult territory than property for distinguishing the intrinsic and instrumental views. This is because the indirect effects of strong speech rights are mostly appealing. Strong speech rights generate healthier democratic institutions, spur cultural progress, and create an environment conducive to Millian flourishing of the individual. The desirability of the patterns engendered by the exercise of strong speech rights will push an instrumental approach toward the same strong rights favored by a status-based approach.

Where the two approaches do diverge is over cases of indirect harms: cases where A's speech convinces B to hold beliefs that make it more likely that B will harm C. As mentioned above Nagel does not wish to restrict sexist or racist expression, even when this expression could convince audiences that women or minorities are inferior and so make it more likely that audiences will go on to harm minorities or women. Pornography is a specific case of this sort. The status-based and the instrumental approaches agree that the right to promulgate pornography can be qualified to prevent direct harms, such as the harm of being confronted with revolting images on newsstands. The controversy concerns whether the right to promulgate pornography can also be qualified for the sake of limiting indirect harms: harms inflicted by pornography consumers on third parties.

One familiar instrumental argument concerning pornography runs as follows. We can predict that most pornography will portray women as subordinate to men, that the consumption of this pornography will lead to a greater prevalence of negative attitudes toward women, and that these attitudes will lead to greater discrimination against women, or even to greater risks of physical attacks against women. The controversy over this instrumental argument tends to revolve around the empirical questions— whether consumption of pornography does in fact lead to greater incidence of discrimination and attack. Some studies say yes, others say that the thesis is not proven.[34]

However, our question is not empirical but philosophical. We need to judge not the *truth* but the *relevance* of the empirical claims being made. Nagel's status-based approach rules the empirical questions out of court. On Nagel's view speech may be restricted to prevent speakers from harming audiences directly, but not to protect third parties against what audiences may be more inclined to do after they hear the speech. Only direct effects are relevant. On an instrumental view, however, the indirect effects of speech are crucial for deciding whether speech rights should be qualified. Our philosophical question is whether harmful indirect effects would be grounds for restricting the right to promulgate pornography *were the causal links conclusively established.* If one believes that there would be a reason to limit speech rights could it be proved beyond doubt that promulgating pornography leads to significantly greater risks of harm to women, then one is taking an instrumental approach to rights.

A recent Supreme Court case allows us to focus the question even more tightly. In *Ashcroft v. Free Speech Coalition* the Court considered the permissibility of "virtual" child pornography: that is, of obscene materials depicting totally "computer-generated" minors. What is helpful about considering virtual child pornography is that it eliminates the distracting question of whether real children are injured or coerced in the making of the pornography—in virtual porn, they are not. The case thus allows us to isolate the role of indirect effects in our reasoning about speech. Our question is: if it could be established beyond doubt that consumption of virtual child pornography makes a significant number of adults much more likely to abuse children sexually, would that in itself be a reason to restrict the promulgation of virtual child pornography? If one answers affirmatively, then one is favoring an instrumental view of rights on this issue.[35]

I believe that we do consider these kinds of indirect effects to be relevant. We do believe that harms to women are a relevant consideration when we reason about the permissibility of promulgating pornography. We do believe that harms to children are a relevant consideration when we reason about whether to restrict the dissemination of virtual child pornography. Since only the instrumental approach has the resources to explain why we take indirect harms into account, the instrumental approach appears to be stronger in these cases.

Rights and Institutions

The third comparison examines the relevance of the larger causal environment to our reasoning about rights. The test case here will touch on content neutrality and indirect harms, but it will focus primarily on the divergence between the two approaches concerning the effects of entrenching rights in the law. Recall that on Nagel's status view, we know that individuals have strong rights before we look at legal institutions, and our task is to make institutions fit the rights that are set by the nature of persons. On an instrumental approach, by contrast, the touchstones for whether to entrench a right in the law are the effects of entrenching the right on people's interests. The status-based approach, unlike the instrumental approach, does not allow facts about the wider effects of institutionalizing a right to affect the shape of the right that should be codified.

So far in our comparisons, the intrinsic view of rights has appeared to be implausibly narrow. I believe that this trend continues here. Our reasoning about legal rights does in fact respond to facts about political institutions and political power. One area where this is apparent is in how we treat the rights to political and to commercial speech.

It is an interesting and important part of our settled understanding of the legal right to free speech that speakers in the political arena should remain legally free to lie, but that speakers in the marketplace should face a legal ban on making knowingly false statements. Campaigning politicians, for example, may intentionally misrepresent their records with no fear of legal prosecution. Yet advertisers who intentionally misrepresent their products should find themselves in the dock.

Why do we draw this distinction between political and commercial speech? A status approach to speech rights will have difficulty explaining the distinction. The major handicap of a status approach is that it has disabled itself from tying the permissibility of speech to the content of speech (political vs. commercial). Nor is there any hope of making the distinction with the "direct harm" qualification, since there is no reason to think that false commercial speech will be any more directly harmful (ear-shattering, insulting, etc.) than false political speech. Indeed, the political–commercial distinction will elude a status approach even if we loosen up considerably on the kinds of harms that it can count as reasons to restrict speech. On the one hand, the harms of false commercial speech are usually trivial—as when a corporation lies about which soft drink is best selling. On the other hand, false speech in the political realm can be quite damaging both emotionally and to reputation. (Consider, for instance, the false statements made by Senator McCarthy, and by either Clarence Thomas or Anita Hill.) Moreover, our laws hold that virtually no false political speech should be legally prosecutable, no matter how harmful—yet all false commercial speech should be legally prosecutable, no matter how harmless. Any simple harm-based qualification to the general right to free speech will draw the line in the wrong place.

An instrumental approach, by contrast, presents clear rationales for distinguishing between false political and false commercial speech. An instrumental approach will acknowledge that false political speech can harm. Yet it will also register that democratic processes are less stable where political speech can be prosecuted on the ground that it is false. This is partly because government officials, even well-intentioned ones, have a tendency to use their power to prosecute the political speech of their opponents. A right to prosecute political speech deemed by officials to be untruthful would encourage this tendency, and the mere possibility of prosecution would have a chilling effect on the potential speech of the government's opponents.[36] Moreover, it is difficult to imagine a workable constitutional design wherein officials from one branch of government have the right to prosecute the allegedly false political statements of officials from another branch in any but the most extraordinary circumstances. A right permitting false political speech therefore has important stabilizing influences in a democratic system. It is not hard to see why such a right would be endorsed by instrumental theories ranging from utilitarianism to justice as fairness.

The consequences of ascribing a right permitting false commercial speech, however, would be quite different. False advertising has obvious costs, since it can confuse and even endanger those who rely on it when making purchases. Perhaps more significantly, false commercial speech can create an atmosphere of "buyer beware" that dampens general economic activity.[37] Yet in contrast to the political case, officials can be given the power to weed out false commercial speech without unduly endangering the larger system. Government officials have less incentive to abuse the power to prosecute false commercial speech than they do to prosecute false political speech, and for this reason commercial speech is less likely to be chilled by this power. Moreover, since "the truth of commercial speech . . . may be more easily verifiable by its disseminator than, let us say, news reporting or political commentary . . . and since advertising is the *sine qua non* of commercial profits, there is little likelihood of its being chilled by proper regulation and forgone entirely."[38]

Our understanding of the relative benefits and dangers of empowering officials to regulate political and commercial speech is, I take it, distilled from the history of struggles over speech rights in liberal societies. All instrumental views will point to these benefits and dangers when explaining why they ascribe broader rights to political than to commercial speakers.[39] A status-based approach, on the other hand, has neither the space to acknowledge these facts about official power nor the resources to reach the relevant distinctions by another route. This looks to be a significant deficiency in the status approach. By insisting on the preinstitutional purity of speech rights, the status approach disables itself from responding to concerns about institutions and power that are integral to our reasoning about rights.

Status-Based Strategies of Response

Although status-based rights may be stronger than utilitarian rights, our test cases have made status-based reasoning look implausibly rigid and underresourced when compared to instrumental reasoning more broadly understood. It is of course open to the status approach to retreat from rights at Nagel's level of specificity, and to claim that status explains only why an abstract right to free speech must be ascribed. Status, it might be said, justifies the broad "manifesto" right to free speech but must bow to instrumental considerations when it comes to specifics. Nagel would strongly resist this retreat, and one can see why. For instrumental views like utilitarianism and justice as fairness can easily account for the importance of a manifesto right to free speech. The status-based approach becomes distinct as a competitor to the instrumental approach only when it comes to cases—and indeed it is at this level that Nagel advertised his approach as superior. This is not, however, what we have found.

An alternative strategy for a status approach would be to try to generate resources that would allow it to mimic the kinds of instrumental reasoning that we have found in the test cases. A status approach might try, that is, to elaborate the theory of the nature of persons and the nature of speech so as to be able to distinguish public figures from private citizens, so as to take into account indirect harms to children, so as to distinguish political from commercial speech, and so on. A status theorist who opts for this strategy will have a lot of work to do, and previous attempts to make this strategy work have not proved successful.[40] Moreover, the more a status approach elaborates a theory of the nature of persons so as to get the right results, the less likely it is that such a theory will be acceptable as a basis for public policy in a pluralistic liberal society.[41]

Furthermore, this "mimicking" strategy is inherently risky, because it threatens the status-based approach as a distinct enterprise. The status-based approach to rights is significant because the patterns of reasoning it recommends are so dissimilar to those recommended by an instrumental approach—indeed, this dissimilarity is one of the main advantages cited by Nagel, Kamm, and Quinn. A revised status-based approach that tried to mimic instrumental reasoning would lose this distinctiveness. A revised status approach would be in danger of appearing as merely a metaphysical echo of the fact that certain rights have proved themselves very effective instruments for promoting what are obviously important human interests. It would appear merely to be retelling the instrumental story in a different language, and in the less illuminating language of "fittingness" and "appropriateness" at that.

A more promising strategy of reply for the intrinsic view would be to stick to its guns and counterattack. A status theorist might argue that the instrumental view promises more than it can deliver, and this in two ways. First, the instrumental approach maintains that we must look to the effects of ascribing rights—but do we really have enough information about what those effects are to ascribe rights with confidence? Do we really, for example, know what the effects would be of enacting laws that treat public figures and private individuals the same as targets of satire? If we do not, then we cannot complete an instrumental justification for these speech rights with any confidence. Second, a defender of the intrinsic approach might object that the instrumental emphasis on weighing the interests of all parties affected by the ascription of a right is more a liability than an advantage. For weighing individual interests against each other requires a defensible scheme for making interpersonal comparisons of interests. And it has proved rather difficult, the status theorist might say, to explain how such a scheme of interpersonal comparison of interests might work.

This second challenge to the instrumental approach is more serious than the first. The best that a status theorist could hope from the first challenge is to elicit the concession that although we do reason about rights instrumentally, we often do so on the basis of incomplete evidence about consequences. This is a concession that any honest proponent of an instrumental approach should be willing to make, yet it does not show the superiority of the intrinsic approach.

The status theorist's second challenge is more serious because all instrumental approaches do face the challenge of interpersonal comparisons. Yet the status theorist cannot use this as an objection to the instrumental approach, because the status-based approach faces an exact analogue of this challenge, as well as a serious related problem that the instrumental approach does not share.

It is true that an instrumental approach will have to explain why we should think, for example, that in a particular case the interests of speakers in speaking are more weighty than the interests of audiences who might be adversely affected by this speech. Yet an intrinsic approach faces an exactly analogous problem of explaining why the sovereignty of the speaker should outweigh the inviolability of the audience in such a case. When the irresistible force of sovereignty meets the immovable object of inviolability, something's got to give—but which? For example, Nagel says that a man working in an office must have the right to express his sexual desires to an unwilling female coworker, even if he expresses himself in an offensive way. Nagel says that the female coworker's inviolability must yield here because "adults should be able to take care of themselves."[42] The question is how confident a status theorist can be that the line should be drawn exactly there, and in fact whether the status theorist can show that his answer to this question does not simply reflect an implicit interpersonal comparison of interests at stake in this kind of speech.

Moreover, we must not forget that the status approach does not wholly ignore interests and the consequences of ascribing rights. Recall that Nagel concedes that if respecting a right would have consequences that are above some threshold level of badness, then the right no longer holds. It is permissible to murder or torture an innocent person to avert a catastrophe, or to restrict speech to do so. This "threshold" qualification allows the intrinsic approach to avoid an implausible absolutism about rights. Yet it also requires the intrinsic approach to explain how the *status* of one person is to be weighed against the *interests* of many others. This kind of interpersonal comparison is a comparison not within the discrete categories of status or of interests, but a comparison across these two philosophically distant categories. It will be at least as difficult for the status theorist to explain such transcategorical trade-offs between status and interests as it will be for an instrumental theorist to weigh interests against each other.

Reconciliation

We have found the instrumental thesis about the value of rights to be generally more satisfactory than the intrinsic thesis. Although the status-based approach begins with an attractive picture of human dignity, it has not proved to be sensitive to the factors that guide our reasoning about specific rights like rights to free speech. Nor have the status-based strategies for responding to these difficulties appeared promising.

Our reasoning about specific rights does, I believe, ordinarily involve evaluating how effective the rights are as instruments for balancing the competing interests of different parties. Some evidence for this can be seen simply in the number of theorists who have converged on instrumental accounts of rights despite the major differences in their broader philosophical approaches.[43] Indeed so many prominent theories of rights take an instrumental approach that it is tempting to dismiss status-based accounts as just a transcendentalized reflection of the fact that certain rights have proved themselves very effective instruments for distributing human good in desirable ways. The importance of these rights may be so obvious to us that their justification may wrongly appear to require no more than the statement that it is fitting to ascribe them. This would account for Nagel's worry, quoted above, that it has proved "extremely difficult" to explain the values that are meant to ground the intrinsic view of rights.

Yet such a dismissal of the intrinsic view would be mistaken. Status-based theories draw their plausibility from insights it would be rash to ignore. In fact, in two important ways the insights of the status-based approach are critical *within* familiar theories of rights that take an instrumental approach. The first way is more practical, the second more profound.

First, there are real interests that correspond to the status-based concepts of status, sovereignty, and inviolability. Any plausible instrumental approach must take these interests into account. For example, the status-based emphasis on sovereignty over one's own life is an important reminder that freedoms and opportunities will be a crucial element in the instrumental justification of rights like speech rights. Theories that take an instrumental approach to rights must acknowledge that we have interests in having the freedom to make choices, and interests in having opportunities to choose. They must therefore incorporate "translations" of the status-based concept of sovereignty into their metrics of interests. People have interests in opportunities for speaking regardless of whether they speak or not. Moreover, theories that take an instrumental approach to rights must also acknowledge that we have "dignitary" interests in our standing relative to others. Instrumental theories must therefore translate the concept of status itself into their categories of human interests. We have interests in being seen as equal in our capacities to speak, for instance, even if we do not exercise these capacities in any significant way.

To a certain extent theories taking an instrumental approach have already incorporated translations of these status-based concepts. Scanlon acknowledges that being in poor circumstances for making choices is a ground for reasonable rejection; Cohen and Arneson have based their egalitarian theories on opportunities; and Rawls's index of primary goods recognizes that citizens have dignitary interests in the social bases of self-respect. By contrast, utilitarian theories have been slow to recognize that these kinds of interests must be part of any sensible metric of utility. This has diminished the plausibility of the utilitarian approach.[44]

The second way in which status-based insights are crucial within theories taking an instrumental approach is more profound. For all of the familiar instrumental theories of rights rest at the deepest level on status-based rights. Consider, for example, the basic right in Dworkin's theory to equal concern and respect. Or consider the fundamental right in justice as fairness to be treated fairly by the institutions of society as a free and equal citizen. Or consider the basic right in Scanlon's contractualism to be treated in accordance with rules that no one can reasonably reject. Unlike the more particular rights to speech, bodily integrity, and so on, instrumental theories cannot explain these foundational rights as instruments for achieving their optimal distributions. Rather, these most fundamental rights are critical for *defining* what each instrumental theory regards as an optimal distribution. Each of these foundational rights presents a certain vision of the moral relation—of the basic status of individuals with respect to each other. Each foundational right thus defines the end toward which all of the other rights in the theory are instruments.[45]

At one point in defending his intrinsic view Nagel says, "I believe that it is most accurate to think of rights as an aspect of *status*—part of what is involved in being a member of the moral community."[46] For the most fundamental rights in familiar theories of rights, this characterization is correct. Status-based rights define the kinds of moral communities that more specific rights are instruments toward achieving. It is at the deepest level of instrumental theories that status-based rights have their home.

Acknowledgments

I am grateful to a great many people for suggestions, and for written comments to David Enoch, Rob Hopkins, Simon Keller, Glen Newey, Thomas Pogge, Jonathan Riley, Seana Shiffrin, Hillel Steiner, and Joan Tronto. The article was written during a year supported by a Laurance S. Rockefeller Fellowship from the Center for Human Values at Princeton University.

Notes

1. Nagel 2002, p. 87; see Kamm 1992, 1995, 2002, and Quinn 1993, pp. 149–174. Nagel remarks in passing that the status and instrumental approaches to rights may be "perhaps complementary," and that the instrumental justification of the right to expression is "very strong" but "not the whole story" (2002, pp. 34, 42). Yet he also presents an argument that aims to show that the status-based approach "is more likely to be true" than the instrumental approach. Because Nagel says he "favor[s]" the status-based over the instrumental approach (ibid., p. 34), and because all of his arguments champion the status-based approach, I am here treating Nagel as a status-based theorist. However, Nagel's passing remarks may indicate that a more complex position lies behind his arguments.

2. Nagel 2002, p. 34.

3. The status-based approach cannot claim to be a completely general account of rights, but only an account of fundamental rights. Many legal rights, for instance, define institutional roles and procedural rules: e.g., a traffic warden's right to issue tickets, or one corporation's right to sue another for breach of contract. No one would think to justify these kinds of rights by appealing to the intrinsic worth of the rightholders; these rights must be instrumentally justified.

4. Quinn 1993, p. 170.

5. Kamm 2002, pp. 508–509.

6. Quinn 1993, p. 173.

7. Nagel 2002, p. 36.

8. Ibid., p. 39; see also p. 36.

9. Ibid., pp. 39–41.

10. Kamm 2002, pp. 486–487. (The word "of" is not italicized in the printed text; comparison with a prepublication manuscript, and the sense of the passage, show this to be a typographical error.)

11. Nagel 2002, p. 43.

12. Ibid., emphasis added.

13. Ibid., p. 44.

14. Ibid., p. 45.

15. Ibid., pp. 43–45.

16. Jeremy Waldron highlights this aspect of *On Liberty* in "Mill and the Value of Moral Distress," found in Waldron 1993, pp. 115–133.

17. Hart 1982, pp. 96–98.

18. My discussions of the instrumental approach to free speech follow Scanlon (1979) and Cohen (1993).

19. Parfit 1991.

20. Sen 1999, pp. 54–58.

21. Posner 1990.

22. Hurka 1993.

23. Rawls 1971.

24. Scanlon 1998.

25. Dworkin's theory requires the use of two matrices of advantage for evaluating a potential right, one including external preferences and the other excluding them. To simplify: if in the matrix including external preferences there is more utility in the world where the right does not exist, and if in the matrix excluding external preferences there is more utility in the world where the right does exist, then Dworkin's theory will say that the right should be ascribed. See Dworkin 1984, pp. 153–167.

26. Rawls 1993, p. 294. The instrumentality of rights within justice as fairness is slightly obscured by rights being both what the parties in the original position select (i.e., rights are part of the first principle of justice) and a measure of individual interests (i.e., rights are part of the index of primary goods). This makes it appear as if rights are ascribed because they are instrumental to producing a distribution of

rights. However, Rawls includes rights in the index of primary goods only because rights enable citizens to further their most basic interests in developing and exercising their two moral powers. (To take one example, "The role of [the right to personal property] is to allow a sufficient material basis for a sense of personal independence and self-respect, both of which are essential for the development and exercise of the two moral powers" [ibid., p. 298].) Rights in justice as fairness are thus ascribed because they are instrumental to producing a distribution of opportunities for citizens to further their fundamental interests. Nagel (2002) thus errs in attempting to characterize justice as fairness as advancing an intrinsic view of rights (p. 90).

27. Are theories that take an instrumental approach "consequentialist" theories? One reason this question is difficult is the absence of a standard definition for the term "consequentialist." Many (though not all) instrumental theories fit within Hooker's characterization: "A theory is consequentialist if and only if it assesses acts and/or rules . . . in terms solely of the production of agent-neutral value" (2000, p. 110). On the other hand, most instrumental approaches are not captured by Scheffler's remark that, "One thing [that all consequentialist theories share] is a very simple and seductive idea: namely, that so far as morality is concerned, what people ought to do is to minimize evil and maximize good, to try, in other words, to make the world as good a place as possible" (1988, p. 1). Given the absence of a standard definition, we might borrow a phrase from Pogge and say that the instrumental approach is "broadly consequentialist." See Pogge 1989, pp. 36–47, and 1995, p. 244.

28. *Hustler Magazine v. Falwell.* 485 U.S. 46 (1988, pp. 55, 53, 51). Cohen discusses *Falwell* in his 1993, pp. 244–255.

29. It not clear whether Nagel (2002) would want to allow this example, nor whether he could bar it. On the one hand, he remarks that wounding speech should be permitted if this involves "criticism of public actors" (p. 45). On the other hand, it is hard to see how a purely status-based approach could make good on this exception. On the difficulties of status-based approaches to speech in making these kinds of distinctions, see Cohen 1993, p. 221.

30. On this point see also the Supreme Court's decision in *Cohen v. California*, overturning the 1968 conviction of a young man who wore in the Los Angeles County Courthouse a jacket bearing the motto "F*** the Draft."

31. Nozick, like Nagel, also allows that rights might be excusably infringed to avert "catastrophic moral horror." So Nozick, like Nagel, allows that there is some threshold of bad consequences above which status-based rights need not be respected. (Nozick 1974, p. 30).

32. Nozick 1974, pp. 153–159.

33. Nozick 1974, pp. 160–164. Nagel's critique of Nozick is his 1981.

34. For differing views on the empirical evidence, see the essays in part II of Zillman and Bryant 1989, Segal 1990, and Strossen 1995.

35. Most of the Court's decision in *Ashcroft* concerns unrelated issues of overbreadth of the statute involved. When the Court does discuss indirect effects, its reasoning appears to countenance only restrictions for speech that fulfill the *Brandenburg* criterion of inciting "imminent lawless action." However, the line of precedents it cites stretching back through *Stanley v. Georgia* leaves open the question of whether conclusive evidence of non-"imminent" indirect effects would be considered in later cases.

36. As the Supreme Court wrote in *NY Times Co. v. Sullivan*: "A rule compelling the critic of official conduct to guarantee the truth of all his factual assertions—and to do so on pain of libel judgments virtually unlimited in amount—leads to a comparable 'self-censorship.'. . . Under such a rule, would-be critics of official conduct may be deterred from voicing their criticism, even though it is believed to be true and even though it is in fact true, because of doubt whether it can be proved in court or fear of the expense of having to do so. They tend to make only statements which 'steer far wide of the unlawful zone.' The rule thus dampens the vigor and limits the variety of public debate" (1964, p. 279).

37. J. W. Burns correctly argues that the principal federal law on false advertising (the Lanham act) makes little sense as a protection for consumers harmed by false or misleading commercial speech. The act, for example, only gives competitors of the advertiser—not consumers—legal standing to sue. Moreover, it often allows competitors to win a case without showing consumer injury. Further, as Burns says, the act must be grossly inefficient if its purpose is protection from unfair competition, since it encourages expensive litigation about trivial advertising claims that have little possible competitive impact. See Burns 1999. What Burns does not consider is that the act may be a rather effective means toward a third goal: engendering consumer confidence by maintaining an environment in which advertisers are loathe to make false or misleading statements.

38. Justice Blackmun writing for the majority in *Virginia State Board of Pharmacy v. Virginia Citizens Consumer Counsel*, p. 774, n. 24. Those who have disagreed with the Court in *Virginia State Board* about the relative objectivity and durability of commercial speech have questioned the truth of these empirical theses, not the relevance of the empirical questions to the issue of commercial speech. See especially Kozinski and Banner 1990.

39. Rawls, for instance, recommends regulating "dangerous" political and commercial speech differently, because of facts about state power. Officials may be allowed, he says, to penalize commercial speech for the sake of protecting consumers and keeping markets efficient. Yet the price of giving officials power over political

speech is too great. "The history of the use by governments of the crime of seditious libel to suppress criticism and dissent and to maintain their power demonstrates the great significance of this particular liberty to any fully adequate scheme of basic liberties. So long as this crime exists the public press and free discussion cannot play their role in informing the electorate. And, plainly, to allow the crime of seditious libel would undermine the wider possibilities of self-government and the several liberties required for its protection. . . . [The crime of seditious libel] has been tried, so to speak, by the court of history and found wanting" (Rawls 1993, pp. 364, 343).

40. See here especially Scanlon's insightful criticisms of Meiklejohn's theory, and of his own earlier status-based theory, in Scanlon 1979, pp. 528–537. Another example of an unsuccessful attempt to give a more flexible status-based account of speech is Strauss 1991. Strauss's "persuasion principle" states that government may not restrict speech on the grounds that it fears that people will be persuaded by it. By this principle, false advertising is not protected speech, because "false statements of fact do not appeal to reason, their use does not constitute persuasion" (1991, p. 339). Yet Strauss does not then explain his position (p. 338) that all political speech, including false political speech, should be protected. Examples of unsuccessful status-based principles like Strauss's could be multiplied.

41. For instance, Nagel offers some psychological theorizing to support his views on why sexual expression should remain relatively uninhibited by legal restrictions: "What about the range of cases in which sexual expression offends or does harm, from unorthodox sexual practices to private consumption of pornography to the display of nude photos in the workplace to sexual harassment? Here my views are determined by a strong conviction of the personal importance and great variety of sexual feeling and sexual fantasy and of their expression. Sex is the source of the most intense pleasure of which humans are capable and one of the few sources of human ecstasy. It is also the realm of adult life in which the defining and inhibiting structures of civilization are permitted to dissolve and our deepest presocial, animal, and infantile natures can be fully released and expressed, offering a form of physical and emotional completion that is not available elsewhere. The case for toleration and an area of protected privacy in this domain is exceptionally strong" (Nagel 2002, p. 46). Even if Nagel's observations about human psychology are correct, they seem an unlikely foundation for a publicly acceptable justification of the law of free speech.

42. Ibid., p. 51.

43. For example, Mill, Rawls, Scanlon, Parfit, Dworkin, Sen, Posner, G. A. Cohen, Arneson, Hurka, and also Hare, Hayek, Harsanyi, and many others.

44. Sen has repeatedly made this kind of criticism, and has worked to develop consequentialism into a more subtle and capacious view. See most recently Sen 2000.

45. The only instrumental theory that seems to be an exception to this is a simple (and I believe implausible) teleological utilitarianism, where the imperative to maximize utility is grounded in the bare rationality of acting so as to produce more valuable states of affairs.

46. Nagel 2002, p. 33.

References

Ashcroft v. Free Speech Coalition. 535 U.S. 234 (2002).

Brandenburg v. Ohio. 395 U.S. 444 (1969).

Burns, J. 1999. "Confused Jurisprudence: False Advertising under the Lanham Act." *Boston University Law Review* 79: 807–888.

Cohen, J. 1993. "Freedom of Expression." *Philosophy and Public Affairs* 22: 207–263.

Cohen v. California. 403 US 15 (1971).

Dworkin, R. 1984. "Rights As Trumps." In J. Waldron, ed., *Theories of Rights*. Oxford: Oxford University Press.

Hart, H. 1982. *Essays on Bentham*. Oxford: Clarendon Press.

Hooker, B. 2000. *Ideal Code, Real World*. Oxford: Oxford University Press.

Hurka, T. 1993. *Perfectionism*. Oxford: Oxford University Press.

Hustler Magazine v. Falwell. 485 U.S. 46 (1988).

Kamm, F. 1992. "Non-Consequentialism, the Person as an End-in-Itself, and the Significance of Status." *Philosophy and Public Affairs* 21: 381–389.

———. 1995. *Morality, Mortality*, vol. 2. New York: Oxford University Press.

———. 2002. "Rights." In J. Coleman and S. Shapiro, eds., *The Oxford Handbook of Jurisprudence and Philosophy of Law*. Oxford: Oxford University Press.

Kozinski, A. and Banner, S. 1990. "Who's Afraid of Commercial Speech?" *Virginia Law Review* 76: 627–653.

Mill, J. S. 1989. *On Liberty and Other Writings*. Cambridge: Cambridge University Press.

Nagel, T. 1981. "Libertarianism without Foundations." In J. Paul, ed., *Reading Nozick*. Totowa, N.J.: Rowman and Littlefield.

———. 2002. *Concealment and Exposure*. Oxford: Oxford University Press.

NY Times Co. v. Sullivan, 376 U.S. 254 (1964).

Nozick, R. 1974. *Anarchy, State, and Utopia*. New York: Basic Books.

Parfit, D. 1991. "Equality or Priority?" *The Lindley Lecture*. Lawrence, Kans.: Department of Philosophy, University of Kansas.

Pogge, T. 1989. *Realizing Rawls*. Ithaca, N.Y.: Cornell University Press.

———. 1995. "Three Problems with Contractarian-Consequentialist Ways of Assessing Social Institutions." *Social Philosophy and Policy* 12: 241–266.

Posner, R. 1990. *The Economics of Justice*. Cambridge, Mass.: Harvard University Press.

Quinn, W. 1993. *Morality and Action*. Cambridge: Cambridge University Press.

Rawls, J. 1971. *A Theory of Justice*. Cambridge, Mass.: Harvard University Press.

———. 1993. *Political Liberalism*. New York: Columbia University Press.

Scanlon, T. 1979. "Freedom of Expression and Categories of Expression." *University of Pittsburgh Law Review* 40: 519–550.

———. 1998. *What We Owe to Each Other*. Cambridge, Mass.: Harvard University Press.

Scheffler, S. 1988. *Consequentialism and Its Critics*. Oxford: Oxford University Press.

Segal, L. 1990. "Pornography and Violence: What the 'Experts' Really Say." *Feminist Review* 36: 29–41.

Sen, A. 1999. *Development As Freedom*. Oxford: Oxford University Press.

———. 2000. "Consequential Evaluation and Practical Reason." *Journal of Philosophy* 97: 477–502.

Stanley v. Georgia, 394 U.S. 557 (1969).

Strauss, D. 1991. "Persuasion, Autonomy, and Freedom of Expression." *Columbia Law Review* 31: 334–371.

Strossen, N. 1995. *Defending Pornography*. New York: Anchor Books.

Virginia State Board of Pharmacy v. Virginia Citizens Consumer Counsel, 425 U.S. 748 (1976).

Waldron, J. 1993. *Liberal Rights*. Cambridge: Cambridge University Press.

Zillman, D. and Bryant, J. 1989. *Pornography: Research Advances and Policy Considerations*. Hillsdale, N.J.: Lawrence Erlbaum.

Part II

10   Introduction: Wittgenstein and Legal Theory

Douglas Lind

Legal theory in the United States has in recent years increasingly emphasized questions of interpretive methodology and meaning. This so-called
interpretive turn has stimulated, quite understandably, interest among
legal scholars in the later philosophy of Ludwig Wittgenstein. Yet the use
and application that legal thinkers have given Wittgenstein's work is anything but uniform and of one mind. The spring 2002 Inland Northwest
Philosophy Conference highlighted the diversity and breadth of the
Wittgensteinian influence on legal thought by bringing together several of
the leading legal scholars in this area. Presenters included Brian Bix of the
University of Minnesota; Philip Bobbitt, University of Texas at Austin;
Dennis Patterson, Rutgers University School of Law; and Anthony Sebok,
Brooklyn Law School. All but Professor Bobbitt's essay are reprinted here.

The first essay in this section, Brian Bix's "Cautions and Caveats for the
Application of Wittgenstein to Legal Theory" offers some cautionary points
and remarks about the relevance of Wittgenstein's work for legal theory.
Bix raises four specific concerns. First, he charges that some legal theorists
rely too casually on Wittgenstein, allowing mere (and fallacious) reference
to Wittgenstein's "authority" to stand in for careful explication and
rational argument. Second, he attributes to other theorists uncritical
acceptance of certain Wittgensteinian themes, for example, rule following,
without sufficient consideration of whether those themes, developed by
Wittgenstein in reference to matters quite distant from law, bear directly
on the legal context. Third, he admonishes yet others to avoid co-opting
Wittgenstein's "language game" motif toward the end of prescribing
behavior or participants within the practice of law, rather than using that
motif only to restrict philosophical speculation about language games (or
practices) such as law that are autonomous and distinct from philosophy.

Fourth and finally, Bix laments all use of Wittgenstein to justify skeptical theories of law. Although his statement of these concerns stems from his own skepticism about the usefulness of Wittgenstein for legal theory, Bix does not argue against Wittgenstein's relevance, but insists quite rightly on careful and reflective application of his work to legal theory.

In "Prolegomenon to Any Future Legal Theory," Dennis Patterson discusses the problem of semantic content in the context of law. How is it, he asks, that legal concepts come to have the content they have, rather than some other content? The philosophical challenge posed by this question is to devise a middle position, a jurisprudence that can account for the development of legal meaning somewhere between the rigid and unavailing extremes of objectivism and subjectivism. For Patterson, the later philosophy of Wittgenstein offers one promising avenue for crafting such a middle jurisprudence. Most enlightening, he suggests, is Wittgenstein's idea that one's understanding of a rule or concept is often best exhibited by mastery of the technique for its application. Patterson finds this idea illuminating, but incomplete. He wants to fill it in with the metaphor of three concentric circles, each depicting a level of ability and understanding in legal practice. As we move outward with the circles, the level of mastery in legal practice increases. For Patterson, the outermost circle represents a level of mastery where one not only knows the meaning or content of a legal concept, but understands to some extent its doctrinal explanation. This notion of mastery—linking the idea of meaning with explanation—is key, Patterson concludes, and constitutes a position attainable not only through Wittgensteinian analysis, but by way of pragmatic inquiry, as represented by the recent work of Jules Coleman.

Anthony Sebok's essay, "Legal Process and the Practices of Principle," draws comparisons between Wittgensteinian analysis, a certain form of legal process argument, and the legal positivism of H. L. A. Hart. Sebok calls to mind Harry Wellington's important 1973 essay, "Common Law Rules and Constitutional Double Standards: Some Notes on Adjudication," where Wellington advanced the idea that common law adjudication provides the central explanatory model for understanding all of American law. Of interest to Sebok is Wellington's extensive reliance on Stanley Cavell's *Must We Mean What We Say*, a work in turn heavily influenced by Wittgenstein. Wellington adopted a Cavell–Wittgensteinian stance as the grounding for the moral conventionalism that was central to his legal process jurisprudence. The significance of this stance to Sebok is how it aligns Wellington's approach with H. L. A. Hart's dependence on Wittgenstein in conceiving the rule of recognition in *The Concept of Law*. Though Wellington was principally concerned with the role of normative commitment in adjudication, whereas Hart sought to explain the relationship between normativity and validity, Sebok notes their strong methodological similarities. The jurisprudences adopted by each were profoundly normative, yet neither conceived of law or adjudication as merely structures of moral reasoning. Rather, both undergirded their jurisprudences with a Wittgensteinian conception of rule following as a critical and social practice. In this shared dependence on Wittgenstein, Sebok maintains, Hart's positivism and Wellington's legal process jurisprudence rest on methodological common ground.

The relevance of Wittgenstein to legal theory thus assumes a very different form in each of the essays in this section. All they truly share is a recognition of Wittgenstein's importance. From Bix's cautionary remarks to Patterson's extension of Wittgenstein's idea of mastery of a technique to Sebok's placement of Wittgenstein at the center of two quite distinct jurisprudential movements, these essays leave us with three messages: the influence of Wittgenstein on legal theory has already been quite profound; applying his work to legal theory is difficult and must be done with care; and, as Patterson puts it, "[m]uch work needs to be done."

11   Cautions and Caveats for the Application of Wittgenstein to Legal Theory

Brian Bix

I am reminded of a moment in a discussion some fifteen years ago at which a brilliant, successful, exasperated member of the philosophical profession said, "You know, it's possible that Wittgenstein was wrong about *something*!" Recalling the unpleasantness of cults, one must not ignore the sorts of behavior that can, in the most patient, justifiably produce such exclamations. But one must not make too much of such exclamations either. You could just as helpfully say, "You know, it's possible that philosophy is wrong about something!"
—Stanley Cavell (1979, p. xvii)

In the spirit of Stanley Cavell's quotation, this essay will be in part a discussion of what a particular philosopher, Ludwig Wittgenstein, can offer to legal theory, and in part a discussion of what philosophy can offer to legal theory. The essay is intended as a caution, against those who might be too quick in their applications of Wittgenstein's work, but it certainly is not intended to suggest any prohibition on attempting such applications. There is much of great value, at least in the sense of provoking useful further discussions, in the articles discussed in this piece (and in many of the other efforts to apply Wittgenstein's ideas to law and legal theory, a number of which are cited in the "References" section at the end of this piece).

It is not surprising that there is a large and growing number of examples of legal theorists applying Ludwig Wittgenstein's ideas to jurisprudential problems. American legal theorists are generous (or, if one prefers, promiscuous) borrowers of ideas and approaches from other disciplines. Ever since the legal realists, in the early decades of the twentieth century, undermined the confidence (of the legal formalists) that legal materials were sufficient to resolve all legal disputes, legal academics have been looking to other disciplines to supplement or supplant more traditional forms of legal analysis (Bix 2003a, pp. 177–187).

As is well known, many academics have looked to economics for the needed supplement to legal reasoning, but others have looked to philosophy. Wittgenstein is a likely suspect for such assistance, as his work with language, meaning, and rules, seems to tie in well with "the interpretive turn" in legal thought (see Moore 1989).

This search for extralegal grounds for analysis sometimes coincides with a quite different, and unfortunate, tendency in academia generally— though it may well be worse in legal academia—caused, most people think, by an insecurity among theorists in what they are saying and in their right to say anything at all. The unfortunate tendency is the hiding of positions behind labels—the names of particular famous writers or of whole schools of thought. One does not merely put forward a theory of liability in tort law, one puts forward a Hegelian theory or a Wittgensteinian theory, or a liberal theory.

I do not wish to seem like I am against all labels all of the time. They can certainly serve a useful purpose. If nothing else, labels can be a convenient shorthand, allowing readers a quick estimate of the type of work they are considering. I am less concerned with the labels as a means of positioning oneself so that potential allies and potential critics can get a better sense of where one is coming from, and more concerned with those who hide behind the label or the big-name theorist as a small child might hide behind a big-brother protector. (Some of these writers structure their arguments to give the impression that if one was to be so bold as to question the conclusion, the challenge must be brought, say, to Wittgenstein, not to them.)

Like many significant thinkers from other fields, Wittgenstein has probably inspired more bad ideas than good ones, and more misunderstandings of his work than true understandings.[1]

Proving the Negative and the Misuse of Authority

I have already written in the negative about Wittgenstein and the law, arguing that his work is not as useful for legal theory as many commentators seem to believe (Bix 1993, pp. 36–62). Of course, it is never easy to prove a negative, and not terribly interesting either. There is also a danger of discouraging those who have in good conscience tried to learn what they could from another discipline. One hears stories of philosophically trained legal theorists giving sharp rebukes to colleagues who would dare discuss a philosopher's work without doctoral training or comparable levels of rigor and commitment (cf. Leiter 1992), and the fear is that imposing such very high standards may work only to scare off most legal theorists from making any effort at all to learn from philosophers and philosophy. And I am not entirely sure that we want to leave philosophy only to the trained philosophers (or history only to the trained historians or economics only to the trained economists) either inside legal academia or generally. It is thus a difficult balance to try to maintain: to encourage others to try to become more sophisticated in their theories, but to encourage them also to have the proper respect (and, one might add, the proper humility) before the complex ideas of other disciplines (history and economics, as well as philosophy).[2]

Although one could perhaps argue persuasively that a few named commentators, in a handful of specific articles, have misread Wittgenstein's teachings, that is hardly proof that those teachings cannot be properly used in a helpful way. In part, the lesson one could learn from most past alleged misuses of Wittgenstein's work is the one already mentioned: that legal academics might be prone to using authority in place of argument in their work. Although this can be found in many of the more casual (and some of the more detailed) references to Wittgenstein in the literature, it is nothing peculiar to this approach to legal theory—with nearly every philosopher (from Hegel to Derrida to Gadamer), there is a tendency to throw out citations as a shorthand for developing an argument. As there is nothing specific to Wittgenstein studies or Wittgensteinian applications in this topic, I will not tarry here.

Rule Following and Interpretation

Probably the most common use of Wittgenstein's work in recent legal commentary has been the reference to his considerations of rule-following (Wittgenstein 1958, §§ 185–242)[3] in the course of discussions of legal interpretation. The initial problem is quite easily stated: Wittgenstein did not write on legal philosophy or legal interpretation. Even what he did write on both philosophy of language and philosophy of mind remains frequently exegetically uncertain, and, even where the message is relatively clear, the validity of the claims is far from unanimously received. Thus, a mere rough analogy between Wittgenstein's writings and one's jurisprudential work may be something worth noting, but it is far, far short of showing that one's conclusions are right. There is much argument that needs to be made, and it is on those arguments that the focus must lie.

As regards Wittgenstein's rule-following considerations, this influential collection of comments in *Philosophical Investigations* involves questions about the proper understanding of "the rules" ("rules" here broadly understood) by which we apply concepts ("blue," "chair," or "add two") in a context new to us (that is, in a context where, for our purposes, the application of the concept has not already been determined or decided).

The fact of the matter is that there is a great deal of consensus in the application of words and concepts, and that this consensus often occurs after quite minimal training (often involving ostension: "'leaf' means objects like *this one* [pointing]"). The mystery is how or why we all go on the same way on these occasions—and what insight, if any, the answer to that question might give to the nature of language and the nature of meaning.

My argument in the past (Bix 1993, pp. 36–62) has been that the rule-following considerations do not have any *direct* applications to law, at least not to the issues in legal interpretation to which Wittgenstein's work is usually applied. The rule-following considerations are about the proper explanation of a phenomenon: the phenomenon of general agreement in practices regarding the simplest terms and mathematical concepts. The subject of Wittgenstein's discussion are rules so simple that he can state:

Disputes do not break out (among mathematicians, say) over the question of whether a rule has been obeyed or not. People don't come to blows over it, for example. This is part of the framework on which the working of our language is based (for example, in giving descriptions). (Wittgenstein 1958, § 240)

By contrast, law and legal interpretation seem, and seem obviously, to be some distance from the practices inspiring the rule-following considerations. Law and legal interpretation are not practices characterized by consensus or lack of disagreement. To the contrary, one might say that the practice of law is substantially, perhaps even pervasively contested.[4] The question in legal interpretation is not how to explain agreement, but how to resolve *dis*agreement. Given the differences in the practices and the questions being answered, one would have thought that there was a heavy burden on those who believe that the rule-following considerations apply directly to the legal context (see Langille 1988; Patterson 1990). In the end, it may well turn out that the only jurisprudentially helpful use of a proper understanding of Wittgenstein's rule-following considerations is for rebuttal to legal theorists who ground their theories on an improper understanding of those same texts (see Bix 1993, pp. 36–62).

The "Language Game" of Law

At least as frequently as his rule-following considerations are co-opted for jurisprudential purposes, Wittgenstein's work on language, meaning, and rules is cited for a more general proposition: that meaning is use (Wittgenstein 1958, § 43) and that many philosophical problems would dissolve when linguistic practices are seen as merely rules in our game (Wittgenstein 1958, §§ 7, 96) rather than as reflecting some deep metaphysical or ontological truth.

Of course, something like this deflationary move can be seen in the work of some of the American legal realists: for example, in writers like Felix Cohen (1935), who chided the formalists writing at the time for deriving significant moral and legal conclusions from the "nature" of certain legal concepts. However, some recent theorists have made a more substantial argument based on a similar analytical approach.

Theorists like Dennis Patterson and Philip Bobbitt have argued that legal practice generally, or constitutional theory more particularly, are best understood under this sort of rubric: as a game with set rules (Patterson 1996; Bobbitt 1991). Patterson has put greater emphasis on the connection between his own work and Wittgenstein's (1994); Bobbitt, though he does cite Wittgenstein, does not emphasize the connection.[5]

Bobbitt describes six forms of argument that are used for interpreting the United States Constitution (Bobbitt 1991, pp. 12–13).[6] A judicial decision involving the interpretation or application of the Constitution is justified when it is made according to one (or more) of the accepted forms of argument. The legitimacy of a practice—the evaluation of the practice as a whole under the criteria of justice or some other value—is another matter, to be sharply distinguished from justification, which can only be done in terms of the "accepted moves" within the practice of American constitutional interpretation (ibid., pp. 31–42, 151–54). Patterson's analysis can be understood, broadly, as generalizing Bobbitt's approach, and seeing *all* legal analysis in the same way Bobbitt views American constitutional law: Patterson discusses "the role of the forms of arguments as the grammar of legal justification" (Patterson 1996, p. 178); and asserts that "law is an identifiable practice, one with its own argumentative grammar . . . [and] that this grammar is [not] reducible to the forms of argument of another discipline" (ibid., p. 182). At the same time, Patterson clarifies (in a way that seems to distinguish his view from Bobbitt's) that he accepts that legal argument can change over time, and can be responsive to social pressures in those changes (ibid.).

A Wittgensteinian "language game" analysis depends on the practice in question being substantially autonomous.[7] And it is just this autonomy that is in contention in the analyses of both language and law. Wittgenstein's assertion that language, and the grammatical rules within language,[8] are autonomous is itself highly controversial and requires a great deal of argument, particularly in the face of the general or naive view that language can and should be viewed according to its success in representing or capturing reality, as well as the less naive "natural kinds" view that meaning is determined in part by the way the world is.[9] To speak of a similar autonomy of legal practices would be controversial, but for different reasons. The general or naive view here is that law both reflects and responds to external forces: conventional morality, custom, and power are three likely candidates, depending on one's sociological, political, and/or skeptical inclinations. More sophisticated commentators might also argue that the law reflects, or by its nature strives to reflect, basic moral truths, justice, or transcendent legal categories.

Of course, the idea of law as an autonomous discipline has its own history, and not an entirely happy one. An overstatement of the autonomy and resources of law was the major error of the formalist judges and commentators: the formalism criticized by the American legal realists of the early twentieth century (Bix 2003a, pp. 179–180). More modest assertions of legal autonomy are not so obviously erroneous, and they have fared better, but the autonomy asserted is still very far from being a self-evident truth (Bix 2003b).

One can follow Wittgenstein's lead in a more nuanced manner, as Thomas Morawetz has done (1990, 1992, 1999). Morawetz's point is that Wittgenstein's lesson is to pay close attention to actual practices—the attitude and actions of people within a practice. The Wittgensteinian inquiry (still following Morawetz's discussion) is whether law is best seen as being like chess—a game with (generally) fixed rules, which must be accepted in whole if one purports to be playing that game—or whether it is more like conventional morality—an activity where there is ongoing discussion about the merits of present practices, with those practices being very much subject to internal criticism and change over time (Bix 1999, pp. 19–21; see also Martinez 1996).

However, the difference between Wittgenstein (and Morawetz's reading of Wittgenstein) on one hand, and some of the other commentators trying to apply his work to legal theory on the other hand, is that Wittgenstein meant this close observation as a means of avoiding misunderstanding by (philosophical) observers, not as a basis for prescribing behavior to participants. A proper Wittgensteinian observation of constitutional law practice would help avoid tangled or overly metaphysical misunderstandings of that practice, one would think, but it would not (or should not) be the basis, for example, for telling advocates what arguments they may and may not make before a court.[10] To the contrary, Wittgenstein insisted that proper philosophical investigations leave the subject of investigation just as it was[11]—and "as it was" is a matter for the participants to tell us (directly or through their actions), not for us to tell them.

Thus, it is not so much that Wittgenstein's analysis could not possibly apply to law, but rather that the question of whether application is appropriate or not will be determined simultaneously by the justification for using that approach, and in the same way. (Thus, Wittgenstein's work, if properly used, will end up doing little work, for one will be proving his conclusions as much as one's own, and likely against roughly the same sets of objections.)

Wittgenstein and Skepticism

Another unfortunate application of Wittgenstein—though, luckily, a rare one—involves applying Saul Kripke's (1982) highly dubious skeptical reading of the rule-following considerations as the basis for a skeptical (radically indeterminate) view of legal interpretation (e.g., Yablon 1987; Radin 1989). The view here, whether properly ascribed to Wittgenstein or not, is that since one cannot ground the truth of our use of words (or mathematical series) in some Platonic version of the terms to be applied, the only possible source of truth is the agreement of people within the practice—those who are considered competent practitioners of the language. It is not surprising that some scholars otherwise inclined toward a skeptical view of legal practice would be attracted by this approach, for it seems but a short step to the critical (or Foucaultian) view that truth is whatever the powerful say it is (e.g., Foucault 1980; cf. Yablon 1985, pp. 918–920, 929–945; Tushnet 1988, pp. 54–56, 60–69).

Kripke's analysis is all but universally rejected as a reading of Wittgenstein. Of course, the skeptical analysis might yet stand on its own merits, but the question of those merits takes us too far from the current topic. Suffice it to say that legal theorists have no basis for using Wittgenstein (without further argument) to justify a skeptical theory of law.

Conclusion

When legal theorists offer claims about the nature of language and meaning in the course of arguments about legal (and constitutional) interpretation, one would prefer that they know some philosophy of language and meaning rather than not knowing, and one might similarly prefer that they have read some Wittgenstein (and have reflected on it) than not.

At the same time, there is an irony when Wittgenstein is dragged out to buttress or to justify a radical claim about legal practice, or even a radical rethinking of legal theory. I am doubtful that there is much Wittgenstein has to tell us about law and language that someone even moderately familiar with the legal realists does not already know. Yet there are obvious benefits for legal theorists sharpening their analytical and critical teeth on the classic works in the philosophy of language (where there may be a better warranty of strong argument than there is in many volumes of American law journals) and so one should continue to encourage legal academics *to read* Wittgenstein . . . but to put the volume aside before trying to argue for a novel (or conventional) theory of legal practice or about the nature of law.

Acknowledgments

I am grateful to Dennis Patterson, Kenneth Simons, and the participants at the Fifth Annual Inland Northwest Philosophy Conference, University of Idaho, April 2002.

Notes

1. For an example of how misreadings of Wittgenstein have contributed to some bad ideas about mental states—a central concept for determining criminal culpability—see Simons 1992, pp. 529–533.

2. One also wants to encourage legal scholars to look at the philosophical side of the history of ideas, and here there has been some quite good work on using the Wittgensteinian origins of certain ideas to help understand those ideas better (e.g., Sebok 1999).

3. The previous sections of the *Investigations* (Wittgenstein 1958, §§ 143–184) deal with related topics regarding the understanding and normativity of rules.

4. A point that is central to some of Ronald Dworkin's arguments against legal positivism (1986, pp. 33–44).

5. In an earlier text, Bobbitt offers the following statement—"This is a profound error, because it assumes that the commentator comes to the question of judicial review from a fresh perspective, one outside, as it were, the process of legal argument."—and then adds a footnote: "*See generally* L. Wittgenstein, *Philosophical Investigations* (1958)" (Bobbitt 1982, pp. 123 and 266, n. 1).

   At the INPC Conference, Professor Bobbitt disclaimed grounding his constitutional theory on Wittgenstein's work, referring to Wittgenstein's work as one of many sources or inspirations for his views, but not an express foundation.

6. Bobbitt uses the term "modalities" to refer to these forms of argument.

7. Although Patterson expressly denies asserting that law is "autonomous" (1996, p. 182), he is clearly ascribing a kind of "autonomy" to law—which he describes various ways: e.g., that it is a practice "with its own argumentative grammar" (ibid.), and that "legal argument is 'horizontal' in nature" (ibid., p. 179).

8. Wittgenstein used "grammar" (e.g., Wittgenstein 1958, § 90: "Our investigation is therefore a grammatical one") in an idiosyncratic way, to mean the rules of language and meaning understood broadly (Glock 1996, pp. 150–155).

9. For an effort to defend a Wittgensteinian autonomy view, see Hacker 1986, pp. 179–214. For the seminal article on the "natural kinds" view that meaning is in part determined by the way the world is, see Putnam 1975, pp. 215–271.

10. There are comments within Bobbitt's work that seem to do exactly this: e.g., (1) stating, after describing six forms of argument ("modalities") within American constitutional law practice: "There is no constitutional legal argument outside these modalities" (Bobbitt 1991, p. 22); and (2) "they are the only modalities that are sanctioned by the Constitution" (ibid., p. 147). Bobbitt's position is summarized and critiqued in Bix 1999, pp. 11–21.

Although Professor Bobbitt's books generally support the constraining interpretation given above, his later writings disclaim that interpretation (and yet concede that the interpretation is so pervasive that it must have some foundation in the text) (Bobbitt 1994, pp. 1912, 1916, and 1919; Bix 1999, pp. 12–13 and nn. 21–31).

11. For example, there is Wittgenstein's famous comment:

Philosophy may in no way interfere with the actual use of language; it can in the end only describe it.
For it cannot give it any foundation either.
It leaves everything as it is. (Wittgenstein 1958, § 124; see generally §§ 122–132)

References

Arulanantham, A. T. 1998. Note, "Breaking the Rules? Wittgenstein and Legal Realism." *Yale Law Journal* 107: 1853–1883.

Bix, B. 1993. *Law, Language, and Legal Determinacy*. Oxford: Clarendon Press.

———. 1999. "On Description and Legal Reasoning." In L. Meyer, ed., *Rules and Reasoning: Essays in Honour of Fred Schauer*. Oxford: Hart Publishing.

———. 2003a. *Jurisprudence: Theory and Context*, third ed. London: Sweet and Maxwell.

———. 2003b. "Law as an Autonomous Discipline." In P. Cane and M. Tushnet, eds., *The Oxford Handbook of Legal Studies*. Oxford: Oxford University Press.

Bjarup, J. 1988. "Kripke's Case: Some Remarks on Rules, Their Interpretation, and Application." *Rechtstheorie* 19: 39–49.

Brainerd, S. 1985. "The Groundless Assault: A Wittgensteinian Look at Language, Structuralism, and Critical Legal Theory." *American University Law Review* 34: 1231–1262.

Bobbitt, P. 1982. *Constitutional Fate*. Oxford: Oxford University Press.

———. 1991. *Constitutional Interpretation*. Oxford: Blackwell.

———. 1994. "Reflections Inspired by My Critics." *Texas Law Review* 72: 1869–1967.

Cavell, S. 1979. *The Claim of Reason*. Oxford: Oxford University Press.

Cohen, F. S. 1935. "Transcendental Nonsense and the Functional Response." *Columbia Law Review* 35: 809–849.

Dworkin, R. 1986. *Law's Empire*. Cambridge, Mass.: Harvard University Press.

Eisele, T. 1990. " 'Our Real Need': Not Explanation, But Education." *Canadian Journal of Law and Jurisprudence* 3: 5–34.

Foucault, M. 1980. *Power/Knowledge: Selected Interviews and Other Writings 1972–1977*, Colin Gordon, ed. New York: Pantheon.

Glock, H.-J. 1996. *A Wittgenstein Dictionary*. Oxford: Blackwell.

Hacker, P. M. S. 1986. *Insight and Illusion*, revised ed. Oxford: Oxford University Press.

Halpin, A. 2001. "Some Themes from Wittgenstein's *Philosophical Investigations*." In A. Halpin, ed., *Reasoning with Law*. Oxford: Hart Publishing.

Kripke, S. A. 1982. *Wittgenstein on Rules and Private Language*. Cambridge, Mass.: Harvard University Press.

Landers, S. 1990. "Wittgenstein, Realism, and CLS: Undermining Rule Scepticism." *Law and Philosophy* 9: 177–203.

Langille, B. 1980. "The Jurisprudence of Despair, Again." *University of British Columbia Law Review* 23: 549–565.

————. 1988. "Revolution without Foundation: The Grammar of Scepticism and Law." *McGill Law Journal* 33: 451–505.

Leiter, B. 1992. "Intellectual Voyeurism in Legal Scholarship." *Yale Journal of Law and the Humanities* 4: 79–104.

Lin, P. 1989. "Wittgenstein, Language, and Legal Theorizing: Toward a Non-Reductive Account of Law." *University of Toronto Faculty of Law Review* 47: 939–972.

Marmor, A. 1990. "No Easy Cases?" *Canadian Journal of Law and Jurisprudence* 3: 61–79.

Martinez, G. A. 1996. "The New Wittgensteinians and the End of Jurisprudence." *Loyola of Los Angeles Law Review* 29: 545–577.

Moore, M. S. 1989. "The Interpretive Turn in Modern Theory: A Turn for the Worse?" *Stanford Law Review* 41: 871–957.

Morawetz, T. 1990. "The Epistemology of Judging: Wittgenstein and Deliberative Practices." *Canadian Journal of Law and Jurisprudence* 3: 35–59.

————. 1992. "Understanding Disagreement, the Root Issue of Jurisprudence: Applying Wittgenstein to Positivism, Critical Theory, and Judging." *University of Pennsylvania Law Review* 141: 371–456.

————. 1999. "Law as Experience: Theory and the Internal Aspect of Law." *SMU Law Review* 52: 27–66.

Patterson, D. M. 1988. "Wittgenstein and the Code: A Theory of Good Faith Performance and Enforcement under Article Nine." *University of Pennsylvania Law Review* 137: 335–429.

————. 1989. "Good Faith, Lender Liability, and Discretionary Acceleration: Of Llewellyn, Wittgenstein, and the Uniform Commercial Code." *Texas Law Review* 68: 169–211.

————. 1990. "Law's Pragmatism: Law as Practice and Narrative." *Virginia Law Review* 76: 937–996.

————. 1994. "Wittgenstein and Constitutional Theory." *Texas Law Review* 72: 1837–1868.

————. 1996. *Law and Truth*. Oxford: Oxford University Press.

Patterson, D. M., ed. 1992. *Wittgenstein and Legal Theory*. Boulder: Westview Press.

Penner, J. S. 1988. "The Rules of Law: Wittgenstein, Davidson, and Weinrib's Formalism." *University of Toronto Law Faculty of Law Review* 46: 488–521.

Putnam, H. 1975. "The Meaning of 'Meaning.'" In his *Mind, Language, and Reality: Philosophical Papers*, vol. 2. Cambridge: Cambridge University Press.

Radin, M. J. 1989. "Reconsidering the Rule of Law." *Boston University Law Review* 69: 781–819.

Root, S. C. 2000. "Trade Dress, the 'Likelihood of Confusion,' and Wittgenstein's Discussion of 'Seeing As': The Tangled Landscape of Resemblance." *Seton Hall Law Review* 30: 757–805.

Schauer, F. 1990. "Rules and the Rule-Following Argument." *Canadian Journal of Law and Jurisprudence* 3: 187–192.

Sebok, A. J. 1999. "Finding Wittgenstein at the Core of the Rule of Recognition." *SMU Law Review* 52: 75–109.

Simons, K. W. 1992. "Rethinking Mental States." *Boston University Law Review* 72: 463–554.

Smith, G. A. 1990. "Wittgenstein and the Sceptical Fallacy." *Canadian Journal of Law and Jurisprudence* 3: 155–186.

Tully, J. 1989. "Wittgenstein and Political Philosophy: Understanding Practices of Critical Reflection." *Political Theory* 17: 172–204.

Tushnet, M. 1988. *Red, White, and Blue: A Critical Analysis of Constitutional Law.* Cambridge, Mass.: Harvard University Press.

Wittgenstein, L. 1958. *Philosophical Investigations,* third ed. G. E. M. Anscombe, trans. New York: Macmillan.

Wolcher, L. E. 1997. "Ronald Dworkin's Right Answers Thesis through the Lens of Wittgenstein." *Rutgers Law Journal* 29: 43–65.

Yablon, C. M. 1985. "The Indeterminacy of the Law: Critical Legal Studies and the Problem of Legal Explanation." *Cardozo Law Review* 6: 917–945.

———. 1987. "Law and Metaphysics." *Yale Law Journal* 96: 613–636.

Zapf, C., and E. Moglen. 1996. "Linguistic Indeterminacy and the Rule of Law: On the Perils of Misunderstanding Wittgenstein." *Georgetown Law Journal* 84: 485–520.

12 Prolegomenon to Any Future Legal Theory: Wittgenstein and Jurisprudence

Dennis Patterson

This panel has been convened to discuss the importance of Wittgenstein's approach to philosophy for jurisprudence. As this audience well knows, Wittgenstein's work—especially in *Philosophical Investigations*—has received a great deal of attention in legal academic journals; some of this attention has been good, some less so. Despite a fair amount of good writing on the convergence between Wittgenstein's thought and issues in jurisprudence, much work remains. In this essay, I will speak to one issue I think is central both to Wittgenstein's thought and to its role in jurisprudence.

The problem I want to address is that of semantic content in the legal context. Put simply, the question is how do lawyers decide that a certain concept has the content it does and not some other? I wish to explain how Wittgenstein's approach to meaning impacts the question of the semantic content of legal concepts.

As we all know, Wittgenstein begins the *Philosophical Investigations* with an attack on the picture theory of meaning advanced in the *Tractatus*. The elements of the picture theory are that words stand for things and that concepts are reducible to simples (atomism). In the *Philosophical Investigations*, Wittgenstein identifies this picture as the Augustinian account of meaning.

The Augustinian picture of language can be seen as an element of a wider philosophical view, that of realism. Although there are certainly varieties of realism, a key component of the realist picture is the idea that the world imprints itself on us and our modes of expression. Put differently, realists believe that the meaning of our words is, in some sense, determined by the way the world is.

Few in jurisprudence believe that realism provides us with a perspicuous account of legal practice. Alternatives to realism abound, and there are more than a few shades of realism's opposite, subjectivism. The real work of philosophy is done in crafting a middle position between objectivism and subjectivism. What do I mean?

In describing the practice of tort law, Jules Coleman asks the question whether the meaning of corrective justice depends on the way the world is (objectivism) or whether it depends on us (antirealism). Coleman expresses the aspiration of the middle position when he writes: "For me, then, the content of corrective justice depends on the practices in which it figures, but it is not fully fixed by how I or anyone else happened to regard it."[1] The obvious challenge for Coleman is to explain how the content of corrective justice is fixed by something other than the practice of tort law and to do it in a way that avoids the problems of objectivism.

In this essay, I want to tackle the problem of semantic content from a fairly orthodox Wittgensteinian point of view. That is, I want to explore how Wittgenstein's approach to philosophical problems of meaning translates into a methodological approach to questions of meaning in the context of jurisprudence.

Wittgenstein's Place in the Philosophy of Language

Wittgenstein's later philosophy represents a radical break from the analytic tradition of which his work prior to 1929—especially the *Tractatus*—is most representative. Broadly construed, the analytic tradition of philosophy saw language as having two functions: the representation of states of affairs or the expression of the opinions and preferences of the speaker. One reason why analytic philosophers embraced this picture of language is that they tied meaning to reference and reference to facts or states of affairs. For language to be meaningful, it had to express or state a fact. Factual discourse was built on the correspondence theory of truth. To state a truth, one had to state facts.[2]

I see Wittgenstein's *Philosophical Investigations* as breaking with the tradition.[3] For the later Wittgenstein, the meaning of a word is a function not of the way the world is but of how that word is used in a language. Wittgenstein rejects the paradigm of meaning as reference and replaces it with meaning as use. It is *not* the case that Wittgenstein rejects the idea of reference as an element of meaning. However, he does show that reference is meaningful as a function of use.[4] This shift in emphasis has become a centerpiece of current debates in the philosophy of language.[5]

Wittgenstein and Semantic Content: The Importance of Technique

Wittgenstein says that we master concepts when we master techniques for their application. Much of what Wittgenstein has to say about concept mastery is bound up with his remarks on the nature of rule following. Following a rule is a technique. One's understanding of a rule is exhibited in one's mastery of the technique for its application. To understand a language is to be the master of a technique.[6] Counting, calculating, making geometrical constructions, measuring, inferring, and correlating members of sets are all techniques.[7]

I find Wittgenstein's remarks on rule following and concept mastery illuminating but incomplete. Part of the problem with Wittgenstein's account of the relationship between concept mastery and practices is that his examples of practices are often simple. Consider the builders in the early sections of *Philosophical Investigations*. There is little complexity to the orders found in the case of the builders. Of course, Wittgenstein never said the builders were an example of all practices. In fact, Wittgenstein describes the builders as participants in a "primitive language game."[8]

When we move from a practice like the builders' to one like law, the sheer level of complexity urges a more capacious account of the nature of the practice. Not one that is categorically different, but one that is sensitive to the extent of increased complexity.

I want to describe the work of jurisprudence in a way that brings it in touch with the everyday work of lawyers. My picture of law is that of three concentric circles, each inside the other.[9] The innermost circle represents the most basic level of ability. Here one would find a lawyer who is cognizant of a variety of rules but unable to give any systematic account of why the rules are as they are or how to go about changing them or altering them to fit a new context.

The next circle out raises the level of sophistication in legal ability. Here one would find lawyers capable of presenting novel interpretations of legal rules and doing some of the theoretical work one sees at the hands of sophisticated practitioners.

In the third circle, which stands for the highest level of craftsmanship and achievement in law, one would find the legal equivalent of the master craftsperson. At this level, one should not only be able to articulate rules and interpret them in a manner deemed sophisticated, one would also hope to answer questions about the nature and structure of legal doctrine, the relationship of law to justice, and the point or purpose of law.

The point of the metaphor of three concentric circles is to convey the sense that as one moves from the innermost to the outermost circle, one has mastered a skill set that is both necessary to a lawyer's work yet capable of expansion to a higher level of sophistication.

What Is at Stake?

What problem does the three-part account of legal practice solve? And how does this account advance some or all of the current debates in analytic legal theory?

In *The Practice of Principle*,[10] Jules Coleman joins the ranks of self-described pragmatists in adopting the philosophical approach of Sellars, Quine, Davidson, and Putnam.[11] Why does Coleman enlist the aid of these important figures in analytic philosophy? What is the problem to which their work is a solution?

The problem Coleman identifies is a significant philosophical issue: explanation. By implicating the figures of Quine, Sellars, Davidson, and Putnam, Coleman is signaling a certain approach to the question of what it means to "explain" a phenomenon or practice. In a long footnote,[12] Coleman criticizes and differentiates himself from Dworkin in terms he characterizes as epistemic and metaphysical. Although Coleman is light on details, it is clear that he thinks the terms of similar debates in analytic philosophy of language have relevance to current issues in legal theory. In this way, he returns to the point Dworkin himself made twenty-five years ago when he said "the debate about the nature of law . . . is, at bottom, a debate within the philosophy of language and metaphysics."[13]

Of course, those of us with a Wittgensteinian approach to matters of meaning have always come at the issue of explanation in the terms Coleman describes. It is indeed refreshing to see a prominent voice for legal positivism turn to pragmatism in matters of metaphysics and meaning.

For those who see Wittgenstein as right on matters of meaning, where do we go from here? The indeterminacy argument is dead, except as a relic of a failed intellectual agenda.[14] The Wittgensteinian critique of the pseudoscience of cognitive theory is certainly worth pursuing. But I think Coleman has identified a key focus, that is, the idea of meaning and its relationship to explanation. Much work has been done on this issue by members of this panel.[15] The challenge for Wittgensteinians is to leave everything as it is and yet avoid the criticism of quietism.[16] Much work needs to be done.

Notes

1. Coleman 1995, p. 62.

2. Representative works include Wittgenstein's *Tractatus* (1922), Frege's "On Sense and Reference" (1892), A. J. Ayer's *Language, Truth, and Logic* (1946; originally published in 1936), and the ethical emotivism of R. M. Hare's *The Language of Morals* (1952), which argues for a view that is consistent with Wittgenstein's account of factual discourse but makes a place for ethics as a discourse of opinion. Reference is the central metaphor in the modernist philosophy of language (Frege, Russell, early Wittgenstein, and Kripke).

3. I would also include the work of J. L. Austin and John Searle.

4. Consider also Wittgenstein's "broom example" (1958, § 60).

5. Two examples:

We can and should insist that some facts are there to be discovered and not legislated by us. But this is something to be said when one has adopted a way of speaking, a language, a "conceptual scheme." To talk of "facts" without specifying the language to be used is to talk of nothing; the word "fact" no more has its use fixed by the world itself than does the word "exist" or the word "object." . . . The suggestion I am making, in short, is that *a statement is true of a situation just in case it would be correct to use the words of which the statement consists in that way in describing the situation.* . . . [W]e can explain what "correct to use the words of which the statement consists in that way" means by saying that it means nothing more nor less than a sufficiently well placed speaker who used the words in that way would be fully warranted in counting the statement as true of that situation. . . . [T]ruth does not transcend use. (Putnam 1988, pp. 114–115)

Surely if the history of philosophical reflection on the correspondence theory of truth has taught us anything, it is that there is ground for suspicion of the idea that we have some way of telling what can count as a fact, prior to and independent of asking what form of words might count as expressing truths, so a conception of facts could exert some leverage in the investigation of truth. (McDowell 1988, p. 11)

6. Wittgenstein 1958, § 189.

7. See Wittgenstein 1978; I: p. 106, I: pp. 136–140, II: p. 12ff., II: p. 31ff., IV: p. 40–42, V: p. 106, V: p. 46ff.

8. See Wittgenstein 1958, § 2.

9. This image is taken from Charles 2001, pp. 49–79.

10. Coleman 2001.

11. Ibid., p. 6, n. 6. Curiously, Coleman puts Rorty outside this group for reasons that are not explained. I detect no fundamental difference of opinion on metaphysical issues between Rorty and Putnam. And I think there are great affinities between the work of Sellars, Quine, and Rorty.

12. Ibid., p. 10, n. 13.

13. Dworkin 1977, p. 1.

14. See Unger 1996.

15. See, e.g., Bobbitt 1991—identifying six modalities of constitutional argument.

16. See Wright 1993.

References

Ayer, A. J. 1946. *Language, Truth, and Logic*, second ed. London: Golancz.

Bobbitt, P. 1991. *Constitutional Interpretation.* Oxford: Blackwell.

Charles, D. 2001. "Builders and Craftsmen." In D. Charles and W. Child, eds., *Wittgensteinian Themes: Essays in Honor of David Pears*. Oxford: Clarendon Press and New York: Oxford University Press.

Coleman, J. 2001. *The Practice of Principle: In Defense of a Pragmatist Approach to Legal Theory.* Oxford and New York: Oxford University Press.

———. 1995. "The Practice of Corrective Justice." In D. G. Owen, ed., *Philosophical Foundations of Tort Law*. Oxford: Oxford University Press.

Dworkin, R. 1977. "Introduction." In R. Dworkin, ed., *The Philosophy of Law*. Oxford: Oxford University Press.

Frege, G. 1952/1892. "On Sense and Reference." In P. Geach and M. Black, eds., *Translations of the Philosophical Writings of Gottlob Frege*. Oxford: Blackwell.

Hare, R. M. 1952. *The Language of Morals*. Oxford: Clarendon Press.

———. 1963. *Freedom and Reason.* Oxford: Clarendon Press.

Putnam, H. 1988. *Representation and Reality.* Cambridge, Mass.: MIT Press.

McDowell, J. 1988. "Projection and Truth in Ethics." *The Lindley Lecture*. Lawrence, Kans.: Department of Philosophy, University of Kansas.

Unger, R. M. 1996. *What Should Legal Theory Become?* New York: W. W. Norton.

Wittgenstein, L. 1922. *Tractatus Logico-Philosophicus*. C. K. Ogden, trans. London: Routledge and Kegan Paul.

———. 1958. *Philosophical Investigations*, third ed. G. E. M. Anscombe, trans. New York: Macmillan.

———. 1978. *Remarks on the Foundations of Mathematics*. G. E. M. Anscombe, R. Rhees, and G. H. von Wright, eds. Cambridge, Mass.: MIT Press.

Wright, C. 1993. *Truth and Objectivity*. Cambridge, Mass.: Harvard University Press.

13 Legal Process and the Practices of Principle

Anthony J. Sebok

In 1973, Harry Wellington of Yale Law School set out to defend the legal process school's approach to adjudication. Legal process, which had first come to prominence in the 1950s, had by the late 1960s been associated with a certain style of retrograde politics. Legal process was permanently associated with the concept of "neutral principles," a concept that lent superficial support to the right-wing attack on civil rights cases such as *Brown*[1] as well as incipient privacy cases such as *Griswold*.[2] Wellington's answer was the article, "Common Law Rules and Constitutional Double Standards: Some Notes on Adjudication."[3]

For the project of "Common Law Rules," Dean Wellington focused on the central trope of the legal process school, which is the idea of common law adjudication as the central explanatory lens by which to understand all American law. Following Hart and Sacks, Wellington argued that the realists misapprehended the nature of common-law reasoning, in that they felt that decisions such as *MacPherson*[4] or *Roberson*[5] were only explicable as expressions of policy. Legal process did not deny that policy sometimes legitimately plays a role in adjudication, but it insisted that often principle plays a much more significant role than the realists were willing to admit.

For Wellington, principle did not mean, as Ronald Dworkin (1997, pp. 125–128) would have it, morality *simpliciter* or principle as viewed in its "best light." Wellington argued that principle, when used by the legal process school must refer to society's "conventional morality." By conventional morality Wellington meant something very different from what he describes as moral ideals, which may be honored far more often in their breach than in their instantiation.[6] Furthermore, by conventional morality Wellington made clear that, epistemically, the relationship between the individual and the group is the opposite than how Dworkin imagined it. Legal principles, such as rights, were not, for Wellington, defined in teeth of majority preferences: they were wholly constructed by them, although not crudely, as if by instant votes that might take the temperature of society's current passions. This is such an important point that it is worth reprinting the critical paragraph from "Common Law Rules" in its entirety, since only by reading it all the way through can one fully appreciate the uncanny way in which Wellington's approach to principle was almost an "Alice in Wonderland" reversal of what Dworkin has written.

> I claimed in effect that when dealing with legal principles a court must take the moral point of view. Yet I doubt that one would want to say that a court is entitled or required to insert *its* moral point of view. Unlike the moral philosopher, the court is required to insert *ours*. This requirement imposes constraints: judicial reasoning in concrete cases must proceed from society's set of moral principles and ideals, in much the same way that the judicial interpretation of documents (contracts, statutes, constitutions—especially constitutions) must proceed from the document. And that is why we must be concerned with conventional morality, for it is there that society's set of moral principles and ideals are located.[7]

This is the ultimate reversal of Hercules. The familiar natural law approach to principle was to use it like a telescope with which the judge could do nothing else other than look—carefully and in great detail—at her own moral compass. Wellington's idea was that the careful and detailed gaze of principle would be retained, but that the telescope would be turned around and used to look at the moral compass of society. For Wellington, a society's morality, like its fashion and art, could sustain its normative force and conventionality because it is a shared and observed social practice.[8] This is in contrast to an individual's personal morality, which binds each person only to the degree that they can ultimately accept it and commit to it using their powers of reason and judgment.[9]

Wellington stressed, however, that although conventional morality is a product of society, and not of pure reason, it is a special form of conventionalism. It is not the conventionalism of voting or of taking a poll. Wellington contrasted his method of discerning society's principles from the social scientist's method of analyzing the real world of power at a given moment in a given society.[10] He explicitly separated his project from that of political scientists like Robert Dahl and David Truman, whose path-breaking work on interest group politics was (correctly) identified with the legal process school.[11]

The rejection of value-neutral pluralism may seem both obvious and quaint today. Since the early 1970s there has been a definite "turn to normativity" such that Wellington's conventionalism is more likely in need of defense from natural law theory than are pure conventionalists. Nonetheless, Wellington's defense of his conventionalism in the face of "value-free" conventionalism allows us to see the role Wittgensteinian thought plays in his theory.

Wellington recognized that he needed to work with a very different set of tools if he was to come up with an account of "principle as conventional morality" that would not fall into the reductive and circular problems that social science's critics had noted.[12] Wellington began by distinguishing between a society's moral ideals and its practice. The ideals are worth studying, but they must never be confused with the practice. The practice of morality is, Wellington argued, a social convention. It is knowable by anyone who is a member of the community and it is constructed out of the actual practices of the community. To explain his point, Wellington cited heavily from H. L. A. Hart's *The Concept of Law*.[13] He accepted Hart's claim that social morality is "immune from deliberate change" although it is constantly changing.[14] To Wellington, this insight into the actual dynamics of the plasticity of morality supports Hart's final claim that, like language, "morality is something 'there' to be recognized, not made by deliberate human choice."[15]

But if social morality is a form of convention, why not give in to the value-free social scientists and study the conventions of one's own society the way one would study the behavior of migratory birds? To answer this point, Wellington turned to Stanley Cavell. According to Wellington, Cavell had shown that the study of any human practice, such as language use or conventional morality, should occur in the "philosophical temple" instead of the "research institute," and that the researcher should not use "scientific methodology" but something like ordinary language philosophy.[16] Cavell argued that behaviorism cannot explain how language exercises normative force on its users. The goal of behaviorism, which Cavell mockingly referred to as "count[ing] noses," is to identify the rules that preexist the use of language by a speaker.[17] Under the behaviorist model, correct language use is the product of the conscious or unconscious obedience to rules. We discover the rules by observing what "most people" do. Cavell, following Wittgenstein, rejected the idea that the rules of a language could be determined simply by observing the behavior of others. The rules that are at issue are not sensible outside of their use. One cannot extract them from a sample set, state them bare and without context, and then apply them to a new set of circumstances without doing violence to one's initial project, which was (one assumes) to master the language. Wittgenstein argued against the idea that behind every language there are a set of "superlative facts" that govern the formation of a sentence in that language; the only fact about the language available to a competent user of the language *is the language itself*.[18] Language is normative, but its rules are neither discoverable nor describable through the methods of natural science. The rules of language are discoverable only through practice and knowable only through ostention.[19] Under the Wittgensteinian approach, "behavioral science methodology is suspect" when studying social conventions, since it distracts the researcher from her true task, which is to immerse oneself in one's subject matter and to understand it by practicing it, not seeking distance through " 'value free' research."[20]

Wellington's special insight was to notice that someone who is charged with the responsibility of interpreting law has to think about conventional morality the way the linguist or grammarian thinks about the grammar of their society's language game. One might be skeptical about the parallel between morality and language. I will return to the problems with the parallel at the end of this essay. For the moment, I want to point out that Wellington made such a move in "Common Law Rules" and want to locate his contribution in the wider context of the jurisprudential scholarship of the time. However, I will note that, in language, Wellington found a congenial analogue. First, like language, social morality is ultimately subjective. No one would want to say that any given grammatical modality is "better" than another (nationalism aside, few people come to blows over the issue of whether German is "more grammatical" than French because of its approach to the subjunctive); and on many matters of deep moral conflict (some of which may in fact even be measurable from an objective point of view) it seems both senseless and imperialistic to say that American attitudes toward punishment are "more moral" than the Germans' (where average criminal sentences are much shorter). Second, like language, social morality cannot be legislated or governed by a single deliberative authority. As Hart argued, "moral rules or principles *cannot* be brought into being or changed or eliminated" by "deliberate enactment," like the traffic code, which can make an entire nation shift from driving on the right to the left overnight.[21]

It may strike some as odd that Wellington based his analysis of moral convention in Wittgenstein and Hart, but it should not. As I have argued elsewhere, there was a strong affinity between postwar legal positivism, as articulated by H. L. A. Hart at Oxford, and legal process, as articulated by Henry Hart and Albert Sacks at Harvard.[22] It should not surprise us, therefore, given that Wellington was trying to carry forward Hart and Sacks's legal process project, that Wellington would embrace H. L. A. Hart. "Common Law Rules" offers a deeper insight into the connection between legal process and positivism because it highlights their common interest in a certain kind of Wittgensteinian analysis of social convention. It is no accident that Wellington quotes, at length, H. L. A. Hart and Stanley Cavell within two pages of his argument. The rule of recognition, which Hart held out as the normative foundation of a legal system, is a validation rule that itself cannot be validated by legal reasons.[23] Hart noted that:

[W]e only need the word "validity," and commonly only use it, to answer questions which arise *within* a system of rules. . . . No such question can arise as to the validity of the very rule of recognition which provides the criteria; it can neither be valid nor invalid but is simply accepted as appropriate for use in this way.[24]

In "Must We Mean What We Say," Cavell says much the same thing: "(Successfully) justifying a statement or an action is not (cannot be) justifying its justification."[25]

Hart argued that those who thought that the rule of recognition could not be normative *within* its own domain if it were not validated by the norms of *that* domain did not understand how conventions worked. He noted that "we assume, but can never demonstrate, that the standard metre bar in Paris, which is the ultimate test of correctness of all measurement in metres, is itself correct."[26] Hart did not pull this example out of thin air: earlier, Wittgenstein tried to explain how conventions can possess normative force by comparing the grammar of a language game to the "metre-bar" in Paris:

There is *one* thing of which one can say neither that it is one metre long, nor that it is not one metre long, and that is the standard metre in Paris. But this is, of course, not to ascribe any ordinary property to it, but only to mark its peculiar role in the language-game of measuring with a metre-rule.[27]

Wellington's moral conventionalism, therefore, was rooted in an epistemology that rejected both value-free empiricism and pure conceptual analysis. The practice of *social* morality had to be approached critically, not only empirically, but it could not be an exercise in *individual* morality. By invoking Cavell, Wellington wanted to emphasize that by viewing social morality as something akin to a language game, we could get a sense of the task that he was setting out for the judge. The job of the judge was no more conceptually intractable than that of the grammarian.

I want to end with expressing two reservations about the adoption of the Cavell–Wittgensteinian approach to social morality.

First, although it is very appealing today to bash value-free social science, why would we really want to say of language, for example, that the investigations of the single philosopher are more likely to tell us about the correct usage of language than the work of the pollster? Cavell has a very witty line: before starting to count noses we assume the native speaker of English "can rely on his own nose; if not, there would be nothing to count." But even if this observation were true for ordinary language philosophy, is it really translatable to the problem of identifying conventional morality? It would be very convenient if it were, since the role of the common law judge is very much like that of the ordinary language philosopher who says, at the end of the day, whether or not someone can be characterized as having acted responsibly if they were not required to perform the act. Similarly, when they faulted the New York court for failing to recognize the right to privacy, Warren and Brandeis were not saying that the judge on the court should have told the Rochester Folding Box Company how they ought to behave, they were telling them what the common law of tort actually required of them.[28]

This leads to the second concern. What is the status of the rules of social morality that Wellington wants to explicate? Cavell spoke primarily of rules of grammar. Wittgenstein spoke often of grammar and calculus. Yet these systems are validated in an all-or-nothing fashion that seems quite foreign from social morality.

Cavell recognized this problem and tried to respond. He noted that "it is sometimes felt that drawing an analogy between moral conduct and games makes moral conduct seem misleadingly simple (or trivial?) because there are no rules in moral conduct corresponding to the rules about how the queen moves in chess."[29] Cavell's response is that no one doubts that moral conventions are principles and chess is comprised of rules. Rules and principles differ in many respects, complexity being just one, but they share one common genetic strand: both must be done "correctly." Wittgenstein said the same thing in the *Blue Books* when he noted that language is not like calculus, either.[30] But why does this one feature—the capacity for users of the practice to recognize that an instantiation of the practice is correct—swamp the vast array of differences between the practices? In another essay, "The Availability of Wittgenstein's Later Philosophy,"[31] Cavell argues that it is the capacity for correctness in action that characterizes participation in a form of life. To the extent that we are persuaded that the analysis of practice as a form of life fits mathematics, language, and law, there is some reason to believe that Wellington and Hart were right to point us in the direction of Wittgenstein.

Acknowledgments

I would like to acknowledge the assistance of Robert Hardman, Brooklyn Law School Class of 2003.

Notes

1. *Brown v. Board of Education.*

2. *Griswold v. Connecticut.*

3. Wellington 1973.

4. *MacPherson v. Buick Motor Co.*

5. *Roberson v. Rochester Folding Box Co.*

6. See Wellington 1973, p. 245.

7. See Wellington 1973, p. 244.

8. The idea that law is best understood as a complex set of conventions has always lurked in the background of Anglo-American jurisprudence. The role of

conventionality in law has been thoughtfully and persuasively explored by Jules Coleman in his recent work. See Coleman 2001.

9. See Wellington 1973, p. 243, citing Hare 1963, p. 94.

10. See Wellington 1973, p. 246.

11. See Sebok and Postema 1998, pp. 171–174; see also Landauer 2002.

12. See Deutsch 1968.

13. Hart 1961.

14. See, e.g., Wellington 1973, p. 226.

15. See Hart 1961, p. 171.

16. See Wellington 1973, p. 247.

17. See Wellington 1973, p. 247, quoting the original version of Stanley Cavell's essay "Must We Mean What We Say?" that was first published in Chappell 1964. "Must We Mean What We Say?" was later republished in Cavell 1969/1976 and all subsequent references are to this version.

18. See Baker and Hacker 1985, pp. 171–172. ("The pivotal point in Wittgenstein's remarks on following rules is that a rule is internally related to acts which accord with it. The rule and nothing but the rule determines what is correct.")

19. "When we teach another person by ostensive definition we teach by example. . . ." Sebok (1999), citing Wittgenstein 1958, § 6.

20. See Wellington 1973, p. 248; quotes in the original.

21. See Hart 1961, p. 171.

22. See Sebok and Postema 1998, pp. 160–168; see also Sebok 1999, pp. 99–102.

23. See Sebok 1999, pp. 105–106.

24. Hart 1961, pp. 108–109.

25. See Cavell 1969/1976, p. 24.

26. See Hart 1961, p. 109.

27. Wittgenstein 1958, § 50.

28. Warren and Brandeis 1890.

29. Cavell 1969/1976, p. 29.

30. Wittgenstein 1969, p. 51.

31. Cavell 1969/1976.

References

Baker, G. P., and P. M. S. Hacker. 1985. *Wittgenstein, Rules, Grammar, and Necessity.* Oxford: Blackwell.

Brown v. Board of Education, 347 U.S. 483 (1954).

Cavell, S. 1969/1976. *Must We Mean What We Say?* Cambridge: Cambridge University Press.

Chappell, V. C., ed. 1964. *Ordinary Language: Essays in Philosophical Method.* Englewood Cliffs, N.J.: Prentice-Hall.

Coleman, J. 2001. *The Practice of Principle.* Oxford: Oxford University Press.

Deutsch, J. G. 1968. "Neutrality, Legitimacy, and the Supreme Court: Some Intersections between Law and Political Science." *Stanford Law Review* 20: 169–261.

Dworkin, Ronald. 1977. *Taking Rights Seriously.* Cambridge, Mass.: Harvard University Press.

Griswold v. Connecticut, 381 U.S. 479 (1965).

Hare, R. M. 1963. *Freedom and Reason.* Oxford: Oxford University Press.

Hart, H. L. A. 1961. *The Concept of Law.* Oxford: Oxford University Press.

Landauer, C. 2002. "Deliberating Speed: Totalitarian Anxieties and Postwar Legal Thought." *Yale Journal of Law and Humanities* 12: 171–248.

MacPherson v. Buick Motor Co., 111 N.E. 1050 (N.Y. 1916).

Roberson v. Rochester Folding Box Co., 64 N.E. 442 (1902).

Sebok, A. J. 1999. "Finding Wittgenstein at the Core of the Rule of Recognition." *SMU Law Review* 52: 75–109.

Sebok, A. J., and G. Postema, eds. 1998. *Legal Positivism in American Jurisprudence.* Cambridge: Cambridge University Press.

Warren, S., and L. Brandeis. 1890. "The Right to Privacy." *Harvard Law Review* 4: 193–220.

Wellington, H. 1973. "Common Law Rules and Constitutional Double Standards: Some Notes on Adjudication." *Yale Law Journal* 83: 221–311.

Wittgenstein, L. 1958. *Philosophical Investigations*, second ed. G. E. M. Anscombe, trans. Oxford: Blackwell.

———. 1969. *The Blue and Brown Books*, second ed. Oxford: Blackwell.

Part III

14 Introduction: The Practice of Principle

Kenneth Einar Himma

Jules L. Coleman's *The Practice of Principle: In Defense of a Pragmatist Approach to Legal Theory* is one of the most important books in conceptual jurisprudence (i.e., the area of legal theory dealing with the philosophical analysis of legal concepts) in recent years. The book's scope is comprehensive, covering all the important current controversies in conceptual jurisprudence on methodological and substantive issues, as well as substantive issues in tort theory. Although Coleman's principal concern is to defend a pragmatic methodology for conceptual analysis, his coverage of the substantive issues represents the state of the art.

The 2002 INPC hosted a panel discussion of Coleman's book, featuring a number of very prominent legal theorists—including Coleman himself. The other participants were Stephen Perry, New York University Law School; John Gardner, Chair of Jurisprudence at Oxford University; Benjamin Zipursky, Fordham University School of Law; and me. In addition, Scott Shapiro, an influential young theorist from Cardozo Law School, moderated the discussion. The event was among the highlights of the conference and, as one might expect, was well attended.

Three of the contributions to the panel appear in this section.[1] In "Backward and Forward with Tort Law," Gardner distinguishes two kinds of objection to the so-called law-and-economics explanation of tort law: type-(a) objections that challenge the underlying assumption that economic values are the only ones that matter; and type-(b) objections that the content of tort law cannot be justified by reference to economic values (even if these are the only ones that really matter). He goes on to consider two type-(b) objections made by Coleman in *The Practice of Principle* and argues that both fail because "legal economists can in principle account for any norm that can be accounted for." Gardner concludes that the only way to refute law-and-economics explanations of the content of tort law is to show they rest on a bad theory of value.

In "Pragmatism, Positivism, and the Model of Social Facts," Zipursky challenges Coleman's view that legal validity can be fully explained in terms of some set of social facts (the "social fact thesis"). Drawing on elements of Ronald Dworkin's semantic sting argument, Zipursky argues that Coleman must explain how judicial officials can disagree about the content of the rule of recognition if that content is conventional and hence fully explained by a set of social facts about what those officials agree upon. Zipursky argues that Coleman's holistic account of legal argument is incapable of adequately explaining judicial disagreement in hard cases without resorting to devices that are in clear tension with the social fact thesis. On Zipursky's view, Coleman's explanation of judicial disagreement is on the right track, but it requires him to give up the social fact thesis—which is at the core of positivism's defining commitments.

Finally, in "Conceptual Jurisprudence and the Intelligibility of Law's Claim to Obligate," I critically evaluate Coleman's claim that legal obligation can be explained by conceiving of the rule of recognition as a shared cooperative activity (SCA). Qua parties to an SCA, officials are jointly committed to accepting and supporting the rule of recognition; it is this joint commitment that, on Coleman's view, enables a positivist to adequately explain the sense in which laws characteristically give rise to (legal) obligations. I argue that Coleman's theory may succeed in explaining how the rule of recognition obligates officials, but does not succeed in explaining how primary legal norms obligate citizens; the joint commitments of officials, by themselves, cannot obligate persons who are not parties to those commitments. This is problematic, on my view, because the idea that primary legal rules *obligate* citizens is central to our legal practices.

Coleman honors the three panelists with an extended reply piece in which he carefully considers their comments and objections. In reply to Gardner, Coleman points out that although attributions of fault and responsibility are central to the arguments of lawyers defending tort positions, they are irrelevant from the standpoint of law-and-economics explanations; such considerations suggest that tort law is a system of corrective justice—and not a system for allocating costs in the most efficient way. In reply to Zipursky, Coleman reconciles his explanation of judicial disagreement with the social fact thesis by arguing that the semantic sting argument wrongly presupposes that the only way social facts could fix the content of the rule of recognition is by identifying the grounds of law with the scope of convergent behavior; the nature of the activities and attitudes making up a shared cooperative venture can also fix that content. In reply to my essay, Coleman argues that the burden of providing an account of legal obligation rests with normative political philosophy and not with legal positivist accounts of legal concepts.

As is evident from the selections in this section, Coleman's views in *The Practice of Principle* will generate considerable debate and critical discussion. This, of course, is due to the importance of the book; the best books contribute to theoretical progress not by ending debate, but by promoting it. As the range of selections may suggest, nearly every chapter of Coleman's book is likely to provoke lively (indeed, impassioned) discussion. The hope is that the selections in this section contribute something of value to that discussion.

Note

1. Perry was unable to submit a contribution.

15 Backward and Forward with Tort Law

John Gardner

Torts as Wrongs

Here is a lawyer's view of the law of torts. We might call it the "textbook" view. A tort, on this view, is a kind of legal wrong, a breach of a legal obligation on the part of the tortfeasor. This ("primary") legal obligation, unlike a contractual obligation, is not created by the exercise of the tortfeasor's own legal power to bind herself. Rather it is imposed directly by the law. But, like a contractual obligation, it is owed to somebody in particular, some rightholder whose rights are violated by the commission of the wrong. This rights violation has legal consequences for both the tortfeasor and the rightholder. It places the tortfeasor under a new ("secondary") legal obligation toward the rightholder, namely an obligation of reparation. It also confers on the rightholder a legal power to enforce this new obligation against the tortfeasor by applying to the court for an award of damages against the tortfeasor. Such an award crystallizes the tortfeasor's secondary legal obligation of reparation (by putting a money figure on it) and thereby activates further powers of enforcement (those available for liquidated debts). In principle the rightholder could also have enforced the original primary obligation against the tortfeasor by applying to the court for an injunction before the tort was committed. An injunction would have crystallized the primary legal obligation (by specifying more exactly which action would count as a violation of it), and would also have activated further powers of enforcement (penalties for contempt of court). But whereas a court retains discretion to deny the rightholder an injunction to crystallise and enforce the primary obligation, the court has no discretion to deny her an award of damages to crystallize and enforce the secondary obligation. If she makes out her case in tort, the court has a legal obligation to make her an award of damages, even if only a nominal one.[1] Thanks to her original (primary) legal right having been violated by the tortfeasor, to put it another way, the rightholder not only gains a new (secondary) legal right against the tortfeasor but also gains—for the first time— a legal right to be assisted by the court in the enforcement of her legal rights against the tortfeasor.

In sketching this view I have not separated the essential from the inessential nor the central from the peripheral. If the aim were to distinguish the law of torts from other parts of the law, what I have just said would be incomplete in some respects and too elaborate in others. But one feature that I picked out is clearly pivotal. Everything else turns on it. A tort, according to the textbook view, is a kind of legal wrong. It is the breach of a primary legal obligation by the tortfeasor. That somebody's (performed or anticipated) action qualifies as the breach of one of tort law's primary obligations is what lends legal consequences to that action so far as tort law is concerned. Both the rightholder and the court accordingly need to rely on the legally wrongful character of the tortfeasor's (performed or anticipated) action in making the legal case for the award of damages or the issue of an injunction. They must identify it as the breach of a primary legal obligation. If they do not then they have not made out a case in the law of torts. For they have not identified a tort.

Some theorists are suspicious about the textbook view of the law of torts precisely because it makes this feature pivotal. They doubt whether there really are primary legal obligations in tort law. They say that in spite of appearances torts are not really wrongs at all. Here I will not go through all the colorful and clever but uniformly fallacious arguments that have been given for favoring this revisionist conclusion. But let me mention one particularly influential and particularly confused line of thought. It begins from the observation that many potential tortfeasors— perhaps more than ever before in this age of the ruthless multinational corporation—do not think of their so-called primary legal obligations as obligatory and do not rely on them as obligations when they think about what to do. In fact they don't engage with the law of torts in terms of obligations at all, whether primary or secondary. If they give the law of torts any credence, what many potential tortfeasors worry about, and rely on in thinking about what to do, are their potential legal *liabilities*—in other words, the legal powers that others may exercise against them. So why hold out for the view that potential tortfeasors have obligations in the law of torts? Why not regard all the law's talk of obligations as mere verbiage and switch over to thinking of the law of torts as a system of legal liabilities, unencumbered by obligations? It is no answer to say that the liabilities that potential tortfeasors worry about are none other than liabilities to have their obligations crystallized and enforced, so that there must be obligations in the law of torts. This doesn't get us where we need to be. It leaves open that there are no obligations in the law of torts until they are crystallized by a court, in which case a tort—not yet injuncted—is not yet a breach of any obligation, and thus the textbook view still fails.

This challenge to the textbook view misses something really obvious, or at any rate really obvious to lawyers. Even if few (or for that matter no) potential tortfeasors rely on the fact that they have obligations in the law of torts, plenty of other people *do* rely on that fact. In particular, those who have the associated legal powers of crystallization and enforcement— rightholders bringing cases in tort and courts hearing cases in tort—rely extensively and systematically on the existence of the tortfeasor's primary legal obligation. For unless they identify someone's (performed or anticipated) action as the breach of such an obligation there is no case in tort for rightholders to bring or for courts to hear. A primary obligation and an action constituting its breach have to be identified to get the legal arguments started. That is the very point that is pivotal to the textbook view. So the revisionists face the following counterchallenge on behalf of the textbook view: how come what figures in the reasoning of potential tortfeasors should admittedly be regarded as pivotal to the law of torts, whereas what figures in the reasoning of the courts and those who argue cases before the courts should not be?

It is tolerably clear what the revisionists are thinking here. They are thinking of legal systems as systems of incentives, and legal obligations, in particular, as incentives to those who are bound by them. If those who are supposedly bound do not attend to their supposed obligations in their practical reasoning, the revisionist thinks, then there are no such obligations, for there are none of the definitive effects of such obligations. By failing to incentivize, the law fails to obligate. But this conclusion is wide of the mark. Although legal obligations often do come bundled with incentives for their performance, legal obligations are not incentives and are not validated as obligations by their incentive effects. They are validated as obligations by their *normative* effects (including their effectiveness in furnishing legal arguments for the creation by law of incentives for conformity with them).[2] It is no skin off the law's nose, in general, if those who have legal obligations never attend to those obligations in their reasoning. They may even be anarchists for all the law cares. So long as people do whatever they have a legal obligation to do—so long as in their actions they conform to the legal norm—it is all the same to the law whether they do so for legal reasons, for moral reasons, for prudential reasons, or indeed for no reason at all.

Normally, in short, we have no legal obligation, nor even a legal reason, to attend to legal obligations, or any other legal reasons, in our reasoning. But there are exceptions. The main exceptions are those that apply to officials of the legal system (including acting officials such as plaintiffs in civil suits). Some officials have a legal obligation to reason legally. Some have legal powers that are validly exercised only if exercised for legal reasons. Some are legally empowered to acquire further legal powers or rights only if they establish or at least assert legal reasons why they should acquire them. So if we want to know whether a certain legal obligation exists, there is normally no reason to be especially interested in the reasoning of those (nonofficials) who are said to be bound by it. But there is often a reason to be interested in the reasoning of legal officials who rely on the existence of that legal obligation in fulfilling their own legal obligations or exercising their own legal powers or making a legal case for the extension of their own legal powers or rights.

The central role of official law users in determining the incidence of legal obligations and powers was emphasized by H. L. A. Hart. Hart is most commonly remembered for the application of this point to the law of the constitution, where (he argued) all legal systems need official law users (law-applying officials) to settle the incidence of ultimate legal obligations and powers.[3] But Hart's main insight applies no less to the law of torts. If we want confirmation of the existence of primary legal obligations in the law of torts, we should be focusing not on the reasoning of potential tortfeasors but on the reasoning of the courts and the rightholders who appear before them. And in this reasoning we cannot deny the pivotal role of the tort itself. Some (performed or anticipated) action on the part of an alleged tortfeasor has to be identified as a breach of one of tort law's primary legal obligations or else a tort case never gets off the ground. The alleged tort-feasor has no case to answer.

Law and Economics

Possibly some members of the so-called law and economics movement think of legal systems as systems of incentives. If they do, then the difference between them and most other legal theorists is not that the economists are assessing the law against their own specialized economic benchmarks. The difference, rather, is that they are not assessing the law at all. The law has dropped out of their world. All they can see are certain accessories of the law, namely the incentives that are sometimes but not always attached to legal obligations and liabilities. Talk of legal obligations and liabilities is therefore of no interest to them except as a euphemistic (perhaps efficiently euphemistic, but still euphemistic) way of talking about threats, predictions, expectations, and deprivations.

But I doubt whether many legal economists consistently lose sight of the law in this way. More often, in the law and economics literature, the law is taken and assessed at face value. It is held to be made up of the very obligations and liabilities that legal officials rely on in their legal reasoning and that make their way, accordingly, into the legal textbooks. The mainstream legal economists' question is whether people's having these legal obligations and liabilities—understood not as incentives but as normative positions—is economically defensible.[4] Of course, the economic defense of a norm, like other purely instrumental defenses of it, must be sensitive to the extent of conformity with it by those to whom it applies, and securing such conformity may sometimes require the addition of incentives. But this is where economists of law tend to wear their lawyers' hats for a moment. They often make the simplifying assumption, for the sake of conducting their economic assessments, that what the law says goes. The economic defensibility of a legal norm is then its economic defensibility assuming perfect, or at least very extensive, implementation. So, for example, the primary and secondary obligations of potential tortfeasors are apt to be treated as economically defensible if and only if conformity with them by all and only those who are bound by them would be economically defensible. And the enforcement powers of rightholders and courts in respect of breaches of those obligations are apt to be treated as economically defensible if and only if the valid exercise of those powers on every available occasion by all and only those who have them would be economically defensible. And so forth. If it turned out that in fact the legal norm in question were widely disregarded, its economic merits and demerits would call for a radical reassessment.[5]

With or without these simplifying assumptions in place, the question of whether the law is economically defensible could of course be asked with more or less dispositive ambitions. Some who ask it may suppose that the only considerations relevant to assessing the law are economic considerations, so that all and only those legal obligations and liabilities that are economically defensible are defensible tout court.[6] Others may think, less embarrassingly, that discovering whether the law is economically defensible is part but only part of the job of discovering whether the law is defensible tout court. Some noneconomic strengths in the law, on this view, might make up for its economic deficiencies.[7] Still other economists of law, out of abundant caution, may wish to keep their distance from both of these views by saying that they are invoking economic considerations entirely noncommittally. For all they know, economic considerations will turn out to be irrelevant to the defense of the law, but still it is interesting to see to what extent—if they were relevant—such considerations *could* be used to defend the law. To what extent does the law say what economic thinking would have it say? Tackling this question may help to expose the blind spots as well as the insights of economic thinking about law, and so may be interesting even to those who are skeptical about the ultimate importance of economic considerations. The question may also be interesting to those who want to investigate what considerations (for better or worse) influence lawmakers, such as judges and legislators. That the law says what economic thinking would have it say does not of course show that any lawmaker is thinking economically–nor, for that matter, vice versa. It may all be a coincidence. But it may be a legitimate working hypothesis that how lawmakers think will show up, albeit approximately, in the laws they make. Coupled with other plausible hypotheses about the institutional influence of prevailing social ideologies, this may give some scholars a reason to investigate the extent to which legal norms are amenable to an economic justification, without themselves advancing or endorsing that justification.

Legal economists in this noncommittal vein sometimes like to present themselves as engaged in a radically different enterprise from their more committal peers. Their work, they may say, is "explanation" or "analysis," not "justification" or "defense." It belongs to "positive" rather than "normative" economics.[8] But these are notorious false contrasts. Anyone who explains or analyzes legal norms in terms of considerations (also known as reasons) cannot but be concerned with the justifiability or defensibility of those norms. In that sense, their project cannot be other than normative. The only caveat is that a concern with justifiability can in principle be a detached concern. Possibly some people working in the law-and-economics tradition want to know whether certain laws are economically justifiable in the same detached way that I (an atheist who sees nothing wrong with sex outside marriage and who objects to both corporal and capital punishment) might want to know whether stoning adulteresses to death really is justifiable according to Islamic teachings.[9] If it turns out that such an abhorrent action is justifiable according to Islamic teachings, then (I would say) so much the worse for Islamic teachings. It does not follow that my interest in those teachings was not an interest in their justificatory force. On the contrary: I judge them to be deficient teachings precisely because of what is justifiable according to them.

To put it another way, the issue of whether the law of torts is economically defensible has to be kept distinct from the question of whether an economic defense of the law of torts is a defense worth wanting. Corresponding to these two distinct questions, there are two types of objections to the so-called economic analysis of tort law. On the one hand, (a) there are objections to the dispiriting economic theory of value that the economic analysis implicates. Are economic considerations really the only ones, or even the main ones, that matter? Isn't there a lot more to life than can be represented by anyone's "utility function," or measured, even approximately, by their ability and willingness to pay? On the other hand, (b) there are objections that concede for the sake of argument that economic considerations are indeed the only ones that matter and then proceed to argue that the obligations and liabilities of tort law are not defensible in terms of such considerations, or in terms of such considerations alone, so that an economic analysis of tort law fails. Naturally a type-(b) objection leaves a major hostage to fortune. Those who offer an economic analysis of tort law may reply that, since their analysis fails to show the law of torts in a defensible light, the law of torts is indefensible as it stands and calls for reform or abolition. At that point critics of the economic analysis are forced back to a type-(a) objection. But at least they are forced back in a way that prevents supporters of the economic analysis from denying that they really are committed to the dispiriting theory of value that their analysis implicates. They can no longer parade the justificatory detachment of the "mere" social scientist who does not personally endorse the values that he or she invokes. So in this way we can smoke out the disingenuous minority of legal economists who do personally advocate the dispiriting economic theory of value even as they insist—with a hurt look on their faces—that all they are doing is "positive" economics.

A great deal of philosophical energy and ingenuity has been invested in building type-(b) objections to the economic analysis of tort law, objections that attempt to show the inadequacy of economic considerations to explain the main features of the law of torts. Some writers have strange ideas about what counts as a main feature for this purpose. Many arguments rage, for example, about the adequacy of an economic analysis of the law's negligence standard, even though negligence is but one constituent among many of some but not all torts. Other arguments rage about the adequacy of an economic analysis of the legal idea of proximate causation, even though proximate causation is again just one constituent among many of some but not all torts. I will leave these distracting local difficulties on one side. They do not belong to the general part of the law of torts. They bear on what list of primary obligations would feature in the law of torts were it economically defended. My interest here will be in a prior question: can an economic analyst explain the pivotal role of primary obligations in the law of torts *at all*, never mind which primary obligations end up on the list?

Coleman's Twin Objections

In *The Practice of Principle* Jules Coleman sketches two important and closely related type-(b) objections to the economic analysis of tort law. Both challenge the ability of the economic analyst to accord primary obligations—never mind which particular primary obligations—their proper place relative to secondary obligations in the argumentative logic of tort law. Here are Coleman's most trenchant renditions of the two objections:

[First objection]   These [economic] accounts do not use efficiency to discover an independent class of duties that are analytically prior to our liability practices. In the standard economic analysis, there is no boundary, as it were, between what the duties are and what the liability practices should be. What counts as a "duty" or a "wrong" in a standard economic account depends on an assessment of what the consequences are of imposing liability in a given case. Duty and wrong, as independent categories, are doing no work in the story. So while in principle we could have an efficiency theory of duties, what economists offer is not an efficiency theory of duties at all, but an efficiency theory of liability or cost allocation.[10]

[Second objection]   How then does the economist account for the fact that in the typical tort suit the victim sues the injurer and not the alleged cheapest cost avoider? How does one square the forward-looking goal of tort law (on the economic model) with the backward-looking structure of tort law? The economist cannot appeal to the obvious answer that the victim believes the injurer harmed him wrongfully and in doing so incurred a duty to make good the victim's losses. In the economist's account, the victim sues the injurer because the cost of searching for those in the best position to reduce the costs of future accidents is too high.[11]

These two objections might easily be collapsed. But the first is more radical than the second, and Coleman is right to set it apart. The second objection only doubts the ability of legal economists to justify tort law's secondary obligations. As pure instrumentalists about norms, legal economists insist that a secondary obligation can only be justified by the good consequences of its being incurred. According to Coleman, this means that legal economists cannot explain the law's justification of a secondary obligation, which points not to the good consequences of its being incurred ("forward-looking"), but to the fact that a primary obligation was already violated ("backward-looking"). Coleman's first objection, however, goes further and doubts whether legal economists can properly account for the primary obligation itself. A purely instrumental justification of the primary obligation as a way of bringing optimal secondary obligations into existence cannot, claims Coleman, account for the primary obligation *as a* primary obligation. If this is true then the difficulty that economic analysts have in explaining the legal justification of a secondary obligation by reference to the breach of a primary obligation is the least of their problems. They cannot even explain why, in tort law, the primary obligation is there to breach.

You may wonder whether the first objection's greater radicalism isn't promptly surrendered in Coleman's concession that economic analysts could "in principle" offer an economic defense of at least some primary obligations suitable for use in the law of torts ("an efficiency theory of duties"). Doesn't this concession instantly take all the sting out of his first objection, understood as a type-(b) objection to the economic analysis of tort law? The problem, it seems, is not that economic analysis lacks the resources adequately to account for tort law's primary obligations. The problem is merely that legal economists "standard[ly]" fail to use these resources, and so drop the primary obligations out of their picture of tort law. In the process they inflict unnecessary damage on their own positions. But I don't think that Coleman means to concede this much. I suspect he only means to make a more limited concession that I also made in the previous section. An economic study of the law of torts, as I mentioned, could readily tackle the following question about the tortfeasor's primary obligations: are the tortfeasor's primary obligations economically defensible assuming perfect or at least very widespread conformity, that is, on the footing that they are rarely if ever breached? The problem is that nobody would regard an affirmative answer to this question, without more, as an adequate economic defense of the law of torts. In addition we would need to know the answer to this follow-up question: are tort law's *secondary* obligations (assuming perfect or at least widespread conformity with these) economically defensible as legal consequences of the breach of tort law's primary obligations (now necessarily assuming significant nonconformity with these)? The charge against the economic analysts, as framed in Coleman's first objection, is that they cannot but let the follow-up question swallow the original question, and in the process destroy any prospect of an adequate economic defense of tort law's primary obligations. At any rate, this is the intended force that I will ascribe to the first objection in the discussion that follows. And it is with the first objection that we will begin.

Forward from the Primary Obligation

Policy and Legitimacy

The impact of Coleman's first objection, if sound, goes beyond the destabilization of the economic analysis of tort law. It also has implications for the workaday tort lawyer's reliance on policy arguments in debates about where the primary obligations of tort law should begin and end. In this context "policy argument" is a technical lawyers' expression. It refers to an argument for or against recognizing certain acts as falling under certain legal norms (e.g., as meeting the legal test for causation) on the strength of the legal consequences of such recognition (e.g., a wider or narrower net of tort liabilities), and the extralegal consequences, in turn, of those legal consequences (e.g., the possible bankrupting of local authorities or insurance companies, or the possible absence of recourse for victims of large-scale pharmaceutical accidents involving multiple manufacturers). Not all instrumental arguments about what should qualify as a primary obligation in tort law are policy arguments. Even for economists, the classification of a given action as legally obligatory may have good and bad consequences quite apart from the good and bad extralegal consequences of the legal consequences of its classification. Nevertheless, it is hard to deny that the most important extralegal consequences of classifying a given action as legally obligatory are those that are consequences of the legal liability that attaches to a failure to perform the obligation. So if they can't put policy arguments in the driver's seat, legal economists and others seeking a purely instrumental defense of the law of torts have little to say for themselves. This is the unhappy state of speechlessness that Coleman's first objection seeks to reduce them to.

Coleman is not the only theorist of tort law to challenge the ability of policy arguments to establish the content of tort law's primary obligations. Most familiar objections, however, are objections to the legitimacy of *judicial resort* to policy arguments.[12] When judges are attaching legal consequences to people's actions, the story goes, their job is to ensure that justice is done between the parties. The further nonlegal consequences of their doing so (the consequent availability and cost of insurance, the consequent increases in public expenditure, the consequent shift in negotiating power between consumers and producers, etc.) are problems for other institutions, such as legislators, to worry about. Such separation-of-powers objections are open to a range of relatively straightforward replies on behalf of those who advance policy arguments. The most important is the reply made famous by John Rawls and extensively exhibited in the work of modern game theorists.[13] Justification is rarely transparent. That a certain judicial decision is ultimately justified by policy arguments in its favor does not entail that the judge should be aware of those policy arguments, still less rely on them. It suffices that the judge relies on legal or moral norms, reliance upon which is in turn justified by policy arguments. There is no reason to imagine that such norms will disclose the policy arguments that justify reliance on them, let alone instruct or authorize judges to *use* those policy arguments. So the claim that it is illegitimate for judges to resort to policy arguments need not detract from the importance of such arguments in determining what judges are to do. In other words, the contrast between policy arguments and arguments of justice is a false one: those who see to it that justice is done between the parties may well in the process be doing the very thing that, unbeknown to them, the assembled policy arguments would have them do.

We will be coming back to this line of thought when we turn to Coleman's second objection. For present purposes, however, we can make do with a simpler reply to those who offer separation-of-powers objections to the use of policy arguments in determining the content of tort law's primary obligations. The simpler reply is that there is no reason to assume that the content of tort law's primary obligations is wholly or even mainly the business of judges. True, some torts are torts at common law, which have been shaped by successive judicial decisions. But many are statutory torts, or common-law torts modified by statute. Indeed one of the common law's most enduringly important torts—breach of statutory duty—is explicitly organized around the idea that the content of the relevant primary obligation should be determined, in large measure, by legislation. So if the problem with policy arguments were only a problem with the legitimacy of judicial resort to such arguments, the obvious answer would be this: nothing about the law of torts requires that the question of what actions are to count as tortious be left wholly or mainly to judges. Indeed who should decide what actions are to count as tortious is itself a matter amenable to policy argument, turning on a determination of who is best placed to give effect to the policy arguments for and against counting certain actions as tortious (whether by relying on those policy arguments or otherwise).

A Problem of Circularity?
Coleman knows all this. His first objection, accordingly, is not an objection to the legitimacy of judicial resort to policy arguments (or to the legit-

imacy of anything, for that matter). Coleman objects, rather, to something in the *logic* of policy arguments. On the simplest interpretation of what he is saying, his charge is one of vicious circularity. In the law of torts, as I mentioned earlier, the primary obligation has justificatory priority. Its existence and breach have to be relied on in arguing that a secondary obligation has been incurred, and hence in making a case that the rightholder is entitled to the crystallizing and enforcing assistance of the court. But when policy arguments are being employed, the secondary obligation, with its attendant liabilities, seems instead to assume justificatory priority over the primary. One needs to furnish arguments for the incurring of a secondary obligation, with its attendant liabilities, in order to establish that what the defendant did should indeed be counted as a breach of a primary obligation. Can the latter order of argumentation be squared with the former? For Coleman, simply interpreted, the answer is no. There is a vicious circle in treating primary obligations as justified by the very thing that primary obligations also serve to justify.

There is something immediately paradoxical about this challenge of circularity. Another way to express the idea that primary obligations have justificatory priority in the law of torts is to say that, in the law of torts, the incurring of a secondary obligation, with its attendant liabilities, is a *legal consequence* of the breach of a primary obligation. When legislatures or courts create new primary obligations in the law of torts (i.e., when they hold additional actions to be tortious) they also create, by operation of law, new secondary legal obligations that arise in the event of the primary obligation's breach, and new rights for rightholders in search of judicial assistance with the crystallization and enforcement of those secondary obligations. Legislatures and courts cannot avoid creating these legal consequences except by not creating any new primary legal obligations in the law of torts. How can it possibly be viciously circular to regard these legal consequences as relevant to the question of whether to create new primary legal obligations? And if they are relevant to *whether*, then surely also to *which*? Surely the case for or against creating a certain primary obligation cannot *but* be affected by the legal consequences of doing so? Far from casting doubt on the logical acceptability of policy arguments, then, the justificatory priority of primary legal obligations seems to be the very thing that makes policy arguments so central to any credible debate about which primary legal obligations we should have: new primary obligations justify new secondary obligations, so the various arguments for and against having such new secondary obligations must surely be relevant to the arguments for and against having the new primary obligations.

We can make the flavor of paradox here more intense if we apply Coleman's first objection in another (noninstitutional) context. Consider, for example, the morality of promising. One may well suppose that the existence of a moral power to incur moral obligations by promising is justified, at least in part, by the case for people's incurring those moral obligations by promising. How else would one go about defending the power to promise if one did not rest one's case on the defensibility of promising's having the moral consequences that promising has, namely, the incurring of new moral obligations? At the same time, the very fact that the incurring of a new moral obligation is a moral consequence of the exercise of the power means that one necessarily relies on the exercise of the power in defending the incurring of the obligation. Is this viciously circular? Coleman's first objection seems to suggest that it is. So long as one grants that the incurring of the obligation is the moral consequence of the exercise of the power, applying Coleman's first objection, the existence of the power cannot be defended in turn by pointing to the value of its giving rise to that same obligation. For in that defense one puts the obligation before the power in one's order of argumentation, but at the same time one puts the power before the obligation. They cannot both come before each other in the order of argumentation. So we are left—it seems—with a bit of a justificatory vacuum in the morality of promising. How on earth are we now going to set about justifying the existence of the moral power to promise?

Something has gone wrong here, and it does not take long to work out what it is. The existence of the power to promise is one thing, and its exercise is quite another. There is no vicious circle—no circle at all—in holding that the *existence* of the power to promise is justifiable only because the obligations incurred by promising are justifiable obligations, while also holding that each such obligation is justifiable, in return, only thanks to the *exercise* of the same (justifiable) power. So there is no logical obstacle to defending the existence of the power to promise by arguing that the moral consequences of the exercise of that power would be defensible consequences. And exactly the same point can be made regarding the primary and secondary obligations of tort law. The existence of the primary obligations is one thing, and their breach is another. There is nothing circular in holding that the *existence* of the primary obligation not to defame or cause a nuisance is justifiable only because the secondary obligations of reparation that would arise from the legal recognition of these acts as tortious would be justifiable, while also holding that tort law's secondary obligations of reparation are justifiable, in return, only thanks to the breach of the same (ex hypothesi justifiable) primary obligations. So there is no logical obstacle to the defending of the primary obligations of tort law by arguing that the legal consequences of the breach of such obligations—the secondary obligations and attendant liabilities—would be (independently) defensible. One may properly begin by defending the secondary obligations and attendant liabilities, and then proceed to defend the primary obligations by showing them to be the very primary obligations, breach of which would happily have, among its legal consequences, the same secondary obligations and attendant liabilities that one just defended. That the legal justification for the secondary obligation then looks backward to the breach of the primary obligation, while the policy justification for the secondary obligation looks forward to its consequences is a separate problem, not a problem of circularity but a problem of incongruity. It is the problem raised in Coleman's second objection, to which we will turn shortly.

Moral Unintelligibility

The knockdown character of this refutation leads to the suspicion that Coleman's first objection has been uncharitably interpreted. I can think of just one alternative interpretation. It is hinted at in Coleman's addition of scare quotes around the words "duty" and "wrong" as, in his view, these words are used by many legal economists. On this interpretation, Coleman's first objection is not that policy arguments are circular and hence can justify *nothing* in the space of primary obligations. Rather it is that policy arguments are uncontainable and can justify *just about anything* in the space of primary obligations. In particular they can justify "obligations" that are not obligations, hence "wrongs" that are not wrongs, hence a law of "torts" that is not a law of torts.[14]

How so? As ordinary nondoctrinaire observers of legal argument we naturally imagine policy arguments being used to adjudicate small-scale disagreements of the kind that tort lawyers constantly have about what action should count as a tort. (What should be the standard of care in the tort of negligence? Should the unreasonable creation of a personal risk of death be a tort even where the risk does not materialize? Should there ever be strict tort liability?) Many economic analysts of law indulge in this kind of microadjudication, taking the rest of the existing law of torts for granted in the background.[15] But suppose one takes *nothing* in the existing law of torts for granted. Instead one looks in an uncontained way for the liability norms that would have the best consequences and works back to decide what is to count as a tort. It may turn out, for all one can tell at the outset, that one or another of the following liability norms—among infinitely many alternatives—will turn out to have the best consequences: the injured rightholder's family must have reparative damages awarded against them; the person who will least miss the money must have reparative damages awarded against her; the person of whom we can make the most spectacular example must have reparative damages awarded against him. So far as policy arguments are concerned, then, we should be considering all of the following as possible torts: being a member of an injured rightholder's family, being the person who will least miss the money, being the person of whom the most spectacular example can be made. But none of these is a possible tort, because none of them is a possible breach of an obligation. And that in turn is because none of the following is a possible obligation: not being a member of an injured rightholder's family; not being the person who will least miss the money; not being the person of whom the most spectacular example can be made. What this shows is that, by pursuing policy arguments at large, we may end up not with a law of torts in which primary obligations are breached, but rather with a law of "torts" in which "primary obligations" are "breached." This is because it is a matter of indifference, so far as policy arguments are concerned, whether there are really any primary obligations to be breached. All that matters from the point of view of policy arguments is that there be consequentially optimal liability norms such that liabilities to pay reparative damages are always conditional upon whatever they should be conditional upon in order to ensure that they are consequentially optimal, be that the breach of a primary obligation or something else altogether.

The general strategy of this objection is sound. Not just any old thing can be a legal obligation. There are limits to the law's ability, in the fashion of Humpty Dumpty, to make things legally obligatory simply by designating them as legally obligatory. Legal obligations must also satisfy what I like to call the "moral intelligibility" condition. They must be such that, if only the law were justified, they would be moral obligations. Or to put the same point another way, it must make sense for those who regard the law as having a claim on their allegiance to regard their legal obligations as being among their moral obligations. Many theorists rely on this moral intelligibility condition to attack various aspects of the law of torts as it exists today: its resort to strict liability, for instance, or its use of impersonal standards of care. There can be—it is said—no such thing as a moral obligation to avoid injuring people irrespective of how much care one takes (as in strict liability), or a moral obligation to take more care than one is personally able to take (as with impersonal standards of care). So there can be no such thing as a legal obligation to do these things either. There can only be a legal "obligation."[16] For myself, I do not believe that strict liability or impersonal standards of care fall foul of the moral intelligibility condition.[17] But I certainly agree that some things fall foul of it. In particular, the law cannot make something obligatory if that something is not among the conceivable actions of any rational agent. And the following are not among the conceivable actions of any rational agent, because they are not actions at all: not being a member of an injured rightholder's family; not being the person who will least miss the money; not being the person of whom the most spectacular example can be made. So any argument by which such things are advocated or even countenanced as primary obligations of the law of torts does indeed violate the moral intelligibility condition. Such an argument yields "obligations" that are not obligations, "wrongs" that are not wrongs, and hence "torts" that are not torts.

So far so good for Coleman's first objection, as reinterpreted. Yet the soundness of the general strategy still leaves us asking whether it counts as a success when directed against the economist's inevitable emphasis on policy arguments as the way to justify tort law's primary obligations. Is it true that policy arguments are doomed to be indifferent as between a liability norm that makes liability to have reparative damages awarded against one a legal consequence of the prior breach of a primary obligation, and one that does not? It seems to me that the answer must depend on a study of *particular* policy arguments. If there are any policy arguments in favor of having liabilities that are legal consequences of breached primary obligations, then obviously these policy arguments are not indifferent as between a liability norm that makes liability to have reparative damages awarded against one a legal consequence of the prior breach of a primary obligation, and one that does not. We are simply looking for good nonlegal (e.g., economic) consequences of making liability a legal consequence of some legal wrong done in the past. How can the existence of such good consequences be ruled out a priori, without even asking what they are supposed to be? How can we be sure, without a detailed interrogation of the merits that are claimed for it, that there are no forward-looking merits in a legal norm that sets a backward-looking condition of liability?

Here our attempt to make good Coleman's first objection returns us once again to his second objection. Legal justification for the secondary obligation (with its attendant liabilities) looks backward to the breach of the primary obligation. But any economic justification of the secondary obligation (with its attendant liabilities) necessarily looks forward to the good economic consequences of its being incurred. How can a backward-looking legal justification be squared with a forward-looking economic justification? That is the question posed in Coleman's second objection. But it is also the question on which the success of Coleman's first objection turns, no matter how we interpret it. So Coleman's first objection stands or falls with his second. Although more radical, the first objection is not autonomous: the first cannot succeed if the second fails. With that in mind, I turn now to the second objection.

Backward from the Secondary Obligation

The Supposed Inconstancy of the Instrumentalist

In pitting the economist's "forward-looking" preoccupations against the law's "backward-looking" features, Coleman's second objection echoes a stock criticism of instrumental defenses of tort law. But he takes pains to distance himself from the vulgar version of this criticism, which he rightly regards as confused. It is often claimed that pure instrumentalists about practical reasoning, including but not restricted to legal economists, are incapable of explaining why the incurring of a secondary obligation should be conditional (whether necessarily or sufficiently) on a primary obligation already having been committed at an earlier time. For a pure instrumentalist, an act is made wrong by its costs, meaning its actual or expected bad consequences. If these costs have not yet been incurred then the wrong has not yet been committed. The corollary is that once the wrong has been committed these costs are sunk. Nothing anyone can do will save them. But there are other costs that might still be saved, including the costs of future wrongs that might still be prevented. Instrumental rationality would have one orientate what one does entirely toward the saving of these unsunk costs. How can this instrumental orientation toward the saving of unsunk costs be squared with making what is to be done conditional on sunk costs, as tort law does? Sometimes, to be sure, getting someone to pay reparative damages in the wake of their own wrongdoing, or maybe (vicariously) in the wake of someone else's wrongdoing, might be the least costly way of deterring or otherwise preventing future wrongs, and thereby saving further costs. But this makes the past commission of a wrong only *inconstantly* relevant to instrumental thinking. Its relevance varies from case to case. On other occasions the best way to minimize further costs may be to get someone to bear the sunk costs irrespective of whether they, or indeed anyone else, committed a wrong. So there is nothing here that could justify the kind of stance that the law of torts takes, in which the relationship between one's breach of a primary obligation and one's incurring of a secondary obligation is constant, the former being a standing condition (necessary and defeasibly sufficient) of the latter.

The confusion in this line of thought is evident. From the bold charge that pure instrumentalists cannot justify attaching legal consequences to wrongs already committed, the argument quickly retreats to the more modest allegation that they cannot do so with the law's measure of constancy, that is, in every case to which the legal norm under discussion applies. And that more modest allegation itself turns out, on closer inspection, to be just another rehearsal of the view that pure instrumentalists about practical reasoning can't stand up for *any* constancy in norms, but must always license departure from any norm as soon as it requires or permits actions that would not be instrumentally defensible were it not for the norm's existence. I already mentioned John Rawls's famous demolition of this view.[18] I will not flog a dead horse by demolishing it again here. Suffice it to say that if it were sound it would rule out the economic analysis of *any* law, not only those with a backward-looking aspect, since every law, being a norm capable of application to more than one case, sometimes requires or permits actions that would not be economically optimal were it not for that law's existence.[19]

Coleman rightly has no truck with such overkill.[20] He sees that economists and other believers in the pure instrumentality of norms can readily account for normative constancy, including the constancy of the legal norm (which I will call the "linking norm") whereby my breach of a primary obligation is a standing condition of my incurring of a secondary obligation. They can do this by pointing to the various extra economies that come of using this norm instead of engaging in unconstrained economic (or more broadly instrumental) reasoning. In particular, as Coleman notes, they can reduce the high cost of "searching for those in the best position to reduce the costs of future accidents" by narrowing their search, and looking only among wrongdoers. In looking only among wrongdoers they can also, as Coleman might usefully have added, enlist aggrieved rightholders as temporary enforcement officials at reduced cost as compared with disinterested regulators.[21] Either of these considerations, or a fortiori both together, could in principle yield a sound economic case for the linking norm to be part of the law. Naturally, economists of law still have to do the work to show that the cost savings involved are sufficient to justify the law's use of that norm in the face of its undoubted costs (notably the costs involved in litigation). But this is beside the point. Once we start basing our type-(b) objections to the economic analysis of tort law on the accuracy of the costings used by its exponents, we have effectively conceded defeat. We are reduced to fighting economic arguments with economic arguments.

From Condition to Reason

Once Coleman concedes that economists of law can defend the linking norm, what is left of his second objection? Here is one tempting answer: it is not enough for legal economists to defend the linking norm. In the law of torts, the breach of a primary obligation is not only a standing condition of the incurring of the secondary obligation, but also a reason why the secondary obligation is incurred. And this, one might think, is a tougher nut for economists of law to crack. So far as economic thinking is concerned, reasons all lie in the future, in the consequences of what one does (including the consequences of having a norm that regulates one's doing it). But in tort law, one reason for my incurring a secondary obligation—my past breach of a primary obligation—always lies in the past at the time when the secondary obligation is incurred.

It is true that my past breach of the primary obligation is regarded by the law as a reason for, and not only a standing legal condition of, my incurring a secondary obligation. The breach is needed to make the *case* in law. But this fact alone is still not enough to put legal economists on the back foot. For the linking norm itself—now seen to be economically defensible—automatically turns the breach of the primary obligation into a reason for the incurring of the secondary obligation. If a wrongdoer says: "Give me one good reason why I should be the one to incur a secondary obligation in the law of torts," the economist may reply: "Because you breached a primary obligation and an economically defensible legal norm picks those who breach primary obligations as the right people to incur secondary obligations." Here the wrongdoer's breach of a primary obligation, his wrongdoing, is given as a reason for his incurring a secondary obligation. And the linking norm is what makes it a reason. Even though its costs are sunk, a wrong already committed is turned, by its mention in an economically defensible norm, into an economically intelligible reason for the subsequent payability of damages. So there is no incongruity to be found here between the backward-looking legal reasons and the forward-looking economic reasons.

From Reason to Ground

Coleman is unsatisfied, and it seems to me rightly unsatisfied, with this way of forging a rational relationship between my breach of the primary obligation and my incurring of the secondary obligation. In the foregoing story, the breach of a primary obligation becomes a legal reason for the incurring of a secondary obligation because it is a standing legal condition of the incurring of the secondary obligation. But in the law of torts, notices Coleman, the relationship goes the other way. The breach of a primary obligation is a standing legal condition of the incurring of a secondary obligation because it is a legal reason for the incurring of the secondary obligation. This is what is sometimes conveyed by saying that the breach of primary obligation "grounds" the secondary obligation and its associated liabilities. The breach of primary obligation is what gets the case for the secondary obligation up and running. In the law's eyes the breach of a primary obligation is the only possible reason for a secondary obligation to be incurred, and a defeasibly sufficient reason at that. This is reflected in—as opposed to being a reflection of—the linking norm that makes the breach of a primary obligation into a standing condition (necessary and defeasibly sufficient) for the incurring of the secondary.

This, if I understand it right, is what really lies at the heart of Coleman's second objection to the economic analysis of tort law. Although it echoes the stock criticism, it avoids the traps into which vulgar versions of that criticism fall. Unfortunately, it falls into other traps of its own making. To see how, consider what Coleman offers by way of an alternative to an economic analysis of tort law, namely "the sort of explanation offered by the principle of corrective justice."[22] The main feature such an explanation is supposed to have going for it, as against an economic analysis, is its invulnerability to Coleman's second objection. Thanks to this invulnerability, claims Coleman, corrective justice "can provide an account of what tort law is, in a way that economic analysis fails to do."[23] But can it really?

What Coleman calls "the principle of corrective justice" is the principle that "individuals who are responsible for the wrongful losses of others have a duty to repair the losses."[24] We could likewise designate as "a norm of corrective justice" any norm under which those who are responsible for the wrongful losses of others have a duty to repair those losses. Applying these criteria, the linking norm is already, without further ado, a norm of corrective justice. It attaches secondary legal obligations (i.e., duties to repair losses) to those who breach primary legal obligations, or who are vicariously liable in law for the breaching of primary legal obligations by others (i.e., those who are responsible for wrongful losses). Now, as we saw and as Coleman concedes, economic analysts *do* have the resources to mount an adequate defense of the linking norm. It follows that at least one norm of corrective justice, namely tort law's own norm of corrective justice, is economically defensible. So in what sense is a corrective justice account, in Coleman's view, a rival to an economic one? Why isn't a good economic analysis of tort law also a corrective justice account of tort law?[25]

Coleman must mean something like this. He must mean that there is a further norm of corrective justice at work in the law of torts, quite apart from the law's own norm. This we could call the "moral" norm of corrective justice. The law relies on this moral norm, which it regards as a norm not of its own making, in defending its own norm of corrective justice. The moral norm, we may glean from Coleman's formulations, picks out wrongdoing as a necessary and defeasibly sufficient condition for amends to be owed. So thanks to this moral norm the fact that a wrong has been committed becomes a moral reason for amends to be owed. The law in turn cites this moral reason as the reason why, by the law's own norm of corrective justice, (legally recognized) wrongdoing is a necessary and defeasibly sufficient condition for the owing of (legally specified) amends. In this corrective justice story, the wrong having been committed becomes the ground of the ensuing reparative obligations in the law of torts. The wrongdoing is a moral reason for the making of amends that becomes a legal condition of the making of amends only by virtue of the law's recognition of it as a moral reason. So it is a condition because it is a reason. It is not a reason only because it is a condition. And here we have the respect in which the corrective justice story rivals the economic one. The economic story cannot find a rational significance for the wrong's commission apart from that conferred by the law's own norm, whereas the corrective justice story can: the wrongdoing is given rational significance by a moral norm recognized by law, invoked in the legal justification of the legal norm.

But here we come to the crunch for Coleman's first objection. Since the thoughtful economic analyst can admittedly defend the legal norm of corrective justice, why can't she equally defend its moral counterpart in much the same way? I can't think of any obstacle in principle to her doing so. Arguably the existence of such a moral norm, if it were widely conformed to, would help to reduce the duration and intensity of economically wasteful disputes. Arguably the moral norm's existence, if it were widely conformed to, would also give people greater confidence about investing in economically productive activity.[26] One can quibble about the details here, as before, but these sample economic considerations are already enough to show that at the very least a moral norm of corrective justice is open in principle to economic defense. That being so, economic analysts of tort law plainly do have the argumentative wherewithal, *pace* Coleman, to provide a corrective justice defense of tort law's own norm of corrective justice. They can go on to defend the legal norm by relying on the (ex hypothesi economically defensible) moral norm and in the process provide an economic defense of the legal position whereby the commission of the wrong is a ground of, and not merely a condition of or a reason for, the payability of reparative damages. This move completely disarms Coleman's second objection. In the process his parasitic first objection is also neutralized.

Doing without Law and Economics

In an effort to rearm Coleman's second objection you may say that the two sample economic defenses of the moral norm of corrective justice that I just suggested suffer from a common weakness, namely that they are admittedly capable of defending that norm economically only "if it were widely conformed to." This proviso should not surprise us. I already mentioned that economic defenses of legal norms tend to be conducted against the background of strong assumptions about conformity: typically, it is assumed for the sake of argument that what the law says goes. Much the same goes for economic defenses of moral norms: typically, the economic defense of a moral norm is conducted on the footing that it is successfully implemented—if not completely then at least widely—as a social norm.[27]

In the case of legal norms, such an assumption turns out to be relatively innocent. One need not be a pure instrumentalist about the justification of norms to believe that the justification of a legal norm is subject to at least one instrumental condition. The condition is that the existence of the legal norm must serve to improve people's actions enough to warrant all the trouble and intrusion of regulating the matter by law. In the case of a legal norm that attempts to implement a moral norm—in the way that Coleman envisages the legal norm of corrective justice implementing the moral norm of corrective justice—the normal way to show that the moral norm meets this condition is to show that conformity to the moral norm is sufficiently improved by the existence of the legal norm. The improvement may either be direct (enough people successfully use the legal norm to help them conform to the corresponding moral norm) or indirect (the legal norm is relied on in making a case for the application of other legal norms, such as liability norms, that in turn help to secure that enough people conform to the moral norm). All of this should be common ground to defenders of legal norms, be they pure instrumentalists or otherwise. Normally, when anyone tries to defend a legal norm they are taking its successful implementation for granted, and they are entitled to assume that others are doing the same.

But the same does not go for moral norms. Moral norms are not all of them social norms and many are valid irrespective of the extent to which they are implemented. I tend to think that this is true of the moral norm whereby those who commit wrongs should make amends to those whom they wrong. It applies even where nobody conforms to it, where nobody relies on it in argument, even where it has been long forgotten. So I tend to think that the economic defense of this moral norm is a fifth wheel: it defends a moral norm that remains valid quite irrespective of its economic defense. That should not surprise us. As rational agents, people (considered en masse) tend to want what they anyway have reason to want, although not necessarily in proportion to their reason to want it. They have reason to want reparation from wrongdoers for wrongs that were committed against them, that reason being the independently valid moral norm whereby wrongdoers should pay them such reparation. So not surprisingly people often do want reparation. And not surprisingly this shows up in the economic assessment of the very moral norm that gives people reason to want it. The moral norm has epiphenomenal economic appeal: it has appeal as a reflection of what people want, but what mainly explains their wanting it is the moral norm according to which they should anyway want it, whatever its economic appeal.

This is not the place to explain where this moral norm gets its force. That is for another day. Suffice it to say, here, that the explanation could not possibly provide any comfort for Coleman. Why not? First, because Coleman himself joins the legal economists in holding that the moral norm of corrective justice is valid only where it is, in large measure, successfully implemented. "Social practices," he says, "turn abstract ideals into regulative principles; they turn virtue into duty."[28] But second, and more significantly, because my objection to the economic analysis of law is not a type-(b) objection, which is what Coleman is looking for. Coleman wants to show that an economic defense of the law of torts cannot but be inadequate to the task. The legal economist lacks the resources to account for what is going on in tort law. My own view, by contrast, is that the legal economist has all the resources she needs to account for what is going on in tort law. The real question, however, is why the law of torts needs the legal economist, except at the margins to defend it against specifically economic objections. For the law of torts has ample moral support already, assuming only that it meets the instrumental condition I mentioned, that is, that its norms do indeed improve people's actions enough to warrant all the trouble and intrusion of regulating the matter by law.

I hope I have made it tolerably clear that, in my view, there can be no successful type-(b) objection to the economic analysis of tort law. Coleman's attempts to make good such objections are the best we have, but still, as we have seen, they fail. That is because legal economists can in principle account for any norm that can be accounted for. To show that their explanation fails, one is always reduced in the end to arguing that they got their costings wrong, and once the argument gets to that point the war is over. If one wants to defeat the economic analysis of tort law in a less Pyrrhic way, one has no alternative but to mount a type-(a) objection. One must establish that the economic analysis rests on a bad theory of value. This one does by exploring what really matters in life, for what really matters in life is also, by and large, what really matters in law. In the process of exploring this one will discover that whatever success the economic analysis of law enjoys in explaining the norms of the law of torts, is mainly as follower, not as leader: what really matters is mainly tracked, not constituted, by whatever economic goods tort law may yield (and even that, I hasten to add, only very incompletely).

Acknowledgments

This essay is a remote descendent of my contribution to the symposium on Jules Coleman's recent work at the Fifth Annual Inland Northwest Philosophy Conference 2002 in Moscow, Idaho. A more mature version was presented at a seminar at the University of Pennsylvania Law School. Many thanks to everyone who commented on both occasions.

Notes

1. Hence the practice of giving contemptuous damages—a farthing, say—to those making out unmeritorious but legally successful claims in tort. It is true of all rights (moral as well as legal) that relying on them can be unjustifiable or even inexcusable. Nevertheless they are rights and those against whom they are held remain bound by them. See Aristotle *NE* 1137^b35 commenting on those who are "sticklers for their rights in a bad way."

2. On the justificatory relationship between obligations and incentives, see Hacker 1973.

3. Hart 1994, pp. 98–99.

4. Consider the titles alone of the following articles, picked at random from a much longer list: Priest (1977), "The Common Law Process and the Selection of Efficient Legal Rules"; Ayres and Gertner (1992), "Strategic Contractual Inefficiency and the Optimal Choice of Legal Rules"; and Kaplow and Shavell (1996), "Property Rules versus Liability Rules: An Economic Analysis."

5. On the effects of varying the conformity assumptions in an economic analysis of law, see Kornhuaser 2001.

6. See Posner 1979, Johnsen 1986, and Kaplow and Shavell 2001. Kaplow and Shavell have a slightly more sophisticated idea of what counts as an economic consideration.

7. Calabresi 1970, e.g., at pp. 291–292. This also seems to have become Posner's view by the time of, for example, Posner 1995.

8. For invocations of this contrast aimed at insulating the "positive" enterprise, see Posner 1977, pp. 17–19; Coleman 1980, p. 547; Friedman 1994, p. 15; and Geistfeld 2001, p. 252. ·

9. This example was brought to mind by the case of Amina Lawal. See McGreal 2002.

10. Coleman 2001, p. 35.

11. Ibid., p. 18. This encapsulates an objection originally advanced by Coleman in his 1988.

12. For different versions, see Dworkin 1984, pp. 73–74, and Weinrib 1995, pp. 210–214.

13. Rawls 1955.

14. This interpretation would bring Coleman's thinking in one respect closer to Weinrib's. Weinrib (1995) also claims that those who resort to policy arguments do not respect the very idea of a tort (pp. 218–222). However Weinrib invokes a highly idealized notion of a tort, laced with common-law romanticism, to get this claim off the ground. Coleman does not need and does not use any such idealizing measures.

15. For example, Posner's famous economic defense of the law governing the tort of negligence (1972, p. 29) proceeds as follows. Legal norm A is defended economically while norms B, C, and D are held constant. Then norm B is defended economically while norms A, C, and D are held constant. And so on. In a neat illustration of the fallacy of composition, these several defenses of A, B, C, and D are then paraded as adding up to a defense of the system of norms A+B+C+D.

16. See, e.g., Perry 1997, p. 352 ("There can be no *ex ante* duty, except in the most formal sense, not to cause harm to others.") and Ripstein 2004 ("One cannot be responsible for an unforeseeable injury because one person cannot owe another a duty to avoid them.")

17. See my 2002.

18. See Rawls 1955.

19. With the obvious exception of a law prohibiting whatever action would not be economically optimal were it not for that law's existence.

20. Contrast the interpretation of Coleman's position in Kutz 2002, pp. 2008–2009.

21. Cf. Posner 1972, p. 48.

22. Coleman 2001, p. 15.

23. Ibid.

24. Ibid.

25. For more on this theme see Posner 1981.

26. Recently the Swiss conglomerate Nestlé argued that (with or without the imprimatur of the law) the government of Ethiopia had a moral obligation to pay the company reparative damages for the nonconsensual and uncompensated (and hence according to Nestlé wrongful) expropriation of one of its Ethiopian subsidiaries in an earlier nationalization program (Denny 2002). The Nestlé argument for the existence of this moral obligation was a purely economic one: that any government that denied the existence of such an obligation (or failed to perform it having granted its existence) would be undermining the confidence of prospective investors and hence failing to maximize economic value. I shared with many the view that Nestlé's demand for damages was base. But this was not because the economic considerations the company mentioned were incapable of justifying the moral norm of corrective justice that it identified, nor because the norm did not apply. It was simply because there were conflicting moral norms (of mercy and humanity) that were more important in the circumstances. Nestlé was therefore being a mean-spirited stickler for its rights (see note 1 above).

27. See, e.g., Posner and Rasmusen 1999, and Levmore 2000. The assumption of successful implementation is not gratuitous. When moral norms are not social norms Rawls's argument in his 1955, does not apply. See the first few footnotes of Rawls 1958.

28. Coleman 2001, p. 54.

References

Aristotle. 1925. *Nicomachean Ethics*. D. Ross, trans. Oxford: Oxford University Press.

Ayres, I. and R. Gertner. 1992. "Strategic Contractual Inefficiency and the Optimal Choice of Legal Rules." *Yale Law Journal* 101: 729–773.

Calabresi, G. 1970. *The Costs of Accidents*. New Haven, Conn.: Yale University Press.

Coleman, J. 1980. "Efficiency, Utility, and Wealth Maximization." *Hofstra Law Review* 8: 509–551.

———. 1988. "The Economic Structure of Tort Law." *Yale Law Journal* 97: 1233–1253.

———. 2001. *The Practice of Principle*. Oxford: Oxford University Press.

Denny, C. 2002. "Nestlé Claims £3.7m from Famine-Hit Ethiopia." *Gaurdian* (December 19).

Dworkin, R. 1984. *A Matter of Principle*. Cambridge, Mass.: Harvard University Press.

Friedman, D. 1994. "A Positive Account of Property Rights." *Social Philosophy and Policy* 11: 1–16.

Gardner, J. 2002. "Obligations and Outcomes in the Law of Torts." In P. Cane and J. Gardner, eds., *Relating to Responsibility*. Oxford: Oxford University Press.

Geistfeld, M. 2001. "Economics, Moral Philosophy and the Positive Analysis of Tort Law." In G. Postema, ed., *Philosophy and the Law of Torts*. Cambridge: Cambridge University Press.

Hacker, P. M. S. 1973. "Sanction Theories of Duty." In A. W. B. Simpson, ed., *Oxford Essays in Jurisprudence: Second Series*. Oxford: Oxford University Press.

Hart, H. L. A. 1994. *The Concept of Law*, second ed. Oxford: Oxford University Press.

Johnsen, B. 1986. "Wealth *Is* Value." *Journal of Legal Studies* 15: 263–288.

Kaplow, L. and S. Shavell. 1996. "Property Rules versus Liability Rules: An Economic Analysis." *Harvard Law Review* 109: 713–790.

———. 2001. "Fairness versus Welfare." *Harvard Law Review* 114: 961–1388.

Kornhuaser, L. 2001. "The Economic Analysis of Law." In E. N. Zalta, ed., *The Stanford Encyclopedia of Philosophy*. Available at http://plato.standford.edu/archives/win2001/entries/legal-econanalysis/.

Kutz, C. 2002. "Pragmatism Regained." *Michigan Law Review* 100: 1639–1660.

Levmore, S. 2000. "Norms as Supplements." *Virginia Law Review* 86: 1989–2021.

McGreal, C. 2002. "Woman Faces Death by Stoning 'After Weaning.'" *Guardian* (August 20).

Perry, S. 1997. "Libertarianism, Entitlement, and Responsibility." *Philosophy and Public Affairs* 26: 351–396.

Posner, R. 1972. "A Theory of Negligence." *Journal of Legal Studies* 1: 29–96.

———. 1977. *Economic Analysis of Law*, second ed. Boston: Little Brown.

———. 1979. "Utilitarianism, Economics, and Legal Theory." *Journal of Legal Studies* 8: 103–140.

———. 1981. "The Concept of Corrective Justice in Recent Theories of Tort Law." *Journal of Legal Studies* 10: 187–206.

———. 1995. "Wealth Maximisation and Tort Law: A Philosophical Inquiry." In D. Owen, ed., *Philosophical Foundations of Tort Law*. Oxford: Oxford University Press.

Posner, R., and E. Rasmusen. 1999. "Creating and Enforcing Norms, with Special Reference to Sanctions." *International Review of Law and Economics* 19: 369–382.

Priest, G. L. 1977. "The Common Law Process and the Selection of Efficient Legal Rules." *Journal of Legal Studies* 6: 65–82.

Rawls, J. 1955. "Two Concepts of Rules." *Philosophical Review* 64: 3–32.

———. 1958. "Justice as Fairness." *Philosophical Review* 67: 164–194.

Ripstein, A. 2004. "Justice and Responsibility." *Canadian Journal of Law and Jurisprudence* 17: 361–386.

Weinrib, E. 1995. *The Idea of Private Law*. Cambridge, Mass.: Harvard University Press.

16 Pragmatism, Positivism, and the Conventionalistic Fallacy

Benjamin C. Zipursky

Jules Coleman's *The Practice of Principle: In Defense of a Pragmatist Approach to Legal Theory* (2001a) is a fascinating and sustained analysis of contemporary jurisprudential issues of substantial importance. One of the major aspirations of the book is to apply certain aspects of the philosophy of language and the epistemology of the past few decades to leading jurisprudential debates. More precisely, Coleman aims to present two of his ongoing agendas in legal philosophy in the fresh light of contemporary pragmatist theory within the philosophy of language. The first agenda relates to the relative merits of conceptualist versus instrumentalist accounts of law—particularly tort law. I have written extensively on that issue (Zipursky 2000), as Coleman himself indicates (2001a, p. 10, n. 12) and our views are rather close. The second issue, of even greater breadth, is the nature and plausibility of legal positivism as an overall jurisprudential view. There are many twists and turns to his discussions of this matter, and many subsidiary arguments relating to Raz, Dworkin, Shapiro, and others. I shall focus, in what follows, on one aspect of Coleman's jurisprudential view: his assertion that law is a matter of social fact, and that this social fact thesis is central to the legal positivist tradition.

I shall argue that the social fact thesis, on the interpretation most naturally attributed to Coleman, is untenable, and is untenable for reasons that are suggested by Dworkin's (1978, 1986) critique of Hart. Moreover, I shall argue that its untenability is, in interesting ways, related to Quine's (1953) critique of Carnap on the analytic–synthetic distinction in "Two Dogmas of Empiricism." Although some jurists have asserted that Hart's (and now Coleman's) analysis of law in terms of social facts involves the naturalistic fallacy, I shall offer a somewhat different view. I shall argue that what I call a "conventionalistic fallacy" saddles one plausible interpretation of Coleman's view, just as it did Hart's. On the other hand, some version of a social facts thesis is tenable, I argue, and this version is enriched by Coleman's account, and is also consonant in some ways with Hart's aims. Yet this version of the social fact thesis eliminates central aspects of Coleman's positivism, and, indeed, appears to undercut his claim to being a positivist at all.

The Model of Social Facts and the Argument from Disagreement

In *The Practice of Principle*, Jules Coleman endorses what I have elsewhere labeled "The Model of Social Facts" (Zipursky 2001). According to this view, whether a putative law is valid law is a matter of social fact. In an early, Austinian version of this jurisprudential position, the facts in question were whether a given command had been issued by persons or entities situated a particular way within a legal community. This involved, in turn, whether a certain group of people, subjects, that is, habitually obeyed the class of commands issued by the persons or entities so situated. Coleman rightly views Hart as improving upon Austin's model. The status of a putative law as law depends on whether it satisfies certain criteria. These criteria might be expressed by predicates that are quite subtle, including perhaps moral predicates. But the question of what the criteria are is itself a question of social fact. The social fact is whether a rule of recognition demanding conformity to those criteria has the status of a practiced rule of recognition in the relevant legal community (Coleman 2001a, pp. 77–78). Having the status of a rule of recognition that is practiced in the community is a matter of whether the relevant legal officials in the community have a certain set of behaviors that converge in certain respects related to the rule, and whether they have a certain attitude toward the rule. This attitude is the internal point of view (ibid., p. 83). On Hart's view, according to Coleman—and it is a view that Coleman himself accepts—it is a matter of social fact about behaviors and attitudes in the group of persons whether a given rule of recognition is practiced in the community (ibid., pp. 75–76).

One of the central tasks of Coleman's book is to respond to certain aspects of Dworkin's powerful critique of Hart (Coleman 2001a, pp. 153–174). Coleman famously responded to Dworkin's "Model of Rules I" critique of Hart in "Negative and Positive Positivism," arguing that the

Hartian picture of rules of recognition that determined legality could easily be squared with a Dworkinian thesis that moral considerations often bear on what is legally valid (Coleman 1982). One need only recognize—as Hart himself did in less decisive fashion than Coleman—that rules of recognition can incorporate moral criteria, and some legal systems (including the American legal system) in fact exemplify this possibility.

Moreover, Coleman, along with Hart and several other distinguished philosophers, have responded to major aspects of Dworkin's *Law's Empire* critique in a quite persuasive fashion elsewhere. But both "The Model of Rules II" (Dworkin 1978, pp. 46–80) and one aspect of *Law's Empire* offer Dworkin's argument from disagreement, which seems particularly challenging to a conventionalistic account of the model of social facts. *The Practice of Principle* contains Coleman's most nuanced and sustained response to the argument from disagreement. In what follows, I shall argue that there is one version of Coleman's response that successfully meets the Dworkinian, but only at the cost of giving up the model of social facts as a genuine form of positivism.

Dworkin's argument from disagreement is as follows: it is common for legal officials within a given system to disagree explicitly, and to argue, about what the criteria of legality are. If the rule of recognition being practiced is constituted by convergent behavior, then the rule of recognition must run out where there is not convergence. But then the arguments about what the criteria of legality are must be incoherent arguments, for it should be clear that where there is not agreement there are not agreed-upon criteria of legality. Yet this is not true to the fact or phenomenology or hermeneutical understanding of secondary legal-rule discourse. On the other hand, if it is not the sheer fact of agreement that controls the criteria of legality, then the criteria of legality are not conventional. It follows that facts about behavior do not determine what the rule of recognition is, and therefore the model of social facts is defeated (Dworkin 1978, pp. 61–64).

Coleman's response is that social facts may determine what the rule of recognition is, even if the social facts are not simply the facts of convergent behavior (Coleman 2001a, p. 80). The social facts in question involve the existence of a certain attitude on the part of (all) the legal officials in the community. For the rule of recognition to be practiced in the community requires that officials take the internal point of view toward the rule of recognition. This involves, roughly speaking, their taking themselves to be guided by, and their being guided by, the rule of recognition. It is hence a psychological fact about them. Yet it does not follow from the fact that they are all guided by the same rule of recognition that they will not disagree on determinations of legality (ibid.).

In prior work, Coleman argued that it was possible that legal officials who agreed on what the rule of recognition was would disagree on how it should be applied in particular cases (Coleman 1982). Hart himself put forward this solution in the "Postscript" (Hart 1994). Dworkin has never disagreed with Coleman or others on this point. But Dworkin has asserted that it is artificial and untrue to legal practice to assert that all disagreements must be analyzed as disagreements in application of an agreed-upon rule of recognition (Dworkin 1983, pp. 252–253). In Coleman's essay in *Hart's Postscript*, he rejected this position of Dworkin's (Coleman 2001b). In *The Practice of Principle*, Coleman now effectively concedes the point to Dworkin (Coleman 2001a, pp. 157–158). It is important, particularly in the context of the larger view of the aims of *The Practice of Principle*, to see why he is right to concede the point. This will also figure later in my critique of Coleman's ultimate position.

Holism is one of the central features both of pragmatism generally and of Coleman's pragmatism in law more particularly (Coleman 2001a, pp. 6–8). Frege famously argued against the atomistic view that language and world met where word met object, contending instead that sentences met propositions, and word–object connections were possible only against the propositional backdrop. Quine argued, analogously, that sentences could not be matched with propositions, except against the backdrop of entire sets of sentences or theories matched against the entire domain of the world we experience. Put in epistemic terms, we do not match belief against fact, but web of belief against entire domain of experience. The canonical argument for this point, within the pragmatist tradition, is Quine's argument in "Two Dogmas." Quine adopted Duhem's basic point that an experience confirms or disconfirms any single sentence only against the backdrop of an entire theory. Quine combined this point with his observation that a rational belief-former, or theorist, needs to weigh a variety of different desiderata in deciding how to prune a theory or web of beliefs in order to retain the best overall system. It remains, Quine argued, a logically and empirically open possibility that rejecting statements that, from a metalinguistic point of view, could be dubbed "true by definition" might sometimes be the best option. In that case, an experience or aspect of the world could be properly viewed as disconfirming that statement. It follows that these analytic statements or meaning postulates or statements "true by definition" did not enjoy the status of being necessarily true or known a priori (Quine 1953).

Quine's point is essentially a pragmatist's point, in my view, because a pragmatist stance toward rationality in theory acceptance plays a pivotal role in the argument. Not even the apparently privileged status of "truth by definition" can come before the possibility of doing what works best in deciding which sentences to retain in one's theory or which beliefs to retain in one's set of beliefs. It is the priority of what it is best to do as believer that runs the argument, in part. Two implications of the theory, however—implications Quine developed in many other works—are epistemic and semantic. The epistemic implication (which may in fact have been the Duhemian premise) is that there is no privileged place for beliefs to plug in to reality, and Quine's views have therefore lent great credence to antifoundationalism in epistemology, and this antifoundationalism is sometimes treated as a form of holism. The semantic inference drawn by Quine is semantic holism: that fundamentally language and world connect as a whole, and not word by word or sentence by sentence.

If Coleman is to remain consistent with his pragmatism and his holism, he cannot maintain that all disagreements about conditions of legality must be disagreements about the application of an agreed-upon rule of recognition. It is not just that, as Dworkin has persuasively argued, participants in the American legal system disagree enough on conditions of legality that Coleman will be forced to identify something as vacuously broad as the rule of recognition (Dworkin 1987). The problem is structural and mirrors the Quinean problem. To demand that all disagreements can only be disagreements in application is essentially to suppose that a legal decision maker cannot be a good pragmatist in deciding what to do in order to accommodate optimally all of the pressures a given case presents to her or him. For a good pragmatist may decide that the best move in the epistemic activity of legal theory construction is sometimes to reject what would appear to be foundational—in this case, an aspect of a secondary legal-rule statement, rather than accepting the rule statement but swallowing the perhaps unacceptable contention that the conditions of application do not apply. As Dworkin has argued tirelessly, and I think persuasively, it is often implausible to assert that a judge under such conditions is *changing* the law; *applying* the law often requires just such decisions.

Technically, I suppose, there is a slippage in the analogy to Quine, for the argument I have just offered is not an argument that Coleman as a pragmatist is committed to the foregoing analysis, but rather that a judge operating under the epistemic and semantic guidance of pragmatism would have to operate this way. Yet I do not think the slippage amounts to much. First, Dworkin's own analysis of what law is resembles a Putnamian pragmatist's analysis of knowledge of the physical world in the following respect; the reasonable judge operating with appropriate (and holistic) norms of rationality is, as a theoretical matter, very closely linked to the very idea of what the law is, just as for the Putnamian, what the world is is very closely linked to what the reasonable belief-former would (under ideal conditions) take it to be. Coleman has himself displayed sympathy with a soft realist, coherentist approach, and in certain respects has endorsed its replication in law. Moreover, Dworkin has gone to great lengths to argue, as a hermeneutical and an empirical matter, that this is accurate to the American legal system, and Coleman has not contested this point. The result is that: (1) in an account of what the law is, it would seem misguided to deny the legal official the breadth of the holist-pragmatist; (2) an account of American law should make room for such holism-pragmatism on the part of legal officials. Under any of these routes, then, Coleman cannot plausibly rest his response to the argument from disagreement on the contention that all disagreement must be disagreement in application, for the "rule/application" distinction is fundamentally at odds with the pragmatism and holism that Coleman places at the center of his book.

Yet with the "rule/application" response eliminated, Coleman is evidently in a difficult spot. Let us note, first, one other dead end. Coleman argues, relying on Wittgenstein and Kripke, that to agree upon a particular rule and to have a shared grasp of a rule does not necessarily dictate any one particular way of extending the rule (Coleman 2001a, pp. 80–81, 157–158). In a similar (though oddly converse) vein, he argues that there is sometimes convergence in behavior that cannot be adequately explained by appeal to a rule whose application demands that convergence in behavior (ibid., pp. 80–81). The upshot is the two-way claim that convergence in behavior underdetermines the linguistic-propopsitional entity from which the behavior supposedly stems, and conversely, the rule underdetermines the pattern of behavior. Coleman seems to want to conclude from this that there might be agreement in behavior but disagreement over what the rule of recognition is (ibid.).

This argument is inadequate for two reasons. First, Coleman's assertion that there is agreement on the rule of recognition is not simply part of an explanation of convergent practices. It is in fact the core of his theory of what it is for there to be a rule of recognition *practiced* in the legal community (ibid., pp. 75–78). Second, it is not clear that there really is either an identifiable convergence in behavior or an identifiable rule that is agreed upon. As a hermeneutical matter, both appear to be disagreed upon, and there seems to be divergence in both. And third, the model of social facts depends on there being a rule of recognition that is practiced, and this depends on the acceptance of that rule. But it is just the acceptance that is challenged by the argument from disagreement.

Another false start—here, I believe, not a view Coleman seriously entertains—is that the disagreement in question is not a disagreement about what the rule of recognition is, but just a disagreement about how to articulate it. In other words, legal officials who appear to be debating criteria of legality are in fact struggling together to articulate a rule of recognition that, at a psychological level, they all already agree upon. This view might have worked if Coleman did not view rules of recognition as propositional entities, but he clearly does view them that way (ibid., p. 77). Given this, and plenty of evidence that Coleman favors a model of belief attribution that would link beliefs quite closely in this context to the linguistic expressions of those beliefs, I think this solution is untenable.

Coleman also rejects a Razian framework that might have helped him out of the problem. On that view, the rule of recognition is simply a proposition that in fact characterizes what is and is not law in the relevant community, but it is not something accepted or deployed as such by members of the community. Hence, they may engage in their own struggles to articulate what they view as acceptable criteria of legality, but those struggles are not necessarily connected in any clear way to what is in fact the rule of recognition in this community, which is an objective fact. Coleman clearly rejects this, and must do so given that his view is that what makes the rule of recognition exist in the community is that it is practiced (ibid., pp. 84–85).

Instead, Coleman crafts what in many ways is a synthesis of his own views, Scott Shapiro's (1998), Hart's and, in a much different context, the views of Allan Gibbard (1990) and Michael Bratman (1992, 1993). According to this view, we cannot properly understand what it is for the rule of recognition to exist in a community of legal officials without getting a more complex view of: (1) what it is to adopt a rule; (2) in what sense an attitude with respect to a mode of behavior can be characterized as being in the grip of a norm; and (3) in what sense an ongoing coordinative activity of a group of people involves cooperation and mutual responsiveness. Coleman's picture, in effect, is that of a set of roughly convergent behaviors: within an institutional structure in which officials each regard themselves as involved in a joint activity that imposes upon them certain obligations, there is a practice of accepting a certain set of criteria for legality as governing. This kind of cooperative practice in one sense makes these criteria of legality exist, and makes the legal system possible, and imposes duties upon them; at the same time, however, it leaves open any formulation of a rule of recognition, leaving it to the vicissitudes of ongoing constructive self-interpretation (Coleman 2001a, pp. 87–102). To this extent, Coleman believes that he has accepted a great deal of the hermeneutics while still accepting a Hartian picture, and, in particular, the model of social facts. As Coleman of course concedes, the "shared cooperative activity" (SCA) account is the germ of an idea.

Even assuming Coleman's model of what occurs is correct, it does not succeed in defending the model of social facts. Coleman may be correct, as a descriptive matter, that this is what the practice appears to be like. And there may indeed be a sense in which conventionally accepted clusters of criteria constitute some form of social convention. But this does not suffice to save the view that there is a rule of recognition as a propositional entity that members of the community all accept, and toward which they take the internal point of view, which determines whether first-order statements of validity about primary rules (and other secondary rules) are true, and which is nevertheless open to dispute within cogent legal discourse. For if they all do conventionally accept that proposition, if what it is for them to have discourse about validity in that system depends on their acceptance of that proposition, and if indeed the truth of statements about validity is dependent on that proposition's being accepted, it cannot also be true that whether the proposition (which is about validity) is so can be a matter over which they have disputes.

This brings us to an important juncture. It obviously cannot be the case that satisfaction of the criteria set out by *the proposition that is conventionally accepted as the rule of recognition* is the fact that determines whether some putative norm is law, if there is no such proposition as *the proposition that is conventionally accepted as the rule of recognition*. Moreover, it cannot be the case that certain facts about attitude and behavior constitute the acceptance of a rule of recognition. Thus, whether a putative legal norm is law is not simply a matter of fact about behavior and attitude. This destroys the model of social facts *insofar as it was aimed at justifying an account of how statements about law could be made true by social facts*. Although Coleman's synthetic sketch may be right, and may permit him to endorse a form of conventionalism, if Coleman maintains it, he does so at the cost of the model of social facts.

Metaphysical Motivation for Adopting the Model of Social Facts

Does Coleman really need the model of social facts? How important, philosophically, is it that Coleman retain this view? I have elsewhere argued that Hart appears to have been committed to the model of social facts, and probably believed that it was a significant philosophical achievement to have retained this Austinian proposition without inheriting many of Austin's defects. Briefly, I think there is a historical reason to believe that Hart shared the suspicion of many philosophers in his era of domains of discourse that could not be fit into an ontology exhausted by facts about what people did and thought. This is not to say that Hart was a reductionist or a logical positivist or empiricist. But it is to recognize that he put a premium on the elimination of philosophical fat in the account of law, and on the continuation of the Austinian position. On a rather different front, I think there is reason, notwithstanding the "Postscript" and important passages in *The Concept of Law*, to believe that Hart valued the model of social facts in part because of its tendency to enhance philosophers' and lawyers' ability to distinguish the question of a norm's status as law from its moral status.

Coleman is no doubt a naturalist, in some sense, and is also keen to inherit the mantle of positivism. But it is far from clear that there is sufficient philosophical motivation for Coleman to insist on the model of social facts. Let us deal with the naturalism first. Coleman's naturalism is, in an important sense, modest. Its point is that certain kinds of metaphysical apparatus above and beyond the natural world, the world of people, and the world of ordinary discourse, need not be added to the universe in order to account for domains such as law or morality. This is a far cry from any form of reductionism or antirealism about these other areas. And it is clearly a hallmark of the sort of pragmatism and holism that Coleman adopts that these areas can retain their distinctive nature, and hang together as areas of truth and knowledge without being reformed or translated into, say, physicalistic discourse. An important challenge, for Coleman, is to explain how normativity emerges out of nature, broadly construed. But this is no reason to insist that facts of legality be fixed by facts about legal officials' attitudes. Of course, Coleman's central, and extraordinarily broad inclusive positivism renders implausible any effort to explain his adherence to the model of social facts by focusing on the value of separating legal from moral questions.

My hunch is that Coleman has run together three different ideas, one of them the Ockhamistic, almost logical empiricist taste for the desert landscapes of the Quinean, perhaps shared by Hart; the second, an anti-Dworkinian and anti-Thomistic idea that legality does not necessarily entail any particular moral status; and the third, an extraordinarily appealing model of the conventionality of legal systems that seems to entail the model of social facts. I have already commented on the first. As to the second, Coleman has argued forcefully in "Negative and Positive Positivism" that one can concede Dworkin's observations about the centrality of principle without being committed to the necessity of the connection between morality and legality (Coleman 1982). While I think it is fair to say that Dworkin has never fully confronted that argument, or perhaps not even felt the need to do so, the point is irrelevant with regard to the model of social facts. At this date in the development of Coleman's pragmatism, and his endorsement of coherentism and antireductionism, the rejection of the necessity of morality as a criterion for legality certainly does not entail that social facts constitute legal facts. It remains a possibility that legality is not reducible to or (more accurately) fixed by any other kind of fact, and I and others have argued elsewhere that this is the case.

Explanatory Motivation for Adopting the Model of Social Facts

I think that the strongest motivation for Coleman's view that law is a matter of social fact is not any ulterior philosophical, moral, or metaphysical motive. It is simply the plausibility of the Hartian framework for understanding legal systems, and the idea that, on the Hartian framework, law is a matter of social fact. From Coleman's point of view, Dworkin's hermeneutical observations about legal practice stand on the same footing as the ordinary language philosophers' and Wittgensteinians' observations about linguistic practices: they enrich in interesting and important ways the nature of the practice in question and therefore the complexity of the social facts, but they do not undermine the conclusion that what constitutes this area of thought and language and what gives content to the propositions that speak of it are essentially the social practices that constitute them. Coleman's use of Shapiro, Bratman, and Gibbard are simply efforts to further that project. And if I were Coleman, my response to the discussion above would be to the turn the tables, and ask: "Zipursky, given that you are comfortable with my version of the separation thesis, and you recognize my rejection of reductionism, and you recognize my concession to Dworkin on phenomena of disagreement, and you too think social practices constitute the legal system, why are you so worried about whether law is a matter of social fact? What is *your* reason for thinking this is an important question?"

My response is twofold. First, of course, I would take the same tack I have attributed to Coleman himself: ultimately, we must see where the chips fall when we put the motivations aside and ask whether Coleman can make out the case on social facts. I have argued that he cannot, at least not in the form he wishes. But second, it may be useful to indicate that I think many of the core practical issues separating positivists from their adversaries are implicated by the truth or falsity of the model of social facts, so construed.

A classic form of debate between the positivist and the antipositivist is about whether arguments of moral principle enter into debate about what the law is. If the model of social facts is true, then arguments of moral principle *can* enter the debate, but only if the system in question in fact has secondary legal rules that permit such arguments, and only to the extent that such principles permit them. Having been deeply influenced by figures such as Dworkin and other constitutional theorists who embrace robustly moral patterns of judicial reasoning as legally appropriate, Coleman is entirely comfortable with the proposition that the American legal system does incorporate morality as a criterion for legality. Hence, for all practical purposes within our legal system, Coleman believes it entirely possible to take Dworkin's side of this practical debate while remaining a positivist. That is the core of Coleman's inclusive positivism.

I share Coleman's philosophical openness to inclusivism as to rules of recognition and secondary legal rules, and indeed I think his defense of that position in *The Practice of Principle* is extraordinarily powerful. And yet that does not mean that I think the practical debate between positivists and their advocates has been blunted, at least in the American legal system. I do not think that there is a particularly plausible set of legal arguments or sociological arguments for the conclusion that secondary legal rules in any American jurisdiction demand moral evaluation in the way Coleman imagines. Although many primary and secondary legal rules contain moral predicates, there is great variety in the narrowness and breadth of those predicates, and there are many domains within which the predicates and principles of morality have narrow or circumscribed roles. Hence, if it were simply a hard fact that a certain secondary legal rule applies, there would be many domains in which moral arguments are in effect entirely irrelevant, even in the American legal system.

In other words, my own reading of large domains of American law is such that, if the model of social facts were accepted, it would, as a contingent matter, lend credence to a powerful, practical, positivistic argument emphasizing separation. More precisely, the model of social facts, as so construed, makes whether, when, and how moral considerations apply to questions about validity purely a matter of social fact, and it is a matter of the very nature of law itself that the moral-legal link—to the extent that it exists at all—is a matter of social fact. It is this version of the social fact thesis that I have argued against.

The Truth in the Model of Social Facts

In the second section, I outlined Coleman's argument for the model of social facts and I argued against it. In the third section, I tried to explain why it might be important for Hart or Coleman to try to make good on that model, beyond merely extolling conventionalism. In the fourth section, conversely, I explained why an antipositivist might think it matters whether the model of social facts is accepted, even when that model is appended to inclusive positivism. But throughout, I have suggested that the greatest appeal in the model of social facts is the attractive idea that jurisprudential puzzles and attributes of lawfulness are somehow constituted by social practices, and that nothing beyond social practices is needed to explain them. It is the richness and nuance of the world of social norms and their capacity to constitute legal phenomena that makes Hart's work in jurisprudence so philosophically inspiring; just as the similar richness of Wittgenstein on linguistic practice is remarkable not, in the first instance, for its capacity to eradicate bloated metaphysics, but in its capacity to generate powerful philosophical insight simply from within analysis of social practices.

In this section, I shall attempt to vindicate both Hart's and Coleman's faith that the analysis of social and linguistic practice in law will yield philosophically rich products and that a down-to-earth analysis of legal phenomena in terms of social facts will produce many interesting results. I shall even argue that, in one relatively narrow but important sense, the social fact thesis is true. I shall nevertheless maintain that insofar as the social fact thesis is understood as what I have labeled "the model of social facts"—a view that is intended to secure the conclusion, in a judge's or lawyer's argument, that a putative law is valid because it complies with a rule of recognition that as a matter of social fact is in force—the social fact thesis is false.

In a prior essay, I depicted a fundamental ambiguity in the phrase "rule of recognition" in *The Concept of Law*: it is sometimes used to refer to a propositional entity, and sometimes used to refer to a social practice (Zipursky 2001, pp. 227–229). Thus, for example, a rule of recognition might be something of the order of the sentence "Only statutes passed by both houses of Congress are valid federal law," or the proposition *that only statutes passed by both houses of Congress are valid federal law*. Both the sentence expressing the proposition and the proposition itself are propositional entities. On the other hand, a social practice among judges of treating statutes as valid federal law only if passed by both houses of congress is a social practice—a pattern of conduct (and attitude) and not a propositional entity. Hart sometimes seems to think of a rule of recognition as something of the first sort, but he also seems to think it essential that rules of recognition be social rules. Coleman recognizes this distinction, and agrees that there is sometimes unclarity in *The Concept of Law*. But Coleman also agrees with my statement that Hart's position can be rendered consistent on this point. Our methods differ somewhat. We both believe that as a matter of determining what sort of entity a rule of recognition is—as a matter of sorting into ontological types—a rule of recognition belongs to the category of propositional entities. But, asserts Coleman, it is possible for this propositional entity to be *practiced* in a particular community, and equally possible for it *not to be practiced*. Whether it is practiced determines whether the rule of recognition exists in that community. Put differently, it determines whether the rule of recognition exists in that community (Coleman 2001a, p. 83).

My own prior analysis anticipated *The Practice of Principle* at least insofar as I took it to be significant to say that a rule of recognition's being a social rule is not a matter of its being of a certain ontological category. On the contrary, it is an important attribute of this propositional entity that it is a social rule (or the lack of such an attribute, if it is not). Whether it has this attribute is a matter of how it is treated by members of the community. I think it is clearer to say that this propositional entity—the rule of recognition—has or lacks the attribute of being a social rule in the particular community, than it is to say that it exists or does not exist in the community (Zipursky 2001, p. 233).

Part of the elegance of Hart's theory is its capacity almost to encapsulate an entire legal system into the rule of recognition. That is, if one can attribute the rule of recognition to the community, one can attribute acceptance of whatever is entailed by the rule of recognition to the system (in conjunction with sufficient evidence that the other pieces of the system are authorized by the rule of recognition). Again, Coleman emphasizes this point when he argues that a primary rule can be binding as law even if the citizens do not adopt a social rule for it. And this structural aspect of Hart's theory is what Coleman has in mind when he says that for a rule of recognition to exist, it must be practiced.

In *The Model of Social Facts*, I argued that the phenomenon of a legal system being the legal system of a community of persons was analogous to the phenomenon of a language being the language of a community.

And I suggested that, in principle, David Lewis's account of what it is for a language to be the language of a community could be adapted to the context of a legal system (Zipursky 2001, p. 19). Lewis put forward a basic model of a language, L, characterized by a function from strings of symbols (sentences) to sentence meanings, with sentence meanings construed as something like truth conditions (in fact, it was important for Lewis to define sentence meanings in terms of truth values and possible worlds, but this is unimportant for the analogy) (Lewis 1975, p. 163). He then depicted what it was for L to be "used by" a population P, or to be the "language *of*" P. P would have a convention of truthfulness-and-trust-in-L. Such a convention would involve asserting a given sentence in L if and only if one believed that the sentence was true (one believed of the truth condition assigned to it by L that it obtained) and expecting others to assert a sentence if and only if they sincerely believed it was true (ibid., pp. 166–168). Of course, Lewis produced an account of what pattern of behavior and attitude constituted a convention (1975, 1969). But my focus is not so much on the account of what a convention is, but on his account of how a certain kind of system, which is composed of a function from certain propositional entities (and their parts) to certain other values, could become the system of a community; what it means for that system to be the system of a community.

I suggested that we treat legal systems, on the Hartian account, analogously. Think of a legal system, as Hart suggested, as a union of primary and secondary rules, and suppose that each legal system has a rule of recognition, which is a function from putative laws to validity values. One could argue that for the legal system to be the legal system *of the community* is for the rule of recognition of that legal system, qua function from putative laws to validity values, to have the attribute of being conventionally accepted by legal officials of the community as the rule of recognition, and for the primary and secondary rules rendered valid under that rule to be generally obeyed by members of the community, and to be in the legal system. This means, roughly, that the legal officials have a cooperative coordinative practice (a form of convention) of treating a putative law as a valid law if and only if it complies with the criteria set out in the rule of recognition of legal systems. As should be apparent, Coleman's account of shared cooperative activities is thus far consistent with my account.

The account so stated promises many advantages, and many of the merits Hart has claimed for it. It permits a phenomenologically rich and normatively significant account of the internal point of view; it allows us to see how meaningful formal points about legal systems can be made and yet can be relevant to the legal system, as practiced. It also explains the fluidity and continuity of the system, and explains parallels between different systems in different legal communities, despite deep differences in the actual legal systems. Many of these merits, interestingly, match merits of Lewis's account, and, arguably, of the Wittgensteinian and Gricean accounts of language that Lewis was attracted by and that he formalized.

And yet I believe that this account is entirely consistent with the possibility of discourse and repartee over criteria of legality—that is, it does not fall to the argument from disagreement. It simply requires us to concede that, insofar as criteria of validity change, the legal system (as a formal entity) that once qualified to be the legal system of the legal community in question, no longer does so qualify, and a new (or amended) legal system qualifies (or counts) as the legal system of that community. This is somewhat paradoxical, because secondary legal rules are supposed to govern change, on the Hartian model, and yet secondary legal rules, as propositional entities, are part of what individuates the formal legal system, which may be the system of the community at one time but not a subsequent time. There is nothing genuinely self-contradictory about this pairing of positions, however.

The Hartian challenge, as I am interpreting it, is not to nail down immutable facts about legal validity within a given community of people. It is to explain how a developed legal system with a certain structure could have the attribute of being realized in a community of people at a time. The account is most elegant if the possibility of this realization can be explained even for systems of law that are complete, in the sense that Hart indicated (including secondary rules). And, as Coleman has pointed out drawing upon Shapiro, it permits us to understand certain fundamentally challenging aspects of legal systems, such as the concept of being governed by law, just as the Lewissian account permits a profound understanding of the possibility of communication and meaning. These are, in important respects, central to the metaphysical challenge of understanding law. What is particularly impressive in both Lewis and Hart is the ability to explain simultaneously the sense in which social facts constitute a phenomenon about which philosophers have often been overly metaphysical, and the ability to design the social philosophy-norms-conventions component of the theory so that it is capable of framing a formal aspect of analysis in the area—for Lewis, compositional semantics, and for Hart, Kelsen-like theorizing about legal systems as abstract entities with a certain formal structure, including secondary legal rules.

Legal Positivism and the Conventionalistic Fallacy

My position can be put in terms of a critique of a particular form of positivistic argument that I have sketched above. The argument is:

(1)   Putative law PL satisfies the conditions set forth in RRX.

(2)   RRX is a rule of recognition in LCX (legal community X).

And therefore,

(3)   PL is valid (in LCX).

Proposition (1) must be argued for as a legal matter, for example, one might have to show that a particular statute was approved by both houses of Congress, and signed into law by the president. Proposition (2) is asserted to be true as a matter of social fact. Proposition (3) is said to follow from (1) and (2) because PL satisfies the rule of recognition that applies in LCX.

Generalized, the argument purports to show that for any putative law, whether that putative law is valid in a particular legal community is a matter of social fact plus a matter of whatever kind of fact is set forth as a condition of legality in the rule of recognition that, as a matter of social fact, is accepted in the community. This is what I have called, earlier in the article, the positivist's practical application of the model of social facts to arrive at a type of argument in which validity status is inferred from social facts.

The problem with this argument is that it illicitly mixes postures, that of the lawyer and that of the sociologist of law. Proposition (1) is a proposition of law, about whether a certain putative law does or does not satisfy certain legal conditions, uttered standardly by a member of LCX. Proposition (2) is not about law, it is about whether certain persons have certain shared attitudes and practices; of course, it could be uttered by a member of LCX. In order to be a valid argument, we would need proposition:

(2′)   RRX (simply the rule of recognition itself, as a secondary legal rule statement).

That would license the conclusion:

(3′)   Putative law PL is valid, when drawn by participants in LCX.

Alternatively, if (2) remains the same, then (1) and (2) do license the conclusion,

(3*)   According to the conditions of legality accepted as governing in LCX, PL is valid.

Of course, one could adopt a secondary legal rule statement,

(3a)   Whatever complies with the conditions of legality accepted as governing in LCX is valid, as a proposition of law.

And (3a) would arguably lead from (3*) to (3). But a legal system need not have such a secondary legal rule, and I do not believe ours does. Moreover, such a statement, as a rule of identification, is patently conventionalistic in a sense that Hart, Dworkin, and Coleman have all rightly bridled at when offered as a piece of law. The upshot is that (1) and (2) do not yield the conclusion that PL is valid (in LCX).

This is a version of what I would call "the conventionalistic fallacy." The fallacy here is not so much about drawing prescriptive conclusions from descriptive premises. It is a matter of drawing conclusions that are internal to a particular reason-giving practice, and that will actually license an important sort of inference, from a premise that asserts that, as a matter of social fact, that particular reason-giving practice exists in a particular community. The fallaciousness of the inference is often difficult to see, especially where the reason-giving practice has a high coordinative component. For when it has a high coordinative component, a substantial aspect of the reason-giving involves drawing upon practices that already exist. There are, however, many ways of *drawing upon practices that already exist*, and asserting that as a matter of fact a certain set of attitudes and behaviors does exist, is only one of those ways. In law, participants in the community refer to precedent, citing both examples and general propositions that convey criteria of legality; just as in language, we teach words and offer accounts of meaning, and offer explanations and interpretations of one another, in a manner that certainly draws upon already existing practices, but in so doing we are not making assertions that these practices exist.

The Conventionalistic Fallacy in Semantics

Without going too much further afield, it may be useful to offer one further analogy to the linguistic case. The legal positivist's inference to validity from the rule of recognition appears to be much like the logical empiricist's inference to analyticity from definitions or meaning postulates. In a form that is expressly relativized to a particular formal system, the inference may be sound. But if the aim is to infer an analytic statement as a necessary truth in a sense that is not purely formal, then the meaning statement from which it is inferred must be necessary, and if it is necessary, it must not be empirically disconfirmable. For Quine–Duhem reasons, this is an implausible position for an empiricist to take. But the appearance of necessity comes from, in some sense, the plausibility of taking a meaning postulate or an analytic statement to be fixed by its connection to a linguistic system. But it is a social fact that the language is the language of the community, and it is not a necessary truth. Moreover, it is possible that the language of the community will be amended. The necessity of the analytic truth is necessity *in a language*, and even if that language is the language of the community of the participants, it does not follow that it is *necessity simpliciter*. In attempting to depict a sentence like "All bachelors are unmarried men" as a special kind of necessary truth, there is an attempt at a certain kind of shift. There is an attempt at a shift from necessity *as a feature that flows from features of the linguistic system through the social fact of the connection between the language and the community, to a conclusion that is not relativized to language or community*, but simply expresses the putative fact. This shift appears to be another example of the conventionalistic fallacy.

As I have argued in *The Model of Social Facts*, and have discussed at length with Coleman and Shapiro, there is a parallel between Dworkin's critique of Hart and Quine's critique of Carnap. Both Hart and Carnap recognized elegant formal systems, within which certain kinds of analyses were possible and certain kinds of formal results could be obtained. Both recognized that there was an important sense in which the system was realized in a community. And both attempted to argue that certain kinds of substantive truths—truths detached from the system merely as a formal system—could be obtained. For Carnap it was analytic truths emerging from meaning postulates. For Hart—on at least one standard reading— it was the supposedly clear-minded observation made by judges and lawyers in certain cases that a putative law was the law because it complied with what the formal system laid out as conditions of legality. And for each there is a broader lesson; for Carnap, the existence of a domain of analytic truths and the incompleteness of the domain of empirical truths; for Hart, the more general conclusion that what is law is a matter of social fact.

The essence of Quine's "Two Dogmas"—at least the Duhemian strand—is that there is no sentence that is unrevisable, including putatively analytic truths. And the essence of Dworkin's argument from disagreement against Hart is similarly that all legal statements are in principle contestable, including rule of recognition statements. Both of these results seem paradoxical, because each of the targets (Carnap and Hart) had a powerful argument that the very possibility of the activity depends on the existence of a system, within which certain fundamental standards are constitutive. I have argued that there is merely a tension or an apparent contradiction between the members of each of these respective pairs.

The gist of the problem, as both Carnap and Hart were at some level aware and were actively engaging, is a problem of theoretical perspective. In the theoretical activities of (1) explaining the possibility of law and (2) explaining the nature of a certain kind of formal system, it is true that certain kinds of statements express constitutive truths within the respective systems. However, those statements, as used by participants in the community, in connection with the activities to which they are related—asserting facts about the physical world, in Carnap's case, and asserting the applicability of pieces of law, in Hart's case—take on a different cast. For as participants in the community, although we are conventionally constrained in a variety of ways, and although the existence of the conventions may make the activities possible, it does not follow that the very constraints expressed by whichever sociologist of language or law who would most plausibly identify and individuate the formal system, would function as similarly rigid constraints within the discourse of the participants.

The upshot is that if a phenomenon came along that would cause a reasonable scientific theorist to reject what would have been an analytic truth, the participant may reject it. That would mean, at some level, that what the ideal linguistic theorist would identify as the language of the community would be slightly modified. There is nothing wrong with that. And the result is that efforts to link necessary truth, as a modal status to analyticity within semantic theory should be rejected. Similarly, as discussed above, if a legal issue came along, and deliberation on that issue fulfilled the Dworkinian example of causing judges to alter what they might before have taken as conditions of legality, that might well change what the sociologist of legal systems would say the legal system was, but it does not follow that the judge would have done anything inappropriate or anything out of keeping with the concept of applying the law. And the result, similarly, is that efforts to link legal status too tightly to what in fact are conventionally accepted standards of legality are inappropriate.

In both cases, the conventionalistic fallacy involves inferring the substantive proposition within the first-order activity from what is a constitutive truth within the formal system conventionally accepted. The problem is not that no such inference can be drawn. Typically—almost invariably—what is a constitutive truth within the formal system (e.g., the rule of recognition, the definition), will also be assertible, and usually true, as asserted within the practice, and so the drawing of the conclusion as an ordinary conclusion will often be sound. But if an effort is made to elevate the status of the conclusion to one that is constitutive, beyond revision, or demonstrable in a manner that goes beyond the general demand for justification, then the arguer is equivocating between the constitutive status of the premise within the formal system, and its (probable) truth within the first-order domain. That is the heart of the conventionalistic fallacy.

The Contingent Relevance of Morality to Law under Inclusive Positivism

There would seem to be a great deal here for Coleman to agree with, and the question arises as to whether the affirmative account I have offered, and the critique of Hart I have offered, really undercut anything that Coleman has said, or is trying to do. I conclude by articulating two respects in which the foregoing account does cut against Coleman's jurisprudential aspirations and claims: (1) the reasons that moral considerations may go into the assessment of what is law; and (2) the question of whether conventionalism and the model of social facts constitute a form of legal positivism. Both points have been discussed above, to some extent: they are presented here in part as summary, and in part as suggestions of where I take myself to be leaving off with Coleman.

Arguably, the central tenet of Coleman's inclusive positivism is that, although moral principles and moral criteria may well enter into the inquiry of what is legally valid, they do not do so, contra Dworkin, Fuller, Perry, and Aquinas, because of the ineliminability of the normative roots of legal questions. Rather, moral considerations play a role in determining what is and is not valid only if, and only because, as a contingent matter, the rule of recognition accepted in the relevant community happens to include some moral criteria for some cases. Absent such agreed-upon conditions, morality and legality would truly be independent, though perhaps overlapping.

As I have already indicated, I believe that Coleman and I hold different views as to whether, within American legal systems, the largely accepted secondary legal rules are as chock-full of moral predicates and principles as Coleman says. Certainly, there are many moral predicates in, say, accepted constitutional norms that have the status of secondary legal rules in both state and federal systems. And beyond constitutional norms, as I have argued elsewhere, moral predicates can certainly play an important role in secondary rules. However, the real question is whether the role of moral considerations as reasons for or against the assertion that some putative law is valid depends on an underlying accepted secondary legal rule to which the moral consideration is relevant. The modified version of the social facts thesis that I have put forward offers a negative answer to this question. To be more precise, there is nothing in the version of a social facts thesis that I have offered that implies a positive answer to this question. That our understanding of the possibility of a legal system (qua formal entity) being the legal system of a community depends on secondary rules being accepted by the legal officials in the community simply does not entail that the only reasons that can be offered for or against a legal assertion are ones that, according to those secondary rules, are relevant to validity. To think so is to commit what I have called the conventionalistic fallacy.

The point is perhaps more easily expressed in affirmative, rather than negative terms, and this is, in fact, the manner in which Dworkin, in his earliest and in some ways most powerful work, made the point. Legal reasons—assertions or considerations offered on behalf of one side of a legal argument or another—may take many different forms. Matters of judgment as to what sorts of arguments are powerful or proper are matters that substantial learning is required in order to make well. This is not to say that one must be conventionalistic about what constitutes the truth in this area. It is simply to say that there is no reason within the metaphysics of law that necessarily bounds what kind of consideration can enter. Moreover, there is a great variety of legal arguments that have been properly used, and there is no evidence that it is true as a legal matter that moral considerations enter only when conditioned on a secondary legal rule that authorizes them to enter in. Whereas this account is more modest than Fuller's or Dworkin's on the role of morality in law, it is not as constrictive, in structure, as that offered by Coleman.

There is no overarching metaphysics of law according to which we can make prior boundary judgments about what sorts of reasons can count as legal reasons and what cannot. Lawyers and judges must try to offer the best arguments they can, and, although they are not disallowed from using jurisprudential or metaphysical theories to support or criticize arguments about what the law is, they are not necessarily bounded by such prior jurisprudential considerations either. The web of legal discourse, like the Quinean web of belief, is not externally bounded.

Is Coleman a Positivist?

One of the boldest statements in *The Practice of Principle* is the assertion that the true core of positivism is the social fact thesis, not the separation thesis (Coleman 2001a, pp. 152–153). Coleman has been asserting something along these lines for quite a while. At one level it is clear why he is doing so. In "Negative and Positive Positivism," Coleman identified only a very thin version of the separation thesis as one to which the positivist must be committed—that it was not inconsistent with the concept of law that validity not be conditioned on morality. When Dworkin indicated that he would readily accept this, and when it became clear that even many natural law theorists would accept it, it became clear that this was not enough to hang positivism on. And indeed, Coleman recognized this within the original essay. Yet Coleman for some reason wants to remain in a position where he can call himself a positivist. In support of this aspiration, Coleman asserts that the core of positivism is in fact the social fact thesis (Coleman 2001a, p. 153).

It is hard to know how to evaluate claims that some thesis or other is the core of an intellectual school or movement that goes under some name. And it is hard to know why it matters whether such a statement is true. At a minimum, I think one could say that if there is a set of intellectual motivations driving the movement, and a set of intellectual commitments adhered to by leading figures of the movement and rejected by leading antagonists of it, and a set of ideas exemplified by leading texts within the movement, then that thesis should play a central role in bringing these motivations and commitments together, rendering them unified, and justifying them (or, conversely, displaying them ultimately unjustified). And it would seem to be important because the stronger and more defensible aspects of the view could be separated from the weaker ones if a justifiable core could be found, and the different ideas could be vindicated or defeated based on the nature and soundness of their connection to a core thesis.

From within this rough-and-ready framework, I find it quite implausible that the social fact thesis, in the form that I have accepted it, constitutes the core of positivism. For it cuts little ice on the separation thesis; it has very little tendency to imply the independence of law and morality. Similarly, it has no particular implications about the sources thesis. It has no particular affinities with the Benthamite and Austinian view that a law's status as law depends on pedigree. It has little or no tendency to drive a wedge between law and custom; it leaves open the question of whether appeal to custom is a sound basis for a claim of legality. And, of course stemming from Hart, it leaves open the question of a legal obligation as simply a matter of facing an armed "commander."

Conclusion: Pragmatism *or* Positivism

There is, then, at least prima facie reason to believe that Coleman faces a choice. Either he can adopt the version of the social facts thesis that he appears to have adopted—what I have called "the model of social facts"—and face I think irrepressible criticism of the sort I have offered, and remain untrue to the web-of-belief pragmatism that he has been advocating; or he can remain true to philosophical pragmatism, offer a cogent account of the respect in which social practices constitute law, and adopt the commensurate view of the social facts thesis. If he takes the latter route, however, he may no longer condition the moral-legal link only on accepted rules of recognition and must overhaul inclusive positivism; more broadly, it is not clear that he is entitled to call himself a positivist any longer.

References

Bratman, M. 1992. "Shared Cooperative Activity." *Philosophical Review* 101/2: 327–341.

———. 1993. "Shared Intention." *Ethics* 104: 97–113.

Carnap, R. 1947. *Meaning and Necessity*. Chicago: University of Chicago Press.

Coleman, J. 1982. "Negative and Positive Positivism." *Journal of Legal Studies* 11: 139–164.

———. 1995. "Truth and Objectivity in Law." *Legal Theory* 1: 33–68.

———. 2001a. *The Practice of Principle: In Defense of a Pragmatist Approach to Legal Theory*. Oxford: Clarendon Press.

———. 2001b. "Incorporationism, Conventionality, and the Practical Difference Thesis." In J. Coleman, ed., *Hart's Postscript: Essays on the Postscript to* The Concept of Law. Oxford: Clarendon Press.

Dworkin, R. 1978. *Taking Rights Seriously*. Cambridge, Mass.: Harvard University Press.

———. 1983. "A Reply by Ronald Dworkin." In M. Cohen, ed., *Ronald Dworkin and Contemporary Jurisprudence*. Totowa, N.J.: Rowman and Allanheld.

———. 1986. *Law's Empire*. Cambridge, Mass.: Harvard University Press.

———. 1987. "Legal Theory and the Problem of Sense." In R. Gavison, ed., *Contemporary Legal Philosophy: The Influence of H. L. A. Hart*. Oxford: Clarendon Press.

Gibbard, A. 1990. *Wise Choices, Apt Feelings: A Normative Theory of Judgment*. Cambridge, Mass.: Harvard University Press.

Hart, H. L. A. 1994. *The Concept of Law*, second ed. Oxford: Clarendon Press.

Kripke, S. 1982. *Wittgenstein on Rules and Private Language: An Elementary Exposition*. Cambridge, Mass.: Harvard University Press.

Lewis, D. 1969. *Convention: A Philosophical Study*. Cambridge, Mass.: Harvard University Press.

———. 1975. "Languages and Language." In K. Gunderson, ed., *Minnesota Studies in Philosophy of Science* 7: 3–35.

Putnam, H. 1995. "Are Moral and Legal Values Made or Discovered?" *Legal Theory* 1: 5–19.

Quine, W. V. O. 1953. "Two Dogmas of Empiricism." In W. V. O. Quine, *From a Logical Point of View*. Cambridge, Mass.: Harvard University Press.

Shapiro, S. 1998. "On Hart's Way Out." *Legal Theory* 4: 469–507.

Zipursky, B. 1997. "Legal Coherentism." *SMU Law Review* 50: 1679–1720.

———. 2000. "Pragmatic Conceptualism." *Legal Theory* 6: 457–485.

———. 2001. "The Model of Social Facts." In J. Coleman, ed., *Hart's Postscript: Essays on the Postscript to* The Concept of Law. Oxford: Clarendon Press.

17 Conceptual Jurisprudence and the Intelligibility of Law's Claim to Obligate

Kenneth Einar Himma

One of the most stubborn problems facing positivists has been to explain how legal norms give rise to legal obligations. John Austin's account of obligation as being constituted by the threat of sanctions is problematic because, as H. L. A. Hart famously argued, a coercive command can, by itself, only *oblige* a person to obey; it cannot *obligate* a person to obey. But Hart's account of obligation as arising out of the acceptance of a rule of recognition by officials is also vulnerable to objections. First, it is not clear how the official's voluntary acceptance of a rule can obligate her to obey that rule. Second, it is not clear how the acceptance of officials to abide by metarules governing the manufacture, modification, and adjudication of law can give rise to an obligation on the part of *citizens* to obey the norms that satisfy those metarules.

In this essay, I consider Jules Coleman's defense of Hart. Coleman (2001) supplements Hart's view with the proposition that it is a conceptual truth that the rule of recognition constitutes a shared cooperative activity (SCA). As parties to an SCA, officials are jointly, rather than just unilaterally, committed to supporting the acceptance and efforts of each other to further the legal enterprise; it is this feature of the rule of recognition that, on Coleman's view, allows the Hartian positivist to give a satisfactory account of legal obligation. In this essay, I argue that Coleman's theory succeeds in explaining how the rule of recognition obligates officials, but does not succeed in explaining how primary legal norms obligate citizens.

The Problem of Legal Obligation

John Austin's (1995) command theory of law analyzes the notion of legal obligation in terms of a sovereign's ability to coerce compliance. On

Austin's view, a law subject S is legally obligated to perform an act A if and only if there is some general command of the sovereign (or rule promulgated by the sovereign) that is backed by a threat of a sanction and requires S to do A. As Austin explains the notion of an obligation, it is the threat of a sanction that makes A nonoptional (or mandatory) and hence obligatory. Since it is the general commands of the sovereign that constitute law, it follows that it is the threat of a sanction for noncompliance with the command that gives rise to a legal obligation on the part of the subject.

H. L. A. Hart (1994) rejects Austin's view that legal obligation is conceptually reducible to the presence of a sanction for noncompliance on the ground that it assimilates legal norms to a gunman's demand for money. The subject of such a demand can, according to Hart, plausibly be characterized as being "obliged" to comply, but not as being "duty bound" or "obligated" to do so; thus, since the existence of legal obligation is entailed by the existence of a legal system, and the application of coercive force can't give rise to obligation, it follows, on Hart's view, that Austin's command theory of law fails to explain the existence conditions for law and hence for legal obligation.

Instead, Hart seems to explain the concept of legal obligation in terms of a social rule of recognition that governs the behavior of officials in making, changing, and adjudicating law. On Hart's view, the rule of recognition is constituted by a convergence of behavior and attitude on the part of officials: officials converge in their behavior by satisfying the requirements of the rule and converge in their attitude by criticizing deviations from these requirements. It is, on this line of interpretation, these two elements of official practice that bring the rule of recognition into existence and thereby create standards that *obligate* officials.

While it is the officials alone who bring a rule of recognition into existence, citizens also play a role in bringing the legal system and hence legal obligation into existence. According to Hart's minimum conditions for the existence of a legal system, there is a legal system in S if and only if (1) there is a social rule of recognition R accepted by persons serving as officials in S; and (2) citizens generally obey the rules valid under R. Accordingly, since, as a conceptual matter, the existence of a legal system entails the existence of laws and hence of legal obligations, it follows, on Hart's view, that the satisfaction by a society of the minimum conditions described above is a sufficient condition for the existence of legal obligation in that society.

Hart's elegant attempt to explain legal obligation has been criticized on two fronts. The first is that the acceptance of a rule in the Hartian sense is not, by itself, sufficient to give rise to *official* obligations (hereinafter referred to as the problem of official obligations). As Andrei Marmor strongly puts the criticism, "the existence of a social practice, in itself, does not provide anyone with an obligation to engage in the practice" (1998, p. 530). The second criticism is that Hart's account of law's conventionality cannot explain how law imposes obligations on its *citizens* (hereinafter referred to as the problem of citizen obligation).[1] A minimal legal system in which *only* officials accept the rule of recognition is no less coercive toward its citizens than an Austinian normative system. Just as the commands of a gunman can't give rise to an obligation to comply even if the gunman takes the internal point of view toward his authority to make such a threat, the first-order norms of a legal system are no less coercive just because officials take the internal point of view toward their authority.

Although it is true that the problem of official obligations does not affect positivists, like Marmor, who deny that the rule of recognition is a duty-imposing rule, every positivist must deal with the problem of citizen obligation. As a conceptual theory of law, positivism is obliged to provide an account of all the central concepts that figure prominently into legal practice. If, as seems reasonable, it is a conceptual truth that legal rules give rise to legal (as opposed to moral) obligations, then there is no concept more central to law than that of legal obligation. Accordingly, the proponent of any conceptual theory of law is obliged to provide an analysis of the concept of legal obligation.

Law as Shared Cooperative Activity and the Problem of Official Obligation

Coleman believes that an explanation of law's conventional character must be sought at a higher level of abstraction than is evident in Hart's account. Coleman argues that the conventional metarule of recognition is most plausibly thought of as being a shared cooperative activity (SCA).[2] Coleman identifies three characteristic features of an SCA: (1) each participant in an SCA attempts to conform her behavior to the behavior of the other participants; (2) each participant is committed to the joint activity; and (3) each participant is committed to supporting the efforts of the other participants to play their appropriate roles within the joint activity. An SCA, then, enables participants to coordinate their behavior and also provides "'a background framework that structures relevant bargaining' between [participants] about how the joint activity is to proceed" (Coleman 2001, p. 97).

What is conceptually essential to the social practice constituting a conventional rule of recognition, then, is that it has the normative structure of an SCA. It is a conceptual truth about law that officials coordinate their behavior with one another in various ways that are responsive to the intentions and actions of the others; what a judge, for example, does in a particular case depends on what other judges have done in similar cases. Similarly, it is a conceptual truth that officials are committed to the joint activity and to supporting one another; officials responsible for promulgating laws require an assurance of continuing support from officials responsible for enforcing and executing those laws. In the absence of the normative features constitutive of an SCA, according to Coleman, legal practice is not conceptually possible.

Coleman's analysis of the rule of recognition as an SCA provides a plausible solution to the problem of official obligation. Hart's analysis of the internal point of view is unable to explain how a rule of recognition could give rise to autonomous obligations because it is hard to see how one person's completely unilateral acceptance, by itself, can transform a situation in which not-X is a permissible option to a situation in which X is mandatory and hence obligatory. Indeed, if an official is bound only to the extent of her acceptance, then withdrawing acceptance is sufficient to extinguish any obligation. Since, as a conceptual matter, there is nothing that precludes the withdrawal of acceptance at any time, there is little reason to think that the official is bound in any meaningful sense: if I can get out of an obligation merely by repudiating it, it is hard to see how I can meaningfully be said to be bound in the first place.

In contrast to Hart's theory, Coleman claims that the rule of recognition in an SCA involves more than just a convergence of independent unilateral acceptances of the rule of recognition. It involves an interdependent commitment by the participants in the practice that gives rise to the rule of recognition. As Coleman puts the point with respect to judges, "[t]he best explanation of judges' responsiveness to one another is their commitment to the goal of making possible the existence of a durable legal practice" (Coleman 2001, p. 97). Here the commitment is joint in the sense that the commitment of one person is conditioned in part on the commitment of other persons—though it is not necessarily explicitly bargained for.

It should be clear that joint commitments of the sort involved in an SCA, by themselves, can give rise to obligations. Notice that such commitments are interdependent in the sense that the commitment of one person is conditioned, at least in part, on the commitment of another person; in the absence of the participation of the other persons, there is no compelling reason for one person to commit to the relevant norm. Accordingly, as a conceptual matter, such commitments induce reliance and hence a set of expectations that are, as a moral matter, at least presumptively justified.

There is, of course, nothing controversial about the idea that presumptively justified reliance expectations give rise to moral obligations. If I knowingly induce you to rely to your detriment on my performing a particular act, then, other things being equal, I have morally obligated myself to perform that particular act. What obligates me, of course, is not just my unilateral behavior. It is rather my leading you to put yourself in a position of comparative peril. Insofar as you reasonably rely on my behavior, you have given up—at my instigation and *to your detriment*—an option that you otherwise had; uncontroversial principles of fairness dictate, under those circumstances, that I perform the act.

This is not necessarily to claim that the obligation that binds officials to the rule of recognition is a moral one. Strictly speaking, the point is merely to show that an SCA can give rise to one kind of obligation. But if an SCA can give rise to a moral obligation, the most stringent kind of obligation,[3] then it is reasonable to think that it can give rise to lesser sorts of obligation, such as purely social obligations (whatever they turn out to be). Ideally, of course, one would like to have an account of what social obligations are and how they differ from moral obligations; however, there is little reason to think it is the job of the conceptual jurisprude to produce such an analysis.

Coleman's Response and the Problem of Citizen Obligation

Although Coleman's analysis of the rule of recognition, then, is a viable solution to the problem of official obligation, it is somewhat less successful in solving the problem of citizen obligation. To begin with, merely showing that officials can obligate themselves through some mechanism does not show that their acts qua officials can, in the relevant Hartian sense, obligate *citizens*. That you and I can obligate ourselves to behave in a particular way cannot, by itself, entail the existence of an obligation on the part of other people.

Whether or not officials can obligate citizens by means of their acts under the rule of recognition seems to depend, in part, on *whom* the officials owe their obligations to. If, on the one hand, the official obligations to apply the rule of recognition are owed to citizens, then it seems reasonable to think that citizens are obligated by the norms valid under the rule of recognition. Given the logic of obligation, it would be very hard to make sense of the idea, for example, that a judge owes an obligation to all citizens to incarcerate any citizen who violates some primary norm N if N does not obligate citizens. A coherent concept of legal obligation simply cannot function this way. But if, on the other hand, the official obligations are owed only to the officials, then the existence of such obligations provides no obvious reason to think that official acts are any less coercive relative to citizens than the demands of a gunman.

To see the problem here, let us assume that an exchange of promises always gives rise to at least a prima facie social obligation of some kind (though not necessarily a moral obligation). Suppose two gunmen mutually promise to carry out a particular plan to commit a robbery against a third person and thereby create a prima facie social obligation that each owes to the other.[4] Even if we assume that the gunmen have succeeded in obligating themselves to each other, it is clear that this fact, by itself, does not render their behavior with respect to their victim any less coercive.

Accordingly, adding the requirement that the relevant official practice is an SCA to Hart's minimum conditions for the existence of a legal system does not appear to help with the problem of citizen obligation. Conceiving of the rule of recognition as an SCA shows how officials may obligate themselves to conform their official behavior to the requirements of the rule of recognition, but it provides no grounds for inferring the existence of an obligation to *citizens*. Since it is the reliance of other officials that obligates an official *O* to the rule, we can reasonably infer that obligation is owed to the other officials, but we can't reasonably infer that the obligation is owed to citizens. In a minimal legal system, then, the only obligations officials have to apply the rule of recognition are owed to one another. In that conceptually possible legal system, the citizens neither participate in the SCA nor take the internal point of view toward the authority of the officials to make law.

The problem, however, is that the enforcement of primary norms against citizens in this legal system is no less coercive than the demands of two gunmen who are jointly committed to robbing some third person. The mere fact that the gunmen are united by a joint commitment to rob the victim and are hence committed to supporting each other's efforts does not make their threats any less coercive. Thus, if Hart is correct in thinking that the application of coercive force can never give rise to a legal obligation to obey, then citizens in that world do not have a legal obligation to obey the primary norms.

What Is Required for a Successful Analysis of Legal Obligation?

In response, Coleman might acknowledge that conceiving of the rule of recognition as an SCA does not show how law can obligate citizens, but argue that a complete analysis of the concept of legal obligation does not require this. If it is true, as Joseph Raz (1994) believes, that it is a conceptually necessary truth that law claims authority over citizens, then it is also a conceptually necessary truth that law purports, or claims, to give rise to obligations; to explain this feature of law, the theorist analyzing legal concepts must, as Coleman would put it, "make intelligible" law's claim to obligate citizens by explaining how it is possible for law to obligate citizens.[5] But it is not a conceptually necessary truth that laws that purport to obligate give rise to citizen obligations; just as law may purport to have authority over citizens without actually having such authority, law may purport to obligate citizens without actually obligating them. Since it is not a conceptual truth that law obligates, the theorist analyzing legal concepts need not give an account of how law obligates. Accordingly, a positivist must explain how law's claim to impose obligations is intelligible by showing how law could impose obligations, but need not explain how law obligates. On this line of reasoning, then, a successful analysis of legal obligation needs to do no more than make intelligible law's claim to obligate citizens.

This line of analysis is vulnerable to a number of worries. To begin with, the claim that primary legal norms may fail to give rise to obligations seems to be true, as a conceptual matter, only of *moral* obligations. A primary legal norm that requires citizens to behave in morally repugnant ways (say, to torture one's first born) could not under even the best of circumstances give rise to a moral obligation to do so. Indeed, giving rise to a moral obligation to obey is the mark of a morally legitimate legal system; on this traditional view, a legal system is morally legitimate if and only if the primary norms of the system give rise to content-independent *moral* obligations to obey. Thus, it is to be expected that there will be many primary norms in illegitimate legal systems that fail to give rise to moral obligations to obey.

But the claim that valid primary norms don't necessarily give rise to obligations seems to be false of *legal* obligations. As Hart defines the notion, primary norms are addressed to citizens and either prohibit or make mandatory certain behaviors. And, according to our pretheoretical understanding of the relevant notions, legally valid primary norms create, by definition, *legal obligations*—an understanding that Hart seems to endorse:

> It is true that the idea of a rule is by no means a simple one: we have already seen ... the need, if we are to do justice to the complexity of a legal system, to discriminate between two different though related types. Under rules of the one type, which may well be considered the basic or primary type, human beings are required to do or abstain from certain actions, whether they wish to or not. Rules of the other type are in a sense parasitic upon or secondary to the first; for they provide that human beings may by doing or saying certain things introduce new rules of the primary type, extinguish or modify old ones, or in various ways determine their incidence or control their operations. *Rules of the first type impose duties*; rules of the second type confer powers, public or private. (1994, pp. 80–81; emphasis added)

Indeed, as Hart defines it, a primary norm N is legally valid in a system if and only if it gives rise to a legal obligation to comply with the requirements of N.

If this is correct, then it is not true that a theory of law need only make intelligible law's claim to impose obligation. As there is no concept more central to legal practice than the concept of legal obligation, the conceptual jurisprude must explain what it is to be legally obligated. And this requires an account of *how* a norm that satisfies the criteria of legality gives rise to an obligation since we cannot understand what it means to be legally obligated without understanding, so to speak, the conceptual mechanism by which the obligation arises.[6]

The Intelligibility of Law's Claim to Impose Primary Obligations

Assuming, however, that it is true that all the positivist needs to do with respect to the notion of legal obligation is to make law's claim to impose duties intelligible, it is not clear that conceiving of the rule of recognition as an SCA meets this burden. To see the problem, it would be helpful to get a sense for what must be done to make this claim intelligible. To make intelligible law's claim to impose obligations is to show that law is the sort of entity that is capable in principle of imposing obligations. If properties $P_1, \ldots, P_n$ jointly make intelligible law's claim to impose obligations, then an entity that fails to satisfy any one of these properties is not the sort of thing that is capable, even in principle, of imposing duties.

Although such properties are, thus, necessary conditions for an entity to impose duties, they are necessary conditions of a very special kind. The important notion of "being capable in principle of instantiating a property" was first introduced to legal theory by Joseph Raz in connection with his views on authority. Raz believes it is a conceptual truth that law claims morally legitimate authority and hence that law must be the sort of thing that is capable, in principle, of possessing authority:

[I]t is all too plain that in many cases the law's claim to legitimate authority cannot be supported. . . . [But] in order to be able to claim authority, the law must at the very least come close to the target, i.e. that it must have some of the characteristics of authority. It can fail to have authority. But it can fail in certain ways only. If this is so, there are features of authority it must have. (1994, p. 216)

It must be possible, then, for an entity constituting a legal system to have authority. Thus, a legal system can lack authority for reasons that are *contingently* true, but it cannot lack authority for reasons that are *necessarily* true. Any entity that necessarily lacks authority is conceptually disqualified from being a legal system. To be a legal system is, in part, to be the kind of entity to which it makes sense to attribute authority.

Thus, there are two different ways, on Raz's analysis, in which a claim about authority might be false. A claim attributing authority to an entity

E might be false because *E* lacks a property it is capable of possessing. For example, the claim that the legal system in South Africa during the period of apartheid was legitimate is false because it lacked the property of affording equal respect to all citizens. Notice that the failure here is a contingent failure: it is conceptually possible for the institutional normative system in apartheid South Africa to require treating all citizens with equal respect without changing its status as a legal system. Thus, although the claim of legitimacy is false of apartheid South Africa, it is nonetheless an intelligible claim.

In contrast, a claim of authority might be false because it expresses a category mistake: the claim that a banana split is a legitimate authority, for example, evinces such a mistake. It makes no sense to apply the predicate "constitutes a legitimate authority" to the term "banana split" because a banana split is not the sort of thing that is capable, even in principle, of authority. Although there are many conceptually possible circumstances in which it is true that the legal system in apartheid South Africa instantiates legitimate authority, there are no conceptually possible circumstances in which it is true that a banana split instantiates legitimate authority. It is a conceptual truth that an entity can have authority over people only if it can communicate with them; and a banana split cannot communicate with people in any relevant sense. Thus, unlike the claim of legitimacy by apartheid South Africa, the claim that a banana split constitutes a legitimate authority is unintelligible.

Applying the Razian distinction to Coleman's view, then, the thesis that conceiving of the rule of recognition as an SCA makes intelligible law's claim to impose content-independent obligations entails that an institutionalized system of norms lacking an SCA that defines a recognition norm is not capable even in principle of imposing such obligations. Indeed, the attribution of the predicate "imposes content-independent obligations" to such an entity is a category mistake in the sense that such an attribution is no more sensible than attributing the capacity to impose content-independent obligations to a banana.

This seems too strong to be plausible. Strictly speaking, although it might be true that an institutionalized system of norms satisfying only Austin's minimum conditions for a legal system *could not* impose content-independent duties, the claim that such a system could do so is conceptually intelligible—unlike the claim that a banana imposes content-independent obligations. The difference here is that what would explain the failure, even the necessary failure, of an Austinian sovereign to create content-independent obligations are substantive theoretical considerations about the necessary conditions for giving rise to obligations—and not conceptual considerations about the nature of obligations.

Not every theoretical consideration is conceptual. If, for example, the anarchist's view that there could be no morally legitimate states is correct, it doesn't follow that a state's claim to legitimate authority is unintelligible. The anarchist's argument rests on substantive considerations of morality and not conceptual considerations. The anarchist would presumably concede that the state is the sort of thing, unlike a banana, that can, as a conceptual matter, be a legitimate authority (i.e., the state is the sort of entity that satisfies the conceptual prerequisites for being a legitimate authority), but it *necessarily* fails to do so on moral grounds (i.e., given certain properties of the state, it fails to satisfy the necessary moral prerequisites for legitimate authority).

Likewise, although Coleman might be right in thinking that a minimal Austinian state (i.e., one that satisfies only Austin's minimum conditions for a legal system) is incapable of imposing content-independent obligations, the incapacity has to do with substantive theoretical considerations—and not conceptual considerations. There is clearly a difference between claiming such a system imposes content-independent obligations and claiming a banana does so; only the latter is conceptual nonsense. Thus, Coleman's view that a minimal Austinian legal system is conceptually incapable of creating content-independent reasons for action is, I think, much too strong to be plausible—regardless of whether we are talking about moral obligations or legal obligations.

SCA as a Necessary Condition for Primary Legal Obligations

The analysis of the last section raises the issue of whether it is even a necessary (though not sufficient) condition for a system of institutionalized norms to create content-independent obligations that such a system be grounded in a recognition norm that constitutes an SCA. As a point of departure, it is helpful to note that this is not generally thought to be true of content-independent *moral* obligations. As we have seen, the concept of a morally legitimate state is traditionally explained in terms of the capacity to create content-independent moral obligations to obey.[7] But there are many theories of moral legitimacy that make no reference whatsoever to the structural organization of the state.

Consider, for example, Raz's normal justification thesis. According to the normal justification thesis (NJT), authority is justified to the extent that the subject is more likely to do what right reason requires by following authoritative directives than by following her own judgment:

> The normal and primary way to establish that a person should be acknowledged to have authority over another person involves showing that the alleged subject is likely better to comply with reasons which [objectively] apply to him (other than the alleged authoritative directives) if he accepts the directives of the alleged authority as authoritatively binding, and tries to follow them, than if he tries to follow the reasons which apply to him directly. (Raz 1994, p. 214)

Notice that NJT is a purely substantive theory of legitimacy; it states no procedural or structural conditions whatsoever. According to NJT, then, even a minimal Austinian sovereign state can give rise to content-independent moral obligations to obey: if the subjects are more likely to do what right reason requires by following the sovereign's commands than by following their own judgments about what right reason requires, it follows that such commands give rise to moral obligations to obey.

Although it is reasonable to think that the absence of any procedural constraints on morally legitimate authority is at least mildly problematic given the proliferation of democratic theories of legitimacy, one feature of Raz's theory is especially helpful here. Notice that part of what makes NJT plausible (and most conceptual jurisprudes take it for granted that NJT forms at least one adequate account of moral legitimacy) is that it requires a certain relationship between the putative authority *and its subjects*. The law gives rise to content-independent moral obligations if it does a better job than the subjects of identifying the requirements of right reason.

This is also true of other theories of legitimacy. Rawlsian theory, for example, legitimizes the state only insofar as it recognizes the principles of justice that would be chosen by its subjects in the original position of equality. Democratic theories disagree, of course, on the particulars, but all are expressed in terms of such a relationship. Depending on the theory, the law subjects either constitute the ultimate authority or merely exercise their autonomy in choosing the authority. All such theories, like Raz's view, identify the morally significant property of authority in terms of its relationship to the subjects it purports to govern.

Indeed, a theory of moral legitimacy that does not require some sort of relationship between the authority and the subjects simply isn't plausible. For the content-independent moral obligation to which legitimate authority gives rise is one that is owed *by the subjects* to the authority. Whatever fact about the world that gives rise to such an obligation, it must involve some morally significant relation to the subjects. It seems clear that any explanation of morally legitimate authority that refers only to properties that bear no relationship to the subjects fails as an explanation of why those subjects owe an obligation to the authority.[8]

At the very least, then, this much seems clear: Coleman's analysis of the rule of recognition does not succeed in describing even a necessary condition for law to impose content-independent *moral* obligations to obey. To my knowledge, there is not one theory of moral legitimacy, whether procedural, substantive, or hybrid, that requires the joint instantiation of a certain mental state among the officials as a necessary condition for being able to create in citizens content-independent moral obligations to obey.[9] All are concerned with the external relationship between subject and authority—and not internal relations that obtain among the officials constituting the immediate law-making authority.

But it is no less problematic to think that the mental states giving rise to an SCA must occur among officials if the valid primary norms of a legal system are to give rise to *legal* obligations on the part of citizens. Notice that one can reasonably think that the mental states of citizens are relevant with respect to whether the primary norms of a legal system are capable of obligating citizens. Indeed, on Hart's own analysis of social rules, it is clear that a legal system in which citizens took the internal point of view toward the primary norms valid under the rule of recognition would give rise to legal obligations on the part of citizens. And likewise for Coleman's view: it is easy to see why one might think it relevant to the issue of citizen obligations that citizens must instantiate the mental states associated with an SCA.

In contrast, it is not clear why or how the internal attitude of officials bears on the issue of whether valid primary norms obligate citizens. Showing that officials can provide reasons that apply to *one another* may contribute to an explanation of how the officials of a legal system can

provide obligations that bind *them*, but a joint commitment among officials to a certain set of validity criteria seems irrelevant with respect to
whether and how laws could give rise to legal obligations binding citizens.
If so, then there is substantial reason to doubt even that it is a necessary
condition for a system of institutionalized norms to create content-
independent obligations that such a system be grounded in a recognition
norm that constitutes an SCA.[10]

Notes

1. This criticism is due to Payne 1976. For a slightly different formulation, see Shiner
1992.

2. The concept of an SCA is due to Bratman 1992.

3. It is commonly taken to be a conceptual truth that the obligations of morality
override all other obligations, including social obligations. See Frankena 1966.

4. Here it is worth noting that if one gunman A decides, without notice to the other
B, not to exercise his part of the plan and B is caught because of this nonfeasance,
B has a reasonable ground for complaint—as odd as this may sound. After all, B
might not have gone through with the robbery had he known of A's decision. Of
course, this ground for complaint has negligible force in the moral calculus, but the
fact that there is a reasonable ground for complaint suggests that some sort of obligation was created—though, again, the ultimate force of that obligation is very
weak.

5. See, e.g., Coleman 2001, p. 98.

6. Indeed, as an interpretive matter, one of Hart's central objectives in *The Concept
of Law* seems to be to give an analysis of the concept of obligation, in general, and
of the concept of legal obligation, in particular, that will withstand his own objections to Austin. Consider, for example, the following statements from a long discussion about obligations: (1) "[I]t is crucial for the understanding of the *idea* of
obligation to see that in individual cases the statement that a person has an obligation under some rule and the prediction that he is likely to suffer for disobedi-
ence may diverge"; (2) "It is clear that obligation is not to be found in the gunman
situation, though the *simpler notion* of being obliged to something may well be
defined in the elements present there"; (3) "To understand the *general idea of obligation* as a necessary preliminary to understanding it *in its legal form*, we must turn to
a different social situation which, unlike the gunman situation, includes the existence of social rule; for this situation contributes *to the meaning* of the statement
that a person has an obligation in two ways"; (4) "The statement that someone has
or is under an obligation does indeed imply the existence of a rule"; and (5) "Rules

are *conceived and spoken as* imposing obligations when the general demand for conformity is insistent and the social pressure brought to bear upon those who deviate or threaten to deviate is great" (Hart 1994, pp. 85–86; emphasis added). It is clear here that Hart is not merely trying to make talk of obligation intelligible; he is trying, as he must, to give a full-blown conceptual analysis obligation—and, to be internally coherent, it must avoid his own criticism of Austin.

7. The reason for this is that a state can be morally justified in coercively enforcing its laws regardless of content if and only if those laws give rise to a content-independent moral obligation to obey.

8. Indeed, even accounts of why human beings have a content-independent duty to obey the commands of God rest on such a relationship: on this line of analysis, God's relationship to her subjects as creator gives rise to a duty to obey.

9. Coleman himself seems to accept the normal justification thesis as a theory of moral legitimacy: "This analysis [of authority] is a great advance over Hart's. For Raz shows how distinctively legal reasons can be genuine reasons, and how legal obligations, duties, responsibilities, and their corresponding rights can also bear a moral signification. Law's reasons can be genuine because as a practical authority, law may reflect special expertise or may serve to coordinate individuals' actions, enabling them better to satisfy the demands of right reason" (Coleman 2001, p. 122).

10. In this connection, it is worth noting that if Coleman were right, then the Razian view that the rule of recognition is not a rule at all would have to be incorrect. Raz conceives of the rule of recognition as "a general statement that does not describe a law but a general truth about law." As a purely descriptive statement, then, the "rule" of recognition has no normative implications whatsoever; it neither creates obligations nor, by itself, gives rise to reasons for action. Indeed, on Raz's view, it is simply not essential to the explanation of legal normativity that we explain the behavior of officials; since such behavior does not give rise to a legal norm, it does not figure into a general explanation of legal normativity. At the very least, then, one would need an argument for thinking that the Razian view is incorrect in order to make out a case for Coleman's analysis.

References

Austin, J. 1995. *The Province of Jurisprudence Determined.* Cambridge: Cambridge University Press.

Bratman, M. 1992. "Shared Cooperative Activity." *Philosophical Review* 101: 327–341.

Coleman, J. L. 2001. *The Practice of Principle: In Defense of a Pragmatist Approach to Legal Theory.* Oxford: Oxford University Press.

Frankena, W. 1966. "The Concept of Morality." *Journal of Philosophy* 63: 688–696.

Hart, H. L. A. 1994. *The Concept of Law*, revised ed. Oxford: Oxford University Press.

Marmor, A. 1998. "Legal Conventionalism." *Legal Theory* 4: 509–531.

Payne, M. A. 1976. "Hart's Concept of a Legal System." *William and Mary Law Review* 18: 287–301.

Raz, J. 1994. "Authority, Law, and Morality." In J. Raz, *Ethics in the Public Domain.* Oxford: Clarendon Press.

Shiner, R. 1992. *Norm and Nature: The Movements of Legal Thought.* Oxford: Clarendon Press.

18   Facts, Fictions, and the Grounds of Law

Jules L. Coleman

I write to learn. I know of no other way of proceeding. There is a sense in which philosophy is an intensely private activity, but for me, there is no greater academic good than participating with others in the joint pursuit of knowledge and understanding—of ourselves and our place in the world.

I can conceive of no greater compliment than to have those I respect engage my work in a serious and sustained way. The essays by John Gardner, Kenneth Himma, and Benjamin Zipursky on *The Practice of Principle* far surpass what I could have hoped for. Often the authors' characterizations of my views and their defenses of them improve greatly upon the originals. They raise and formulate issues in ways that had never occurred to me; and I am much the richer for it. I am deeply indebted to all of them.

I cannot possibly do justice to these essays in the context of this reply. In addition, I think it important that I not simply walk away from claims that I have made even when the arguments and objections offered against them seem persuasive to me. This is not a matter of stubbornness or defensiveness, but of respect. I don't want to diminish the importance of the objections by "giving in." I want to fight back as best I can to bring out the best in the arguments on all sides in the hopes that doing so will deepen our understanding of the issues at stake. I define myself by a commitment to work with others to see if we can collectively get it right, not by a desire to be the one who does.[1] Very likely we will all have to settle for a good deal less than getting it right.

On the Economic Account of Tort Law

I begin with John Gardner's wonderful essay that focuses entirely on my objections to the economic analysis of tort law. I have long been concerned to explore aspects of economic analysis—its analytic and normative foundations, its relationship to rational choice theory, to the nature of explanation in the social sciences, and to law.[2] Most of my work on economic analysis *of law* has focused on the law of torts.[3]

John Gardner and I share what he refers to as the lawyer's view of tort law. Central to this view are the primary duties of care. It is helpful to distinguish between two kinds of questions we can ask about these duties: (1) to whom do we owe them? (2) What is their content? In exercising my liberty of action I often impose risks on others (as well as on myself). To act responsibly I need to show adequate regard for the fact that my conduct may be dangerous to others. (1) To whom do I owe a duty of appropriate regard for their interests? And (2) what is required of me to regard their interests appropriately?

The distinction between the object of a duty of care and its content helps us eradicate a widespread confusion about the difference between strict and fault liability. On the standard view, the difference between strict and fault liability is that under fault liability an injurer can be liable to his victims only if he has harmed them through some fault of his, for example, his carelessness or his recklessness; whereas under strict liability the same injurer can be liable to his victims whether or not his conduct exhibits any such defect. Thus, under strict liability an innocent, that is, a nonfaulty injurer, can be responsible to repair another's loss, whereas under fault liability, one can be made to shoulder a burden of repair only if one has acted wrongfully in some way.[4]

The conduct for which one is subject to strict liability can be permissible, even justifiable. Why should someone who engages in permissible or justifiable conduct be subject to liability for losses that would otherwise fall to others? By the same token, if a victim can recover from someone who has merely caused his loss, why should other victims be unable to recover unless they can show that the loss they have suffered is the result of another's mischief?

These are interesting questions no doubt, and there are more where they came from—all invited by the standard formulation of the strict–fault liability dichotomy. Much of my early work in tort theory gave credence to this widespread, but mistaken formulation of the distinction between fault and strict liability. I apologize, and one of the aims in the book was to rectify this particular wrong that I have done (and to undue as best I can its untoward consequences within tort theory).

The conventional formulation suggests that the relevant distinction between strict and fault liability is to be explained in terms of the concept of *wrongdoing*. Strict liability is liability without regard to wrongdoing of any sort; fault liability requires wrongdoing—a failure of some sort, typically a failure to exercise reasonable care, or an intention to injure or harm without justification. I now think that the relevant concept in the law of torts is *wrong* not *wrongdoing*. A wrong is a breach of a duty. Strict and fault liability are different ways of articulating the content of one's duty to others. Let me explain.

Suppose I engage in two different activities: blasting and motoring. Arguably, if you fall within the scope of foreseeable risk I impose, I owe a duty of care to you whether I am motoring or blasting. The question is: what is the content of the duty I owe to you?

In torts, blasting is governed by strict liability and motoring by fault liability. The way to understand the difference is as follows. In the case of motoring, my duty of care is a duty to exercise reasonable care; it is a duty-not-to-harm-you through carelessness, recklessness, or intention. The law demands that I take reasonable precautions not to harm you: that I insure the brakes and lights on my car operate properly, that I observe speed limits and other traffic regulations, and so on. In the case of blasting, however, the law imposes on me the duty-not-to-harm-you. The way I am to take your interests into account is to make sure that I don't harm you by blasting.

The difference between fault and strict liability is a difference in the content of the duty of care I owe to you. That there is a difference of moral significance between the duties I owe to you in both cases is illustrated by the difference in success conditions for discharging them. If my duty to you is a duty-not-to-harm-you, then the only way that I can discharge that duty is by not harming you.

If my duty to you is a duty-not-to-harm-you-faultily (that is, by negligence, carelessness, recklessness, or intention), then I can discharge that duty either by not harming you or by not being at fault—whether or not I harm you. So if in the course of driving I injure or harm you, whether or not I have failed to discharge my duty to you depends on whether I have driven carefully—that is, taken reasonable precautions to avoid harm to you.

In either case, if I fail to discharge my duty to you, I thereby wrong you. And it is my wronging you—something that I can do innocently or wrongfully—that is the morally relevant notion in tort law.

The basic moral category in torts is wrong, not wrongdoing.[5] The other side of wrong is duty. Tort law articulates the content of a broad range of the duties of care we owe to one another. Not every duty of care is enforceable in torts, and so the law is in that sense limited. Tort theory is concerned to explain or illuminate the relationship between the duties of care crystallized in and through tort law and their legal consequences: the legal liabilities and powers grounded by their breach. The concern of tort theory is to provide an account of the way in which these first-order or primary obligations of care figure *normatively* in the practice—that is, as grounds of second-order powers and liabilities. This, in effect, is the "general" part of tort law—the structure of practical reasoning within it—and the burden of tort theory is to explain it.

In Coleman 2001 I argue that the principle of corrective justice explains the structure of practical reasoning in tort law (as captured by the lawyer's view), in a way that the economic analysis of tort law cannot.

In advancing these views, I have emphasized two criticisms of the economic analysis of tort law. The first is that economic analysis cannot account for the primary obligations in tort law. The second is that economic efficiency does not explain the relationship between the primary obligations of due care and the secondary obligations of repair.

Economists have responded by arguing that the best predictions of behavior—whether of potential injurers, victims, or even officials—rely on understanding their responses to potential liabilities and rewards. This may be true, but it misses the point of my objections. I am not making a causal claim about the role of primary obligations of due care in the practical deliberations of potential injurers or victims. I doubt it, but for all I know, potential injurers are moved only by considerations of potential liability. But the system of law is not a system of liabilities; it is a system of *grounded* or *warranted* liabilities—liabilities for which the law provides reasons or grounds—and to understand the law is to understand the relationship between liabilities and their grounds.[6] My concern, then, is with the normative and not the causal relationships between law and agents and officials: what reasons they have for acting; what justifications or warrants they have; what the normative structure of legal reasoning and deliberation is.

So when I claim that economic analysis of law fails to explain the relationship in tort law between the primary obligations of due care and the secondary duties of repair (or the judgments of liability to make repair), I am making a claim about its failure to provide a plausible account of the actual normative relationship between the two.

Tired of defending their view against my objections, economic analysts of tort law have sometimes taken the offensive. They claim that the principle of corrective justice is empty; it is formal at best, an account of the relationship between primary duties of care and secondary duties of repair, telling us nothing about the content of the duties we owe one another. Those duties of care, they add, can be shown to derive from considerations of efficiency or optimal deterrence. Perhaps not all duties can be so derived, but at least economic analysis has the resources to explain the content of the duties we have. Corrective justice theory does not even purport to have the resources adequate to explain the content of the duties of care we owe one another.

At times an economic theory of the duties of care we owe one another is offered in a more cooperative and sympathetic vein in order to show the compatibility of economic and corrective justice theories of torts. Still other times it is offered to establish that a corrective justice theory of tort law is itself grounded in an economic one. That is, corrective justice does no more than enforce a system of efficiency-based entitlements and their correlative duties: corrective justice is either empty or parasitic on an economic account of duties of care—or so the argument goes.

This mode of response to corrective justice is confused and misses the point. Let's begin by accepting the economist's charge that the only role the principle of corrective justice plays in tort theory is to explain the relationship between first-order duties of care and second-order duties of repair. That hardly renders the theory empty or insignificant. An account of the ways in which primary duties of care figure normatively in the practice of tort law just is an account of the way in which they license powers to bring actions against others for breach, and an account of the way in which they figure as grounds in the imposition of secondary duties of repair. Far from being an empty theory of tort law, it purports to be a relatively complete explanation of the central elements of the structure of practical reasoning in tort law.

Now let's turn to the claim that the corrective justice account is silent on the content of the duties of care we owe to one another. It is surely true that the full panoply of duties of care we owe to one another cannot be derived a priori from the principle of corrective justice. Still it does not follow that the principle of corrective justice is altogether silent on the matter. For if corrective justice is to be a plausible account of the relationship between secondary duties of repair and primary duties of care, then the duties of care sustained by a principle of corrective justice must meet certain standards. As I argued in both Coleman 2001 and 2002, only a scheme of legitimate property rights can be justifiably entrenched or secured by a principle of corrective justice. Indeed, in the latter book, I devoted an entire chapter to spelling out what this amounted to in terms of the relationship between corrective and distributive justice. The point of the chapter was to articulate the constraints corrective justice imposes on the underlying system of entitlements secured by duties of care and a practice of repair for their breach. To be sure, very few fully formed duties of care will fall out of considerations of an abstract sort, but that's of no import at all. Rather, the duties of care we owe one another will be determined largely by other factors in our social, economic, and moral lives as they are expressed or embodied in our institutions.

So, to sum up: my claim about corrective justice is that it explains the normative structure of practical reasoning in tort law—the relationship between primary duties of care and secondary duties of repair for their breach. It is not a claim about the causal role of primary duties of care in the practical reasoning of potential injurers or victims—though it is a claim about the causal structure of judicial reasoning and is borne out by the phenomenology of judicial decision making. Next, although the content of the duties of care we owe one another do not fall out of the principle of corrective justice, corrective justice imposes constraints on what they can be. In addition, as I argue in Coleman 2001, some particular duties of care, as regards bodily security and autonomy over one's person, can in fact be derived from the principle of corrective justice.[7]

I have tried very hard to make these points over the course of my work. I am extremely grateful to John Gardner for making them on my behalf, and far more persuasively than I have. Much to my chagrin, however, Gardner is not content to let matters stand at that. He has no truck with my claim that the corrective justice account of tort law can explain its normative structure. But he thinks that I am mistaken in thinking that economic analysis cannot. He distinguishes between what I will call a simple (and unsympathetic) reading of my objection and a complex (and sympathetic) reading. Both he claims miss their intended target.

The simple reading of my objection is this. In tort law, the breach of a primary duty of care is a reason for the imposition of liability in the form of a duty of repair. Economic analysis cannot account for the status of the breach of the primary duty as a *reason* for imposing a duty of care. The only thing that counts as a reason in economic terms is efficiency; and so whether someone should incur a duty of repair must depend on whether there are efficiency gains to be had. The existence of a breach of a duty of care is normatively irrelevant to that. The breach is a backward-looking matter; potential gains in efficiency are always forward looking. The latter considerations therefore could not in principle ground the normative emphasis the law of torts places on the breach of a duty of care.

Gardner's response on behalf of the economist is this. The breach of a duty of care is a reason for the imposition of a duty of repair provided there is a norm that makes it so. Let's call any such norm a linking norm. It links the breach of a duty to a duty of repair. My observation is that the law of torts has such a linking norm. But there is no reason in principle why there cannot be sound economic reasons that would support such a norm. It may be that economic considerations do not support such a norm, but they could in principle. So if this is my objection to economic analysis, it isn't compelling.

Gardner then offers a more sophisticated interpretation of my objection that goes as follows. On this reading, it is not the existence of a linking norm in the law that connects the duties of care and repair. Rather, it is a moral consequence of the breach of a duty of repair that one has a right to repair; and it is *this* fact about the relationship between the duties that calls for or requires a linking norm. Gardner puts this by saying that my view is that the breach of the duty of care is the *ground* of the duty of repair. There is no need for a linking norm to connect them; they are already connected. What is it that connects them? Corrective justice. And that is why I do not say that the law of torts is *explained* by the principle of corrective justice as much as I say that tort law is an institution of corrective justice, one that embodies or expresses the principle, and that in doing so realizes and gives content to it.

As Gardner reads me, the economist is in a bind. If tort law is an institution of corrective justice, then pretty much by definition there can be no economic accounting of it. But that's not playing fair. On the other hand, if tort law really does embody a principle of corrective justice, the question is whether there can be an economic defense of the principle of corrective justice. And although there may be no satisfying defense in the offing, there is no reason in principle why there could not be one. And so my general objection that there is no economic account of the normative structure of tort law is at the end of the day unpersuasive.

If that were my objection, it would not be persuasive. I don't take myself to be arguing that economic analysis cannot in principle explain the structure of practical reasoning in tort law. I argue, rather, that it does not.

The first set of questions economic analysis must ask do not concern the relationship of particular injurers to victims. It is simply of no intrinsic interest to economic analysis whether Jones hit Smith. What matters is this: is the accident between Jones and Smith and all similarly situated individuals the sort of accident that ought to be prevented? If the answer is yes, the next question is what, if anything, ought individuals like Jones and Smith do in order to prevent it. This is a question about Jones's ability to reduce risk (at a cost); it is a question of Smith's ability to do so as well. And it is a question about whether risk reduction is best done by coordinating their efforts. The next set of questions necessarily concern what ought to be done to create adequate incentives for the parties to take the optimal levels of precaution. *This* is the structure of reasoning that falls out of the economic analysis of law. This is not the structure of reasoning in the lawyer's view of tort law.

We can get to the lawyer's view from here. For we can surely imagine all sorts of search- and other transaction-cost-related reasons why an institution designed as economists claim the tort system is to promote optimal cost avoidance might end up asking very different questions than the ones just posed. That is, instead of inquiring into the relative ability of injurers and victims to take cost-justified precautions, it was structured so as to inquire into whether the injurer owed the victim a duty of care, and whether if he did, he failed adequately to discharge it, and so on. That's just Gardner's point that there can be, and probably is, given transaction costs, an economic explanation of the linking norm. But the norm remains a norm of corrective justice even if there are good economic reasons for adopting it under our current conditions.

It may well be, given existing transaction costs, that there are good economic reasons for adopting a tort system that embodies a principle of corrective justice. But there is no denying that the practice embodies a principle of corrective justice. The question after all, is whether the system of tort law embodies a principle of corrective justice. And it does. The fact that there may even be good economic reasons at this time for the law to embody such a norm is in a sense simply beside the point.

What we need to do is ask certain kinds of counterfactual questions to get at the heart of the matter. Whether the law embodies economic analysis or corrective justice is best determined by what we take to be the proper answers to some pertinent counterfactuals. So, let us suppose then that search costs were eliminated and it became very easy to determine which parties could reduce risk at the lowest cost. Economic analysis would counsel that these are the questions we would ask. But would tort law follow suit? That is, were transaction costs to be eliminated or drastically reduced, do we imagine that the structure of practical reasoning in tort law would mirror those changes in circumstance?

Do we think, in other words, that the burden of victims to bring actions would change if it were now easy for any of us to identify the cheapest cost avoider? There would be nothing special about the status of being a victim. Do we think that victims would be required to search out the cheapest cost avoiders rather than the parties who injured them?

Do we think that it would fall to victims to present evidence that the person they have identified as the defendant is the cheapest cost avoider? Will the plaintiff's burden be to focus on the relative ability of the injurer, the victim, and others to reduce risk optimally? Or would we think it appropriate that the victim establish that he was harmed by the failure of the injurer to discharge adequately a duty of care to him?

Do we think that it would fall to the court or the jury to allocate accident costs in a way that encouraged both optimal risk taking and litigation? Again, this is what economic considerations would counsel if transaction and search costs were to drop precipitously. Or would we think instead that once the plaintiff has established that he has been wronged by the injurer that he be fully compensated for the loss he has suffered, as corrective justice counsels?

If we thought that all these changes were appropriate we would in effect have a system of efficiency. If not, we have a system of corrective justice; and that's true even if there are good economic reasons for having a tort system that embodies the principle of corrective justice—as indeed, ours does. That, I think was my central point. Tort law embodies a corrective justice structure of practical reasoning according to which the duty of repair arises as a result of the victim of a breach exercising his liberty to bring an action that is itself warranted by the breach. That there are also good economic reasons for structuring our practice this way given existing costs has no bearing on the explanation of the practice we have. I don't think that Gardner would disagree with me.

The Normativity of Law

I turn now to Kenneth Himma's excellent paper on the obligation of ordinary citizens to obey the law. Again, a little background is in order. I am often credited with having developed and defended a version of "inclusive legal positivism." For as long as I can recall, legal positivism has been characterized as a theory of law defined by its denial of what natural law theory asserts. So we need to figure out what natural law theory asserts before we can determine what legal positivism stands for.

In the conventional view, natural law theory maintains that morality is a necessary condition of legality. This is then generalized as the claim that there is a necessary connection between law and morality. Legal positivism denies this, and so denies that there is a necessary connection between law and morality. The claim that there is no necessary connection between law and morality is, what I have called, the "separability thesis."

If one aim of Coleman 2001 was to reformulate the difference between strict and fault liability then another was to force us to rethink the difference between legal positivism and natural law theory. That is something we need to do because there are two insurmountable problems with the conventional view.

The first is that no natural lawyer with whom I am familiar claims that morality is a necessary condition of legality. Positivists may deny that morality must be a condition of legality, but so too do natural lawyers. In addition, the conventional view attributes to legal positivism the claim that there cannot be a necessary connection between law and morality, but there is no reason a positivist must hold any such position.

Suppose that law is a system of governance by rule (which it is), and that whatever else could be said about governance by rules, it respects certain features of humans as agents capable of acting for reasons. This too strikes me as correct. Suppose that respecting this feature of persons is invariably, perhaps even, intrinsically good. Then law would necessarily possess or exhibit moral value. All true, and none of it would be problematic for a positivist.

The separability thesis cannot separate natural lawyers from positivists. Positivists are not committed to it, and natural lawyers are not committed to rejecting it. And if we abandon the separability thesis, we have to give up on the traditional formulations of both the positivist and natural law traditions.

In *The Practice of Principle* I suggest that it is more helpful to identify legal positivism with what I have called the social fact thesis—or what Ben Zipursky refers to as the model of social facts. There are a number of different claims that we can associate with the social fact thesis, and we shall have occasion to discuss at least some of these in conjunction with Ben Zipursky's essay.

One version of the social fact thesis is the claim that whether a putative norm is a law in a community depends only on social facts about it. John Austin's view that a law is the order of a sovereign properly so called backed by a threat is an example of this version of the thesis. Whether or not a norm is law depends on whether it expresses the will of a sovereign, and that is a social fact about it. Moreover, whether or not one is a sovereign depends on certain social facts as well, for a sovereign is someone who has secured the habit of obedience from others and who is not herself in the habit of obeying anyone. In Austin's case, the legality of the norm depends on social facts about it at two separate levels. A norm is law if it is the command of a sovereign—independent of its content (level one); someone is a sovereign if and only if he has secured but not given a habit of obedience.

Versions of positivism can be distinguished from one another by which form of the social fact thesis they hold. Inclusive legal positivists, like Hart and myself, require that the legality of a norm depend on social facts at the second level only: the test of legality in a community must itself be determined by a social fact, though it may include among its tests of legality, conditions that are not themselves social facts. So, to modify the Austinian example, if the sovereign commands that a norm can be law only if it is morally defensible, then its legality at the first level does not depend on social facts alone, but the ultimate test of legality—the sovereign—does.

Other legal positivists, like Joseph Raz, argue that the test of legality must be restricted to social facts at level one. This is the "sources thesis." For Raz, the sources thesis derives from theoretical considerations about the nature of law and authority. Law necessarily claims to be a legitimate authority. Raz's particular theory of authority requires that nothing about the value or content of a law can be a condition of its legality. Though positivists differ from one another with respect to which of these two versions of the social fact thesis they hold, it is helpful to think of positivism in terms of a commitment to some or other form of the thesis if only because doing so helps us to understand various objections to it.[8]

There are three different kinds of objections that have been offered to the social fact thesis in various of its forms. The first is that the test of legality cannot in fact rest on social facts. At the end of the day, this is Dworkin's most serious challenge to positivism (taken on its own terms). Dworkin emphasizes the centrality of disagreement to legal practice. Officials disagree with one another not only about whether a norm satisfies the criteria of legality but about the criteria of legality themselves. And this latter disagreement that penetrates to the grounds of law is incompatible with any plausible version of the social fact thesis. Ben Zipursky offers a subtle reading of this objection and I postpone further discussion of it until we come to his essay below.

The second objection is the one offered by Mark Greenberg. A legal system must have determinate content. Its content is a set of propositions or statements of what the law requires, prohibits, and permits. Even a social-fact-based test of legality will do no more than provide a list of authoritative texts. These texts must be interpreted in two distinct ways. The first form of interpretation provides their semantic content. Once authoritative texts have semantic content, that is, meaning, it is necessary that they be interpreted as a whole to determine what it is the law requires. The content of the law requires an appeal to moral and other values to put meaningful legal sentences together in a way that produces determinate legal content. I will have just a bit to say about this line of objection below in my discussion of the Zipursky essay.

The third objection to the social fact thesis focuses on the relationship between facts and reasons. Roughly the objection can be expressed as follows. Legal rules and standards purport to articulate rights, powers, and liberties on the one hand, and duties, encumbrances, and liabilities on the other. It sets out claims about how we are to act toward one another—what we have reason to do. The content of the law is a set of putative reasons for action. The question then is how can reasons derive from social facts?

Frankly, this way of putting the objection is unfair since it appears to saddle legal positivism with a controversial metaethical thesis. Positivism is said to be the view that legal facts are social facts. Yet the content of the law is a set of reasons. The objection takes it to be the burden of a jurisprudential thesis to show how legal facts can give rise to reasons. In the case of legal positivism this amounts to the requirement that one derive reasons (which are normative facts) from legal facts (which are social facts). Positivism can only meet this burden by rejecting the so-called naturalistic fallacy. Some legal positivists may well reject the naturalistic fallacy, but it cannot be a condition of being a legal positivist—which is a theory about the nature of law as a scheme of governance—that one take on board a controversial metaethical claim.[9]

We need to formulate the concern about the relationship between facts and reasons in a less tendentious way. To do so, let's begin by recalling one of Hart's most well-known objections to Austin. According to Austin, the central organizing concepts in law are command, sanction, and habit of obedience. Hart argues persuasively that these resources are inadequate to explain the centrality of the notion of obligation in law. He sometimes puts his point this way: that the Austinian view of law is adequate to explain the sense in which individuals would feel "obliged" to conform their behavior to the sovereign's commands, but it would not explain their being "obligated" to do so. And so Hart rejects the command theory as inadequate to explain the normativity of law.

Famously, Hart responds to this shortcoming in Austin's account by replacing the concepts of command and sanction with that of rule and the concept of habit of obedience with that of the internal point of view. Commentators have asked whether the introduction of the concepts of rules and the internal point of view succeed where Austin's conceptual framework failed. Unsurprisingly, they find Hart's own efforts to explain how social rules give rise to reasons inadequate to the task.

The arguments differ in detail but they are all of the same type. For Hart, law consists not in commands, but in rules. What kind of rules? Social rules. What are social rules? Social rules have two dimensions: one behavioral, the other psychological. Social rules consist in the general convergence of behavior and a set of psychological attitudes and beliefs (themselves exhibited in but not reducible to other behaviors). This critical reflective attitude is expressed in the behavior of appealing to the rule as an explanation for what one does and as grounds for criticizing the behavior of others.

Critics of Hart then point out that taking the internal point of view toward a rule does not make the rule obligatory. One cannot bootstrap oneself into being obligated under a rule. Treating the rule as an obligation, sincerely believing that it is, cannot without more make it obligatory. So the internal point of view is as unsatisfactory (if different) an answer to how to derive law's obligations from social facts as is Austin's.

A cottage industry has grown up around this mistaken reading of Hart. Hart's objection to Austin is not that Austin cannot *derive* legal obligations from the paucity of resources at his disposal. Rather, his objection is that Austin's account lacks the resources to explain the aptness of the use of the term "obligation" in law—a term that is central to our ordinary understanding of the practice. That is, we would never use the term "obligation" to describe or characterize the state of an individual who had been commanded to act in a particular way and then threatened for noncompliance. We might characterize this person as feeling or being obliged to conform, but not as being obligated to do so. Yet the term whose use we want to understand in law is the term "obligation."

By the same token, rules and the internal point of view succeed where Austin's impoverished vocabulary of legal concepts fails. As rules purport to govern behavior by imposing obligations on those to whom they are directed, and adopting those rules from an internal point of view means treating the rules as grounds for conformity and as the basis for criticizing nonconformity, then the notion of obligation in law is no longer mysterious. We have the adequate resources to explain the centrality of the concept of obligation to our understanding of law.

The internal point of view is not offered as an explanation of how law creates reasons or obligations. Rather, the adoption of an internal point of view is expressed in behavior that provides a reliable indicator that participants view their practice as normative, as reason giving. It explains the aptness of terms like "obligation," "right," "duty," and "reason."[10] The internal point of view does not explain the normativity of law; it is evidence of law's normativity. It is part of the argument for the claim that social facts are adequate to render intelligible the normative language of the law.

Hart's objection to Austin then can be put in terms of its failure to meet an adequacy condition of a theory of law. In order to be adequate a theory of law must possess resources adequate to explain the intelligibility and meaning of the normative language of the law. It need not be required to explain how law gives rise to reasons. Law may not in fact do so. Austin's account fails to satisfy this adequacy condition. Hart's account succeeds.

I am not sure, however, that a jurisprudential view must not be able to do more. Exactly what, is quite controversial; and as far as I can tell there has been precious little discussion among jurisprudential theorists about exactly what is required of a theory in regards to explaining the "normativity of law"—which is not to say that different theorists haven't provided at least an implicit account of what they take the normative dimension of law that needs explaining to be. Consider Raz in this regard.

Raz understands the normativity of law through the lens of the theory of authority. Law for him necessarily claims to be a legitimate authority. As regards its normativity, law is a claiming and aspiring practice. It aspires to provide reasons for action and it claims to do so. To explain the normativity of law is to provide the resources in one's theory that makes sense not of law's giving rise to reasons—it may not in fact do so—but of law as a claiming and aspiring institution. In contrast, Dworkin's account of law presupposes that law is a reason-giving activity—that it imposes defeasible obligations on judges, and when it exhibits integrity and the characteristics of genuine political communities, on ordinary citizens as well.

My point is not to take issue with these views, but only to point out that although all jurisprudes I am familiar with agree that an adequate theory of law will explain the "normativity of law," it is considerably less clear what one is being asked to explain in doing so. There is a sense, I would suggest, that what counts as the normativity of law that is to be explained by one's theory, more often than not turns out to be a consequence of one's theory and not an adequacy condition of it.

With this in mind, let's turn to Ken Himma's objection, which is that the resources I offer are inadequate to explain the intelligibility of the obligation of ordinary citizens to comply with the law. I completely agree with his objection. But I did not take it to be a burden of my view to provide any such account.

Return to Hart for a moment. Recall that he introduces the idea of law consisting in rules that have an internal aspect. He suggests that all law be thought of in this way—as social rules. As it happens of course the vast majority of legal rules are not social rules and Hart ultimately acknowledges as much. The one rule of a legal system that must be a social rule is the rule of recognition. Among other things, what this means is that the resource Hart introduced to explain the normativity of law, by which he meant at least the aptness of the language of obligation as applied to it, was not in fact available for most of the law. The focus was shifted to the behavior of officials and the normative structure of their relationship to law and to one another. The question of the normativity of law as a whole simply drops out of the picture.

Rightly or wrongly, fairly or not, I have narrowed my focus accordingly. Indeed, all positivists do. The focus is on official behavior both as a condition of the possibility of law and as to the normativity of law. None of this is intended to undervalue questions about the normativity or legitimacy of law more generally, or of the citizen's obligation, if any, to comply with its demands. Positivists as a general matter have relegated these issues to political philosophy more generally, and not surprisingly, because part of the standard framework of positivism is the importance of distinguishing between the validity of a norm as law and its legitimacy— the latter bearing on its obligatoriness. Dworkinians allow no such distinctions because for them jurisprudence is part of political philosophy. What law is, for Dworkin, is connected to the conditions of political obligation. There is simply no other way of reading chapter 6 of *Law's Empire*, and no other way of making sense of his criticisms of positivism.

Long answer shortened then. Like Hart, I have focused primarily on the practice of officials, and insofar as one is required to explain the normativity of law, positivists take this in the first instance to be a burden they must meet about the behavior of officials with respect to the practice of lawmaking. Though, even with respect to officials and not citizens, it remains quite controversial what one is attempting to do in explaining the normativity of law.

Let me say a bit about what I have taken the burden of explanation to be—though my views are far from settled either about what needs to be explained and what provides the best explanation of it. At times I have written as if the burden of a jurisprudential theory was to establish how the rule of recognition could in fact give rise to obligations among judges and other officials. Certainly this is the approach I sometimes take in parts of the book. But it is not my consistent theme. I accept that the law plays a significant role in the practical reasoning of judges: that there can be no law unless judges adopt a rule of recognition (or criteria of legality) as a standard governing their behavior. These criteria must act as reasons for them. What do I mean by that claim? I'm not sure. At the very least, however, the criteria of legality must operate as rational constraints or demands on their reasoning.

In my earlier work I claimed that the practice of officials in regards to the rule of recognition constituted a Lewis-like coordination convention. Law exists when there is a rule of recognition that sets out criteria for legality that are adopted by officials. Their adoption, which Hart referred to as acceptance from an internal point of view, was best thought of as constituting a coordination convention. This view expressed the sense in which law ultimately rested on social facts, and did so in a way that explained the normative structure of the relationships of officials to the criteria of legality and to one another. For in standard coordination conventions, each person has a reason to comply with the rules provided others do. No one has a reason unilaterally to defect. So conventions are social facts that are also reasons for compliance with them. That fact about them was part of my motivation for advancing the view that there was a convention at the foundations of law.

Scott Shapiro offered a devastating critique of this position. Shapiro notes that coordination conventions are solutions to certain games in which the preferences of the participants line up in a particular way. And though it may be the case that we cannot have governance by law in the absence of a social practice among certain individuals of adopting criteria for assessing which norms are to be employed to assess the conduct of others, it cannot possibly be a conceptually necessary feature of law that the preferences of all those individuals have the same overall structure.

Shapiro's objection to my view put an end to the coordination convention version of the social fact thesis. If the practice of officials is not a coordination convention, what kind of social practice is it? Borrowing from some of the work of Michael Bratman on shared agency, I suggest in Coleman 2001 that the social practice among officials might plausibly be analyzed along the lines of a shared cooperative activity (SCA).

I believed that conceiving of the practice of officials as an SCA might help us better understand the role of the rule of recognition as a source of reasons and reasoning in the lives of officials. In Coleman 2001, I went further than I am now prepared to go. I suggested two things: first that judges and other officials were defeasibly obligated to apply the criteria of legality set forth in the rule of recognition, and second that seeing their practice as an SCA explained why that was so. My argument for the second claim was that SCAs created systems of interdependent expectations and reliance on these was, under appropriate conditions, grounds for obligations.

I no longer believe it follows from the fact, if it is one, that the behavior of judges is an SCA that judges have obligations to one another or to comply with the rule of recognition. Nor do I believe that one can derive reasons from the social facts that constitute SCAs, including those among officials. Instead, I want to develop a very different line of argument according to which certain normative constraints and structures are constitutive of certain kinds of jointly intentional actions. What remains of course is to identify the normative constraints, the kinds of jointly intentional actions that give rise to them and to make the case for claiming that the latter are partially constituted by the former. That is the kind of argument I believe that someone adopting a view like mine about the foundations of law needs to provide in order to explain the normativity of law. It is not an argument that I have as yet provided. Not close.

Understanding the Social Fact Thesis

I turn finally to Ben Zipursky's extremely nuanced and important discussion of what I have referred to above as the social fact thesis. I distinguish among three versions of the thesis. The first is that the test of legal validity must be social fact or social source based. Crudely, this is the position of so-called exclusive legal positivists. Inclusive legal positivists reject this requirement. We hold that the test of legal validity in a community can include factors other than social sources, but that the standard for being the test of legal validity must itself be a social fact—the second version of the social fact thesis. Morality can be a condition of legality then provided it is a social fact that makes it so. The third version of the social fact thesis is that the content of the law must be determined by social facts alone: facts about behavior, attitudes, and beliefs. Exclusive positivists like Raz and Shapiro adopt both the first and third version of the social fact thesis. I don't think Raz adopts the second, but I believe Shapiro does. That is, I believe Raz thinks that the criteria of legality are what they are and that officials can be wrong about them. So what makes them the criteria of legality in a community is not necessarily that they are the criteria adopted by officials.

Shapiro's view is the most sophisticated. As I read him, like Raz he rejects the idea of a rule of recognition. Instead, he views the criteria of legality to be part of a set of plans of individuals (officials or designers in his terminology) to make law (and in doing so to secure the goods that they believe are attainable by law). So the criteria of law are the criteria because they are elements of plans. Plans are in turn reducible to social facts about individuals (behaviors and psychological states). So the criteria of legality are determined by social facts; and the content of law is as well. The law's requirements are the contents of plans and the content of plans is determined by the behaviors and beliefs of parties to them (as closed under the appropriate interpretive constraints). Nothing in this part of his view entails that Shapiro adopt the first version of the social fact thesis. But his commitment to the so-called practical difference thesis does.

In any case, there is no getting around the fact that both Hart and I are committed to the second version of the social fact thesis. The test of the test of legality is social facts; or the grounds of law are the grounds in virtue of some social fact about them. It is also true that Dworkin's main objections to both Hart's and my accounts is that this version of the social fact thesis is incompatible with widespread disagreement about the grounds of law. The argument Dworkin offers is against a conventionalism of all sorts. He offers it up against Hart's and my jurisprudence and against the criterial semantics about "law" that he attributes to Hart.

Roughly, the argument is this. There is always a question of what we have to agree about in order for our disagreements to be meaningful. Conventionalists believe that we have to agree about criteria in order for our disagreements about what falls under the criteria to be meaningful. In the case of language, this amounts to the requirement that we must agree about the criteria for properly applying a term in order for our disagreements about whether the term applies in a particular case to be meaningful. In the case of law, we have to agree about the test of law in order for our disagreements about whether a particular standard is law to be meaningful. Unfortunately, disagreement in both law and language runs deeper. Speakers of a language disagree about the criteria for the proper use of a term; and lawyers disagree about the grounds of law. In neither case, then, can there be the relevant convergence of behavior that is necessary to sustain a conventionalist picture.

This is a powerful line of objection that I have tried consistently to meet. It may be a plausible line of objection to a criterial or conventionalist semantics, but the problem there is in attributing any such semantic thesis to legal positivism.[11] The objection is more on point in the jurisprudential context.

I agree with Dworkin that judges can disagree not only about what is law given the grounds of law, but about the grounds of law themselves. Ultimately, I have tried to meet Dworkin's objection by characterizing the behavior of officials as an SCA. Doing so has the advantage of (1) explaining the depth of disagreement about the grounds of law; (2) the resolution of disagreement by appealing to various normative accounts of the purpose or goal of the practice; and (3) demonstrating that law is made possible by a social practice among officials.

This is where Zipursky enters the argument. He has no real quarrel with my account of officials as an SCA (which is not to say that there are no problems with it). Instead, his objection is that my response answers to a different concern than the one Dworkin raises. The key to his objection is an important distinction between what law is and what it is for a community to have law. My claim that the behavior of officials constitutes an SCA goes to the existence conditions for a community having law; it does not go to an analysis of what law is.

Positivism is a theory of the nature of law or of legal validity. The social fact thesis is a claim about the nature of legal validity: legal validity is always determined by social facts alone. To see the difference, recall Austin's and Hart's accounts of law. Austin claims that law is a command of a sovereign. Social facts fully determine whether a command is law. All laws are commands; and only the commands of sovereigns are law. A sovereign is defined in terms of social facts: habits of obedience.

According to Hart, law consists in two kinds of rules: for our purposes we can simplify his account so that there are primary and secondary rules on the one hand and a rule of recognition on the other. What does the claim that legal validity is determined by social facts amount to in this context? For Hart it is not the claim that the test of legal validity appeals only to social facts about a norm (its pedigree or social source). It must instead be a claim about the rule of recognition.

But what kind of claim about the rule of recognition can it be? The rule of recognition is not a social fact. It is a propositional entity. So it can either be a claim about its content or its existence conditions. If it is a claim about the content of the rule of recognition, then it is the claim that the content of the rule is fixed by social facts. Which social facts? The obvious answer is, convergent behavior among officials. The rule of recognition sets out the criteria of legality. That is its content. If its content is fixed by social facts, then the criteria of legality, the grounds of law, are determined by the facts of convergence.

This is clearly how Dworkin must be reading the social fact thesis. His objection is simply that if there is disagreement or the absence of convergence, there is no criterion of legality: the grounds of law run out where convergence does.

The problem is that disagreement about the grounds of law is among the most important features of our legal practice. If we take the social fact thesis seriously, the positivist cannot interpret this feature of legal practice as disagreements about what the grounds of law are. He must interpret it as a disagreement about what the criteria of legality ought to be. It follows, therefore, that judges cannot be disagreeing about what they are bound to apply, but what they should apply. So the social fact thesis renders positivism insensitive to the phenomenology of the practice.

On the other hand, the social fact thesis might be understood as a claim about the existence condition of the rule of recognition, not about its content. But if it is a thesis about the existence conditions of the rule of recognition it has no bearing on the claim that legal validity is a matter of social fact. Indeed, if Dworkin is right about the structure of judicial argument, it is clear that legal validity is not a matter of social fact.

It may well be that whether a community has law—which would include a practice for determining which of its norms are authoritative legal texts—depends on the existence of social facts, but that is a very different kind of claim. There is after all an enormous difference between the claim that it is a social fact about a community that it has law, and the very different claim that law itself is a social fact (or that legal validity is). The former claim is external to the practice; the latter is internal to it. Zipursky's point is that I offer the claim that officials participate in an SCA to establish the former claim, when what I need is an argument that would establish the latter one. He refers to this as the "conventionalist fallacy" and accuses me of it. If I understand him correctly and if I have fairly represented his objection accurately, it is an excellent point. I want to suggest, however, that there is a way out of the dilemma Zipursky offers. I am by no means certain that I have his objection right; nor am I certain that my response is decisive. I simply offer it up in the spirit of encouraging further discussion of these tremendously important points.

Let me suggest the following line of defense. Zipursky distinguishes between two questions: what is law? When does a community have law? He claims that the social fact thesis must make a claim about a feature of law and not about the existence conditions for law in a community. He takes it to be a claim about legal validity that in the context of my inclusive legal positivism must become a claim about the content of the rule of recognition.

Suppose we agree. It follows I think that the claim the social fact theorist is committed to is this: law is a certain kind of institutional social practice in which certain concepts figure prominently. One of these is the concept of legal validity. (To be honest, I am not sure the concept of legal validity must be prominent. What we need is a notion like "authoritative legal text." Whether a text has the status in virtue of its validity is another matter, best left for another occasion. For the purposes of this argument, let us simply employ the notion of legal validity.) The social fact thesis is the claim that the grounds of law or the test of legal validity or the standards for determining which texts are authoritative are fixed by certain social facts. One does not need to introduce the idea of a rule of recognition in this formulation. In fact, there may be a variety of good reasons for simply doing away with the notion of a rule of recognition as a useful theoretical tool for formulating the kinds of claims positivists and others may want to make.

So the position the positivist is defending in the name of the model of social facts is that the grounds of law are fixed by social facts. This is enough of a claim to distinguish the positivist from the Dworkinian, for example, who claims that grounds of law are fixed by interpretation; interpretation of social facts of course. Indeed the very same social facts that positivists claim fix the grounds of law: that is, facts about judicial behavior and psychological attitudes toward that behavior.

The Dworkinian objection against the positivist is really an objection to one way in which social facts might fix the grounds of law—by identifying the grounds of law with the scope of convergent behavior. But that is far from the only way in which behavior and attitude can fix the content of rules, or plans, or the criteria of law. In fact, I introduced the idea of an SCA in Coleman 2001 in order to introduce a way of fixing on content through a practice of cooperation and disagreement. For me the SCA is not introduced as an existence condition for a community's having law, but as a conceptual truth about law. Law is an institutional social practice that necessarily consists in, among other things, a kind of cooperative activity of officials. That activity can be characterized in purely social fact terms: behavior and psychological states. This is what law is. The content of the criteria or grounds of law will be fixed by the nature of their cooperative venture.

I think the person who has approached jurisprudence in this way with the most insight and creativity is Scott Shapiro. He takes law to be an instance of large-scale coordination and planning activity. Judges are planners, and the content of their plans are fixed by psychological and social facts about them. Shapiro's approach to the problem is the first great advance in jurisprudence since Dworkin's conceptualization of law as an interpretive activity.

The key debate, as I see it, is between those like Shapiro on the one hand who view law as a planning activity aimed at large-scale cooperation and coordination, and who are thus committed to the idea that the criteria of legality can be derived from facts about planners and the history of their institutions, and others, like Mark Greenberg, who believe that plans and other social facts and phenomena cannot yield determinate content without attributing moral values to the activities and plans in question.

This, as I see it, is the new frontier on which the centuries-old debates between those who claim that law is ultimately a matter of social fact—as legal positivists from Hart and Raz to me, Gardner to Shapiro do—and others who claim that law must include value facts as well—as nonpositivists from Dworkin and Perry to Stavropoulos, Zipursky to Greenberg do—will be adjudicated. I cannot begin to express how pleased I am that so many individuals who have participated in moving these debates along—in reformulating them to reveal ever deeper connections to other core areas of philosophy and lived human experience—see my work as playing a central role in their own development. If I have contributed at all, I like to think that it is by encouraging others.

Notes

1. I have worked hard to be a sympathetic critic and interpreter. On the other hand, I have no patience for academic pretense and posturing, hand waving and intellectual filibustering of the sort that runs rampant and unchecked in the legal academy. I have twice in my recollection been unfair by being unkind in print to other academics, and I have regretted it ever since. And so I would like to apologize to Matthew Kramer for a cutting and unkind remark I made in a reply to one of his essays on legal positivism, and to Ronald Dworkin for framing a couple of arguments in Coleman 2001 in ways that were less respectful to his work and his contribution to the field than they should have been. I cannot control the way others participate in this project of intellectual engagement, but I can control the way that I do. And I regret that I have ever done so in a way that is demeaning to those who do so in a serious and sustained way. There are far too few of those.

2. My most basic concerns are ones in the philosophy of the social sciences: understanding the nature of groups, especially their normative structure. Indeed, my work in jurisprudence on the foundations of law as a social practice among officials is really just a part of this larger project.

3. However, I did jointly author a long essay applying economic analysis to contract law, which reappeared as a substantial section of Coleman 2002.

4. The fault need not evidence a defect in character or motivation, as often, a person who has an excuse for his mischief may nevertheless be liable for the misfortune it has occasioned. But some failure in action, if not in agency or character, is required.

5. Wrong and duty are not the only basic moral categories in tort law of course. The others include harm, responsibility, and repair. On an economic picture in contrast the basic category is cost, and any economic theory of tort law must be reductive in attempting to fully explicate the concepts of harm, responsibility, duty, and

repair in terms of the basic notion of cost—something that I have argued is, even if possible, unhelpful. See part 1 of Coleman 2001.

6. Holmes may have been a wonderful jurist, but he was not much of a jurisprudent. It is no insight into the nature of what law is to ask what a bad man's interest in it might be. After all, even if the central causal notion in law is that of sanction, the distinctive claim of law is that it is a system of warranted or justified sanctions. Understanding that claim is minimally necessary to understanding the nature of law but of no intrinsic interest to the bad man who is concerned only to avoid wrath, not the reasons that would or would not justify its imposition.

7. Finally, it is probably false that the duties we have in law are those that fall out of the principle of economic efficiency. Even if all the duties of care we owed others coincided entirely with the demands of efficiency, that would have no bearing on the claim of corrective justice, which is a theory not primarily about the content of those duties, but about their role in licensing normative judgments within the practice itself.

8. There is another version of the social fact thesis that is itself normally associated with the sources thesis. This is the claim that the content of the law must be determined only by social facts. The usual formulation of the sources thesis includes constraints both on the identity and the content of law. I mention this as a separate version of the social fact thesis because it is this claim of legal positivism that is the object of Mark Greenberg's recent criticism of legal positivism. See his forthcoming.

9. In fact some positivists might also claim that social facts are also normative facts or that some of them are or can be, thus rendering the burden less demanding.

10. In fact, it may also be plausible to analyze what Hart is up to in emphasizing the internal point of view in terms of his offering a nonrealist or noncognitivist interpretation of the meaning of the term "obligation" in law, according to which the meaning is to be spelled out in facts about behavior and beliefs among users. Hart clearly was a noncognitivist about the meaning of ethical terms and so such a view is by no means implausible. Still, my concern is much broader than Hart scholarship or exegesis.

11. See Coleman and Simchen 2003.

References

Coleman, J. 2001. *The Practice of Principle*. Oxford: Oxford University Press.

———. 2002. *Risks and Wrongs*. Oxford: Oxford University Press.

Coleman, J. and O. Simchen. 2003. "Law." *Legal Theory* 9: 1–41.

Greenberg, M. Forthcoming. "How Facts Make Law." *Legal Theory* 10.

Index